In historical accounts of the circumstances of ordinary people's lives, nutrition has been the great unknown. Nearly impossible to measure or assess directly, it has nonetheless been held responsible for the declining mortality rates of the nineteenth century as well as being a major factor in the gap in living standards, morbidity and mortality between rich and poor. The measurement of height is a means of the direct assessment of nutritional status.

This important and innovative new study uses a wealth of military and philanthropic data to establish the changing heights of Britons during the period of industrialisation, and thus establishes an important new dimension to the long-standing controversy about living standards during the Industrial Revolution. Sophisticated quantitative analysis enables the authors to present some striking new conclusions about the actual physical status of the British people during a period of profound social and economic upheaval, and *Height, Health and History* will provide an invigorating statistical edge to many current debates about the history of the human body itself.

RODERICK FLOUD is Provost of City of London Polytechnic

KENNETH WACHTER is Professor of Demography and Statistics at the University of California, Berkeley

ANNABEL GREGORY Computing Adviser for the Arts at Birkbeck College, London

NBER Series on Long-term Factors in Economic Development

Editors

ROBERT W. FOGEL and CLAYNE L. POPE

Also in the series

Samuel Preston and Michael Haines *Fatal Years: Child Mortality in Late-Nineteenth Century America* (Princeton University Press, 1990)

Claudia Goldin *Understanding the Gender Gap: An Economic History of American Woman* (Oxford University Press, 1990)

In preparation (tentative titles)

Robert W. Fogel *The Escape from Hunger and Early Death: Europe and America, 1750–2050*

Robert A. Margo *Race and Schooling in the American South, 1880–1950: A Quantitative History*

Kenneth L. Sokoloff *In Pursuit of Private Comfort: Early American Industrialization, 1790–1860*

Height, health and history

*Cambridge Studies in Population, Economy and
Society in Past Time 9*

Series editors

PETER LASLETT, ROGER SCHOFIELD and
E. A. WRIGLEY

*ESRC Cambridge Group for the History of Population and
Social Science*

and DANIEL SCOTT SMITH

University of Illinois at Chicago

Recent work in social, economic and demographic history has revealed much that was previously obscure about societal stability and change in the past. It has also suggested that crossing the conventional boundaries between these branches of history can be very rewarding.

This series will exemplify the value of interdisciplinary work of this kind, and will include books on topics such as family, kinship and neighbourhood; welfare provision and social control; work and leisure; migration; urban growth; and legal structures and procedures, as well as more familiar matters. It will demonstrate that, for example, anthropology and economics have become as close intellectual neighbours to history as have political philosophy or biography.

Height, health and history

Nutritional status in the
United Kingdom, 1750–1980

RODERICK FLOUD, KENNETH WACHTER
and ANNABEL GREGORY

The right of the
University of Cambridge
to print and sell
all manner of books
was granted by
Henry VIII in 1534.
The University has printed
and published continuously
since 1584.

CAMBRIDGE UNIVERSITY PRESS

Cambridge
New York   Port Chester   Melbourne   Sydney

Published by the Press Syndicate of the University of Cambridge
The Pitt Building, Trumpington Street, Cambridge CB2 1RP
40 West 20th Street, New York, NY 10011, USA
10 Stamford Road, Oakleigh, Melbourne 3166, Australia

© Cambridge University Press 1990

First published 1990

Printed in Great Britain by The Bath Press, Avon

British Library cataloguing in publication data

Floud, Roderick
   Height, health and history: nutritional status in the
   United Kingdom, 1750–1980. – (Cambridge studies in
   population, economy and society in past time; 9).
   1. England. Man. Diet. Socioeconomic aspects, history
   I. Title   II. Wachter, Kenneth W.   III. Gregory, Annabel
   306′.3

Library of Congress cataloguing in publication data applied for

ISBN 0 521 30314 1

Relation of the Directors to the Work and Publications of the National Bureau of Economic Research

1. The object of the National Bureau of Economic Research is to ascertain and to present to the public important economic facts and their interpretation in a scientific and impartial manner. The Board of Directors is charged with the responsibility of ensuring that the work of the National Bureau is carried on in strict conformity with this object.

2. The President of the National Bureau shall submit to the Board of Directors, or to its Executive Committee, for their formal adoption all specific proposals for research to be instituted.

3. No research report shall be published by the National Bureau until the President has sent each member of the Board a notice that a manuscript is recommended for publication and that in the President's opinion it is suitable for publication in accordance with the principles of the National Bureau. Such notification will include an abstract or summary of the manuscript's content and a response form for use by those Directors who desire a copy of the manuscript for review. Each manuscript shall contain a summary drawing attention to the nature and treatment of the problem studied, the character of the data and their utilization in the report, and the main conclusions reached.

4. For each manuscript so submitted, a special committee of the Directors (including Directors Emeriti) shall be appointed by majority agreement of the President and Vice Presidents (or by the Executive Committee in case of inability to decide on the part of the President and Vice Presidents), consisting of three Directors selected as nearly as may be one from each general division of the Board. The names of the special manuscript committee shall be stated to each Director when notice of the proposed publication is submitted to him. It shall be the duty of each member of the special manuscript committee to read the manuscript. If each member of the manuscript committee signifies his approval within thirty days of the transmittal of the manuscript, the report may be published. If at the end of that period any member of the manuscript committee withholds his approval, the President shall then notify each member of the Board, requesting approval or disapproval of publication, and thirty days additional shall be granted for this purpose. The manuscript shall then not be published unless at least a majority of the entire Board who shall have voted on the proposal within the time fixed for the receipt of votes shall have approved.

5. No manuscript may be published, though approved by each member of the special manuscript committee, until forty-five days have elapsed from the transmittal of the report in manuscript form. The interval is allowed for the receipt of any memorandum of dissent or reservation, together with a brief statement of his reasons, that any member may wish to express; and such memorandum of dissent or reservation shall be published with the manuscript if he so desires. Publication does not, however, imply that each member of the Board has read the manuscript, or that either members of the Board in general or the special committee have passed on its validity in every detail.

6. Publications of the National Bureau issued for informational purposes concerning the work of the Bureau and its staff, or issued to inform the public of activities of Bureau staff, and volumes issued as a result of various conferences involving the National Bureau shall contain a specific disclaimer noting that such publication has not passed through the normal review procedures required in this resolution. The Executive Committee of the Board is charged with review of all such publications from time to time to ensure that they do not take on the character of formal research reports of the National Bureau, requiring formal Board approval.

7. Unless otherwise determined by the Board or exempted by the terms of paragraph 6, a copy of this resolution shall be printed in each National Bureau publication.

(Resolution adopted October 25, 1926, as revised through September 30, 1974)

Contents

Figures

Tables

To Bob and Enid

Preface

One of the most striking features of the demographic history of North America, as of many other developed countries, has been the fall in mortality levels between the eighteenth and the twentieth centuries. This fall requires documentation and explanation; both were the task of a research programme begun in the late 1970s, under the auspices of the National Bureau of Economic Research, into 'The Decline of Mortality in North America'. But, as Robert Fogel, who inspired the research programme, soon recognised, explanation of the fall in American mortality involved a search beyond North America; from the beginning of settlement until the First World War, the millions of immigrants who settled in the new world brought with them the culture, the habits of diet and of clothing and the health which they had acquired in the old.

Any explanation of the decline in mortality thus had to confront the question of how far the mortality levels of North America should be attributed to the health of the immigrants and of their immediate descendants who shared their customs and how far to the environment which they found in their new country. But to answer such a question required in its turn knowledge of the environment which they had left and which, in conjunction with their incomes and habits, had shaped their health. For much of the history of North America, this meant knowledge of the health and environment of the peoples of Britain and Ireland, from whom the vast majority of immigrants were drawn.

But it was also necessary to find some way of judging that health and environment and of comparing it to the health and environment of the peoples of other countries. Conventional measures of welfare, such as real wages, the level of infant mortality or the level of life expectation, were insufficiently comprehensive to provide what was

xvii

needed, a general indication of the health of the migrants and of their ability to withstand the pressures of the new life which they would be required to lead. It was in searching for such an indication that Robert Fogel began to explore the potential of anthropometric measurements and their relationship to health and nutrition.

Fogel was not in fact the first historian to make use of anthropometry, since Emmanuel le Roy Ladurie had used the records of French conscripts to describe the physical characteristics of Frenchmen in the early nineteenth century (1973). But Fogel's use of anthropometric material, gathered by himself, Stanley Engerman and Marilyn Coopersmith from the records of the Royal Marines in the Public Record Office, represented the first attempt to use such material – in particular the records of the heights of recruits – for comparative purposes and in the study of economic history and historical demography.

It was at Fogel's suggestion that the research which is described here began; it was matched by similar research in the archives of the United States, in the records of the British West Indian colonies and, later, in the records of Sweden and of Austria–Hungary. As the research developed, and as the full potential of anthropometric data in studies in economic history and demography was realised, the original purpose of the research in Britain – to contribute to the mortality history of the United States – became secondary to the study of British height data for the light that it could throw on the British economy and on the health and nutritional status of the people of Britain and Ireland.

The British research would, however, have been impossible without the encouragement and support of Robert Fogel and of the other members of the research programme on the 'Development of the American Economy,' who have worked on similar problems, shared their insights and given freely of their time and critical abilities in helping to shape the research and this book itself. Lance Davis, Stanley Engerman, Gerald Friedman, Robert Margo, Kenneth Sokoloff, Richard Steckel, James Trussell and Georgia Villaflor deserve special mention, but we are also grateful to other participants at the National Bureau of Economic Research summer workshop in 1987, and to John Komlos and Sidney Rosenbaum, who commented on early drafts.

We have also received most generous support and constructive criticism from many who are more expert than we in the various fields of study which are represented in this interdisciplinary work. James Tanner has put his unrivalled knowledge of both auxology – the study of human growth – and of its history unstintingly at our service and has saved us from many errors. Harvey Goldstein and Michael Healy gave generous and useful statistical advice. Paul David, Alexander Field, Philip Payne, Johan Pottier, Peter Solar and Simon Strickland have been particularly helpful. We have also benefitted from the comments of many seminar participants at the universities of Berkeley, Cambridge, Durham, Edinburgh, Glasgow, Leeds, London, Oxford, St Andrews and Stanford and at the ESRC Cambridge Group for the History of Population and Social Structure, the London School of Hygiene and Tropical Medicine and St Thomas' Hospital, London. Initial results of the research were presented at the Boehringer-Ingelheim Symposium, at the International Economic History Conference at Budapest, at the Quantitative Economic History workshop and at conferences organised by the British Society for Population Studies, the Journal of Interdisciplinary History, the International Commission for the Application of Quantitative Methods to History, the Wellcome Foundation for the History of Medicine and the Social Science History Association. We are grateful to the organisers for their invitations and to the audiences for their comments.

Like much quantitative research in history and economics, the research reported here has required substantial financial support, which it has received from the British Academy and the Economic and Social Research Council in Britain (Research grants HR 7447 and G00230057) and from the National Science Foundation, the National Bureau of Economic Research and the Center for Population Economics at the University of Chicago, in the United States. We have also greatly benefited from the research and networking facilities of the National Bureau of Economic Research and the Centre for Economic Policy Research although, as with all publications under the auspices of these bodies, they are not responsible for the opinions which are expressed here. We have also received generous support from the University of California at Berkeley and especially its Committee for Research, and from Birkbeck College, London, which provided research assistance and two periods of research leave for Roderick Floud; one of those periods of leave was made both pleasant and productive by his appointment as a Visiting Professor in Economics and History at Stanford University.

The Public Record Office at Kew kindly allowed us to install and use cumbersome data entry terminals in its search-room. The Librarian of the Ministry of Defence acted as a guide through some especially arcane military records. The National Maritime Museum and the Marine Society of London provided easy access to the records of the Society. We are particularly grateful for research assistance in the collection and processing of data provided by Carl Boe, Catherine

Crawford, Judy Collingwood, Joseph Lau, Christophe LeFranc, Mary-Lou Legg, Barbara Neagle, Sunchai Rajadhon and Meta Zimmeck. Barbara Whitmore, Lin Bailey and Sheila Hailey entered the Marine Society data. We also thank Eleanor Thomas, who typed many of the tables, and Julia Peacock, who checked and collated the bibliography and tables. The staff of Cambridge University Press have tolerated delays and given much helpful advice.

Despite all this help, this book with its faults and lacunae remains our own. It is the first attempt to write the anthropometric history of Britain and Ireland over the last 250 years. It is unlikely to be the last, both because the potential of the study of human growth by historian and economist has not yet been fully realised and because, although this study breaks some new ground in the use of quantitative methods in the service of history, various aspects of the data remain unexplored. These data are available to any scholar who wishes to use them and it is our hope that they will be used and that this work stimulates similar studies of the anthropometric history of many other countries. Despite the many years which this study has taken, we remain intrigued and fascinated by the data and by the problems of the study of human growth and we hope that we have conveyed some of that fascination in this book.

We have not sought to write a history of human height in Britain for any period earlier than the eighteenth century. Many materials for such a study exist and some of them have recently been discussed by Kunitz (1987). They spring from the work of archaeologists, physical anthropologists, architectural historians and historians of armour. Despite the interest of such work and the actual and potential excitement of the use of information from suits of armour, heights of doorways, coffin sizes, cemeteries and the plague pits of seventeenth-century London, such studies would have taken us too far from our competencies as modern historian, statistician and historical anthropologist. We are grateful to all who suggested the use of such material and hope that it may be further collected and collated in the future.

One particular regret deserves emphasis. We have been able to say virtually nothing about the heights of women. Our sources are primarily military and do not contain any records of women; even when, as in the case of the Marine Society of London, some girls were recruited, they were not measured. Prison records do contain measurements of women but we chose not to use them on the basis, which was possibly mistaken, that such records could not be used as a basis for inference about the female population. Nor, because of our emphasis on males in our study of the eighteenth and nineteenth century, have we considered evidence on the heights of girls and women in the twentieth century, although this has been done in a study associated with ours (Harris 1988). So this is a study of male heights; we can only hope to stimulate a companion study of the heights of females.

We have been particularly sustained, during the years of this study, by Cynthia Floud and Bernadette Bell, who have provided criticism of obscurity, succour in periods of irritation and elation, and hospitality for interminable discussions. Enid Fogel, too, has shown endless patience and encouragement and has helped us, and Bob Fogel, to keep a proper sense of proportion. We end this preface, as we began, with Robert Fogel. Not only did he inspire this study but he has encouraged it at all stages, has remained calm even when we despaired of finding a way through a statistical maze, and has both been a stern critic and one who has often been readier to see the potential and relevance of our work to historical problems than have we ourselves. It is because of their joint contribution that we are delighted to dedicate this book to our two friends, Bob and Enid.

City of London Polytechnic
University of California at Berkeley and
Birkbeck College, London

1

Height, nutritional status and the historical record

1.0 INTRODUCTION

Height matters to humans. It is the stuff of myth and chronicle; 'there were giants on the earth in those days' (Genesis 6:4) who were seen by the scouts of the children of Israel when they ventured from the desert into the land of milk and honey: 'the giants, the sons of Anak, which come of the Nephilim: and we were in our own sight as grasshoppers, and so we were in their sight' (Numbers 13:33). It is, in many primitive societies, part of the power of kingship that the rulers tower above the ruled, a phenomenon reflected in our language; we speak of 'looking up' to our superiors and tell children to 'stand up tall!'. Tallness is not always a positive characteristic; the short count Socrates, Napoleon and Einstein among their number. But whichever way the connotations run, height is a salient characteristic, one of our primary means of identification, one of the features of the body which it is most difficult to disguise. And it is still one of the most important factors which enters into a choice of girlfriend, boyfriend or marriage partner.

It comes as no surprise, therefore, that travellers in strange lands often comment on the unusual height, whether high or low, of those whom they see. Within a single country, differences in heights between groups have the power to surprise and to shock. Thus in 1833 one of the British Factory Commissioners, Dr Bisset Hawkins, reported on his visit to Manchester that (PP 1833: xxi):

I believe that most travellers are struck by the lowness of stature, the leanness and paleness which present themselves so commonly to the eye at Manchester and, above all, among the factory classes. I have never been in any town in Great Britain nor in Europe in which degeneracy of form and colour from the national standard has been so obvious.

while in 1840 it was said of handloom weavers, the archetypal

1

casualties of the Industrial Revolution, that (Royal Commission 1840: xxiii, 240):

They are decayed in their bodies; the whole race of them is rapidly descending to the size of Lilliputians. You could not raise a grenadier company amongst them all.

Even in the twentieth century, it is still commonplace for men and women to observe systematic height differences between the group to which they themselves belong and some other group. Those from the prosperous south-east of England who saw the Hunger Marches against unemployment in the 1930s often comment on the shock that they received when they saw how short were the miners of south Wales or the steelworkers of the north-east. Even more common is the observation of changing height between generations and, in particular, the increase in height which is often attributed to the nutritious and egalitarian effects of food rationing in Britain in the Second World War.

As this shows, humans are almost as quick to explain differences in height as to observe them. The first systematic observations of height differences within a large population were made in the 1820s by a French doctor, L. R. Villermé, who moved straight from observation, of recruits to the French army, to explanation (1829, translated by Tanner 1981: 162):

Human height becomes greater and growth takes place more rapidly, other things being equal, in proportion as the country is richer, comfort more general, houses, clothes and nourishment better and labour, fatigue and privation during infancy and youth less; in other words, the circumstances which accompany poverty delay the age at which complete stature is reached and stunt adult height.

Without the benefit of modern statistical methods, Villermé thus asserted a clear and causal relationship between the environment and human stature; he was followed in this by such British pioneers of epidemiology as Edwin Chadwick, who commented several times in his great *Report on the Sanitary Condition of the Labouring Population of Great Britain* that physical deficiency was the mark not just of the criminal classes but of the whole working class and in particular those born and brought up in urban areas. 'Noxious physical agencies', Chadwick thought, were producing a population 'having a perpetual tendency to moral as well as physical deterioration' (Flinn 1965: 268). Chadwick did not apportion blame, but Marx had no doubt of the cause of the declining height of working class populations throughout

Europe as shown by the height of military recruits (1867 (1961) I: 239):

The limiting of factory labour was dictated by the same necessity which spread guano over the English fields. The same blind eagerness for plunder that in the one case exhausted the soil had, in the other, torn up by the roots the living force of the nation. Periodical epidemics speak on this point as clearly as the diminishing military standard in Germany and France.

Later in the century, the apparent deterioration of the physical strength and health of military recruits in Britain prompted a wave of similar concern about the health of the nation.

But how was it possible for Villermé and his British contemporaries so clearly and so definitely to assert a connection between poverty, ill-health, deprivation and disease and the physical growth of human beings? As we shall show in this book, they could do so because the differences which they observed between the average heights of social and geographical groups, among whom they lived and worked, were so large and thus so striking. It is only mildly flippant to assert that, in the early nineteenth century, the upper classes of France and Britain could literally look down on the lower classes.

That is no longer true. A sample survey of adult heights and weights in Britain, taken in 1980, revealed that there are still social-class differences in height in Britain, as in most other countries, but such differences have greatly diminished from the time when Villermé could see them. Other obvious distinctions have replaced them; we are used to observing that children are on the whole taller than their parents and we can also discern clear differences in average height between different societies in the world.

It does not follow, of course, that such differences stem from the effects of the environment on the human body. Indeed, it was immediately argued by those who read the work of Villermé that he had jumped to the wrong conclusion; the difference between the average heights of conscripts from different regions of France stemmed not from environment but from race. It was accepted that poverty and disease might delay growth, but mature adult height was said to be racially determined (Tanner 1981: 163). The argument was soon extended to Britain where it was asserted, and still is, that the peoples of southern and eastern England, descended from the Anglo-Saxon invaders, were and are taller than the Celtic peoples of Wales and the west. Observation of these latter peoples, with their dark hair and eyes, might lead to the 'common-sense' conclusion that those features are inextricably linked to their height and both together to their Celtic heritage.

If we range more widely in the modern world, then it again may seem obvious that differences in the appearance of different peoples stem from their racial origins. We cannot escape from racial stereotypes, contrasting for example the tall and fair Anglo-Saxons with the short, slim and dark south Asian populations or the short but fairer populations of east Asia. Moreover, the fact that differences *between* ethnic groups now seem to the casual observer much greater than differences *within* ethnic groups (though they are in fact much smaller) leads naturally to a presumption that those differences are related to ethnicity. While Chadwick and Villermé could see that it was the poor in their own nation who were short, now we, in prosperous Europe or America, see that it is the people of other nations who are often shorter than ourselves.

Half-understood aspects of the earlier study of human physical growth, together with a confusion between the factors which affect the heights of individuals and of groups, contribute to the tendency to ascribe height to ethnicity. Francis Galton, in the late nineteenth century, made an extensive study of human growth and, in particular, of the extent of inheritance of height between parents and children. His demonstration of a significant inherited component in individual height, together with a second concept, that of regression to the mean, both entered public consciousness, but both were and are normally misunderstood. Both concepts relate to what a statistician would call 'within-group' variation between individuals, rather than to the 'between-group' variation which is relevant to the study of differences between geographically distinct populations.

Nevertheless, when combined with the fact that between-group variation, for example that between social classes, is now much less than it was during the nineteenth century and that therefore individual or within-group variation appears to be the most obvious cause of differences in heights within a particular ethnic group, the public confusion is natural. Unfortunately, the confusion leads, through an emphasis on the undoubted genetic component of within-group variation (stemming for example from parent–child inheritance), to a misplaced belief in the similar importance of the genetic component of between-group variation. Differences in the heights of populations between the developed and the less developed world are then ascribed to genetic differences.

In fact, most people greatly overestimate not only the speed of genetic change within a Darwinian framework – where it is measured in many millennia rather than in decades – but also the extent of differences between different ethnic groups. To illustrate these points, figure 1.1 contrasts modern adult heights in various parts of Africa with some evidence of adult heights in Europe over the past two hundred years. The most striking finding is that Norwegian recruits of the 1760s were as short as bushmen; today, they are as tall as the Dinka of the Sudan.[1] In other words, the range over time in one European population matches the range over space throughout Africa; it would be hazardous to conclude, without additional evidence, that either range was *obviously* due to racial inheritance, despite the fact that many other features of these populations, such as skin or hair colour, seem likely to be so.

Confusion about the relationship between heredity and environment arises because, when we look around us, we observe men, women and children of many different heights; as we seek to explain those differences, we enter into fields of study such as genetics and human biology which are intrinsically complex and have also become overlaid with prejudice and political controversy. If we are to disentangle these complexities and prejudices then we have to begin with one simple statement: height is not determined either by heredity or by environment, but always by both. As the distinguished geneticist J. M. Thoday put it (1965: 94):

Every character is both genetic and environmental in origin. Let us be quite clear about this. Genotype determines the potentialities of an organism. Environment determines which or how much of those potentialities shall be realised during development.

Consider first the variation in height which we observe among those to whom we are closest, our group of friends, neighbours and relatives. Given our human propensity to cluster together with others like ourselves, it is likely that such a group consists of men and women brought up in much the same way and under many of the same conditions of income, health and psychological treatment, in other words in approximately the same environment. Yet we observe that some of our friends are much taller, some much shorter than ourselves;

---

[1] Eveleth and Tanner (1976: 338) report the Mbaiki as having an average adult height of 151.8 cm (59.8 in), and the Bunia as 145.0 cm (57.1 in). The sample sizes were, however, only 15 and 14 respectively (Rimoin *et al.* 1967; Mann *et al.* 1962). The shortest other African groups were bushmen of Botswana at 157.8 cm (62.1 in) with a sample size of 15, and 159.4 cm (62.8 in) with a sample size of 292 (Wyndham 1970; Tobias 1962); the Fulero of the Congo at 159.1 cm (62.6 in) with a sample size of 100 (Hiernaux 1965); and the Twa pygmies of the Congo at 160 cm (63 in) and a sample size of 36 at ages 25–34 (Barnicot *et al.* 1972). (In all cases cited in Eveleth and Tanner.)

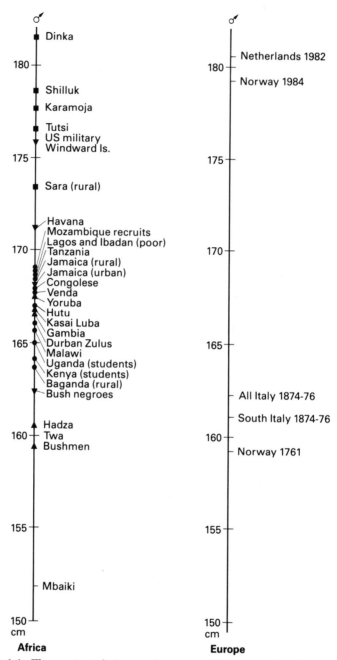

Figure 1.1. The contrast between the range of European heights over time and of African heights today. Sources: left, reproduced from Figure 75 of P. B. Eveleth and J. M. Tanner (1976) *Worldwide Variation in Human Growth* (Cambridge University Press); right, see text.

in statistical terminology, there is variance in heights within the group. If we went to the trouble of measuring all the men and women of the group and calculating the average height of each sex we could make a precise statement about the range in heights, the variation around the mean. What explains this variation?

We know, following Thoday, that the height of an individual is determined by both genotype and environment and by the interaction between them, and that therefore the individual height of each member of our group is so determined. But because we know that members of the group have been brought up in approximately the same environment (so that variety in environment has been minimised), we can deduce that variety in genetic endowment of those individuals within the group is likely to have been relatively important in producing the variance in their heights.

Now let us imagine that we add to this group their children, grown to adulthood. Although these children will have shared the environment of their parents to a considerable extent, they will have grown up at a different time and probably in different places. The variance of heights within the larger group will reflect some of these differences, so that the variety of environments will now be playing a relatively larger, and genetic variety a relatively smaller, part in producing the overall variance. In addition, however, the increasing genetic and increasing environmental variety will be interacting with each other to contribute also to the variance. How can we disentangle these factors?

One way to try to do so is to split our larger group into two – parents and children – and to consider the differences between them. In doing this, we move away from discussing the individuals whose heights make up the variance within the group to discuss the differences between the groups as a whole. As a result, we need a new measure, not the individual heights which continue to make up the variance within each group, but the average heights which represent the difference between the groups. We find that there is a difference between the average heights of the parents and of the children and, knowing that the two groups share a genetic endowment, deduce that the environmental differences between the two groups are relatively important in explaining the difference in their average height.

In this very simple example, we can attribute relatively greater influence to genetic causes in producing *within-group* variance and relatively greater influence to environmental causes in producing *between-group* variance, remembering always the importance of interaction between them. There is thus no conflict between genetic and environmental factors; both operate together to produce variance. This remains true as we move from stylised examples to the world as a whole and as we move from variance within groups to variance between groups. Just as genetic and environmental factors produce variance within groups, so they produce variance between groups. Different peoples in the world exhibit different genetic endowments; these interact with the different environments in which they live to produce differences between themselves and other groups.

The fact that variance in height in humans is the result of both environmental and genetic variety does not stop us from focussing our interest on one in preference to the other, provided that we never forget how they are linked and that we are always concerned to establish their relative importance. Nor, as these remarks have shown, does it make it impossible to distinguish between variance largely attributable to genetic factors and that attributable to environmental factors. In this book, we shall concentrate on environmental variety and variance in height between groups. This is for two reasons.

First, we are writing history; we are concerned with change over time and with examining the heights of successive generations within Britain and Ireland. Since this is so, we can assume that, as in our simple example, environmental causes of variation are particularly important; this is a book about the last 250 years and we can be sure that, over such a short period, Darwinian evolution has not produced significant genetic change within the indigenous population of the United Kingdom.

There have been, it is true, periods of substantial migration into the British Isles since the eighteenth century, as well as substantial internal migration which would have broken up any earlier isolated communities. Some of this migration could have contributed to height increases through the phenomenon known as heterosis, akin to hybrid vigour in plant communities; arguments for heterosis are presented in, for example, Schreider (1968), Billy (1980), Wolanski (1980) and Wolanski, Jarosz and Pyzuk (1968). But the evidence for heterosis in human populations is very weak (see, for example, Damon 1965) and even its postulated effects are not large enough to have been a significant cause of the observed changes in height.

Second, one of our objectives will be to describe and explain differences between socio-economic groups at one moment in time, within societies whose members are so intermixed and intermarried that they can be assumed to share a similar genetic endowment; once again, though not so simply as in our simple example, we can assume that environmental causes are of particular importance.

Even if we concentrate on environmental variety and on between-group variation, many problems remain. Why do substantial differences exist in the average height of populations in time and space? How are they related to other phenomena of interest to social scientists and to historians, such as movements in the output of the economy or the changing mortality and morbidity levels of populations? How much does knowledge of the height of the population add to our understanding of economy and society?

1.1 THE PATTERN OF HUMAN GROWTH

We have all experienced human growth and, if our memories of some of it are weak, are reminded of it by seeing the growth of children. But such knowledge is necessarily individual and subjective; unless we have studied the subject intimately, we have no way of distinguishing between the normal pattern of growth and individual variations. In this section, we will describe that normal pattern and the ways in which is it measured.

The different tissues which make up the body grow at different rates; indeed some, such as the skin, consist of cells which are continuously produced to replace cells which have died, while others, such as nerve and muscle tissue, are formed during the process of growth in childhood and adolescence and cannot later be replaced. But even within these broad groups, different types of tissue are formed at different rates, in a complex process which J. M. Tanner once described as (1978: 1):

like the weaving of a cloth whose design never repeats itself. The underlying threads, each coming from the reel at its own rhythm, interact with one another continuously, in a manner always highly regulated and controlled. The fundamental biological questions of growth relate to these processes of regulation, to the programme that controls the loom.

While many of these fundamental processes are still imperfectly understood, the actual pattern of growth in human populations is now extremely well documented, mainly as a result of the International Biological Programme (Eveleth and Tanner 1976). The pattern of growth of the British population is shown in figures 1.2 and 1.3, which display the normal pattern of growth in height. Despite the fact that we grow in many other ways than in height, as J. M. Tanner observes (1978: 1): 'that is the characteristic we single out in everyday speech, for we talk of a child "growing up".' Although the International Biological Programme gathered data on many other aspects of growth, the authors who summarised the findings of the IBP saw growth in height as fundamental, both because of its popular connotations and

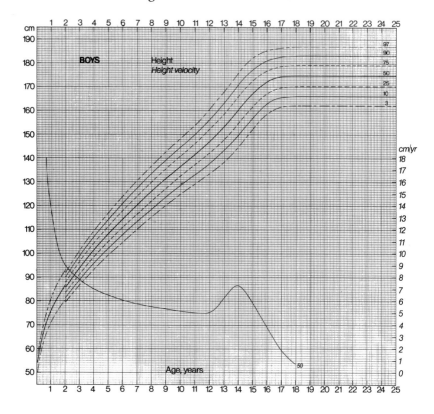

Figure 1.2. The pattern of growth of males in Britain in 1966 (cross-sectional standards). Source: Tanner, Whitehouse and Takaishi (1966).

because it exhibits so much systematic variation with aspects of the environment.

In this book, we shall concentrate on height, both for these reasons and because of the limitations of historical data; only in very recent times has it become customary to record even weights, let alone more complex anthropometric data. For similar reasons, though with great regret, we are forced to concentrate on the growth of males; very few historical records of the growth of females in Britain or the rest of Europe exist.

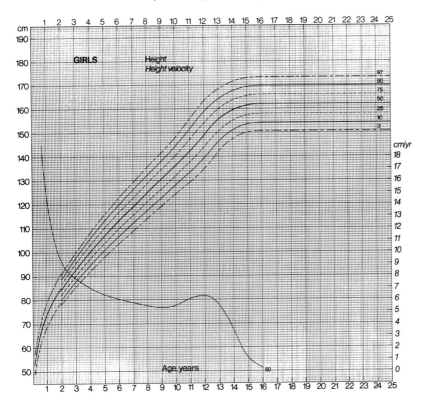

Figure 1.3. The pattern of growth of females in Britain in 1966 (cross-sectional standards). Source: Tanner, Whitehouse and Takaishi (1966).

A growth chart, such as those in figures 1.2 and 1.3, is normally compiled from samples of the child and adolescent population, in this case by Tanner, Whitehouse and Takaishi (1966) from the children of London in the 1960s. Growth charts serve two principal purposes, first to establish the pattern of growth characteristic of a particular population (and to facilitate comparisons between populations) and second to aid in the diagnosis of abnormalities in the growth of an individual child. The first purpose focusses attention on the average height, the second on extreme variations from that average.

Growth charts can be compiled in at least three different ways. Figures 1.2 and 1.3 are examples of the most common method, known as the 'cross-sectional', based on measuring at one time a set of groups of children of different ages; this produces a set of frequency distributions, one for each age, from which a median height for that age group is easily calculated. The medians are then joined to produce a curve of median heights by age; such a curve is that labelled '50' in the top part of figures 1.2 and 1.3. This, and the meaning of the lines labelled 3, 10, 25, 75, 90 and 97, is explained shortly.

Cross-sectional charts are based on *different* children measured at different ages. They do not coincide, therefore, with a second type of chart, known as 'longitudinal', which is based on measuring the *same* children at successive ages. Such charts do give a precise picture of the growth of a particular group of children, but like all longitudinal data, such measurements are extremely difficult and expensive to collect; children move, refuse to cooperate or fall ill, so that they cannot be remeasured. For these reasons, there are few examples of longitudinal growth profiles either for contemporary or historical populations.

The third method, which we shall use extensively in this book, is a variant of cross-sectional charts. A clear defect of a chart derived by the cross-sectional method is that the data relate to children who were born at different times and may have had very different childhood experiences; if the measurements were taken in 1960, for example, then the group of 20-year-olds were born in 1940 and experienced childhood during World War Two, while the two-year-olds were children during the peacetime prosperity after 1958. If successive cross-sections are gathered, however, it is possible to rearrange the data to group on one chart all those children *born* in a particular year but *measured* in successive later years; we refer to such groups of children as 'birth cohorts'.

Growth charts such as figures 1.2 and 1.3 show the results of measurements in two different ways; in the top half they plot height itself against age, in the bottom the change in height from the previous age-group. In individuals this would be called the 'velocity curve', but for cross-sections (where it is averaging out large variations in velocity between individuals) it is properly known as the 'mean increment' curve; it brings out most clearly the tremendous changes which occur in the speed of growth. In early life, growth is very rapid; although the mean increment actually diminishes from the fourth month of foetal life onwards, by the age of two the child has already reached approximately half its adult height. Thereafter mean increments continue to reduce until, at the age of 10–11 for girls and

12–13 for boys, there is a reversal of trend, a rapid increase known as the 'adolescent growth spurt' which is associated with the onset of puberty. After the spurt the mean increments again diminish and growth in height ceases entirely in the late teens or early twenties. Only later in life does velocity again become important, when shrinking occurs.

Figures 1.2 and 1.3 show the pattern of growth of the population of Britain. But the International Biological Programme showed that this overall pattern is characteristic of all human populations, although different populations exhibit different velocity and different timing of the growth spurt and the attainment of final height. The east Asian populations, for example, appear typically to grow faster than European populations during the period before and during the growth spurt though there is then a more rapid deceleration to a final height which is typically less than in European populations. But the overall pattern remains much the same.

A second feature of variation in height is also common to all human populations. As the last section made clear, our main concern in this book is with variance *between* groups, but there is one aspect of *within*-group variance which concerns us and which is implied in the growth charts which we have just examined. Height, like other human characteristics, is determined by both genetic and environmental factors and the interaction between them, but there is, contrary to popular belief, no single 'gene for height'; instead, it is thought that many genes interact with many features of the environment to determine the height of any individual. Individuals are, for this reason, neither 'tall' nor 'short' but take their place on a continuum of tallness around the average height of the group of which they are members. The interaction of many genes with the environment, each with small effect, determines the fact that the height of any given individual is most likely to be close to the average height of his or her group, less and less likely to be much taller or much shorter than that average. It is a feature of the distribution of adult human heights, within a group not specially selected for their heights, that this distribution approximates closely to a Gaussian or normal distribution, sometimes known as the 'bell-shaped curve'. Indeed, adult heights provided one of the classic examples of Gaussian distribution during the development of the basic theory of statistics and probability. Adolescent heights differ slightly from adult heights in this respect, but the differences are well understood and will be discussed in chapter 3.

Figure 1.4 shows such a distribution, drawn from the heights of recruits to the Italian army in the late nineteenth century. In this

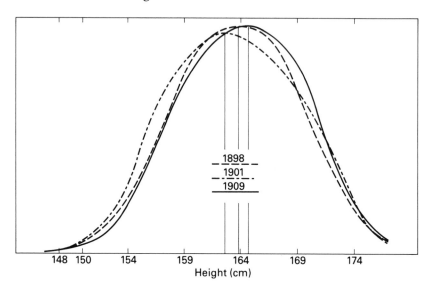

Figure 1.4. A normal distribution of height: Italian army recruits of 1898, 1901 and 1909. Source: Livi *Antropometria Militare* (Rome) (1896), Table XXVI (redrawn).

figure, the vertical distance between each point on the horizontal axis and the curve above it represents the number of recruits with the height shown at that point.

This distribution has a number of features. First, figure 1.4 shows that the height distribution, as a normal distribution, is symmetrical around its centre or mode; because this is so, each observation in the distribution (each individual height) taller than the mode is balanced by another observation shorter than the mode. This ensures arithmetically that the mode is also the arithmetic mean. It also ensures that the mode and the mean coincide with the median, the value which divides the distribution into two parts, with exactly the same number of observations above as below it.

Second, let us imagine that we start at the mean and move to the left in the distribution, counting observations as we go and stopping after we have moved each 0.5 of a centimetre along the horizontal axis. It is clear that the number of observations in the first 0.5 cm will be larger than the number of observations in the next 0.5 cm, and so on until we reach the outermost part of the distribution. This reflects the fact that heights near the average are most common and that extreme shortness (or tallness) is relatively uncommon. It is, in other words, more probable that a given recruit will have a height close to the mean than that he will be extremely tall or extremely short.

But now consider this in the reverse direction; let us start from the outer part of the distribution and move towards the centre, but this time counting observations and seeing how far we move for each 500 observations (the exact number is immaterial). At first, we will move a long way but, as we get closer to the mean, we will move less and less for each 500 men. Then, as we move past the mean the opposite will occur, until as we get towards the taller heights we will again move a long way for each 500 men.

This characteristic of the normal curve is reflected in the growth charts, figures 1.2 and 1.3, which show what are called the centiles of the distribution of heights. Just as the median is the value which divides the distribution into two parts, so the centiles are the values which divide the set of observations into 100 groups, each containing the same number of observations; to put it in another way, these are the values which delineate each percentage of the distribution. Values which divide the distribution into five equal parts are called quintiles; into ten equal parts, deciles; and the general word for such a division point is quantile, a concept which is prominent in the statistical methods we have used and which are discussed in chapter 3.

Following the logic of the last paragraph, we can see that the difference between the centiles which are close to the mean will be small, while as we move further from the mean the differences will get larger. This is shown in the growth curves, where the gap between the 3rd and 10th centiles is only slightly smaller than the gap between the 10th and 25th centiles, which is itself only slightly smaller than the gap between the 25th and 50th centiles (the median). It is clearly relatively unusual to come across a height lower than the 1st or 2nd centile (or higher than the 98th or 99th centile). For this reason, when growth charts of this kind are used to assess the heights of individual children, it is conventional for doctors to refer for further examination any child with a height less than the 3rd (or greater than the 97th) centile.

The third characteristic of height distributions which requires mention is that the range between extreme values of the distribution – say the 1% tallest and shortest – is very similar in all human populations, *whatever the mean of the distribution*. That is, the variance in the heights of African bushmen, who are on average very short, is approximately the same as the variance in the heights of the Dinka, who are on average tall, and we can assume – or sometimes measure – the same phenomenon in the case of other groups shown in figure 1.1, such as the Norwegian recruits of the eighteenth and of the late twentieth centuries. Statisticians conventionally measure the spread in a distribution by calculating its standard deviation, which, in the case of height distributions, almost always falls between 2.3 and 2.8 inches (6.35–7.11 cm).[2] If we follow the logic set out above, we know that as we move the first 2.5 inches above (or below) the mean we shall cover much of the distribution, as we move the next 2.5 inches somewhat less of it, but the nature of the normal distribution allows us to be very precise; 64 per cent of all the observations in the distribution will fall within one standard deviation above and below the mean, while 95 per cent will fall within range of two standard deviations above and below the mean. In other words, 95 per cent of all heights of individuals fall within a range of 10 to 11.2 inches (25.4–28.4 cm) distributed symmetrically around the average height of the group to which they belong.

These properties of human growth and of distributions of height may seem esoteric, but in fact they underlie much of this book. Armed with knowledge of them, we can now safely move away from individual heights or within-group variance to consider the average heights and between-group variance which are the main subject of this book.

1.2 HEIGHT, NUTRITIONAL STATUS, THE ENVIRONMENT AND THE STANDARD OF LIVING

The observation that systematic variations exist between the patterns of growth of different populations leads directly to the question of what causes such variations. While we must remember that all characteristics such as height are produced by genotype and environment, the data collected by the International Biological Programme suggests that variations in growth within very broad racial groupings are primarily the product of the effects of the environment. This is summed up in the statement of Eveleth and Tanner (1976: 1) which introduces the IBP report:

A child's growth rate reflects, better than any other single index, his state of health and nutrition, and often indeed his psychological situation also. Similarly, the average value of children's heights and weights reflect accurately the state of a nation's public health and the average nutritional status of its citizens, when appropriate allowance is made for differences, if any,

---

[2] This statement is not true in the case of cross-sections of heights of adolescents during the period of the growth spurt. At such times, when growth is rapid, the fact that some adolescents enter the growth spurt, and complete it, earlier than others has the effect of increasing the variance.

in genetic potential. This is especially so in developing and disintegrating countries. Thus a well-designed growth study is a powerful tool with which to monitor the health of a population, or to pinpoint subgroups of a population whose share in economic or social benefits is less than it might be.

Eveleth and Tanner were speaking, of course, of growth studies in the modern world; the research reported in this book aims to be such a study in history.

Eveleth and Tanner write of the 'average nutritional status' of a group, a term which will be used frequently in this book and which requires explanation. As their statement makes clear, a child's growth rate reflects many aspects of the environment in which it is brought up; a child requires an adequate intake of nutrients to maintain its body, to undertake physical activity and to grow. In addition, it must combat disease and other forms of stress, such as cold and emotional deprivation. Studies of children show clearly that, if the normal balance between the supply of nutrients to the body and the demands on those nutrients is upset, for example by a decline in food intake or by a need to combat disease, then the child's growth will rapidly be affected. It seems as if the child's body attempts to protect itself by sacrificing growth. Weight will normally be first affected, but height growth and change in other anthropometric indicators of growth will soon follow. Similarly, if the danger recedes, weight, height and other signs of growth will return; indeed, the child will grow faster than before, a phenomenon known as 'catch-up growth', to return to the growth path which it was previously following.

It is because growth is so rapidly affected that it is now common for paediatricians and social workers to examine the growth charts of individual children to see if evidence exists of deprivation or child abuse. This abuse can be both physical and emotional. Figure 1.5, for example reproduces a weight chart from the report of an enquiry into child abuse. The child's growth can be clearly seen responding first to deprivation and then to the removal of the threat to its welfare.

In chapter 6 we consider in much more detail the impact of disease and deprivation on growth and, in particular, the differential impact of such factors at different ages and stages of growth. As might be expected, the growth of a child appears to be particularly sensitive to environmental influences at the times when growth is normally fastest, that is before birth, during the neo-natal period and in infancy and during the adolescent growth spurt. But there is also evidence that continued deprivation, perhaps in the form of a constantly deficient food supply, can exert a depressant effect on growth throughout the growing years.

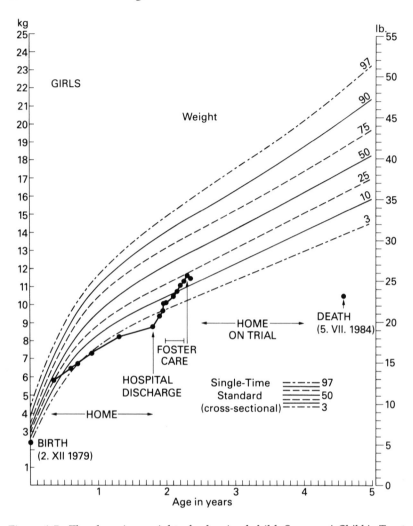

Figure 1.5. The changing weight of a deprived child. Source: *A Child in Trust: The Report of the Panel of Inquiry into the circumstances surrounding the death of Jasmine Beckford* (Brent, London: London Borough of Brent, 1985), p. 71.

Because the growth of a child responds to far more than simple nutrient intakes, human biologists employ the term 'nutritional status' to describe the outcome of the whole complex of factors which affect the welfare of a child from its conception. To employ the jargon of economists, nutritional status is thus a 'net' concept, the outcome of nutrient intakes since conception balanced against the demands on those nutrients for health, growth, work, play, warmth and happiness. During infancy, childhood and adolescence, the relationship between these factors and growth in height is very close.

In this study we are not primarily concerned with individuals. But all the factors which affect the growth of individuals can affect the average growth of a group of individuals. In other words, we can use the concept of 'average nutritional status' to refer to the balance between intakes and requirements for a whole population or for sub-groups within it. There are, indeed, examples of the deprivation of a whole community which illustrate this well; in 1944, the retreating German forces essentially starved the population of western Holland, already under considerable psychological stress and short of fuel and clothing. The result was the cessation of growth among children, accompanied by weight losses among adults and other signs of distress such as amenorrhoea among the female population (Stein *et al.* 1975). Although many of these effects were temporary, the experience illustrates well the sensitivity of growth to environmental change.

The Dutch Hunger Winter is an extreme example. But throughout the world today, and throughout history, malnutrition, disease, deprivation and trauma are and have been reflected in growth. This close relationship between growth and the environment gives height its importance for economists and historians, interested as both are in the changing living standards of human populations. The concept of 'average nutritional status' has an enormous amount in common with the concept of 'average living standard'; it might indeed be thought that they are identical. Thus the measurement of nutritional status through the measurement of height represents, as chapter 7 shows, a powerful method by which to measure the standard of living.

But how sensitive is height to changes in the environment? Is it possible, for example, to estimate the elasticity of height with respect to a change in income or nutrient intake, to say that a change of *x* per cent in income will produce a change of *y* per cent in height? The answer is no, for two main reasons. First, the impact of the environment on height is crucially dependent on age and not only on absolute but on developmental age; that is, different conditions will have different effects depending on the stage of growth which has been reached, which is itself dependent on the severity and duration of previous insults. Second, so many features of the environment, many of them difficult to measure, can be shown to affect growth that we cannot take account of them all in a single causal model, such as is required to estimate an elasticity with any worth or use. What we must do instead is to use the evidence of height sensitively, in conjunction with much other information about a population – its income, housing, health and so on – to contribute to an understanding of its welfare.

Within very broad genetic groups, the effects of the environment dominate variations in human growth. But how large can such variations be? This book is about the heights of the British and Irish, but the fluctuations, trends and differentials in the heights of the peoples of the British Isles are paralleled by similar changes in the heights and thus in the nutritional status of other European populations. Indeed, economic and social change in Europe as in the rest of the world seems always, during the last 250 years, to have been accompanied by change in the indicators of nutritional status; the change in recent years has been so ubiquitous that it has sometimes simply been described as 'the secular trend'.[3]

But that concept can conceal more than it reveals. It tends to imply that all those peoples which have experienced an upward trend in heights have done so at roughly the same rate or for the same reasons, or that there have not been particularly important fluctuations in height around the trend. In addition, to focus on the overall similarity between countries diverts attention from the differences between them. It may divert attention also from the possibility that, just as economists use measures of national income per capita to assess the relative economic welfare of different peoples, so we can use height data to assess differences in nutritional status between peoples.

This section describes the heights of the peoples of the countries of Europe and of European settlement overseas. This is not because studies of the remainder of the world are not fruitful; the work of the International Biological Programme reported by Eveleth and Tanner (1976) has shown the value of such research, while studies such as those of Greulich (1957, 1976) into the heights of the children of Japanese migrants to California are also most illuminating. It is, however, sensible to confine our attention to the area of the world for which data are most abundant, where genetic differences between national populations are minimised and where the relevance to the

---

[3] Many authors have summarised evidence on the secular trend in heights, but particularly comprehensive accounts are in Bakwin (1964), Bakwin and McLaughlin (1964), Cone (1961), Meredith (1976), Tanner (1966, 1978), Van Wieringen (1978) and Wolanski (1978) and, as an example for a single country, Sweden, in Ljung, Bergsten-Brucefors and Lindgren (1974).

British experience is greatest. Our object in this section is, therefore, to provide a context against which the changes in the heights of the British and Irish can best be judged.

1.3.1 Sources of evidence

Study of the height and nutritional status of European nations since the beginning of the eighteenth century must rely almost exclusively on the work of military recruiters.[4] Although material does exist on the heights of other groups, such as newborn babies (Ward 1988), schoolchildren (Komlos 1986) and university students (Aubenque 1957, 1963; Sutter, Izac and Tran 1958), such material is scattered.[5] For this reason, the bulk of our evidence and certainly the evidence of annual or semi-annual mean heights must be drawn from recruitment statistics.

In almost all cases, European height statistics stem from a process of compulsory military service which entailed the annual medical examination and measurement of the entire population of young male adults of conscription age. Most European countries adopted such a system of examination and recruitment during the nineteenth century. It was occasionally possible for certain groups to evade the draft and, on other occasions, only the heights of those accepted for service were recorded; but, with such exceptions, the statistics published by the recruiting authorities normally cover the whole population and were taken at the time as a good indication of the health of that population. It was common, in fact, for such statistics to be published in the section of national statistical yearbooks which dealt with matters of health; most of the evidence used in this chapter is drawn from such sources.

Because almost the whole population of young males was measured, conscription data can provide a good estimate of the mean height of the population. On the other hand, conscription data suffer from the difficulty that there is no possibility of determining or examining the pattern of growth in late adolescence or early adulthood. One can discover with great accuracy the mean height of young men of a particular age, but such data give only a snapshot of the complex

---

[4] For earlier periods, physical anthropologists have relied on archaeological evidence. For examples from British data, see Kunitz (1987) and for Europe, Schwidetzky, Chiarelli and Necrasov (1980) and Werdelin (1985).

[5] A particularly valuable collection of such material was made by Chamla in 1964 while the work of Olivier and his collaborators has demonstrated the achievement of physical anthropologists in this field (Olivier 1970; Olivier *et al.* 1977).

process of human growth and, moreover, give it at a moment at which the process of growth in those measured has largely but not entirely ceased. The age at which recruits were measured is not always exactly known, but it seems likely that most conscription took place at the ages of 18 to 21, at an age when we can be certain, with data drawn from the last century, that final height had not been achieved.

It is therefore important to remember that, because there is evidence that over the course of time the tempo of growth has accelerated and the age of achieving final height has dropped, a comparison of the mean height of a cohort of 18-year-olds today with the height of a cohort of the same age from one century ago will overestimate the change in final height; the boys would have continued growing a century ago whereas now they do not. On the other hand, even if we knew the change which had occurred in final height, that change would itself be an underestimate of the effect of changing environment on growth; this is because some of that effect would have been reflected in the earlier maturity – perhaps at the same absolute height – of the modern cohort as compared with that of the past. The problem arises because, although the tempo of growth and the absolute level of final height are linked as consequences of improved nutritional status, the two phenomena are to some extent independent of each other (Tanner 1982: 574–5).

When examined with these points in mind, military conscription data offer the largest and the most consistent set of evidence for the description of changes in mean height. In some cases, however, other evidence must be used. In the United States, although conscription was used at some periods, in peacetime the armies were composed of volunteers; the pattern of mean heights used below, derived from Fogel (1987), has therefore been calculated after correction, using methods which are described in chapter 3, for the fact that some short recruits were excluded. In Sweden during the eighteenth and early nineteenth centuries, military service was performed in return for land, an obligation passed on from father to son, and appropriate corrections have to be made for this fact, following Steckel (1987).

1.3.2 *The range of European heights*

The average height of national European male populations of conscription age has varied, during the last 200 years, between 159 and 181 cm (62.6–71.3 in). The shortest mean height yet recorded or computed for conscripts measured on a national basis is that of 159.1 cm (62.6 in) for recruits aged 18 to the Habsburg armies in the eighteenth century

(Komlos 1985), while Kiil (1939) estimated that the average height of recruits aged 18.5 to the Norwegian army in 1761 was 159.5 cm (62.8 in). The *Historical Statistics of Italy 1861–1975* (1978) show that the mean height of 20-year-old recruits born in 1854 was 162.39 cm (63.9 in). Spanish recruits, as late as 1913, had a mean height of 163.6 cm (64.4 in) (Rodriguez n.d.).

Since growth would have continued after the age at which these recruits were measured, these measurements give a slight underestimate of final adult heights for those communities. On the basis of modern populations in the less-developed world, who have similar mean heights, it is reasonable to add about 3 per cent for further growth after the age of 18, giving an estimated minimum for mean final height of European national populations of about 165 cm (65 in).

Measurement of the upper end of the observed range can rely on modern data. Army recruits aged 17.5 in the Netherlands had a mean height of 180.7 cm (71.1 in) in 1982 (*Statistical Yearbook of the Netherlands* 1983). These men, the tallest recorded in Europe, were closely followed by Norwegians with a mean of 179.4 cm (70.6 in) in 1983 (*Statistik Arbok* 1984). In the absence of survey data, it is not clear how much further growth after the age of conscription should be assumed for such tall populations, but it is unlikely that more than 1 per cent further growth could possibly occur, giving an estimate for final height of not more than 182.5 cm (71.9 in).

The range of final heights for whole national populations observed in Europe has thus been between about 165 cm (65 in) and about 183 cm (72 in) during the past 200 years. As would be expected, the range over subgroups of national populations has been somewhat wider. The shortest geographical group of all appears to have been recruits from the town of Murcia in Spain, whose mean height in 1895 was only 158.8 cm (62.5 in) (Carrion 1986: 7). At the upper end of the scale, the tallest geographical group yet recorded within Europe appears to be the inhabitants of Aust-Agder in Norway at 180.8 cm (71.2 in) (*Statistik Arbok* 1986), although it seems likely that some Dutch areas would have higher means; the Dutch statistical yearbook ceased to record regional height data after World War Two. If we again allow 3 per cent further growth after conscription for the shortest recorded group and 1 per cent further growth for the tallest, we can estimate the range for large geographical subgroups of national populations to have been from 163.6 cm to 182.6 cm (64.4–71.9 in), with the last figure a probable underestimate. There is, unfortunately, too little evidence to make similar statements about the range across different socio-economic groups although, once again, one would expect the range to widen somewhat if economic and occupational factors could be taken into account.

The range over time and space within Europe of 18 cm (7 in) in mean final height may appear to be extraordinarily small. It represents, after all, only about 10 per cent of current male height and the 'average European man' is at most only 11 per cent taller now than he was 200 years ago. But in fact such differences have changed the appearance of the peoples of Europe in a dramatic way. This was apparent from figure 1.1, which juxtaposed historical European heights against those of contemporary African populations. How different the Norwegian recruits of the 1740s would have looked from Norwegians today!

The process of change in European heights which has led to such dramatic contrasts can be described on the basis of information about twelve European nations or nations of European settlement; ten, Belgium, Denmark, France, Greece, Italy, the Netherlands, Norway, Spain, Sweden, and the United States are considered here, while Britain and Ireland form the subject of the rest of the book. Fragmentary information, not enough to estimate changes over periods of time, exists for other countries and it is likely that further search and the use of archival rather than published material would widen the range of information.[6]

These ten countries can be divided into three broad groups on the basis of their changing heights over time, although the divisions between the groups are often not large. Figure 1.6 shows changing mean heights in the United States, figure 1.7 those of four relatively northern European nations, Denmark, Norway, the Netherlands and Sweden, and figure 1.8 those of a group of relatively southern European nations, Belgium, France, Greece, Italy and Spain. The United States had greater mean heights than any other country until the latter part of the nineteenth century (Sokoloff and Villaflor 1982; Sokoloff 1984); the northern European nations, while initially shorter than the United States, grew rapidly and surpassed them after the Second World War; the southern European nations, initially much shorter, have grown particularly since the Second World War, but remain distinctly shorter than the other two groups. This material is presented in another form in table 1.1, which shows the approximate date at which each country attained a particular mean height.

---

[6] Examples of studies of other European countries are Suchy (1976) for Czechoslovakia, Valaoras (1970) for Greece and Bolsakova (1958) and Vlastovsky (1966) for the Soviet Union. There is also a particularly useful literature on Japan, demonstrating the very rapid increase in Japanese heights in the twentieth century; see, for example, Greulich (1957, 1976) and Tanner *et al.* (1982).

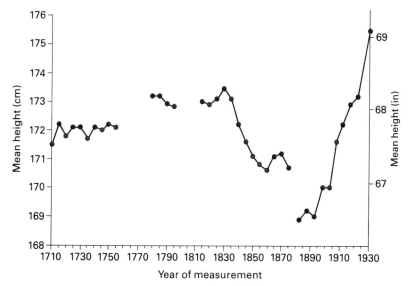

Figure 1.6. Mean final height (age 25–49) in the United States, 1710–1831. Source: Fogel (1986), p. 144. Note: dates are for quinquennial cohorts centred on the date given.

Figure 1.7 Mean height at conscription age in Europe, 1865–1984. The Netherlands, Denmark, Sweden and Norway. Source: see text and Floud (1983).

Table 1.1. *The dates at which nations achieved particular mean heights.*

Nation	Mean height achieved (cm)									
	162	164	166	168	170	172	174	176	178	180
Belgium			1911	1938		1960	1972	1977		
Denmark			1835	1911	1930	1940	1951	1966	1974	1983
France			1910	1940	1960					
Greece			1947							
Holland	1864	1883	1903	1921	1936	1950	1960	1966	1976	
Italy	1874	1909	1930	1956	1971	1977				
Norway					1900	1927		1952	1964	
Spain				1967	1978					
Sweden					1898	1913	1937			
USA						1715	1931			

Sources: see notes to figures 1.6–1.8.

Note: Dates are for cohorts measured at the date shown.

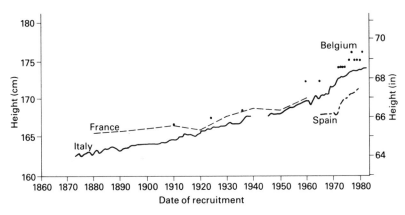

Figure 1.8. Mean height at conscription age in Europe, 1875–1984. Belgium, France, Italy and Spain. Source: see text and Floud (1983).

Since the purpose of this section is to provide a context against which to view British and Irish heights, no attempt will be made to provide an explanation of the trends in, or differences between, the mean heights of these nations. Steckel (1983) has argued that a substantial amount of variation in height in the modern world can be accounted for, in a gross statistical sense, by variations in the levels of income, in the distribution of income, and in levels of infant mortality. His results have been replicated with the present collection of data, though omitting measures of income distribution (Floud 1983, 1985), but such 'ecological' regression analysis is a notoriously hazardous basis for inference. In default of a more general model of the determinants of height variation, it seems safe to say only that the upward trend in European heights reflects the economic development of European nations and the increasing living standards of their populations.

It is clear, however, that all European countries for which records exist have experienced very substantial changes in mean height, great enough to transform the physical appearance of their populations.

1.4 THE SCOPE OF THIS BOOK

The aim of this book is to describe and explain the changes which have occurred in the height of the population of Britain and Ireland since the middle of the eighteenth century. Most of the evidence which is available for such a study relates, as in European countries, to the heights of military recruits, but since Britain did not resort to systematic conscription until 1916, British recruitment evidence is drawn from measurements of volunteers. The next chapter therefore considers the process of voluntary recruitment and locates it within the market for the labour of working-class males in eighteenth- and nineteenth-century Britain and Ireland. It is shown that military recruiters had specific restrictive demands for manpower, but that, despite this, a very large proportion of males attempted at some time in their lives to join the armed services.

Chapter 3 considers men and boys who were successful, based on a sample of about 170 000 individual recruits to the Army, to the Royal Marines, to the Royal Military Academy at Sandhurst and to the Marine Society of London. Supplemented by published statistics of recruits to the Army in the late nineteenth century, this material shows that recruits were drawn widely from the working class throughout Britain and Ireland. Chapters 2 and 3 therefore together argue that it is possible to make inferences from military recruitment data to the working-class population as a whole and thus to base estimates of the height of that population on the evidence of the heights of recruits.

Military recruiters, however, were concerned to select men who were healthy and sturdy enough to stand up to the rigours of military life. Since they identified height with strength and fitness, they imposed minimum height limits on recruits as a means of controlling the flow of recruits. For this reason, the heights of recruits provide initially a biased estimate of the height of the working-class population, since all men shorter than the military height limits are necessarily missing from the sample. Chapter 3 therefore describes statistical methods, especially developed for this study, which correct this bias and make it possible to estimate not only the average height of the whole population but also the average heights of various geographical and occupational subgroups.

Chapter 4 presents the results of this work. It discusses a series of estimates of the average adult height of the British working class between the middle of the eighteenth and the beginning of the twentieth century, supplemented by a variety of surveys of the civilian population taken during the twentieth century. This series of average heights constitutes the longest single national series of height estimates yet published. It is supplemented by shorter series which relate to teenage males and which span the social range between the children of the aristocracy and the children of the London slums. All these series show long-term increases in heights but they also show that this increase has been neither regular nor uninterrupted; in broad terms, an increase in heights between the middle of the eighteenth and the second quarter of the nineteenth century was succeeded by a downswing which was itself succeeded by an increase which has only recently come to an end.

The evidence collected on 110 000 individual recruits to the Army and Royal Marines is exploited in chapter 5 to describe changes in the heights of six geographical and thirteen socio-occupational subgroups within the population of Britain and Ireland. This material shows that there were significant changes over time in the relative height of different groups; Scottish heights, for example, fell markedly relative to those of the English, while many changes occurred in the relative fortunes of different occupations.

Chapters 6 and 7 attempt to explain the variations and differentials which have been discovered. Chapter 6 first summarises the current state of knowledge, based largely on studies in the less-developed countries of the modern world, about the relationship between growth and the environment. It then considers the extent to which such knowledge is relevant to the experience of Britain and Ireland in the eighteenth and nineteenth centuries. In the light of chapter 6, the next chapter relates the trends and fluctuations in height to other historical evidence about the condition of those countries, arguing that height data provide a new and valuable insight into the long-standing historical controversy about the standard of living of the British working class.

This book is the first attempt to write the anthropometric history of Britain and Ireland. It is unlikely to be the last, both because the potential of the study of human growth has not yet fully been realised and because, although this study breaks new ground in the use of statistical methods in the service of history, various aspects of the data remain unexploited. Those data are available to any scholars who wish to use them and it is the hope of the authors not only that they should be used again but that this work should stimulate similar studies of the anthropometric history of many other countries.

2

Inference from military height data

2.0 THE PROBLEM

Writing history is a process of inference. We rarely, if ever, know all that we wish to know about a person or event in the past and we are therefore forced to gather scraps of evidence and fit them together into what seems to be a believable pattern. In this respect, information about historical heights is like any other kind of evidence about the past; we do not know, and will never know with certainty, the average height of particular groups within historical populations. Even today, since it is impossible regularly to measure the entire population, inferences about its characteristics and about those of subsets within the population must be made from sample surveys. In studying the past, we can only try to approximate as closely as possible to such modern means of investigation.

Our knowledge of the range of European heights during the past two centuries comes from evidence which approximates to a modern survey, since conscript data relate to most if not all of the male population. In Britain, by contrast, there are no data of a similar kind from a period earlier than the middle of the twentieth century. Britain traditionally relied on volunteers to man its armed forces. Although various forms of conscription existed in eighteenth- and nineteenth-century Britain – the impressment of seamen and balloting for the militia are examples – such methods never involved a survey of the whole population. Even when conscription was introduced in 1916 and again in 1940, it followed a long period of voluntary recruitment, thus removing a large part of the relevant age-group from the conscription process. Only with National Service after the Second World War did Britain adopt procedures which most European states had been using for over a century.

Military records are, however, for Britain as for other countries, the main source – indeed, for some periods, the only source – of information about the heights of the population. British data do have one advantage over conscription material; deprived of a captive pool of adolescents, the armed forces recruited boys, young men and adults aged between the ages of 16, or sometimes even younger, and 30 or older. For many purposes, data covering such a wide age range are more useful than measurements of conscripts taken in late adolescence. Conscript data, for example, can tell us little about the age at which final height was reached and thus about changes in the tempo of growth.

But, if we are to use British evidence about the heights of military recruits, we must first answer the central question: how reasonable is it to make inferences from military records to the wider population from which the recruits were drawn?[1] This problem is the subject of this and the next chapter. First, we consider the nature of the recruitment process by which men were selected from the wider population; second, we consider the nature of, and the inferences that may be drawn from, the samples of military records which have been gathered and analysed.

2.1 RECRUITMENT IN BRITAIN, 1700–1916

There is no doubt that military recruits during the eighteenth and nineteenth centuries were not a random sample of British men. Most military historians are clear that for much of the period soldiers were seen as a race apart from the civilian population, often reviled as essentially agents of an occupying power; mothers were said to dread the day on which their sons enlisted, fathers to regard such sons as cutting themselves off from the family. Throughout the period, almost all recruits to the ranks were drawn from the working class but, at times of great need for recruits, resort was had to paupers, criminals and the rest of what came to be known as the residuum. Sailors were, perhaps, more respectable but the Army became used to their description as the 'scum of the earth'.[2] Throughout the

---

[1] These issues are not sufficiently considered in the only previous study of the heights of military recruits in the eighteenth century, by Steegmann (1985). This study is based solely on recruits who joined the 54th (West Norfolk) regiment between 1762 and 1799.

[2] Their commander for many years, the Duke of Wellington, was responsible for this description, telling Stanhope on 4 November 1821 that: 'Ours [our army] is composed of the scum of the earth – the mere scum of the earth' (Stanhope 1888). Wellington is also usually credited with the even more famous remark about a draft of troops sent to him in the Peninsular War: 'I don't know what effect these men will have upon the enemy but, by God, they terrify me', although the remark is also attributed to George III.

period, it was rare for the sons of the middle or upper classes to join the ranks.

Yet, as other historians have pointed out, such a picture is puzzling. First, it does not match well with the undoubted success of the British armed forces in battle to suppose that the troops were the dregs of society. As late as 1919, the National Service Medical Boards confronted this paradox in describing the health of the men whom they had examined, and could resolve it only by reference to the fighting spirit of the British race (PP 1919 xxvi: 23):

If such measurements represent truly the physique of our manhood of military age – as there is every reason to believe they do – we cannot be surprised at the general grading results throughout the country. We may well be surprised that, with human material of such physique, it was found possible to create the Armies which overthrew the Germans, and proved invincible in every theatre of War. One cannot but feel that the spirit of the race, which alone made this possible, deserves that no effort should be spared to ameliorate the conditions which have brought about such deplorable effects upon its health and physique.

Second, accounts which stress the aberrant character of recruits seem to ignore the fact that, for much of the eighteenth and all of the nineteenth century, the armed forces could not rely on forced recruitment, but had to recruit in the market-place for labour, in competition with other working-class occupations; this suggests that recruits themselves paid attention to the costs and benefits of enlistment and that historians should do likewise. Most traditional accounts have made little attempt to estimate the size of recruitment and thus its possible place within the general labour market or to assess the nature of the incentives which the armed forces offered.

Last, while impression and anecdote certainly have their place in discussion of the character of recruits, it is essential to check such impressions with the detailed information about the occupations, birthplaces and other characteristics of recruits which can be found in the military records.

2.1.1 *The history and historiography of military recruiting*

During the eighteenth and nineteenth centuries, the British Army moved gradually and haltingly from a devolved to a centralised system of recruitment. In earlier times, the recruitment and organisation of military units had essentially been subcontracted; those men who aspired to lead regiments had first to find the men to man them and, thereafter, had to retain their strength by continued recruitment in competition with other regiments. By the beginning of the eighteenth century, the state was aiding recruitment by the offer of bounties to new recruits, by encouraging local authorities to send the able-bodied poor to the Army and, in time of war, by providing for the release of debtors and criminals to man the Army. But, despite these inducements, recruitment remained essentially a devolved process, in which each regiment was responsible for attracting men to the colours. Recruiting parties, like those described by Shakespeare in *Henry IV* and by Farquharson in *The Recruiting Sergeant*, still scoured the country for men, setting up in pubs and inducing, bribing or otherwise persuading men to take the fatal step of accepting the King's shilling. Their work was subject only to the authority of a 'beating order' issued under the royal sign manual and countersigned by the Secretary-at-War (Public Record Office 1988).

Such methods were just adequate to man the Army in time of peace and even in the successive wars of the eighteenth century, but could not survive under the stress of the expansion of the Army which was required by the American and French wars at the end of the century. At that time, both the overall demand for recruits and, perhaps more important, the unrestrained competition between military units, which led essentially to units bidding against each other, forced the Army authorities to move towards a more centralised, or at least more regulated, system. An 'Inspector-General and Superintendent of the Recruiting of all the Forces employed in Foreign Service' was appointed in 1778 and was assisted by a number of Inspecting Field Officers. Although recruiting for individual regiments continued on the old pattern, 'this appointment introduced an element of central direction and control' (Public Record Office 1988). The appointment may have lapsed in the 1790s, but there was certainly an Inspector-General of Recruiting between 1797 and 1807, when a recruiting branch was established under the Adjutant-General (Public Record Office 1988). Recruiting districts were set up throughout the country and individual regiments were obliged to obtain permission before recruiting parties were sent out, although they were still able to recruit without restriction at their own headquarters.[3]

Paradoxically, the French wars also led the Army to rely for a time on a more localised form of recruitment. The apparent impossibility of obtaining enough men both to fight abroad and to defend, and possibly police, Britain itself led to the formation of local county militia units, manned by a system of forced recruitment by ballot within

---

[3] A full description of recruitment procedures is given in PP 1806–7 iv: 167–198.

each county; men were drawn by lot to form the county militia, although it was normally possible for those who could afford it to send a substitute. Fees for such substitutes were often substantial. Once these units were established, however, the Army was unable to resist the urge to recruit militiamen into the regular forces and, as the pressure for men continued, increasing numbers of men were attracted by greater and greater bounties to transfer from the militia to the line regiments and other Army units. In periods of peak demand, the combination of fees for substituting into the militia and the bounty for transfer to the Army amounted to several times the yearly civilian wage.

At the end of the French wars, military recruitment moved back towards the devolved system which had characterised the eighteenth century, moderated by some central direction to avoid wasteful competition and, increasingly, to enforce common standards and procedures. While the office of Inspector-General of Recruiting had been abolished, and regiments continued to send out recruiting parties, the great expense of recruiting by these means led to an increasing emphasis on centralised recruiting through the recruiting districts and their specialised staff. Army pensioners were also employed to bring men to the recruiting offices. Dissatisfaction with the system continued, however, and led to the establishment of two Royal Commissions to examine recruiting in the 1860s. As a result of these enquiries and reports, the system was further reformed in the 1870s, under an Inspector-General of Recruiting whose office had been re-established in 1867 (Spiers 1980: 42). At the same time, the Army Medical Department's role in the medical inspection of recruits was expanded and formalised. The formation of county regiments in the 1880s, replacing the older numbered regiments of the line, also helped to direct recruiting into more clearly defined channels by providing a natural catchment area for recruits. By the end of the nineteenth century, therefore, the move from a devolved to a centrally controlled system of recruiting had been largely completed.

This gradual re-organisation of the administrative system of recruiting was accompanied by a gradual tightening of the actual process of recruiting and of the systems for the inspection and approval of recruits. Even in the eighteenth century, recruiting officers had to ensure that recruits were up to standard; if they did not, and admitted a man who was too short, they were in danger of being charged for the bounty which they had paid to the recruit. It was for such reasons that a manual of military practice suggested that (Cuthbertson 1776: 59, quoted by Steegmann 1985: 79):

Before an Officer quits the regiment, to enter on the recruiting service, he should take the measure of the Regimental Standard, that he may not act contrary to the instructions, by enlisting Men of too low a Size; he ought to make it a rule to measure every Man himself before he pays him any part of his Levy Money, taking care, that nothing is concealed between his feet and stockings, to help his stature: an Officer will find the advantage of being exact in this particular.

and it was even suggested that recruits should be measured in the morning, as it was realised that people shrink during the day.

In the nineteenth century, the central authorities clearly scrutinised recruiting records with great care. In December 1805, Thos. Pritzler, Assistant Inspector-General, wrote: 'Capt. Ridgeway, R.O. Bolton Le Moors, is requested to observe that John Harrobin, a recruit for the parish of Twiton in the enclosed roll, is returned but *Five Feet high*, if a clerical error (as is supposed) he will correct it and return it to this office.'[4]

Throughout the period, the actual moment of enlistment remained that at which the recruit accepted the King's or Queen's shilling from the hands of the recruiting officer. However, as Spiers points out, even in the nineteenth century, 'Of the men who took the shilling, barely half of them ever joined the ranks' (Spiers 1980: 41). The recruit had an opportunity for second thoughts before being brought, at least twenty-four hours later, before a Justice of the Peace for the process of attest-ation; he could buy himself out by the payment of 'smart money' or, possibly, desert. In addition, the Army itself remained able, both before and after attestation, to reject men on medical or other grounds and it seems likely that this was the major cause of the loss to which Spiers refers. If men enlisted at an Army recruitment depot or regi-mental headquarters, they were examined by an Army Medical Officer; if they were enlisted by a roving recruiting party, they were examined both by a civilian doctor and then by an Army Medical Officer. The systemisation of recruiting as a whole was accompanied by a greater control of the process of medical inspection so that, by the second half of the nineteenth century, elaborate procedures for the inspection of recruits and for recording their physical condition were laid down. In addition to medical inspection at or shortly after enlistment or attest-ation, the Army retained the right to reject recruits during the early months of their service if they proved to be ill or incapable.

Despite these administrative and other changes to recruiting meth-ods, there was no period in the eighteenth or nineteenth centuries

---

[4] (Public Record Office WO3/583) This letter-book contains many other examples of such scrutiny.

in which recruiting was not a central preoccupation of and cause of concern to the military authorities. Even after most of the reforms outlined above, Skelley views recruitment as 'one of the biggest problems facing the regular army', a problem which impinged on many other aspects of military life and which was always in the background of efforts to improve terms and conditions (1977: 235).

There was, throughout the period, a constant tension between the need to man the Army, so as to enable it to carry out the tasks which the nation desired, and the wish to do so at the lowest possible cost; since the great bulk of military expenditure was on manpower, it was there that the pressure and the desire for economy was most felt. As Clode wrote in 1869:

Prior to the present century [1800s] the policy of this country was to fill the ranks of the Army with the cheapest labour, and at the lowest cost to the State. For many years there was little or no inducement for men to enter the Infantry – the principal arm of the Service. The pay was small, the barracks, when they existed, were execrable, the discipline, or rather the punishments, severe, and the service abroad was equal to the late punishment of transportation. (1869: II, 1)

while in times of war matters were even worse, for then:

the great principle of supply throughout the last century was that of conscription limited to the Criminal and Pauper classes. (Clode 1869: II, 10)

From the Mutiny Act of 1703 onwards, the Sovereign was empowered 'to order the delivery from gaol of capital offenders, who had been pardoned on condition of enlistment' while from the following year there was provision for the release of insolvent debtors who agreed to serve (Fortescue 1909: I,565–6). At the same time, Justices of the Peace were allowed to send the unemployed to be enlisted, a practice encouraged by the division of the bounty between the Parish Officers and the recruit himself. In 1744 the 'Act for the more speedy and effectual recruiting His Majesty's land forces and marines' provided that Justices of the Peace were empowered to press as soldiers:

such able-bodied men as do not follow or exercise any lawful calling or employment, or have not some other lawful and sufficient support and maintenance

exemptions being granted only to those who had the vote for a Member of Parliament and for labourers during the corn and hay harvest (Marshall 1846: 33), while in the same year, 1744, the *Gentleman's Magazine* wrote that over 1000 men were secured from the jails of London and Westminster, others being found in this way in every county (quoted in Marshall 1846: 33). There are, unfortunately, no returns which give the numbers which were recruited by such means.

In both peace and war, it was assumed that no-one would join the Army unless forced to do so. In 1749 Lord Barrington, the Secretary of War, opposed a bill which would have allowed soldiers to buy their discharge from the Army on the grounds that:

as it was idleness, extravagance and dissoluteness that filled the ranks of the army, to discharge men, if they pleased, after ten years service, would be to fill the country with a number of idle and dangerous vagabonds. (Marshall 1846: 37)

while the Army was said in 1760 to be composed of:

men who enter into the service through levity, are inveigled or drove into it by necessity, and, lastly, forced into it to supply the deficiency of the other classes. (Dalrymple 1761, quoted in Marshall 1846: 45)

Such descriptions of the recruiting process, and of the soldiers who resulted from it, were repeated in only slightly different form throughout the next 150 years and have, naturally, been repeated since then by military historians. The Royal Commission on Recruiting in 1861, for example, concluded that:

but few enlist from any real inclination for military life, and that Enlistment is, for the most part, occasioned by want of work – by pecuniary embarrassment – by family quarrels – or by any other difficulties of a private nature. (PP 1861 xv: xvii)

while Skelley (1977: 235) quotes the pithier comment of Major-General Lord William Paulet that 'It is drink and being hard up which leads a great many to enlist.'

In brief, much contemporary comment about recruiting and the comments of most historians can be summarised as follows: the Army (and Navy and Marines) were forced by the parsimony of their civilian masters to accept the dregs of society, the only men who had no escape from military life, and, under these appalling conditions, were able to turn such men into one of the most effective fighting forces that the world has ever known.

It is, however, possible and necessary to look at the history of recruitment in other ways. For a start, it has to be accepted that we actually know very little about the recruits, particularly in the eighteenth century. As Neuburg has written (1983: 39), our knowledge of serving men and their officers and of recruitment remains extremely limited. Even in the nineteenth century, at least up to the 1860s, most of our knowledge of recruiting and of the character and motivation of recruits is drawn from memoir, anecdote and allegation rather than from detailed analysis of military records. Most seriously, the description of recruiting is not normally based on a thorough analysis of the motives of the different parties who were involved, in particular the government, the military authorities and their recruiters and, finally, the recruits themselves.

2.1.2 *The rationale of recruitment: was there a 'recruiting problem'?*

Demand

Contemporary and historical discussion of recruitment to the armed forces in the eighteenth and nineteenth centuries is dominated by the concept of the difficulty of recruitment or 'the recruitment problem'. It is difficult to discover when this phrase was first used, although Fortescue speaks of the 'strain' of recruiting in 1703 (1909 i: 565) and of the 'dearth of recruits' during the Seven Years' War (1909 iii: 40). Marshall (1846: 55) speaks of 'the difficulties which obviously existed in procuring recruits during the last century'. More recently, the word 'problem' has been used frequently, among others by Neuburg (1983: 41), de Watteville (1954:95), and Spiers (1980: 35), while Skelley entitles a chapter of his detailed study of the late Victorian Army, 'The Recruiting Problem' (1977: 235).

But what was this problem? More specifically, was the problem any different from that of any employer in the labour market, anxious to obtain a labour force at the lowest possible average and marginal cost? In one sense, the problem was different; an employer seeks to recruit labour until the marginal cost – the cost of obtaining and employing one additional worker – is equal to the marginal product – the revenue from the additional output of that worker. The Army does not have output in the sense that the word is used in manufacturing industry, but this does not mean that it is not subject to revenue constraints, though imposed by government rather than the market. In the eighteenth and nineteenth centuries these constraints were severe, both because of a general desire to limit public expenditure and because of the long-standing dislike of, and suspicion of, a standing Army which might be used to suppress internal dissent. In wartime, such constraints were relaxed to some degree, but they still existed.

Within budgetary constraints imposed by governments, the Army sought to obtain a specified quantity and quality of recruits for as low a cost as possible, a desire which it shared with any other employer. Each year, it faced the need to secure a given number of soldiers – either to replace those who had died, deserted or been discharged or to increase the size of the forces to some number authorised by parliament, the 'establishment' of the forces, within the sums voted by parliament for military pay.

Similarly, the methods which the Army could use to attract recruits did not differ in principle from those used by any employer in a competitive labour market. It is impossible here to discuss the intricate history of Army pay, but recruits were offered what would now be called a 'remuneration package'; its main elements were the 'King's shilling' given to the recruit as a sign of enlistment, the 'Bounty' given on attestation, weekly pay, housing, food and equipment and, if the recruit survived, additional pay for good conduct and long service followed, at the last, by a weekly pension payable for life. Other benefits included extra pay while in transit, pay for extra duties such as acting as an officer's servant and the chance of promotion to noncommissioned or, in entirely exceptional circumstances, to commissioned rank. Some of the elements of this package, including the pension, existed from before the beginning of the eighteenth century, others were added and the value of existing elements increased, throughout the following two centuries.

The exact monetary value of this package has been the subject of dispute for centuries and it seems unlikely that the dispute can ever be resolved; important elements in such a calculation, such as the expectation of life of retired soldiers (which is crucial in calculating the present value of pension provisions), are extremely difficult to assess.[5] Most calculations do not take account of such factors, or even of the fact that soldiers' pay was increasingly paid net of food and other costs, a factor which makes comparison with civilian occupations very difficult. In an otherwise most perceptive discussion of Army pay and conditions of service, for example, Spiers (1980: 55) states that, after a 'radical' improvement in pay in 1902:

After two years' service an infantry private, if awarded the extra 6d service pay, would earn 1s 11d daily less 3.5d stoppages – a net 'weekly' pay of 11s 4.5d. This was not merely an abysmal wage by contemporary urban standards, but it was also over 2s lower than the average weekly wage of an agricultural labourer in Caithness, the poorest paid agricultural labourer in mainland Britain.

The problem with this comparison is that, by this period, the soldier's pay was indeed 'net' of most living expenses, including rent

---

[5] There is no evidence that explicit calculations of this kind were made at the time.

and food, both of which would have taken up most of the income of an agricultural labourer.

Even more problematic is the 'value' or 'cost' of the constraints imposed by Army rules and regulations and of Army life in general, which make it difficult to find an appropriate civilian comparison with the life of a soldier. Bulwer in *Monarchy of the Middle Classes* (1836: II, 245, quoted by Marshall 1846: 92) denied the difficulty: ' A soldier is exposed to a life of much hardship and much constraint; to this he submits if he is paid, because, as a peasant, he would also have been subjected to severe toil and much constraint.' However, no other occupation, for example, required service for life – in practice for 21 or 22 years – nor did any other, with the exception of the employment of dons at Oxford and Cambridge, forbid or severely discourage marriage; for most of the period the Army provided, in a very meagre fashion, only for six wives for every hundred private soldiers. Other, unauthorised, wives suffered terrible privation, particularly if their husbands were posted overseas (Trustram 1984).

The Army often found it necessary to alter the terms which it offered. Such alterations were made in a variety of ways. Pay was increased, the 'stoppages' from pay in respect of food, medical care and other expenses were reduced and good conduct and long service pay was introduced. In wartime, for example in the French wars, alterations were made in the expected length of service. A favourite expedient in wartime, however, was to vary the bounty paid to the new recruit.[6] While in peacetime in the late eighteenth century this stood at £3-0-0,

---

[6] The Mutiny Act of 1703–4 provided for a bounty of £1 (Fortescue 1909 i: 566), but by 1759, when the bounty was raised in London to £5-5-0, it was said that the bounty was traditionally £3 in peacetime (Gilbert 1976). Early in 1787 a bounty of £3-3-0 was offered but thereafter the sum rose rapidly, to £15-15-0 by October 1787 (Fortescue 1909 iii: 526) before falling to £5 in 1793 (Fortescue 1909 iv: 77). By 1795 established regiments were giving £15 and by 1796 the standard bounty was £21 (Gilbert 1976) although this was far below the bounty given for naval recruits, which is said by Lewis to have been £70 (1960: 122). Thereafter the bounty continued to fluctuate in line with the demand for recruits. By 1805, for example, men could get between £40 and £60 for serving as a substitute in the county militia and then immediately volunteer for service in a line regiment, receiving a further bounty of up to £16-16-0 (Marshall 1846: 64). At that time, the market for substitutes was highly organised, with a parliamentary return listing the sum obtainable in each county; the sums range from £45 in Monmouth to £10 in the Isle of Wight (PP 1808 vii: 205). From 15 August 1807 it was £14-14-0 for unlimited service, £10-10-0 for seven years' service (PP 1807 iv: 319), in 1808 £16-16-0 and £11-11-0 respectively (Marshall 1846: 71), while in 1814 it had fallen to £5-5-0 and £3-14-0 respectively (Marshall 1846: 75). The Waterloo campaign saw a renewed rise to £7-7-0 and £4-4-0 (Marshall 1846: 75), but peacetime brought a fall, first to £5 and £3-14-0 on 15 January 1816 and then to £3 and £2-8-0 on 1 December (Marshall 1846: 78), remaining at that level at least until 1839 (Marshall 1846).

by 1805 a recruit was able to get as much as £76, a huge sum by contemporary standards (Marshall 1846: 64). Later in the century, the Royal Commission of 1861 commented that (PP 1861 xv):

we find that an increase of Bounty is, generally, a necessary consequence of any large number of men being suddenly required – believing also that without some Bounty it would frequently be impossible to get recruits.

although the Commissioners, like many other commentators, regretted the drunkenness which, they thought, resulted from giving men such large sums.

There is much evidence that, in altering the terms and conditions of Army service, the military authorities were consciously responding to alterations in civilian conditions of employment. In 1806, for example, Windham told the Commons that (Fortescue 1909 v: 302):

to make voluntary enlistment a success, the Army must be rendered an eligible calling. This object could be easily accomplished by an increase in pay; but such a recourse was economically impossible.

Instead, the length of service could be reduced and pensions increased. In 1834, when William Cobbett proposed a reduction in the pay of soldiers, Lord Hardinge rebuffed the challenge by pointing out that the Poor Law Commission had 'pronounced the soldier to be ill-paid compared with any other class' (Fortescue 1909 xi: 444). J. R. Godley, similarly, told the Royal Commission of 1861 that: 'there must be some approximation to correspondence in the rate of wages' although arguing that there were other attractions in the life of a soldier (PP 1861 xv: 109). As Spiers shows (1980: 54), the net pay of private soldiers was 'more than doubled in the latter half of the nineteenth century' following frequent complaints that pay was too low and that, therefore, too few and too poor recruits were being attracted; this was at a time when there was a downward movement in the general price level.

Examination of the demand side of the market for Army recruits thus does not suggest that the Army behaved unusually in its search for a labour force. It did, of course, have some quality standards which it wished recruits to meet, in particular those of height and medical fitness. But all employers demand some qualifications from their employees and it is difficult to see that the Army's standards differed in principle from those applied by a factory owner seeking men who knew how to operate a power loom. In practice, of course, it is possible that the standards so constrained the supply of potential recruits as to cause a 'recruiting problem' of the Army's own making. To examine whether this was so, we must turn to the supply side of the labour market.

Supply
If military recruitment can be seen as part of the overall market for labour, with the military authorities competing in it with other employers, then the most natural interpretation of the phrase 'the recruitment problem' is that the Army found it difficult to attract recruits of the kind it was willing to accept *whatever the inducements it offered*. It is possible that, in the terminology of economics, it faced an inelastic labour supply schedule. There are at least two major reasons why this might have been so: first, the Army may have imposed such stringent conditions on recruits that it unreasonably reduced the pool from which it could draw its labour; second, the Army may have been considered so unfavourably by most members of that pool that, no matter what pay or conditions were offered to them, they would not consider enlistment.

Both these reasons need to be explored, but it is first sensible to consider whether there is good evidence that the supply of labour was inelastic. If it was, then one would expect to find that the Army had great difficulty in meeting its manpower targets and that changes in the level of pay and conditions did not produce commensurate changes in the level of recruitment.[7] Evidence about this is of two kinds: first, quantitative evidence about the level of recruitment and, second, contemporary observation about the effect of changes in pay.

The simplest form of quantitative evidence about the supply of recruits is the year on year change in the size of the Army. This is, however, a considerable understatement of the requirement for recruits, since men were needed to replace those who were 'D, D, or D' – dead, discharged or deserted. The numbers in these categories were always substantial, although they are only intermittently reported in the published Army statistics. Table 2.1 sets out the evidence that survives.

As table 2.1 shows, there were very large variations in the number of recruits, responding to changes in the establishment which reflects the desired size of the Army. Spiers (1980: 37) points out that between 1815 and 1839 the effective strength fell below establishment in 16 out of 25 years, a situation which improved only marginally later in

---

[7] In strict terms, it is necessary to estimate the elasticity of supply, defined as the proportionate change in the number of those seeking to join the Army divided by the proportionate change in pay and conditions, but the necessary data for such a calculation do not exist.

the century. However, more important than the existence of a shortfall is its size, and table 2.2 shows that, at least in the nineteenth century, the gap between establishment and 'effectives' was rarely large. It seems, in other words, that the Army was able to attract approximately the numbers of recruits that it needed. War put exceptional strains on recruitment, but it is notable how under such circumstances the flow of recruits could expand very much and very rapidly.

If, as this evidence suggests, Army recruitment was reasonably elastic and able to respond to changes in demand, it is sensible to enquire into the motives that led men to enlist. Many contemporary observers stressed non-pecuniary reasons. An ex-soldier, Mr Wallace, argued for example that most men did not know before they enlisted what pay they were going to receive (PP 1867 xv: 101). Marshall (1846: 85) had earlier argued, in similar vein, that few recruits thought about the prospects of a pension, although these prospects were important in deciding a soldier whether to re-enlist, and this was repeated in 1867 by Sergeant Griffiths (PP 1867 xv: 130). Spiers also reports (1980: 54) the remarks of a number of Secretaries of State for War who resisted arguments for increasing the pay of soldiers by claiming that pay was an unimportant factor in a man's decision to enlist.

It was certainly frequently argued that men were persuaded to join, or deterred from doing so, by non-pecuniary factors. A. R. Skelley mentions a number of reasons (1977: 249):

For those running from the law, from family or friends, or from the boring sameness of civilian life and a menial occupation, the army provided a ready means of escape. Some were deceived through the use of alcohol and false promises. Impulse too had a part to play. Evidently a considerable number of soldiers joined the army each year simply because it struck their fancy at the time. And there was always a large number of men who enlisted either to be with family or friends, for the opportunity to travel or out of a desire for the glamour or excitement of a soldier's life.

Discouraging factors, on the other hand, were the length of service to which a man was committed, the prospect of long years of foreign service, the bar on marriage and the severe discipline and punishment. In addition, there was the disapproval of respectable families and friends; there is no reason to doubt that, as Skelley suggests, the experience of John Fraser in 1877 was common; his father was infuriated by his decision to enlist (Skelley 1977: 246, quoting Fraser 1939: 42):

To him my step was a blow from which he thought he would never recover, for it meant disgrace of the worst type. His son a soldier! He could not believe his ears. Rather would he have had me out of work for the rest of my life

Table 2.1. *Numbers of men in, entering and leaving the Army, 1691–1913.*

Date	Establish-ment	Effectives	Recruits	Dead	Deserted	Discharged
1691	69 636	N.A.	N.A.	N.A.	N.A.	N.A.
1692	64 924	N.A.	N.A.	N.A.	N.A.	N.A.
1693	54 562	N.A.	N.A.	N.A.	N.A.	N.A.
1694	83 121	N.A.	N.A.	N.A.	N.A.	N.A.
1695	87 702	N.A.	N.A.	N.A.	N.A.	N.A.
1696	87 440	N.A.	N.A.	N.A.	N.A.	N.A.
1697	87 440	N.A.	N.A.	N.A.	N.A.	N.A.
1698	35 875	N.A.	N.A.	N.A.	N.A.	N.A.
1699	12 725	N.A.	N.A.	N.A.	N.A.	N.A.
1700	12 725	N.A.	N.A.	N.A.	N.A.	N.A.
1701	22 725	N.A.	N.A.	N.A.	N.A.	N.A.
1702	52 396	N.A.	N.A.	N.A.	N.A.	N.A.
1703	63 396	N.A.	N.A.	N.A.	N.A.	N.A.
1704	70 475	N.A.	N.A.	N.A.	N.A.	N.A.
1705	71 411	N.A.	N.A.	N.A.	N.A.	N.A.
1706	77 345	N.A.	N.A.	N.A.	N.A.	N.A.
1707	94 130	N.A.	N.A.	N.A.	N.A.	N.A.
1708	91 188	N.A.	N.A.	N.A.	N.A.	N.A.
1709	102 642	N.A.	N.A.	N.A.	N.A.	N.A.
1710	113 268	N.A.	N.A.	N.A.	N.A.	N.A.
1711	138 882	N.A.	N.A.	N.A.	N.A.	N.A.
1712	144 650	N.A.	N.A.	N.A.	N.A.	N.A.
1713	24 400	N.A.	N.A.	N.A.	N.A.	N.A.
1714	16 347	N.A.	N.A.	N.A.	N.A.	N.A.
1715	18 851	N.A.	N.A.	N.A.	N.A.	N.A.
1716	N.A.	N.A.	N.A.	N.A.	N.A.	N.A.
1717	N.A.	N.A.	N.A.	N.A.	N.A.	N.A.
1718	16 347	N.A.	N.A.	N.A.	N.A.	N.A.
1719	17 886	N.A.	N.A.	N.A.	N.A.	N.A.
1720	19 500	N.A.	N.A.	N.A.	N.A.	N.A.
1721	19 840	N.A.	N.A.	N.A.	N.A.	N.A.
1722	19 840	N.A.	N.A.	N.A.	N.A.	N.A.
1723	23 840	N.A.	N.A.	N.A.	N.A.	N.A.
1724	23 810	N.A.	N.A.	N.A.	N.A.	N.A.
1725	23 810	N.A.	N.A.	N.A.	N.A.	N.A.
1726	23 772	N.A.	N.A.	N.A.	N.A.	N.A.
1727	32 058	N.A.	N.A.	N.A.	N.A.	N.A.
1728	28 501	N.A.	N.A.	N.A.	N.A.	N.A.
1729	28 882	N.A.	N.A.	N.A.	N.A.	N.A.
1730	23 836	N.A.	N.A.	N.A.	N.A.	N.A.
1731	23 756	N.A.	N.A.	N.A.	N.A.	N.A.
1732	23 756	N.A.	N.A.	N.A.	N.A.	N.A.
1733	23 756	N.A.	N.A.	N.A.	N.A.	N.A.
1734	25 634	N.A.	N.A.	N.A.	N.A.	N.A.
1735	34 354	N.A.	N.A.	N.A.	N.A.	N.A.

Table 2.1. (*cont.*)

Date	Establish-ment	Effectives	Recruits	Dead	Deserted	Discharged
1736	26 314	N.A.	N.A.	N.A.	N.A.	N.A.
1737	26 314	N.A.	N.A.	N.A.	N.A.	N.A.
1738	26 896	N.A.	N.A.	N.A.	N.A.	N.A.
1739	26 896	N.A.	N.A.	N.A.	N.A.	N.A.
1740	40 859	N.A.	N.A.	N.A.	N.A.	N.A.
1741	53 395	N.A.	N.A.	N.A.	N.A.	N.A.
1742	51 044	N.A.	N.A.	N.A.	N.A.	N.A.
1743	51 696	N.A.	N.A.	N.A.	N.A.	N.A.
1744	53 538	N.A.	N.A.	N.A.	N.A.	N.A.
1745	53 128	N.A.	N.A.	N.A.	N.A.	N.A.
1746	77 664	N.A.	N.A.	N.A.	N.A.	N.A.
1747	61 471	N.A.	N.A.	N.A.	N.A.	N.A.
1748	64 966	N.A.	N.A.	N.A.	N.A.	N.A.
1749	28 399	N.A.	N.A.	N.A.	N.A.	N.A.
1750	29 194	N.A.	N.A.	N.A.	N.A.	N.A.
1751	29 132	N.A.	N.A.	N.A.	N.A.	N.A.
1752	29 132	N.A.	N.A.	N.A.	N.A.	N.A.
1753	29 132	N.A.	N.A.	N.A.	N.A.	N.A.
1754	29 132	N.A.	N.A.	N.A.	N.A.	N.A.
1755	31 422	N.A.	N.A.	N.A.	N.A.	N.A.
1756	47 488	N.A.	N.A.	N.A.	N.A.	N.A.
1757	68 791	N.A.	N.A.	N.A.	N.A.	N.A.
1758	88 370	N.A.	N.A.	N.A.	N.A.	N.A.
1759	91 446	N.A.	N.A.	N.A.	N.A.	N.A.
1760	99 044	N.A.	N.A.	N.A.	N.A.	N.A.
1761	105 221	N.A.	N.A.	N.A.	N.A.	N.A.
1762	120 633	N.A.	N.A.	N.A.	N.A.	N.A.
1763	120 419	N.A.	N.A.	N.A.	N.A.	N.A.
1764	31 773	N.A.	N.A.	N.A.	N.A.	N.A.
1765	31 654	N.A.	N.A.	N.A.	N.A.	N.A.
1766	31 752	N.A.	N.A.	N.A.	N.A.	N.A.
1767	31 701	N.A.	N.A.	N.A.	N.A.	N.A.
1768	31 700	N.A.	N.A.	N.A.	N.A.	N.A.
1769	31 589	N.A.	N.A.	N.A.	N.A.	N.A.
1770	30 949	N.A.	N.A.	N.A.	N.A.	N.A.
1771	43 546	N.A.	N.A.	N.A.	N.A.	N.A.
1772	30 641	N.A.	N.A.	N.A.	N.A.	N.A.
1773	30 641	N.A.	N.A.	N.A.	N.A.	N.A.
1774	30 641	20 443	N.A.	N.A.	N.A.	N.A.
1775	30 641	33 190	N.A.	N.A.	N.A.	N.A.
1776	50 234	33 897	N.A.	N.A.	N.A.	N.A.
1777	80 669	48 242	N.A.	N.A.	N.A.	N.A.
1778	82 995	53 302	N.A.	N.A.	N.A.	N.A.
1779	115 863	81 086	N.A.	N.A.	N.A.	N.A.
1780	122 677	88 034	N.A.	N.A.	N.A.	N.A.

Table 2.1. (*cont.*)

Date	Establish-ment	Effectives	Recruits	Dead	Deserted	Discharged
1781	128 549	90 867	N.A.	N.A.	N.A.	N.A.
1782	131 989	89 336	N.A.	N.A.	N.A.	N.A.
1783	124 254	90 395	N.A.	N.A.	N.A.	N.A.
1784	30 680	N.A.	N.A.	N.A.	N.A.	N.A.
1785	29 557	25 767	N.A.	N.A.	N.A.	N.A.
1786	33 544	26 465	N.A.	N.A.	N.A.	N.A.
1787	35 544	26 842	N.A.	N.A.	N.A.	N.A.
1788	32 117	29 174	N.A.	N.A.	N.A.	N.A.
1789	38 592	33 682	N.A.	N.A.	N.A.	N.A.
1790	38 784	34 207	N.A.	N.A.	N.A.	N.A.
1791	59 772	38 171	N.A.	N.A.	N.A.	N.A.
1792	56 859	36 557	N.A.	N.A.	N.A.	N.A.
1793	157 396	38 945	17 033	N.A.	N.A.	N.A.
1794	211 893	85 097	38 563	N.A.	N.A.	N.A.
1795	337 189	124 262	40 463	N.A.	N.A.	N.A.
1796	251 316	111 996	16 336	N.A.	N.A.	N.A.
1797	259 985	104 862	16 096	N.A.	N.A.	N.A.
1798	269 582	102 563	21 457	N.A.	N.A.	N.A.
1799	273 117	115 252	41 316	N.A.	N.A.	N.A.
1800	245 811	169 428	17 829	N.A.	N.A.	N.A.
1801	218 504	184 274	10 698	N.A.	N.A.	N.A.
1802	208 668	196 156	N.A.	N.A.	N.A.	N.A.
1803	211 216	126 673	11 253	5 208	843	6 009
1804	308 085	185 127	11 088	6 458	5 378	5 331
1805	304 848	200 320	33 545	6 833	7 081	4 329
1806	326 744	213 314	20 677	6 495	5 748	4 688
1807	335 132	229 470	30 592	7 932	5 728	3 878
1808	359 315	258 062	30 592	9 285	6 611	4 990
1809	366 343	266 371	22 350	16 343	4 901	3 323
1810	368 346	269 631	22 350	13 597	4 729	4 627
1811	369 355	266 247	22 925	13 448	5 026	3 986
1812	371 527	278 307	24 359	15 842	5 918	3 738
1813	385 558	291 783	19 980	15 012	5 822	3 621
1814	394 351	301 730	13 564	12 502	8 857	34 293
1815	275 392	247 113	15 279	8 124	7 403	29 342
1816	145 724	221 947	14 948	5 427	4 721	36 702
1817	102 168	179 740	9 047	3 870	3 415	25 076
1818	100 412	153 110	7 156	4 442	2 457	23 817
1819	88 682	122 918	5 499	4 247	2 152	15 960
1820	100 436	120 765	8 371	3 324	1 825	7 654
1821	100 969	116 388	7 325	2 413	1 415	19 043
1822	79 039	103 778	N.A.	N.A.	N.A.	N.A.
1823	79 375	100 633	N.A.	N.A.	N.A.	N.A.
1824	84 021	102 981	N.A.	N.A.	N.A.	N.A.
1825	94 514	105 207	N.A.	N.A.	N.A.	N.A.

Table 2.1. (*cont.*)

Date	Establish-ment	Effectives	Recruits	Dead	Deserted	Discharged
1826	95 266	118 904	N.A.	N.A.	N.A.	N.A.
1827	95 297	124 626	N.A.	N.A.	N.A.	N.A.
1828	99 359	125 211	N.A.	N.A.	N.A.	N.A.
1829	99 398	118 012	N.A.	N.A.	N.A.	N.A.
1830	97 193	110 481	N.A.	N.A.	N.A.	N.A.
1831	96 873	117 646	N.A.	N.A.	N.A.	N.A.
1832	97 949	117 695	6 047	N.A.	N.A.	N.A.
1833	97 795	117 385	4 651	N.A.	N.A.	N.A.
1834	97 210	109 230	3 655	N.A.	N.A.	N.A.
1835	89 523	109 285	4 530	N.A.	N.A.	N.A.
1836	89 562	109 369	7 583	N.A.	N.A.	N.A.
1837	89 553	109 405	8 602	N.A.	N.A.	N.A.
1838	97 893	120 961	10 903	N.A.	N.A.	N.A.
1839	103 509	124 838	19 099	N.A.	N.A.	N.A.
1840	102 426	131 112	15 822	N.A.	N.A.	N.A.
1841	101 097	130 277	13 653	N.A.	N.A.	N.A.
1842	110 502	141 089	14 534	N.A.	N.A.	N.A.
1843	109 658	118 628	11 514	N.A.	N.A.	N.A.
1844	109 208	138 680	9 224	N.A.	N.A.	N.A.
1845	109 110	138 461	11 420	N.A.	N.A.	N.A.
1846	119 787	148 760	19 333	N.A.	N.A.	N.A.
1847	120 790	150 486	13 294	N.A.	N.A.	N.A.
1848	128 141	152 870	10 060	N.A.	N.A.	N.A.
1849	117 377	148 704	7 867	N.A.	N.A.	N.A.
1850	113 697	143 850	6 321	N.A.	N.A.	N.A.
1851	113 287	143 751	8 376	N.A.	N.A.	N.A.
1852	119 519	145 522	12 683	N.A.	N.A.	N.A.
1853	119 881	149 089	10 949	N.A.	N.A.	N.A.
1854	163 251	152 780	31 620	N.A.	N.A.	N.A.
1855	215 941	175 947	36 159	N.A.	N.A.	N.A.
1856	246 716	220 228	13 955	N.A.	N.A.	N.A.
1857	126 796	169 083	24 383	N.A.	N.A.	N.A.
1858	130 315	195 740	46 731	N.A.	N.A.	N.A.
1859	122 625	204 079	28 137	N.A.	N.A.	N.A.
1860	143 362	202 547	20 725	N.A.	N.A.	N.A.
1861	202 040	201 015	12 830	4 290	5 021	14 875
1862	194 271	189 968	24 240	3 450	2 895	12 231
1863	197 089	194 022	12 821	3 033	4 112	11 892
1864	192 153	188 025	17 270	3 373	3 622	13 118
1865	190 062	185 147	15 440	3 403	4 573	16 086
1866	182 468	176 731	16 316	2 730	4 144	14 323
1867	173 995	172 079	20 702	3 104	4 107	13 607
1868	172 633	172 014	18 281	2 685	3 431	16 419
1869	171 029	167 751	13 186	3 157	3 749	17 380
1870	161 150	157 017	25 682	2 508	3 332	15 720

Table 2.1. (*cont.*)

Date	Establish-ment	Effectives	Recruits	Dead	Deserted	Discharged
1871	171 074	161 794	25 066	2 220	5 147	12 399
1872	170 029	166 985	19 666	2 549	6 602	11 567
1873	169 395	166 267	18 998	2 046	6 640	14 543
1874	161 031	162 079	22 719	2 011	6 770	13 999
1875	160 929	162 148	20 449	2 161	5 761	14 947
1876	160 537	159 640	31 454	1 998	6 516	16 921
1877	166 191	165 639	31 178	1 708	7 251	21 762
1878	164 877	166 366	65 931	2 171	7 493	54 532
1879	165 885	167 834	29 088	4 069	5 818	19 326
1880	164 115	167 909	27 182	3 186	5 903	20 802
1881	164 923	165 320	28 511	2 570	4 862	20 317
1882	163 401	165 655	35 939	2 140	5 366	24 657
1883	168 863	169 834	34 401	1 707	4 295	40 388
1884	165 386	158 029	38 636	1 521	4 762	24 874
1885	167 864	165 255	46 541	2 588	5 895	26 137
1886	180 130	176 865	41 304	2 721	5 897	25 108
1887	186 834	184 461	33 315	1 946	5 630	23 186
1888	186 180	186 839	26 919	1 852	4 484	20 882
1889	187 135	186 509	30 991	1 869	4 347	25 688
1890	189 426	185 432	32 996	1 738	4 411	26 579
1891	190 149	185 547	37 740	1 795	4 969	29 929
1892	191 348	186 447	43 664	1 859	5 424	30 261
1893	191 045	192 456	37 342	1 730	5 147	28 885
1894	190 690	193 896	35 871	1 792	4 034	27 353
1895	191 790	196 185	31 282	1 774	3 783	25 749
1896	192 054	195 980	28 532	1 769	3 637	26 021
1897	210 253	212 231	35 015	2 067	2 492	30 294
1898	195 304	194 705	40 729	2 578	4 646	29 892
1899	223 542	222 373	100 499	2 457	3 432	26 069
1900	280 954	290 914	128 515	10 153	4 376	19 435
1901	357 211	406 443	76 840	5 969	18 856	74 996
1902	357 405	383 462	66 316	3 896	9 842	124 654
1903	292 877	311 386	35 018	1 560	2 477	63 064
1904	267 618	274 774	43 041	1 699	6 392	39 479
1905	286 036	272 133	38 846	1 432	3 627	46 674
1906	268 141	263 117	41 212	1 489	4 771	43 772
1907	255 288	248 487	38 515	1 186	4 313	46 864
1908	255 221	251 324	44 167	1 141	3 778	35 997
1909	253 004	253 405	36 646	967	3 800	30 096
1910	254 547	252 686	29 755	822	3 404	26 239
1911	256 694	254 309	32 047	744	3 996	26 084
1912	256 839	253 762	33 155	757	4 248	30 971
1913	255 830	247 250	31 081	669	4 161	32 732

Notes to Table 2.1

Sources:

1691–1860	Establishment PP 1868–9 xxxv. Accounts of the Net Public Income and Expenditure of Great Britain in each Financial Year from 1688 to 5 January 1801 (. . . and from 5 January 1801).
1774–1783	Effectives PP 1806 x: 401
1785–1787	Effectives PP 1813–14 xi: 302–3
1788–1792	Effectives PP 1814–15 ix: 288–9
1793–1799	Effectives PP 1806 x: 405
1800–1858	Effectives

1793–1800	Recruitment PP 1806 x: 389
1801	Recruitment PP 1807 iv: 176
1803–1812	Recruitment PP 1813–14 xi: 263
1813	Recruitment PP 1813–14 xi: 273
1814	Recruitment PP 1814–15 ix: 309
1815	Recruitment PP 1816 xii: 423
1816	Recruitment PP 1817 xiii: 195
1817	Recruitment PP 1818 xiii: 229
1818–1821	Recruitment PP 1822 xix: 321

1803	Deaths, Deserted, Discharged PP 1813–14 xi: 261
1804	Deaths, Deserted, Discharged PP 1812–13 xi: 261
1805–1808	Deaths, Deserted, Discharged PP 1810 xiii: 435
1809	Deaths, Deserted, Discharged PP 1813–14 xi: 261
1810	Deaths, Deserted, Discharged PP 1812 ix: 195
1811	Deaths, Deserted, Discharged PP 1812 ix: 195, and PP 1813–14 xi: 261
1812	Deaths, Deserted, Discharged PP 1812–13 xiii: 11
1813	Deaths, Deserted, Discharged PP 1813–14 xi: 277
1814	Deaths, Deserted, Discharged PP 1814–15 ix: 313
1815	Deaths, Deserted, Discharged PP 1816 xii: 427
1816	Deaths, Deserted, Discharged PP 1817 xiii: 197
1817	Deaths, Deserted, Discharged PP 1818 xiii: 231
1818–1821	Deaths, Deserted, Discharged PP 1822 xix: 322

1861–1913	Establishment, Effectives, Recruitment, Dead, Discharged and Deserted from PP 1874 xxxvi: 425; PP 1890 xliii: 18; PP 1896 li: 298; PP 1900 x: 182; PP 1874 xxxvi: 434; PP 1890 xliii: 32–3; PP 1896 li: 314–15; PP 1905 ix: 40; PP 1914 lii: 299; PP 1914 lii: 302–3. All General Annual Returns of the British Army.

Since the information in this table is drawn from a multiplicity of sources and the exact method by which each figure was compiled is not known, one can only repeat the words of Col. Sir Henry James of the Topographical and Statistical Department of the War Office, introducing another return in 1866: *Comparative Statement of the Military Forces and of the Population of the British Empire for every year since 1801* that: 'It has not been feasible to make the return on the same principle throughout.'

In particular, in a number of cases where conflicting information is given in different sources, sources which print series of data have been preferred to sources giving only one observation.

Table 2.2. *The gap in the Army between establishment and effectives,*
1774–1913.

Date	Establishment	Effectives	Difference	Difference as % of establishment
1774	30 641	20 443	10 198	33
1775	30 641	33 190	−2 549	−8
1776	50 234	33 897	16 337	33
1777	80 669	48 242	32 427	40
1778	82 995	53 302	29 693	36
1779	115 863	81 086	34 777	30
1780	122 677	88 034	34 643	28
1781	128 549	90 867	37 682	29
1782	131 989	89 336	42 653	32
1783	124 254	90 395	33 859	27
1784	30 680	N.A.	N.A.	N.A.
1785	29 557	25 767	3 790	13
1786	33 544	26 465	7 079	21
1787	35 544	26 842	8 702	24
1788	32 117	29 174	2 943	9
1789	38 592	33 682	4 910	13
1790	38 784	34 207	4 577	12
1791	59 772	38 171	21 601	36
1792	56 859	36 557	20 302	36
1793	157 396	38 945	118 451	75
1794	211 893	85 097	126 796	60
1795	337 189	124 262	212 927	63
1796	251 316	111 996	139 320	55
1797	259 985	104 862	155 123	60
1798	269 582	102 563	167 019	62
1799	273 117	115 252	157 865	58
1800	245 811	169 428	76 383	31
1801	218 504	184 274	34 230	16
1802	208 668	196 156	12 512	6
1803	211 216	126 673	84 543	40
1804	308 085	185 127	122 958	40
1805	304 848	200 320	104 528	34
1806	326 744	213 314	113 430	35
1807	335 132	229 470	105 662	32
1808	359 315	258 062	101 253	28
1809	366 343	266 371	99 972	27
1810	368 346	269 631	98 715	27
1811	369 355	266 247	103 108	28
1812	371 527	278 307	93 220	25
1813	385 558	291 783	93 775	24
1814	394 351	301 730	92 621	23
1815	275 392	247 113	28 279	10
1816	145 724	221 947	−76 223	−52

Table 2.2. (*cont.*)

Date	Establishment	Effectives	Difference	Difference as % of establishment
1817	102 168	179 740	− 77 572	− 76
1818	100 412	153 110	− 52 698	− 52
1819	88 682	122 918	− 34 236	− 39
1820	100 436	120 765	− 20 329	− 20
1821	100 969	116 388	− 15 419	− 15
1822	79 039	103 778	− 24 739	− 31
1823	79 375	100 633	− 21 258	− 27
1824	84 021	102 981	− 18 960	− 23
1825	94 514	105 207	− 10 693	− 11
1826	95 266	118 904	− 23 638	− 25
1827	95 297	124 626	− 29 329	− 31
1828	99 359	125 211	− 25 852	− 26
1829	99 398	118 012	− 18 614	− 19
1830	97 193	110 481	− 13 288	− 14
1831	96 873	117 646	− 20 773	− 21
1832	97 949	117 695	− 19 746	− 20
1833	97 795	117 385	− 19 590	− 20
1834	97 210	109 230	− 12 020	− 12
1835	89 523	109 285	− 19 762	− 22
1836	89 562	109 369	− 19 807	− 22
1837	89 553	109 405	− 19 852	− 22
1838	97 893	120 961	− 23 068	− 24
1839	103 509	124 838	− 21 329	− 21
1840	102 426	131 112	− 28 686	− 28
1841	101 097	130 277	− 29 180	− 29
1842	110 502	141 089	− 30 587	− 28
1843	109 658	118 628	− 8 970	− 8
1844	109 208	138 680	− 29 472	− 27
1845	109 110	138 461	− 29 351	− 27
1846	119 787	148 760	− 28 973	− 24
1847	120 790	150 486	− 29 696	− 25
1848	128 141	152 870	− 24 729	− 19
1849	117 377	148 704	− 31 327	− 27
1850	113 697	143 850	− 30 153	− 27
1851	113 287	143 751	− 30 464	− 27
1852	119 519	145 522	− 26 003	− 22
1853	119 881	149 089	− 29 208	− 24
1854	163 251	152 780	10 471	6
1855	215 941	175 947	39 994	19
1856	246 716	220 228	26 488	11
1857	126 796	169 083	− 42 287	− 33
1858	130 315	195 740	− 65 425	− 50
1859	122 625	204 079	− 81 454	− 66
1860	143 362	202 547	− 59 185	− 41

Table 2.2. (*cont.*)

Date	Establishment	Effectives	Difference	Difference as % of establishment
1861	202 040	201 015	1 025	1
1862	194 271	189 968	4 303	2
1863	197 089	194 022	3 067	2
1864	192 153	188 025	4 128	2
1865	190 062	185 147	4 915	3
1866	182 468	176 731	5 737	3
1867	173 995	172 079	1 916	1
1868	172 633	172 014	619	0
1869	171 029	167 751	3 278	2
1870	161 150	157 017	4 133	3
1871	171 074	161 794	9 280	5
1872	170 029	166 985	3 044	2
1873	169 395	166 267	3 128	2
1874	161 031	162 079	− 1 048	− 1
1875	160 929	162 148	− 1 219	− 1
1876	160 537	159 640	897	1
1877	166 191	165 639	552	0
1878	164 877	166 366	− 1 489	− 1
1879	165 885	167 834	− 1 949	− 1
1880	164 115	167 909	− 3 794	− 2
1881	164 923	165 320	− 397	0
1882	163 401	165 655	− 2 254	− 1
1883	168 863	169 834	− 971	− 1
1884	165 386	158 029	7 357	4
1885	167 864	165 255	2 609	2
1886	180 130	176 865	3 265	2
1887	186 834	184 461	2 373	1
1888	186 180	186 839	− 659	0
1889	187 135	186 509	626	0
1890	189 426	185 432	3 994	2
1891	190 149	185 547	4 602	2
1892	191 348	186 447	4 901	3
1893	191 045	192 456	− 1 411	− 1
1894	190 690	193 896	− 3 206	− 2
1895	191 790	196 185	− 4 395	− 2
1896	192 054	195 980	− 3 926	− 2
1897	210 253	212 231	− 1 978	− 1
1898	195 304	194 705	599	0
1899	223 542	222 373	1 169	1
1900	280 954	290 914	− 9 960	− 4
1901	357 211	406 443	− 49 232	− 14
1902	357 405	383 462	− 26 057	− 7
1903	292 877	311 386	− 18 509	− 6
1904	267 618	274 774	− 7 156	− 3

Table 2.2. (*cont.*)

Date	Establishment	Effectives	Difference	Difference as % of establishment
1905	286 036	272 133	13 903	5
1906	268 141	263 117	5 024	2
1907	255 288	248 487	6 801	3
1908	255 221	251 324	3 897	2
1909	253 004	253 405	− 401	0
1910	254 547	252 686	1 861	1
1911	256 694	254 309	2 385	1
1912	256 839	253 762	3 077	1
1913	255 830	247 250	8 580	3

Source: See table 2.1.

than earning my living in such a manner. More than that, he would rather see me in my grave.

It is, however, difficult to see why the flow of recruits should fluctuate so much if most were impelled or repelled by such reasoning. Contemporary evidence about the effects of changes in pay and conditions, which might be expected to produce such fluctuations as civilian wages varied, is admittedly difficult to obtain and equally difficult to assess, particularly because observers differed greatly in their opinions. However, one striking example of an apparently large elasticity of supply comes from 1790 when, Fortescue reports (1909 iii: 527):

the pay of the men was insufficient and the stoppages excessive. . . It is literally true that the only alternatives open to the private soldier were to desert or to starve.

Realising this, the authorities increased the pay in 1792 and (1909 iii: 528):

Within a fortnight the Adjutant-General was able to report a decrease in desertion and new facility in obtaining recruits.

There are many other comments which suggest that recruitment corresponded to wage levels. Fortescue describes, for example, how it was very difficult to obtain recruits in 1763–1770 because the 'general standard of comfort and luxury' was increasing, leaving the pay of the soldier too small (1909 iii: 40) while he ascribed the shortage of recruits in 1799 'partly also to the rapid development of the manufacturing industry in England through the removal of all competition in France and in the countries which had been overrun by the armies of the Revolution' (1909 iv: 639).

In 1805, Marshall later argued (1846: 64), the price of substitutes for the militia was set at between £40 and £60, a sum designed to induce a 'respectable class of men' to come forward and, it is implied, this result was produced. Later in the century, in 1865, an increase in pay from 1s 1d per day, from which 8.5d was deducted for various purposes, to 1s 3d per day produced an immediate increase in recruits and re-enlistments of soldiers whose period of service had come to an end (Fortescue 1909 xii: 536).

The question of the importance of pay in attracting recruits was also exhaustively discussed before the Royal Commissions of 1861 and 1867. One witness, Vice-Admiral Eden, was asked (PP 1867 xv: 46):

Q1045 You recruit for the marines upon the same principle, I presume, as the army recruits – I believe that it is the same, but the pay of the marine being better, we have less difficulty in obtaining recruits.

Further questioning showed that the nominal pay of the two types of units was much the same, but that the Marines were subject to fewer 'stoppages'; when on board ship they, like sailors, were fed free. Another witness, Captain Lake, argued that pay determined recruiting and that shortages of recruits were determined by the fact that (PP 1867 xv: 52):

the wages all over the country are much higher in proportion to what they used to be, while the soldier's pay is exactly the same.

while Lt-Col. Keane suggested (PP 1867 xv: 125) that an addition to rations would be much more popular than an addition to pension, although both would help recruiting. In the same year, there was evidence of the responsiveness of recruitment to trade conditions, the Army Medical Department reporting that (PP 1868–9 xxxvii: 42):

Compared with the preceding year there has been a marked decrease in the proportion of labourers, husbandmen and servants enlisted; while there has been an increase in the manufacturing artizans and mechanics, a result, there is much reason to suppose, of the generally depressed state of trade during the year.

Such statements, like that of recruit Fraser who disgraced his father, give a clue to the motive which seems to have underlain the decision of most recruits. By the end of the nineteenth century, it was common ground among observers of recruitment that most men enlisted because of poverty, which was itself usually caused by unemployment, but this seems to have been true from a much earlier period. For much of the eighteenth century, of course, unemployed men could be forcibly enlisted by the Parish. In 1761 C. Dalrymple wrote of men 'drove into it [the Army] by necessity'. In a related context, unemployment was certainly a major factor underlying the recruitment by the Marine Society of London of boys to serve on naval and merchant ships.[8] In 1792 the Society described the various classes of boys who sought their help:

(1) Such boys as are literally in a vagrant state, of whom some are recommended by magistrates, either as found wandering or as guilty of some petty offense. (Of these the smallest number offer.)

(2) Those who live chiefly by begging, or seldom do any work, but appear in filth and rags, and sometimes half naked. (Of these there are more than of the former.)

(3) Some who have occasionally earned their bread by going on errands, or in markets, brick-kilns, glass-houses, feeding hackney coach-horses, draw-boys and such like. (These being often in a naked condition, and unemployed are exposed to every temptation which indolence or idleness can create, and apply for employment at this office. To obviate the exceptions which may arise in relation to any such boys, it must be observed that when any one can be provided for at sea, and brought into the track of a sea-life, as proper to his hardiness and inclinations, it creates a vacancy to be filled by younger or less hardy boys of the same class, who are not fit for the sea.)

(4) The sons of poor people who have numerous families, and, upon enquiry, are in too great a state of indigence to provide clothing for the sea. Such boys, whatever their inclinations may be for a sea-life, are not likely to be accepted by any master, but by means of this society. (Of these there seems to be a majority.)

(5) Boys whose parts have been wrong cast, being so contrary to their genius, that they are more inclined to hazard their necks, than

---

[8] Information about the Marine Society, its founder Jonas Hanway, and its work may be found in open letters by Hanway and in semi-annual publications of the Society, both held in the British Library, and in Jayne (1929), Hutchins (1940), Distad (1972), Marine Society (1965) and in a number of unpublished studies by G. Hewett Joiner. We are grateful to Professor Joiner for allowing us to see his work and to the Marine Society of London for their help and advice. A brief description of the Society can also be found in Floud and Wachter (1982). Its connections with the Royal Navy are described in Lewis (1960).

to live a sedentary life. (Of this class there is no inconsiderable number.)

In the following century, Henry Marshall commented that (1828: 89):

Recruits rarely enlist in consequence of a deliberate preference of a military life, but commonly on account of some domestic broil, or from a boyish fancy, sometimes from want of work, and its immediate result, great indigence.

while Sergeant MacMullen, late Staff Sergeant of the 13th Light Infantry, attempted like the Marine Society to rank motives in order (McGuffie 1964: 23, quoting MacMullen 1846):

Why Men entered the Army in the 1840s.

1. Indigent – Embracing labourers and mechanics out of employ, who merely seek for support   80 in 120
2. Indigent – Respectable persons induced by misfortune or imprudence   2 in 120
3. Idle – Who consider a soldier's life an easy one   16 in 120
4. Bad characters – Who fall back upon the army as a last resort   8 in 120
5. Criminals – Who seek to escape from the consequence of their offences   1 in 120
6. Perverse sons – Who seek to grieve their parents   2 in 120
7. Discontented and reckless   8 in 120
8. Ambitious   1 in 120
9. Others   2 in 120

The Royal Commission of 1861 commented (PP 1861 xv: 10) that it was in winter that recruits 'particularly from the agricultural classes' could most readily be obtained and that (PP 1861 xv: 12) 'Enlistment is, for the most part, occasioned by want of work'. This was confirmed by several witnesses in 1867; Mr Haden, for example, commented (PP 1867 xv: 62):

The great mass of recruits are men doubtless in difficulties who only enter Her Majesty's service because at the moment they have no other means of existence, and they view the step as a desperate remedy for their case.

Sergeant Griffiths (PP 1867 xv: 130) confirmed that recruitment was good at that time because of the level of unemployment, while early in the twentieth century the Inspector-General of Recruiting, giving evidence to the Inter-Departmental Committee on Physical Deterioration, saw even short-term loss of work as a stimulus to recruitment (PP 1904 xxxii: Q188):

But we must remember that strikes and things of that kind give us a lot of recruits; sometimes a place is shut up and therefore it is through no fault of their own that men are out of work. We all know that strikes do us a lot of good.

At the end of the nineteenth century, the thesis that there was a relationship between unemployment and the flow of recruits received official backing from the War Office, which attempted to demonstrate the relationship with a graph (PP 1890 xix: Appendix 2), while the Army Medical Department reported in 1907 that 'as high as 95% of the total' and in 1909 'well over 99 per cent' of those inspected were unemployed (PP 1907 lxiv: 1; PP 1911 xlvii: 2). Spiers concludes that unemployed men were the majority of each year's intake (1980: 45).

The intimate connection between military recruitment and the state of the civilian labour market was thus well established at the end of the nineteenth century. The exact nature of the connection was, however, at the root of the controversy during the South African War about the alleged deterioration in the quality of Army recruits and hence of the British race as a whole. The allegations, among others by Major-General Sir Frederick Maurice, that recruiting statistics demonstrated a dangerous decline in the physical condition of the race, led ultimately to the establishment of the Inter-Departmental Committee on Physical Deterioration ('Miles' 1902; Maurice 1903).

That committee concluded that recruitment was crucially affected by the condition of the labour market, although they went on to argue that the vicissitudes in that market over time made it impossible to draw conclusions from recruiting statistics about the population as a whole. They repeated, in their Report, the views of one of their witnesses, Professor Cunningham, that this was (PP 1904 xxxii: 10):

Because the class from which the recruits are derived varies from time to time with the conditions of the labour market. When trade is good and plentiful it is only from the lowest stratum of the people that the Army receives its supply of men; when, on the other hand, trade is bad, a better class of recruit is available. Consequently the records of the recruiting department of the army do not deal with a homogeneous sample of the people taken from one distinct class.

Other witnesses disputed the view that Army recruits were in some way unrepresentative of the working class from whom they were drawn or that there had been systematic changes in the relationship. Asked about this, the Rev W. E. Edwards, of the Salford Education Committee, replied that (PP 1904 xxxii: Q4252–4):

(A) One can only go upon the dictum of experienced army medical officers, and they, or some of them, hold that the Tommy Atkins recruit is just an average type of his class.
(Q) Yes, the slum class? – (A) Of the class from which he is born, 50 per cent of our people. But 35 or 40 per cent of our people live in slums.

The Director-General of the Army Medical Department confirmed this view (PP 1904 xxxii: Q163):

(Q) Do you think that we can get from it [i.e. recruitment statistics] any indication whatever as to the physique of the people, of whole classes of people, in either certain districts of the country or certain occupations? – (A) As to the districts of the country certainly, so far as the class from which recruits generally come is concerned.

The Army was naturally upset that so few recruits actively sought the military life and that recruits were drawn largely from the unemployed or casually employed working class, but, from the point of view of the analysis of recruitment, the fact that unemployment and poverty were the main motives helps to explain the apparently high elasticity of supply for military labour. In taking the decision to enlist, the recruit can be seen as balancing the prospects of military against the prospects of civilian life. An unemployed, unmarried, able-bodied young man in Victorian Britain, particularly from the ranks of the unskilled, had no prospect of support from the state although he might be able to survive for a short time through charity. In such circumstances, the military life might easily be an attractive alternative to starvation or the vague prospect of civilian employment.

In addition, it must be remembered that casual unemployment or underemployment was an endemic feature of the labour market in the eighteenth and nineteenth centuries. The fact that this was so makes it particularly difficult to make sensible comparisons between civilian and military wages, since no civilian occupation could guarantee uninterrupted employment for over 20 years, at however meagre a wage, followed by a pension. Nor was insecurity of employment confined to the unskilled; a skilled worker in the engineering industry in the late nineteenth century could be dismissed, or leave, at any meal-break and employers in many trades still adjusted their workforce day by day to the level of demand. The unemployed were not, therefore, a class apart but those who, temporarily or for a longer time, were less fortunate than other members of the working class.[9]

In other words, although the Army might well be seen as the last resort, it could be such a resort for a large part of the working-class population of Britain, or at least for those who met the conditions which the Army set for recruits. Spiers implies that this was not so when he writes that (1980: 45):

there was a vast reservoir of eligible unemployed men which the army, though perennially short of recruits, failed to attract. Unemployment, in sum, was never a panacea for the recruiting problems of the army.

But what was the pool from which the Army might draw? Market forces, of the kind described above, limited the supply of recruits, but the specialised requirements of the Army imposed further constraints. These were not unusual in principle – all employers have specialised requirements – but they did limit supply.

The Army's requirements were that its recruits should be male, young and physically fit. As Henry Marshall put it (1828: 58):

The leading qualities required in recruits may be comprehended under four heads, namely. Height. A certain period of life. Health. Activity, or the full power of using the several members of the body.[10]

The first requirement, that recruits should be male, did not change but the Army was prepared to vary the second and third in order to stimulate or limit the flow of recruits.

Indeed, the fact that it was common experience that a relaxation in the age limits or in the height standards would immediately produce a flow of recruits is itself strong evidence that there was a high elasticity of supply for Army service. The efficacy of changing the height limits was certainly believed in 1824, when the Army Medical Department

[9] Spiers (1980: 44) is right to throw doubt on the attempts which were made to show a connection between recruitment and pauperism in the late nineteenth century, but the main reason is not that there was no connection but that the national Poor Law statistics are far too blunt an instrument for such a purpose. He points out that: 'Whereas the largest number of recruits recorded in any year from 1859 to 1888 was 39 552 men, there was never less than 745 453 paupers in any particular year in the same period'. Many of the latter would have been too old or too unfit for military service. Also many would have been too young and, over half, female. In addition, many of the young, male able-bodied poor would not have been eligible for relief or appear in the statistics.

[10] He added that: 'With respect to height and period of life, they belong to the province of military officers, while the qualities of health and activity are in general left to the determination of the medical branch of the service.

circulated a list of rules for medical inspection, including a list of diseases which should lead to rejection, concluding (Marshall 1828: 13):

These instructions may be considered fixed. When men are much required for the service the minimum of height is lowered, and the period of life during which they may be enlisted extended, and vice versa. The supply of recruits is thereby commonly proportioned to the wants of the army, without relaxing the regulations in regard to health or efficiency.

This suggests that before the relaxation there was a large pool of men who would have been prepared to enlist, at current rates of pay and conditions, but were debarred from doing so by the age or height standards.

But how far did these standards or other Army requirements limit the supply of labour? The easiest requirement to consider is that of age. Throughout the period, the Army preferred to recruit men between the ages of 18 and 25, although at various times it was prepared to accept both younger and older men.[11] These age standards meant that its pool of potential recruits was, for this reason alone, far smaller than that of the adult male population of Britain.[12]

The size of the pool depends crucially on the age distribution of the population, and specifically on the proportion of the male population who were aged between the Army's age limits. A reasonably exact calculation of the number of eligible males can be made for census years from 1861 and is shown in table 2.3; the calculation shows that age limits significantly restricted the pool from which the Army could draw its recruits. In practice, the pool was even more severely restricted, as the great bulk of entrants to the armed forces were aged between 18 and 21; the Army Sanitary Commission of

---

[11] The upper age limit for infantry of the line, for example, as stated in the Orders of the Day, was 30 from 13 May 1790. The limit was altered to 25 on 21 Nov. 1790, to 35 on 20 Mar. 1796, to 25 on 25 Aug. 1802, to 30 on 25 Oct. 1806, to 35 on 10 Feb. 1813, to 25 on 1 May 1814, to 30 on 1 Apr. 1815, to 25 on 13 Jan. 1816, to 30 on 30 Oct. 1854, to 25 on 28 Apr. 1856 and to 30 on 23 Jan. 1858. The lower age limit is less often stated and was often essentially replaced by a height limit, but recruits were supposed to be 18 or over from 21 Nov. 1790 to 20 Mar. 1796, when the limit was lowered to 16. It was 17 from 25 Aug. 1802 to 10 Feb. 1813 when it was raised to 18, falling to 17 again only after 28 Apr. 1856. Other limits applied to different army units.

[12] Spiers (1980: 35) is correct in calculating that 'the proportion of men under arms in the regular army remained within fairly confined parameters. Even including the army reserve of the late nineteenth century, the proportion of men under arms merely oscillated between 1 and 2 per cent of the male population.' That proportion, however, is largely irrelevant to the question of recruiting or the demands which that made on the labour supply.

Table 2.3. *The impact of age limits on the availability of recruits.*

1	2	3	4	5	6	7
Census date	Total males	Males aged 18–29	Males aged 18–29 less those in armed services	Col. 4 as % of total male population	Males aged 18–21	Col. 6 as % of total male population
1861	14 063	3063	2747	20	773	5
1871	15 302	3211	2970	19	885	6
1881	16 972	3618	3371	20	1050	6
1891	18 322	3968	3688	20	1158	6
1900	20 103	4560	4039	20	1068	5

Source: Census Reports, as reported in Mitchell (1962). Mitchell reports the numbers in age-groups 15–19, 20–24 and 25–29 and linear interpolation was used to calculate the numbers aged 18, 19, 20 and 21. All numbers except percentages are thousands.

Note: No breakdown exists of the age distribution of men in the armed services at census dates. Column 4 therefore assumes that all were aged 18–29, leading to a slight underestimate in columns 4–5. Similarly, it is impossible to estimate the number of men aged 18–21 in the armed services and columns 6 and 7 are thus overestimates.

1858, for example, assumed in its calculation of mortality rates that all recruits were aged 19.[13]

The Army further restricted its labour supply by the operation of the system of medical inspection. Once again, most statistical information about the effects of the imposition of standards of physical and mental health comes from the end of the nineteenth century, from the Annual Reports of the Army Medical Department, particularly as the rejection rate became a subject of great political controversy; the rejection rates for this period are shown in table 2.4

It is clear, however, that medical rejections had always debarred a substantial number of recruits from a military career. In 1807, even at a time of great shortage of recruits, it was laid down that (PP 1806–7 iv: 178):

---

[13] The sample evidence discussed in the next chapter shows that in the latter part of the eighteenth century 18 to 21-year-old recruits made up slightly under half of all recruits, falling to 34 per cent for those born between 1770 and 1774; in the nineteenth century, this age-group was preponderant, ranging from 53.6 per cent of all recruits for those born in 1830–1834 to 85.3 per cent for those born between 1820 and 1824. The former figure is affected by the recruitment of older men for the Crimea and it seems that the typical pattern of peacetime recruitment in the nineteenth century was to take over 70 per cent of recruits from young men aged 18–21.

Table 2.4. *Rejection rates. The percentage of recruits who were rejected by the Army Medical Department on medical inspection.*

Year	Rejection rate	Year	Rejection rate
1868	37.6	1889	41.6
1869	37.5	1890	39.7
1870	33.7	1891	37.9
1871	33.2	1892	38.3
1872	31.7	1893	41.1
1873	30.4	1894	40.5
1874	27.7	1895	41.1
1875	25.7	1896	42.3
1876	27.3	1897	38.3
1877	29.3	1898	35.1
1878	29.8	1899	33.1
1879	36.3	1900	28.1
1880	40.8	1901	29.4
1881	43.3	1902	32.5
1882	42.5	1903	33.6
1883	39.7	1904	35.2
1884	41.7	1905	37.3
1885	40.0	1906	33.0
1886	43.8	1907	28.5
1887	45.6	1908	28.2
1888	45.9		

Source: Annual Reports of the Army Medical Department.

The greatest care is to be taken that no man be enlisted who is not stout and well-made; and that the lads and boys are perfectly well limbed, open chested and what is commonly called long in the fork ... No recruit is to be on any account enlisted, who has the least appearance of sore legs, scurvy, scald head, or other infirmity, that may render him unfit for His Majesty's service.

At all times, medical rejections were subject to attack by recruiting officers, who found their efforts to obtain recruits thwarted by the doctors. Such attacks were made even by the most senior of officers; Henry Marshall reports that the Commander-in-Chief complained in 1825 that too high a proportion of recruits were being rejected (1828: 25–6). On 30 April 1825 the Adjutant-General sent out a circular which commented on high rejection rates:

The amount of the number of recruits rejected could not but strike the Commander-in-Chief with surprise, and his Royal Highness could not associate such results with a careful and fair inspection of recruits.

On 9 May 1825 a circular from the Adjutant-General, Dublin, repeated this concern, though adding that the proportion rejected in 1824 was 29.09 per cent, while in 1818 it had been 39.5 per cent. On 4 July 1825 a circular from the Director-General of the Army Medical Department made it clear that the duty of examining officers lay in assisting the Army to get its recruits.[14]

It was always difficult to ensure that medical officers were reasonably consistent in their standards, and the difficulty of making sure that this was so was one of the reasons why the Inter-Departmental Committee on Physical Deterioration in 1903 was so sceptical of conclusions drawn from the proportion of recruits who were rejected. Nevertheless, there can be no doubt that large numbers of men were either so unfit that they did not think of joining the Army, or that they tried to do so and were rejected. There is no reason to think that the situation revealed by the Medical Boards in the First World War had not existed for many years (PP 1919 xxvi: 4):

of every nine men of military age in Great Britain, on the average three were perfectly fit and healthy; two were upon a definitely infirm place of health and strength, whether from some disability or some failure in development; three were incapable of undergoing more than a very moderate degree of physical exertion and could almost (in view of their age) be described with justice as physical wrecks; and the remaining man as a chronic invalid with a precarious hold upon life.

The report judged, with some gloom, that:

the men examined during the year under review may be regarded in the aggregate as fairly representing the manhood of military age of the country in the early part of the twentieth century from the standpoint of health and physique. (PP 1919 xxvi: 5)

Height limits further restricted the pool, although the effect is more difficult to estimate; the Inspector-General of Recruiting told the Inter-Departmental Committee that 'there are thousands who, knowing they are under standard, never present themselves, much as they wish to be soldiers' (PP 1904 xxxii: Q163). Some estimate of how large this group of men was can be gained from the Army Medical Department's statistics after 1862. Using statistical methods which

---

[14] 'Medical officers, in the performance of this highly important duty, will not allow themselves to reject men whose disqualifications are not decidedly apparent, or to receive such as are manifestly unfit for soldiers. Attention to the spirit of the orders on this head, unfettered by trivial or questionable objections, will ensure the results expected by the Commander in Chief from the exertions of the several classes of officers, who are employed on the service of recruiting, and merit a continuance of the good opinion his Royal Highness is pleased to entertain and to express of the medical staff.'

are described in detail below, we can estimate the number of potential recruits *with an age distribution and other characteristics similar to those of actual recruits* who were excluded by the operation of the height standard. This calculation is shown in table 2.5; it suggests that over the period from 1860 to 1908, almost half as many potential recruits were debarred by the height standard as were found to pass that standard. In other words, the Army's self-imposed limits were a severe constraint on its ability to recruit.

Like any employer, the Army imposed the need for qualifications on its workforce and thereby restricted the potential supply of employees. The quantitative evidence which has been assembled suggests that such restrictions were quite potent but also that the Army was, nevertheless, usually successful in obtaining approximately the number of soldiers that it desired. In doing so, it must have recruited from a much wider group of the working class than has traditionally been believed. The pressures of poverty and unemployment in eighteenth- and nineteenth-century Britain were potent recruiting officers.

The interaction of demand and supply: the flow of recruits

But how large an influence did the Army, and the other armed forces, have on the labour market in the eighteenth and nineteenth centuries? What impact did its demands have and what proportion of the labour force did it attract? Did it attract only a small, possibly aberrant, group of men or did it reach deep into the young male working class? These questions demand that we should now examine the flow of recruits, the result of the interplay between the forces of demand and supply which we have just examined.

Despite the importance of the subject both to military historians and to students of the labour market, no history has been written of military recruiting. In addition, contemporary documents and contemporary opinion are silent about it for many years, particularly in peacetime; recruiting was a matter of public and parliamentary concern only in time of war or fear of war. As a result, the basic quantitative data for a study of the process of recruitment, whether for Army, Navy or Marines, are difficult to obtain, confusing or contradictory. Every student of this topic will echo Sir John Fortescue who, in discussing the size of the Army during the War of the Spanish Succession, comments of a statement in the Journal of the House of Commons that (1909 i: 557): 'The confusion in the statement is worthy of the War Office.'

The following discussion concentrates on Army data, both because

Table 2.5. *The operation of the height standard in the late nineteenth century; the number and proportion of 'potential recruits' falling below the height standard.*

Date	Number of recruits	Number of 'potential' recruits	'Loss'	Loss as a percentage of actual recruits	Loss as a percentage of potential recruits
1860	22 613	37 235	14 622	65	39
1861	11 828	16 098	4 270	36	27
1862	7 290	11 338	4 048	56	36
1863	10 959	20 118	9 159	84	46
1864	41 780	76 356	34 576	83	45
1877	88 958	128 369	39 411	44	31
1879	41 306	64 722	23 416	57	36
1880	44 123	67 360	23 237	53	34
1881	45 415	75 678	30 263	67	40
1883	58 927	88 086	29 159	49	33
1884	63 746	89 689	25 943	41	29
1885	69 507	105 314	35 807	52	34
1886	72 154	105 604	33 450	46	32
1887	54 238	87 981	33 743	62	38
1888	41 652	69 947	28 295	68	40
1889	48 140	77 572	29 432	61	38
1890	51 112	81 553	30 441	60	37
1891	61 358	93 049	31 691	52	34
1892	67 842	99 119	31 277	46	32
1893	61 326	97 115	35 789	58	37
1894	60 879	98 612	37 733	62	38
1895	50 404	79 609	29 205	58	37
1896	45 803	73 374	27 571	60	38
1897	52 668	77 803	25 135	48	32
1898	56 780	70 949	14 169	25	20
1899	61 150	78 630	17 480	29	22
1900	81 529	102 688	21 159	26	21
1902	76 806	105 980	29 174	38	28
1903	64 915	85 119	20 204	31	24
1904	68 679	84 852	16 173	24	19
1906	58 742	71 570	12 828	22	18
1907	54 474	67 878	13 404	25	20
1908	57 238	69 301	12 063	21	17
Total	1 754 341	2 558 668	804 329		
Mean				49	32

Source: Annual Reports of the Army Medical Department.

Notes:
For 1889 and after, this table is based on an estimate of the number of those who applied and were inspected by the Army.
The 'potential' recruits takes account of those who would have been debarred from applying by the existence of a height standard.
'Loss' is estimated by the quantile bend estimator and represents the proportion of the full distribution which is missing as the result of the operation of the height standard.

it is from the Army that half of our samples are drawn and because it was by far the largest wing of the armed services for most of the period. Even less information appears to exist about recruitment to the Royal Marines or to the Navy, although table 2.6 shows the numbers of men voted for these services between 1689 and 1869.

Five different quantitative series, derived from parliamentary returns, throw light on the numbers recruited to the Army. Each year Parliament voted funds for a certain number of troops, known as the 'Establishment of the Army', representing the desired number of troops, and the number of the establishment is known from 1691 to 1715, from 1718 to 1799 and from 1801 onwards. It was not always possible to recruit sufficient men to meet the establishment (nor, in the aftermath of war, to discharge enough), and in recognition of this a different number of 'effectives' was computed, representing the men actually serving. Data for effectives exist from 1774 to 1859 and from 1861 onwards. Establishment and effectives were balanced by recruitment and by losses caused by deaths, by desertion and by discharge (see table 2.1). Data for the number of recruits are often flawed, but exist in some form for 1793 to 1801, 1803 to 1821 and from 1832 onwards. Data for the 'three Ds' exist for 1803 to 1821 and from 1861 onwards.[15] There are, unfortunately, few periods except during the later nineteenth century when all these data derive from the same source and can be relied upon to be approximately compatible. At other periods, changes in definition and errors of measurement, leading to inconsistencies, are very common.

It is possible to use the published data on the size of the Army to assess the size of recruitment between 1775 and 1913, even for years for which published data do not exist. This is because the five quantitative series mentioned above have a logical structure: the Army begins each new year with a given number of effectives; it loses men through death, desertion and discharge but seeks to recruit other men to make up for those losses and to match the establishment which it has been granted by parliament.

The crucial and normally unobserved number is the depreciation rate, the proportion of the equipment or men who are lost. The number of such men can, however, be directly observed for the periods from 1803 to 1821 and from 1861 to 1913. During those periods, which included times of war and of peace, the relationship between total losses and the number of effectives can be estimated by regression analysis (a statistical technique explained in chapter 3) as:

[15] Army recruitment data are drawn from the sources listed in footnotes to tables.

$$loss = -20\,568.861 + 0.273\,957\,7\ effectives - 14\,032.86\ war \quad (2.1)$$

$$R^2 = 0.506$$

where *loss* = total of those died, deserted or discharged in the year
effectives = number of effectives recorded for the given year
war = a dummy variable taking the value 1 during wartime, 0 otherwise.[16]

This equation suggests that, on average, 27 per cent of the strength of the Army was lost to it each year and needed to be replaced by new recruits. This is a surprisingly large figure, implying that the average length of service was less than four years, but it is consistent with some contemporary evidence in the latter part of the nineteenth century. The equation also suggests that war diminished Army losses, an apparently paradoxical finding which is explained by the fact that in wartime the Army reduced its rate of discharge, holding on for as long as possible to seasoned soldiers.

The estimated relationship between the number of effectives and losses can then be used to estimate the number of recruits in a given year. This stems from the logical relationship:

$$effectives_{(t)} = effectives_{(t-1)} - loss + recruits \quad (2.2)$$

which can be transformed into:

$$recruits = effectives_{(t)} - effectives_{(t-1)} + loss \quad (2.3)$$

But since equation (2.1) expresses *loss* in terms of *effectives*, this equation can be used to estimate:

$$recruits = effectives_{(t)} - 20\,568.861 - 0.726\,042\,3 effectives_{(t-1)} - 14032.86 war$$

Table 2.7 shows the results of this estimation, compared with published figures on recruitment where these are available. During the years for which those figures are available, 1804–1821 and 1862–1913, the estimated number of recruits per annum was 33 968, as compared with an actual number of 31 295, and the correlation between the two series is 0.576. The series are graphed in figure 2.1, which shows their close correspondence, particularly between 1862 and 1913. As this figure shows, as well as figure 2.2 which displays the entire estimated series (RECEST), the estimation procedure leads to the calculation of negative numbers of recruits in some years in which the Army

---

[16] Regression analysis with dummy variables is explained in chapter 5.

Table 2.6. *Estimates of the number of men in the Royal Navy and Royal Marines.*

Date	Royal Navy Establishment	Royal Marines Establishment	Men 'actually Borne' including Navy and Marines
1715	10 000		
1716	10 000		
1717	10 000		
1718	10 000		
1719	13 500		
1720	N.A.		
1721	N.A.		
1722	N.A.		
1723	10 000		
1724	N.A.		
1725	N.A.		
1726	N.A.		
1727	N.A.		
1728	15 000		
1729	15 000		
1730	10 000		
1731	10 000		
1732	8 000		
1733	8 000		
1734	20 000		
1735	30 000		
1736	15 000		
1737	10 000		
1738	10 000		
1739	12 000		
1740	35 000		
1741	40 000		
1742	40 000		
1743	40 000		
1744	30 000		
1745	40 000		
1746	40 000		
1747	40 000		
1748	40 000		
1749	47 000		
1750	10 000		
1751	8 000		
1752	10 000		
1753	10 000		
1754	10 000		
1755	12 000		
1756	41 000	9 000	
1757	43 581	11 419	

Table 2.6. (*cont.*)

Date	Royal Navy Establishment	Royal Marines Establishment	Men 'actually Borne' including Navy and Marines
1758	45 155	14 845	
1759	45 155	14 845	
1760	51 665	18 355	
1761	51 665	18 355	
1762	50 939	19 061	
1763	25 713	4 287	
1764	11 713	4 287	
1765	11 713	4 287	
1766	11 713	4 287	
1767	11 713	4 287	
1768	11 713	4 287	
1769	11 713	4 287	
1770	11 713	4 287	
1771	31 927	8 073	
1772	18 336	6 664	
1773	15 466	4 354	
1774	15 466	4 354	
1775	13 226	4 774	
1776	21 335	6 665	31 084
1777	34 871	10 129	52 836
1778	48 171	11 829	72 258
1779	52 611	17 389	87 767
1780	66 221	18 779	97 898
1781	69 683	20 317	99 362
1782	78 695	21 305	105 443
1783	84 709	25 291	65 677
1784	21 505	4 495	28 878
1785	14 380	3 620	22 183
1786	14 380	3 620	17 259
1787	14 140	3 860	19 444
1788	14 330	3 670	19 740
1789	16 140	3 860	20 396
1790	16 135	3 865	39 526
1791	19 200	4 800	34 097
1792	11 575	4 425	17 361
1793	40 000	5 000	59 042
1794	72 885	12 115	83 891
1795	85 000	15 000	99 608
1796	95 000	15 000	112 382
1797	100 000	20 000	120 046
1798	100 000	20 000	119 592
1799	100 000	20 000	120 409
1800	88 842[a]	22 696[a]	123 527
1801	103 224[a]	28 314[a]	131 959

Table 2.6. (*cont.*)

Date	Royal Navy Establishment	Royal Marines Establishment	Men 'actually Borne' including Navy and Marines
1802	74 000[a]	20 462[a]	77 765
1803	60 154[a]	18 000[a]	67 148
1804	78 000	22 000	99 372
1805	90 000	30 000	114 012
1806	90 000	30 000	122 860
1807	98 600	31 400	130 917
1808	98 600	31 400	139 605
1809	98 600	31 400	144 387
1810	113 600	31 400	146 312
1811	113 600	31 400	144 762
1812	113 600	31 400	144 844
1813	108 600	31 400	147 047
1814	108 600[b]	31 400[b]	126 414
1815	55 000[c]	15 000[c]	78 891
1816	24 000	9 000	35 196
1817	13 000	6 000	22 944
1818	14 000	6 000	23 026
1819	14 000	6 000	23 230
1820	15 000	8 000	23 985
1821	14 000	8 000	24 937
1822	13 000	8 000	23 806
1823	16 300	8 700	26 314
1824	20 000	9 000	30 502
1825	20 000	9 000	31 456
1826	21 000	9 000	32 519
1827	21 000	9 000	33 106
1828	21 000	9 000	31 818
1829	21 000	9 000	32 458
1830	20 000	9 000	31 160
1831	22 000[d]	10 000[d]	29 336[d]
1832–3	18 000	9 000	27 328
1833–4	18 000	9 000	27 701
1834–5	17 500	9 000	28 066
1835–6	15 500	9 000	26 041
1836–7	22 700	9 000	30 195
1837–8	23 165	9 000	31 289
1838–9	23 165	9 000	32 028
1839–40	23 165	9 000	34 857
1840–1	26 456[e]	9 000	37 665
1841–2	30 500	10 500	41 389
1842–3	30 500	10 500	43 105
1843–4	26 500	10 500	40 229
1844–5	23 500	10 500	38 343

Table 2.6. (*cont.*)

Date	Royal Navy Establishment	Royal Marines Establishment	Men 'actually Borne' including Navy and Marines
1845–6	27 500	10 500	40 084
1846–7	27 500	10 500	43 314
1847–8	27 500	11 500[e]	44 969
1848–9	27 500	13 000[e]	43 978
1849–50	26 000	12 000	39 535
1850–1	26 000	11 000	39 093
1851–2	26 000	11 000	38 957
1852–3	27 666[e]	11 500	40 451
1853–4	31 000	12 500	45 885
1854–5	46 000	15 500	61 457
1855–6	44 000	16 000	67 791
1856–7	37 499	16 000	60 659
1857–8	29 030	15 000	50 419
1858–9	30 900	15 000	N.A.

Sources:
1715–1775   Navy and Marines. PP 1816 xii, 399. This source gives the number of men voted for the Navy.
1783–1793   Navy and Marines. PP 1860 xlii, 547.

Notes:
[a] Calculated as an average from figures given for variable numbers of lunar months.
[b] This figure is for seven lunar months; the figure for the remaining six lunar months is not known.
[c] This figure is for three lunar months; the figure for the remaining ten lunar months is not known.
[d] Financial year changed to run from 1st April to 31st March. These figures are for the first three months of 1831.
[e] Calculated as an average from figures given for variable numbers of calendar months.

was reducing its numbers substantially, but this effect is soon corrected as establishment (the desired number of men in the forces) and recruitment stabilise.

Figure 2.3 shows the results of a calculation, along similar lines, of the number of recruits which the Army would have liked to have secured (DESREC). This is related to the difference between the establishment and effectives in a given year (ESTEFF) but also takes account of deaths, desertions and discharges.

The implication of figures 2.1 and 2.2 is that the Army faced serious

Table 2.7. *The number of recruits to the Army, 1775–1913.*

Year	Observed recruits	Estimated recruits	War dummy
1775	N.A.	− 16 254.20	1
1776	N.A.	− 24 802.06	1
1777	N.A.	− 10 970.38	1
1778	N.A.	− 16 325.45	1
1779	N.A.	7 784.773	1
1780	N.A.	− 5 439.585	1
1781	N.A.	− 7 651.127	1
1782	N.A.	− 11 239.00	1
1783	N.A.	− 9 068.434	1
1784	N.A.	− 60 432.45	0
1785	N.A.	− 12 811.79	0
1786	N.A.	− 13 318.57	0
1787	N.A.	− 12 941.57	0
1788	N.A.	− 10 883.29	0
1789	N.A.	− 8 068.419	0
1790	N.A.	− 10 816.42	0
1791	N.A.	− 7 233.589	0
1792	N.A.	− 11 725.62	0
1793	17 033.00	− 22 198.65	1
1794	38 563.00	22 219.56	1
1795	40 463.00	27 876.26	1
1796	16 336.00	− 12 825.19	1
1797	16 096.00	− 11 053.55	1
1798	21 457.00	− 8 172.966	1
1799	41 316.00	6 185.205	1
1800	17 829.00	51 148.45	1
1801	10 698.00	26 660.39	1
1802	0.00	27 763.56	1
1803	11 253.00	− 50 346.27	1
1804	11 088.00	58 555.32	1
1805	33 545.00	31 308.25	1
1806	20 677.00	33 271.49	1
1807	30 592.00	39 993.30	1
1808	30 592.00	56 855.36	1
1809	22 350.00	44 405.36	1
1810	22 350.00	41 632.67	1
1811	22 925.00	35 881.77	1
1812	24 359.00	50 398.70	1
1813	19 980.00	55 118.63	1
1814	13 564.00	55 281.49	1
1815	15 279.00	− 6 557.456	1
1816	14 948.00	21 963.65	0
1817	9 047.00	− 1 971.765	0
1818	7 156.00	2 042.301	0
1819	5 499.00	− 8 815.193	0
1820	8 371.00	10 952.47	0
1821	7 325.00	8 138.644	0

Table 2.7. (*cont.*)

Year	Observed recruits	Estimated recruits	War dummy
1822	N.A.	1 293.469	0
1823	N.A.	4 716.924	0
1824	N.A.	9 348.327	0
1825	N.A.	9 869.58	0
1826	N.A.	21 950.41	0
1827	N.A.	17 727.81	0
1828	N.A.	14 158.39	0
1829	N.A.	6 534.66	0
1830	N.A.	4 230.438	0
1831	N.A.	16 863.26	0
1832	6 047.00	11 710.17	0
1833	4 651.00	11 364.59	0
1834	3 655.00	3 434.667	0
1835	4 530.00	9 410.541	0
1836	7 583.00	9 454.609	0
1837	8 602.00	9 429.621	0
1838	10 903.00	20 959.48	0
1839	19 099.00	16 446.34	0
1840	15 822.00	19 905.47	0
1841	13 653.00	14 515.28	0
1842	14 534.00	25 933.53	0
1843	11 514.00	− 4 377.440	0
1844	9 224.00	31 982.20	0
1845	11 420.00	17 204.60	0
1846	19 333.00	27 662.60	0
1847	13 294.00	21 911.09	0
1848	10 060.00	23 041.94	0
1849	7 867.00	17 145.06	0
1850	6 321.00	15 315.75	0
1851	8 376.00	18 740.96	0
1852	12 683.00	20 583.84	0
1853	10 949.00	22 865.02	0
1854	31 620.00	23 966.22	0
1855	36 159.00	30 420.54	1
1856	13 955.00	57 881.32	1
1857	24 383.00	− 11 380.70	0
1858	46 731.00	52 409.73	0
1859	28 137.00	41 394.63	0
1860	20 725.00	33 808.16	0
1861	12 830.00	33 388.45	0
1862	24 240.00	23 453.75	0
1863	12 821.00	35 528.34	0
1864	17 270.00	26 587.96	0
1865	15 440.00	28 064.04	0
1866	16 316.00	21 737.59	0
1867	20 702.00	23 195.96	0
1868	18 281.00	26 508.51	0

Table 2.7. (*cont.*)

Year	Observed recruits	Estimated recruits	War dummy
1869	13 186.00	22 292.70	0
1870	25 682.00	14 653.82	0
1871	25 066.00	27 224.16	0
1872	19 666.00	28 946.86	0
1873	18 998.00	24 459.97	0
1874	22 719.00	20 793.27	0
1875	20 449.00	23 902.93	0
1876	31 454.00	21 344.84	0
1877	31 178.00	29 164.75	0
1878	65 931.00	25 536.22	0
1879	29 088.00	26 476.39	0
1880	27 182.00	25 485.56	0
1881	28 511.00	22 842.11	0
1882	35 939.00	25 056.83	0
1883	34 401.00	28 992.61	0
1884	38 636.00	14 153.48	0
1885	46 541.00	29 950.40	0
1886	41 304.00	36 314.02	0
1887	33 315.00	35 480.67	0
1888	26 919.00	32 343.66	0
1889	30 991.00	30 287.13	0
1890	32 996.00	29 449.72	0
1891	37 740.00	30 346.67	0
1892	43 664.00	31 163.17	0
1893	37 342.00	36 518.73	0
1894	35 871.00	33 595.95	0
1895	31 282.00	34 839.45	0
1896	28 532.00	32 972.54	0
1897	35 015.00	49 372.38	0
1898	40 729.00	20 047.46	0
1899	100 499.00	46 407.22	1
1900	128 515.00	94 860.08	1
1901	76 840.00	160 625.40	1
1902	66 316.00	53 765.48	1
1903	35 018.00	12 407.52	0
1904	43 041.00	28 125.74	0
1905	38 846.00	52 066.60	0
1906	41 212.00	44 968.08	0
1907	38 515.00	36 884.07	0
1908	44 167.00	50 343.07	0
1909	36 646.00	50 364.29	0
1910	29 755.00	48 134.40	0
1911	32 047.00	50 279.42	0
1912	33 155.00	48 554.06	0
1913	31 081.00	42 439.20	0

Source: See text and sources to table 2.1.

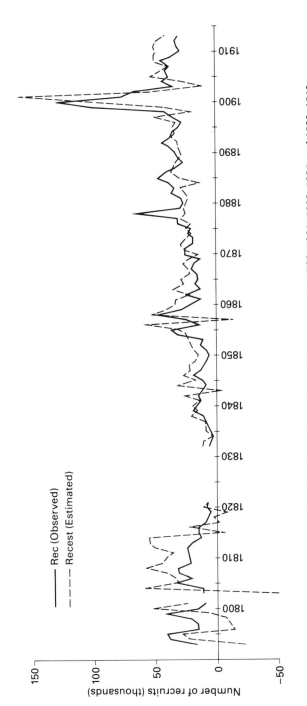

Figure 2.1. The observed and estimated numbers of Army recruits, 1793–1801, 1803–1821 and 1832–1913. Source: see text and table 2.7.

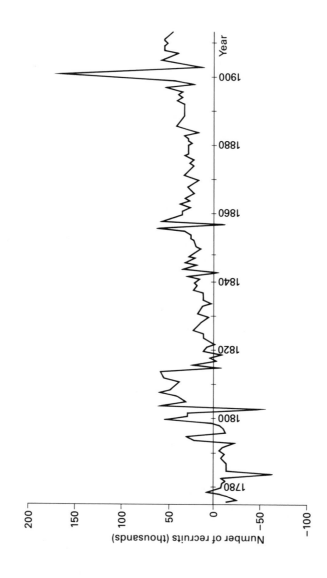

Figure 2.2. An estimate of the number of recruits to the Army, 1775–1913. Source: see text and table 2.7.

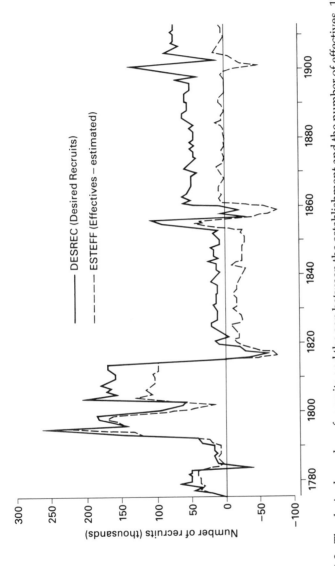

Figure 2.3. The desired number of recruits and the gap between the establishment and the number of effectives, 1775–1913. Source: see text and table 2.2.

difficulties in obtaining manpower only in the latter stages of the French Wars and during the Crimea, when there were substantial divergences between establishment and effectives and between the desired and estimated number of recruits. This is not to argue, of course, that the Army was not forced to improve terms and conditions of service at other times, in order to maintain the flow of recruits, but that in general such stratagems were successful. This can also be seen in table 2.2 and figure 2.3, which show that except in wartime there was rarely a substantial gap between the establishment and the number of effectives.

It is possible, of course, that the Army was realistic about the number of recruits which it was likely to obtain and therefore adjusted the establishment to the number of effectives and recruits, rather than vice versa. The quantitative evidence cannot throw light on such a possibility and it would be necessary, in order to do so, to study the political and administrative procedures by which the number of the military establishment was fixed. In default of this, the quantitative evidence suggests that, despite the complaints of the Army authorities about the difficulty of obtaining enough men, those men were forthcoming except in time of major war.

Military recruitment and the labour market
The impact of military recruitment on the labour market depends not only on its absolute size but also on the specific character of the recruits whom it sought to attract. As table 2.1 shows, the absolute size was never negligible, particularly in the nineteenth century. Even after the substantial reductions in the size of the Army at the end of the French Wars, its size remained above 100 000 men for the rest of the century; the average number of effectives between 1815 and 1899, excluding the period of the Crimea, was 164 077. At the time of the 1871 census, the armed forces ranked 14th in size among 24 occupational groups (Mitchell 1962: 60) and represented 1.5 per cent of the occupied male population, although these figures understate the size of the armed forces, since troops overseas at the time of the census were not counted. It must also be remembered that the armed forces, unlike other 'industries', were essentially a single, or at most three, employers.

Such comparisons are somewhat misleading, however, because of the restrictions which the Army put on the recruits whom it was willing to accept and, particularly, because of the age distribution of Army recruits, which was totally unlike that of the population as a whole. Not only were recruits much younger than the average of the population, but they stayed in the armed forces for a much smaller than average part of their working lives. A simple comparison of the size of the Army with the size of other groups of employed men does not take account of this fact.

The importance of the fact that almost all recruits were aged between 17 and 25 can be demonstrated most clearly by an examination of the statistics of recruitment published by the Army Medical Department after 1862. The Department published, each year, a table of the ages of recruits who had been medically examined (or, for years from 1887, of those finally approved for enlistment). Table 2.8, column D, shows a rearrangement of these data into the form of birth cohorts; that is, the column adds together the recruits who were born in a particular year, whether they were ultimately recruited at the age of 18, 19, 20 or later. This figure can then be compared with column C of the table, which shows the number of men, born in the same year, who had survived to the age of 18. Some proportion of them were recruited at the age of 18, some at later ages, but column E shows the total number of recruits from the men born in a given year; in the language of demography, column E is an 'age-specific participation rate'.

Column E of table 2.8 thus shows the proportion of young men born in a given year in the late nineteenth century who, at some time in their lives, were medically examined after trying to join the Army. The results are striking. Of men born between 1851 and 1884 who had survived to the age of 18, at least 10 per cent were medically examined by the Army Medical Department. For much of the period the proportion was much higher, reaching a peak of 17.0 per cent for the cohort born in 1880 – the contingent who fought the South African War.

It must also be remembered that the great bulk of recruits came from the working-class and that the appropriate denominator for the calculation of the age-specific participation rate should be the size of the working-class, rather than the total, population of 18-year-olds. Estimates of the size of the working-class population in Britain in the late nineteenth century are contentious. The best estimates of class structure for the third quarter of the nineteenth century are those of R. Dudley Baxter (1868: 64). Baxter divided the occupied population into two groups: the upper and middle classes with 19.8 per cent of the occupied population and the manual labour class with the remaining 80.2 per cent. The latter group comprised higher skilled labour and manufacturers with an annual average wage of £50–£73, lower skilled labour and manufacturers with £35–£52 and agricultural

Table 2.8. *Age-specific recruitment rates, 1862–1902.*

A	B	C	D	E
		Estimated number of 18-year-olds	Number of recruits born in year	col. D as % of
Date	Date − 18	(thousands)	shown in col. B	col. C
1862	1844	289.00	18 469	6.4
1863	1845	290.46	22 874	7.9
1864	1846	291.92	30 814	10.6
1865	1847	293.38	27 818	9.5
1866	1848	294.84	23 612	8.0
1867	1849	296.30	24 037	8.1
1868	1850	297.76	26 011	8.7
1869	1851	299.22	30 131	10.1
1870	1852	300.68	38 274	12.7
1871	1853	302.14	37 178	12.3
1872	1854	306.57	37 775	12.3
1873	1855	310.99	39 230	12.6
1874	1856	315.42	36 723	11.6
1875	1857	319.84	38 137	11.9
1876	1858	324.27	39 235	12.1
1877	1859	328.70	40 725	12.4
1878	1860	333.12	39 193	11.8
1879	1861	337.55	41 376	12.3
1880	1862	341.97	53 248	15.6
1881	1863	346.40	55 120	15.9
1882	1864	350.81	44 401	12.7
1883	1865	355.22	52 958	14.9
1884	1866	359.63	57 287	15.9
1885	1867	364.04	58 977	16.2
1886	1868	368.45	58 950	16.0
1887	1869	372.86	51 981	13.9
1888	1870	377.27	49 478	13.1
1889	1871	381.68	56 234	14.7
1890	1872	386.09	59 274	15.4
1891	1873	390.50	62 352	16.0
1892	1874	392.91	65 720	16.7
1893	1875	395.32	57 483	14.5
1894	1876	397.72	56 768	14.3
1895	1877	400.13	55 767	13.9
1896	1878	402.54	58 554	14.5
1897	1879	404.95	65 710	16.2
1898	1880	407.36	69 240	17.0
1899	1881	409.76	67 169	16.4
1900	1882	412.17	68 622	16.6
1901	1883	414.58	65 043	15.7
1902	1884	415.19	66 179	15.9

Notes to Table 2.8

Notes and sources:

Col. A:	Date.
Col. B:	Date less 18 years. 18-year-olds formed the largest age-group among recruits and this date – 18 is therefore taken as the basis for computing the size of the cohort of recruits in col. D.
Col. C:	Estimated number of 18-year-olds, in the population of England and Wales, Scotland and Ireland. The estimate is based on census data (reported in Mitchell 1962: 12–14) which give the number of males aged 15–19 in each country. Each such census figure was divided by 5 and intervening years were estimated by linear interpolation, before the country estimates were summed to give the figure here.
Col. D:	Number of recruits born in years shown in col. B. These data are derived from the Annual Reports of the Army Medical Department. The reports before 1887 give a tabulation of numbers of recruits who were inspected, by age, including those ultimately rejected. These data have been rearranged by implied date of birth; thus, the figure in col. D. for recruits born in 1860 comprises 18-year-olds recruited in 1878 plus 19-year-olds recruited in 1879, plus 20-year-olds recruited in 1880, etc. From 1887 onwards tabulations are given only for those approved for service, together with a statement of the proportion approved which is not broken down by age. In order to make the pre-1887 and post-1887 figures comparable, it has been assumed that approval rates did not vary by age, and the numbers approved have therefore been inflated, age-group by age-group, on the basis of the average approval rate in the year in which they were recruited. It is possible, alternatively, to deflate in a similar way the numbers recruited before 1887, but the focus here is on the number of men who were inspected.
Col. E:	Col. D as a percentage of col. C. A small proportion of recruits from overseas are included in the figures in col. D, importing a slight but unknown upward bias to col. E. By contrast, the procedure for computing col. C is likely to give a downward bias to col. E: the calculation of 18-year-olds as one-fifth of 15- to 19-year-olds ignores the mortality at ages 15–17. In addition, mortality after age 18 is not reflected in col. C whereas it diminishes the opportunity for potential recruits to appear in col. D.

General note:
It must be remembered throughout that these tables do not include the majority of those whose height was below the required standard and who were, therefore, rejected – or ruled themselves out – at an earlier stage of the recruitment process. As table 2.5 shows, during this period 1 754 341 men were inspected and it is estimated that a further 804 327 men from a similar background and with the same age-profile would have been inspected but for being ruled out by the height standard.

and unskilled labour with £10-10s to £36. It seems certain that the bulk of Army recruits came from the manual labour class. At the end of the period covered by the Army Medical Department data, Routh (1965: 105) estimates that manual workers accounted for 79.6 per cent of the occupied population. It is sensible, therefore, to recalculate the percentages in table 2.8 on the basis of a working-class population of 80 per cent of the total occupied population; 17 per cent of the 1880 population cohort translates, for example, into 21 per cent of the working class. It is more difficult to make such comparisons for earlier periods, since we know less about the age structure of the population earlier in the century, but it is likely that the same high proportions obtained then.

In addition, these figures do not take account of the very large numbers of men in the working classes who, by reason of their height, were debarred from applying for enlistment. The size of this group can be seen from table 2.5; during the period covered by the Army Medical Department data an average of 32 per cent of those who might, by reason of their age and status, have been attracted to the Army would have been debarred by the height standard. Taking account of these men would, for example, raise the figure of 21 per cent of the working class to one of about 28 per cent.

These calculations show that the armed services – and we must remember that we have not been able to calculate the additional demands of the Navy and Marines – were an extremely important force within the labour market. If they were, as was suggested above, often the 'employer of last resort', they seem to have had that role for very many young men. There is no evidence, however, that in peacetime the armed forces had an oligopolistic position within the British labour market. At the time of major wars, of course, the situation was very different; then the proportion of the labour force engaged in the armed forces rose very rapidly and appears to have exerted upward pressure on civilian wages.

2.2 CONCLUSION

The central conclusion of this study of the market for military labour, limited though it may be by deficiencies of evidence, is that the armed forces entered the labour market much as did other major employers, though with disadvantages in competing for labour caused by the slowness with which they could react to labour market conditions. Partly as a result of this, partly through the disamenities of Army life, they tended to be an employer of last resort. Nevertheless, in the unstable labour markets of eighteenth- and nineteenth-century Britain, such a position made them attractive, at some time or another, to a large fraction of the British working class.

Since this was so, it is no longer possible to regard military recruits as a race apart, whose records may, for that reason, not be used to make inferences about the wider population from whom they were drawn. At the least, the records must be examined with care, to discover how far the distribution of characteristics such as place of birth, occupation or literacy among recruits was similar to that of a wider population. This is the task of the next chapter.

3

Inference from samples of military records

3.0 INTRODUCTION

In the last chapter, we argued that military recruitment can be analysed within the framework of the operations of the labour market in eighteenth- and nineteenth-century Britain. But it remains possible that, because of variations in labour market conditions over time or because of the vagaries of sampling from the large bodies of military records, samples of military recruits could still not provide a good guide to the nutritional status of the British working class. The two issues, though logically distinct, are intimately related because of the unavoidable fact that our only direct knowledge of the recruits, of their occupations, places of birth and place within the labour market, comes from those very samples. In this chapter, therefore, we examine those samples and compare them with various other evidence about the working class.

3.1 INFERENCE FROM THE SAMPLES TO MILITARY UNITS

Most of the newly collected data used in this book are the result of a selection of evidence about individuals from military records. The bulk comes from the Description Books of the British Army and the Royal Marines, held in the Public Record Office. They are supplemented, however, by the records of the Royal Military Academy, held at Sandhurst,[1] and by the records of the Marine Society, held at the National Maritime Museum. These are not the only records, containing information on height and other indicators of nutritional status, which could have been used; there also exist Board of Trade records describing merchant seamen, the records of the East India

---

[1] The original foundation was the Royal Military College, but it later became known as the Royal Military Academy.

Company armies and voluminous prison and other criminal records. However, the military records and those of Sandhurst and the Marine Society together span the widest possible socio-economic range and give the best hope of describing changes in nutritional status in Britain.

In some cases, it was feasible to record and analyse some details about all the men or boys who were recorded. This is true of the boys and Landmen Volunteers who were aided by the Marine Society and of the boys and young men who joined the Royal Military Academy at Sandhurst. Even in these cases, however, it was possible to record only a small part of the information about the recruits which exists in the original records; information about the occupations and parents of the Marine Society boys could be recorded only for a sample, while information about the parents of Sandhurst recruits was also omitted.[2] Nevertheless, statements about the height-by-age of Marine Society and Sandhurst recruits rest on the firmest possible foundation, that of a data set containing the full population of such recruits.

Statements about the heights and other characteristics of recruits to the Army and the Royal Marines rest, by contrast, on samples drawn from the military records held in the Public Record Office (PRO).[3] The sampling procedure used ensures that the data give a good representation of the contents of the Description Books – over 1150 in number – of the Army and Royal Marines which are held by the PRO, but the ravages of time, carelessness and inertia have inevitably meant that not all the Description Books of all the multifarious military units which existed between 1750 and 1900 have survived to reach the PRO. Some have been destroyed, while others may be held in regimental museums or similar places. No attempt has been made to trace such records, and it is assumed in what follows that the PRO holdings sufficiently represent the Description Books, wherever they now are.

The details of approximately 5000 recruits to the Army and 5000 to the Royal Marines have been recorded for each decade. Samples of this size are sufficient to reduce the effects of pure sampling error to very low levels. If sampling error were the only source of variability, we should be able to estimate the mean heights of recruits to an accuracy of plus or minus 0.05 inches (0.13 cm) at a confidence level of 95 per cent. However, the uncertainties in corrections for the operation

[2] Full details of the data that were recorded can be found in appendix 3.1.
[3] Full details of the sampling procedures and of the data that were recorded can be found in appendix 3.1.

of minimum height standards broaden this error range considerably, as do the uncertainties which surround the relationship of the group of recruits to the pool from which they were drawn. The same applies to the estimation of more complex characteristics, such as the proportion of recruits from a particular area or socio-economic group.[4]

The data which we have used give a good representation of recruits to the Army, the Royal Marines, the Marine Society and the Royal Military Academy. But a far more complex question is that of the extent to which recruits to those military or quasi-military units represent a larger population of British males.

3.2 WHO WERE THE RECRUITS?

The last chapter showed that, contrary to much popular belief, military recruitment was conducted within the framework of the labour market and that recruits were drawn widely from within the working class. But where did the men come from and what had they done before they became recruits? The system of recruitment ensured that the area of the country and the occupations from which recruits were drawn was, to some extent at least, a matter of choice by the recruiting officers. Different units of the Army and Marines had their headquarters in different parts of the country and tended to recruit near to those headquarters. At the same time, different Army and Marine officers had their own ideas about the background of desirable recruits. If we are to use the evidence of Army recruits in order to make inferences about the wider population, then it is important to examine the geographical and socio-economic composition of the recruits, in order to see whether these preferences biassed the selection of recruits in any obvious way. This can only be done, before the recruitment years beginning in the 1860s, by the examination of sample evidence; from the 1860s onwards, information was published about the occupations of recruits and, sometimes, about their national origins.

3.2.1 Geographical composition

The recruiting process exercised an obvious influence upon the areas of the country from which recruits were drawn. This is most apparent when a contrast is drawn between the Marines and the Army. When, in 1755, the Marines were reformed and an establishment of 5000

---

[4] As appendix 3.1 shows, the sampling procedure was not strictly random, but it was sufficiently close to enable these calculations to be made. The accuracy and statistical significance of results is considered where those results are presented.

was authorised, the men were grouped into '50 companies, each of which was assigned to one of three "Grand Divisions", quartered respectively at Chatham, Plymouth and Portsmouth ... From 1805 to 1869 there was a further Division, quartered at Woolwich. In 1848 the Portsmouth Division moved to Forton barracks, Gosport, and in 1861 a Depot was established at Walmer, Kent' (PRO 1981: 1).

The location of all the headquarters and administration in southern England exercised a clear influence on Marine recruiting, especially since during the eighteenth century it was apparently forbidden to recruit Catholics, greatly limiting recourse to Irish recruits. As a result, the great bulk of Marine recruits was drawn from England and Wales, with a very small representation of recruits born in Scotland. Irish recruits appear in some numbers during the French Wars and again among those recruited in mid-century. Table 3.1 shows the national composition of Marine recruits in the samples.

By contrast, the Army spread its net very widely and recruited men born throughout the British Isles, as table 3.2 shows.[5] The most notable feature of this table is the marked downward trend in the proportion of Scottish recruits to the Army, accompanied by a similar fall in Irish recruits towards the end of the period. The fall in the proportion of Scottish recruits is so marked as to invite suspicion about the nature of the sample. Some check on the matter is available since the Army Medical Department reported the national origin of the recruits whom it inspected and these annual figures are shown in table 3.3. These figures suggest that the sampling procedure – perhaps because the Description Books of regiments with their head-quarters in Scotland were less likely to reach the Public Record Office – has led to an underestimate of the proportion of Scottish recruits towards the end of the nineteenth century, with the consequence that the estimate of English, Welsh and Irish recruits is slightly too high. On the other hand, table 3.3 suggests that the trend fall in the proportion of Irish recruits, shown in table 3.2, is not an artefact of the sample.

The main difference between the two tables, an under-represen-tation of Scottish recruits in the samples, is, however, small and

[5] It must be remembered that this and subsequent figures are based on sample data and that, because the sampling scheme was based upon the selection of the entire Description Books of particular units, there is a possible source of bias. The sampling procedure ensured, however, that a new selection of books, and hence of military units, was made for each decade, so that while the data for a particular decade may not be an entirely unbiassed sample, the data for successive periods will be. In the event, as tables 3.8 and 3.13 show, there is considerable consistency over time in the data, suggesting that the sampling method has not introduced substantial bias.

Table 3.1. *The national composition of recruits to the Royal Marines,*
1747–1862 (percentages).

Date of birth	England and Wales	Scotland	Ireland	Foreign	Number
1747.5	90.70	2.20	5.60	1.50	2224
1752.5	87.30	2.20	8.50	2.00	2782
1757.5	84.00	1.60	11.20	3.10	2665
1762.5	82.60	1.20	11.40	4.80	2383
1767.5	81.40	1.90	13.70	2.90	1290
1772.5	78.60	2.10	15.40	3.80	1797
1777.5	73.80	2.10	19.40	4.60	2247
1782.5	78.10	2.80	11.70	7.40	2051
1787.5	77.60	0.90	13.20	8.30	1844
1792.5	92.20	0.80	5.20	1.80	1241
1797.5	91.30	2.50	6.10	0.20	1028
1802.5	91.20	3.10	5.70	0.00	2502
1807.5	91.90	4.20	3.70	0.10	3395
1812.5	89.70	4.50	5.50	0.20	3270
1817.5	92.00	2.10	5.70	0.20	4151
1822.5	95.80	1.60	2.50	0.10	3397
1827.5	85.80	3.50	10.60	0.20	1326
1832.5	88.10	3.50	8.30	0.20	1801
1837.5	85.40	2.40	11.90	0.30	2734
1842.5	84.30	2.40	12.80	0.50	2954
1847.5	90.30	3.70	5.50	0.60	2087
1852.5	84.20	6.30	8.80	0.90	2227
1857.5	82.30	8.60	8.40	0.70	2973
1862.5	82.10	9.40	7.50	1.00	3715

Source: Sample of Description Books.

Note: The date of birth refers to the quinquennium centred on the date given and to the cohort of recruits born in that quinquennium.

insufficient to disturb one of the more surprising findings from this evidence. Table 3.4 shows the results of a comparison of recruitment data with the distribution of the male national population at census dates. Only in 1821 and 1831 do the distributions diverge substantially from each other, in each of those years showing a disproportionately large number of Irish recruits. Spiers (1980: 48) argued on the basis of figures for 1830, 1840 and 1870–1912 that:

The urbanisation of the Victorian army mirrored a massive transformation in its national composition. In 1830 and 1840, over half of the non-commissioned officers and men came from Scotland and Ireland. By 1912, 79.6 per cent of the non-commissioned officers and men were either English or Welsh ... Massive unemployment had produced the bulk of the 42,897 soldiers

Table 3.2. *The national composition of recruits to the Army, 1747–1862 (percentages).*

Date of birth	England and Wales	Scotland	Ireland	Foreign	Number
1747.5	47.90	33.00	17.60	1.50	472
1752.5	62.20	27.30	11.30	0.00	951
1757.5	49.50	30.00	19.80	0.60	2189
1762.5	44.80	27.50	27.10	0.60	2294
1767.5	43.20	38.70	17.50	0.60	2231
1772.5	37.60	23.80	37.20	1.30	2194
1777.5	40.60	16.50	42.00	1.00	2791
1782.5	51.30	15.90	31.50	1.40	2514
1787.5	58.80	14.60	25.20	1.40	2716
1792.5	56.20	10.90	32.50	0.50	3278
1797.5	46.20	9.80	43.60	0.40	2825
1802.5	43.20	12.10	44.40	0.40	2118
1807.5	33.30	21.50	45.00	0.20	3063
1812.5	40.30	20.50	38.50	0.60	2004
1817.5	58.10	9.10	32.20	0.50	2088
1822.5	63.10	13.50	22.80	0.50	2087
1827.5	64.20	8.10	27.20	0.50	946
1832.5	69.60	3.10	26.70	0.60	1916
1837.5	63.30	3.90	32.30	0.40	2147
1842.5	62.20	4.90	32.20	0.80	2031
1847.5	74.40	3.20	21.70	0.80	2715
1852.5	80.80	2.80	15.60	0.80	3358
1857.5	79.10	1.60	18.40	0.80	1609
1862.5	85.30	2.10	11.90	0.70	286

Source: Sample of Description Books.
Note: The date of birth refers to the quinquennium centred on the date given and to the cohort of recruits born in that quinquennium.

from Ireland in 1830, a contribution which amounted to 42.2 per cent of the British army.

The evidence of the samples is, however, that the situation in the second quarter of the nineteenth century is aberrant, in that the previous decades had shown a much higher proportion of English and Welsh recruits, while the latter part of the eighteenth century was marked by a disproportionate number of Scottish soldiers.

Figures 3.1 and 3.2 exhibit a national classification of recruits by their place of birth, which creates few difficulties. More problematic is that of the classification of birthplaces within national boundaries. For the purpose of analysis, the British birthplaces have been grouped

Table 3.3. *The national composition of recruits to the Army, 1862–1899*
(percentages).

1	2	3	4	5
				Approximate date of birth
Year of recruitment	England and Wales	Scotland	Ireland	(col. 1 minus 20 years)
1862	53.9	15.8	28.3	1842
1865	64.7	10.2	25.1	1845
1868	73.8	9.4	16.8	1848
1870	82.1	6.8	11.1	1850
1872	82.4	10.2	7.4	1852
1874	91.4	9.1	19.5	1854
1876	72.4	9.6	18.0	1856
1878	69.6	10.0	20.4	1858
1881	73.3	9.2	17.5	1861
1883	77.6	9.3	12.9	1863
1885	75.7	9.9	13.4	1865
1887	76.7	10.0	13.3	1867
1891	79.4	8.6	12.0	1871
1893	78.5	8.8	12.7	1873
1895	78.6	8.9	12.5	1875
1897	76.7	10.0	12.3	1877
1899	77.1	10.8	12.1	1879

Source: Cols. 1–4 from annual reports of the Army Medical Department as reprinted for selected years by Skelley (1977: 286).

into the wage areas identified by E. H. Hunt (1973) in his study of *Regional Wage Variations in Britain, 1850–1914*, further grouped into five larger areas; Irish and foreign birthplaces have been treated as separate categories. The full categorisation is set out in appendix 3.1.[6] Its aim is to group together recruits who were born in counties with similar economic characteristics, although it is inevitable in any such scheme that the diversity within such areas is ignored. In particular, it must always be remembered that 'urban' counties are those with large urban areas, 'rural' counties those that are predominantly rural, but that there were still, in the eighteenth and nineteenth centuries, many rural workers in 'urban' counties and vice versa.

[6] The place of birth and place of recruitment of each recruit was recorded in full from the Description Books. As a second stage, each birthplace and place of recruitment was assigned a county code and, as a third stage, the counties were grouped into larger categories. A data-set containing the uncoded and county coded records is available from the ESRC Data Archive.

Table 3.4. *The national origin of Army recruits and the distribution of the male population.*

Census year (birthdate of recruits + 19)		Percentage of recruits		Percentage of population
		excluding foreign born	including foreign born	
1801	England and Wales	52.0	51.3	56.8
(1801.5)	Scotland	16.1	15.9	9.7
	Ireland	31.9	31.5	33.5
1811	England and Wales	56.5	56.2	57.0
(1811.5)	Scotland	11.0	10.9	9.6
	Ireland	32.7	32.5	33.4
1821	England and Wales	43.4	43.2	57.8
(1821.5)	Scotland	12.1	12.1	9.6
	Ireland	44.6	44.4	32.5
1831	England and Wales	40.5	40.3	58.2
(1831.5)	Scotland	20.6	20.5	9.5
	Ireland	38.7	38.5	32.3
1841	England and Wales	63.4	63.1	60.0
(1841.5)	Scotland	13.6	13.5	9.5
	Ireland	22.9	22.8	30.9
1851	England and Wales	70.0	69.6	65.9
(1851.5)	Scotland	3.1	3.1	10.3
	Ireland	26.7	26.7	23.8
1861	England and Wales	62.7	62.2	69.6
(1861.5)	Scotland	4.9	4.9	10.3
	Ireland	32.5	32.2	20.1
1871	England and Wales	79.8		66.8
(1871)	Scotland	8.2		11.1
	Ireland	12.0		17.1
1881	England and Wales	74.0		73.2
(1881)	Scotland	8.8		11.0
	Ireland	17.2		15.8
1891	England and Wales	80.3		75.0
(1891)	Scotland	8.2		10.8
	Ireland	12.6		14.2
1901	England and Wales	78.5		77.5
(1901)	Scotland	10.2		11.1
	Ireland	11.3		11.3

Sources:
Percentage of population from Mitchell 1962: 8–9.
Percentage of recruits: for 1801–1861 from samples of Description Books; for 1871–1901 from reports of Army Medical Department.

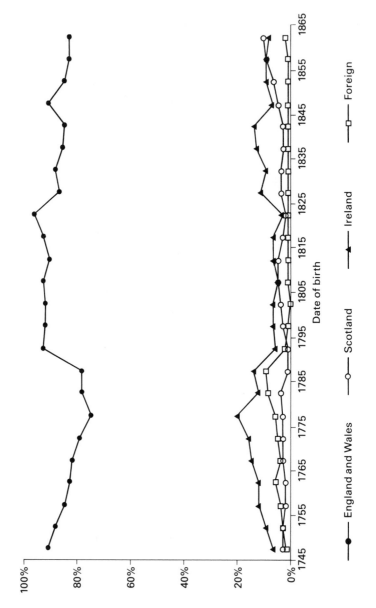

Figure 3.1. The national origin of recruits to the Royal Marines, 1747–1862. Source: see table 3.1.

England and Wales ·——·   Scotland ·——○   Ireland ·——▲   Foreign ·——□

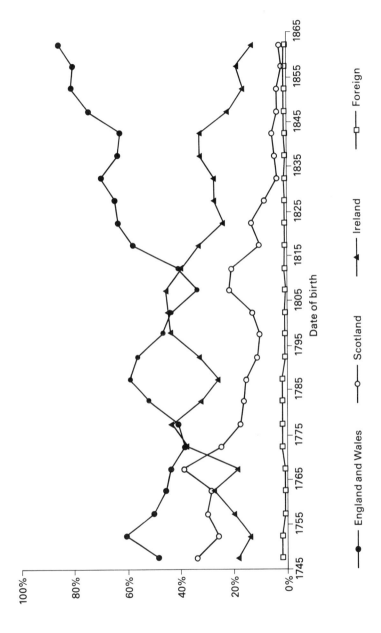

Figure 3.2. The national origin of recruits to the Army, 1748–1862. Source: see table 3.2.

England and Wales ●——●   Scotland ○——○   Ireland ▲——▲   Foreign □——□

Table 3.5 shows the urban/rural composition of Army and of Marine recruits, based on this broad definition. It was a matter of general comment at the end of the nineteenth century that the proportion of country-born recruits was falling; Army officers complained that they were forced to take the puny products of the towns. Such a fall would have been expected in view of the urbanisation of the British population. Skelley found in the course of an analysis of the records of various recruitment centres between 1873 and 1898 that evidence of a substantial decline in rural recruits is 'by no means conclusive'; however, evidence from the Scottish census of 1851 and 1891 about the birthplaces of soldiers stationed in Scotland shows 'very substantial decline in the proportion of soldiers from the country' (Skelley 1977: 295).

Table 3.5 does not show a pronounced trend in earlier periods; indeed there are some signs of a rising proportion of recruits from the predominantly rural counties in England and Wales. The overall proportion of rural recruits certainly fell, when Scottish rural recruits are included.

The problem is complicated by Irish recruits. Spiers (1980: 48) describes Irish recruits as 'overwhelmingly rural in composition'. On 14 November 1796, however, the Chief Secretary to the Lord Lieutenant of Ireland wrote to the Commander in Chief, the Duke of York, about recruitment in Ireland. He had been hopeful of raising large forces from the large rural population but:

I was told by people well acquainted with the population that it was impossible; the men who had enlisted were mechanics and inhabitants of towns, and that the peasants could seldom be persuaded under any circumstances to quit their families and place of nativity ... even in the militia they were chiefly manufacturers and mechanics ... two-thirds or three-fourths of each regiment were of that description (Gilbert 1893: 100).

It is possible that the situation changed between the end of the eighteenth and the end of the nineteenth century, perhaps following the devastation of Irish rural society by the famine.

It is not clear, however, that the fall in the proportion of rural recruits was greater than would be expected given the overall movement of the British population. Table 3.6 compares the overall distribution of the population at various dates with the distribution found in the Army recruitment data. This shows that the Army distribution (and also the Marine, see table 3.7) approximated most closely to the population distribution in 1831. Before that time, the rural populations of England and Wales were under-represented, as was the population of London. It is interesting to note that the situation was reversed

Table 3.5. *The urban/rural composition of Army and Marine recruits: 1747–1862 (percentages).*

Date of birth	London		England and Wales urban		England and Wales rural		Scotland urban		Scotland rural		Number	
	Army	Marines	Army	Marines	Army	Marines	Army	Marines	Army	Marines	Army	Marines
1747.5	8.9	19.90	27.80	29.50	11.20	41.30	13.10	0.80	19.90	1.40	472	2224
1752.5	9.1	21.20	28.60	22.90	22.60	43.20	11.00	0.80	14.40	1.40	951	2782
1757.5	6.6	23.20	24.30	18.60	18.60	42.20	14.80	0.50	15.20	1.10	2189	2665
1762.5	4.0	19.70	24.70	23.20	16.10	39.70	13.80	0.60	13.70	0.60	2294	2383
1767.5	3.7	15.30	21.50	26.80	18.00	39.30	20.60	1.20	18.10	0.70	2231	1290
1772.5	1.9	12.00	22.90	27.00	12.80	39.60	12.40	1.30	11.40	0.80	2194	1797
1777.5	2.7	9.10	23.20	27.30	14.70	37.40	6.40	0.90	10.10	1.20	2791	2247
1782.5	2.7	10.40	30.20	23.90	18.40	43.80	6.20	1.60	9.70	1.20	2514	2051
1787.5	3.4	10.10	34.70	22.90	20.70	44.60	6.30	0.40	8.30	0.50	2716	1844
1792.5	3.7	11.90	27.70	37.10	24.80	43.20	4.80	0.40	6.10	0.40	3278	1241
1797.5	3.2	7.50	25.70	39.60	17.30	44.20	5.40	1.30	4.40	1.20	2825	1028
1802.5	4.3	10.80	22.50	32.90	16.40	47.50	7.50	1.80	4.60	1.30	2118	2502
1807.5	3.6	9.60	14.30	31.70	15.40	50.60	14.90	3.10	6.60	1.10	3063	3395
1812.5	5.6	10.40	15.90	23.90	18.80	55.40	9.90	3.30	10.60	1.20	2004	3270
1817.5	10.2	14.80	24.80	14.90	23.10	62.30	4.50	1.70	4.60	0.40	2088	4151
1822.5	7.5	16.00	33.30	18.70	22.30	61.10	8.80	1.10	4.70	0.50	2087	3397
1827.5	11.8	15.80	30.90	18.50	21.50	51.50	5.80	1.80	2.30	1.70	946	1326
1832.5	6.5	18.90	30.90	26.70	32.20	42.50	2.00	1.80	1.10	1.70	1916	1801
1837.5	7.1	18.70	26.70	25.50	29.50	41.20	2.50	1.60	1.40	0.80	2147	2734
1842.5	10.2	14.80	30.40	27.90	21.60	41.60	2.90	1.40	2.00	1.00	2031	2954
1847.5	23.6	14.00	23.10	32.90	27.70	43.40	1.90	2.00	1.30	1.70	2715	2087
1852.5	22.2	17.80	30.30	24.40	28.30	42.00	1.90	3.80	0.90	2.50	3358	2227
1857.5	3.9	17.10	62.70	30.40	12.50	34.80	1.40	6.10	0.20	2.50	1609	2973
1862.5	5.2	22.40	67.50	26.60	12.60	33.10	0.70	6.00	1.40	3.40	286	3715

Sources: Samples from Description Books.

Note: Sample sizes are as in tables 3.1 and 3.2.

Table 3.6. *The geographical distribution of Army recruits and of the British and Irish population (percentages).*

Area	Census 1801	Recruits, birthdate 1777.5/1782.5	Census 1821	Recruits, birthdate 1797.5/1802.5	Census 1831	Recruits, birthdate 1807.5/1812.5	Census 1861	Recruits, birthdate 1837.5/1842.5
London	11	2.7	11	3.8	12	4.6	15	8.7
England, rural	26	16.6	25	16.9	24	17.1	25	25.6
England, urban	20	26.7	21	24.1	24	15.1	30	28.6
Scotland, rural	4	9.9	4	4.5	5	8.6	6	1.7
Scotland, urban	6	6.3	5	12.9	5	12.4	5	2.7
Ireland	34	36.8	32	44.0	31	41.8	20	32.3

Sources:
Census data from Mitchell (1962: 20): proportions of total population.
Recruits from samples of Description Books.

Table 3.7. *The geographical distribution of Marine recruits and of the British and Irish population, 1801, 1821, 1831, 1861 (percentages).*

Area	Census 1801	Recruits, birthdate 1777.5/ 1782.5	Census 1821	Recruits, birthdate 1797.5/ 1802.5	Census 1831	Recruits, birthdate 1807.5/ 1812.5	Census 1861	Recruits, birthdate 1837.5/ 1842.5
London	11	9.8	11	9.2	12	10.0	15	16.8
England, rural	26	40.6	25	45.9	24	53.0	25	41.4
England, urban	20	25.6	21	36.3	24	27.8	30	26.7
Scotland, rural	4	1.2	4	1.3	5	1.2	6	0.9
Scotland, urban	6	1.3	5	1.5	5	3.2	5	1.5
Ireland	34	15.6	32	5.9	31	4.6	20	12.4

Sources:
Census data from Mitchell (1962: 20): proportions of the total population.
Recruits from samples of Description Books.

among the Marines, where the rural population of England and Wales was over-represented and that of London fairly represented; the absolute numbers of Marine recruits were, of course, much smaller – where they can be measured – than those of Army recruits, but it does seem that the two complemented each other in geographical recruitment patterns.

   Taking the period as a whole, it seems that the geographical distribution of the birthplaces of recruits did not differ to a marked extent from that of the population as a whole. In conjunction with other evidence, this makes it reasonable to use the evidence of samples of Army recruits to make inferences about the population as a whole. Moreover, where differences do exist between the population and sample geographical distributions, the sample data can reasonably be reweighted to represent the distribution of the population.

3.2.2 *Socio-occupational composition*

Each recruit to the Army and Royal Marines was asked to state his occupation and this information was entered into the Description Books. In a small proportion of cases, no occupation was entered, but the information exists for the vast majority of recruits in the samples. The dictionary of occupations in the samples contains 5889 entries; an exact computation of the number of separate occupations is complicated by the existence of numerous variant spellings, but there are at least 2000 separate occupational titles in the sample data. These descriptions of occupations pose at least two major problems. First, are they accurate? Second, how can they be best analysed?

   First, accuracy. It seems likely, on the basis of the evidence discussed in the last chapter, that the majority of recruits were unemployed at the time of their decision to enlist. Yet the description 'unemployed' does not appear in the data. This is not surprising, except to modern eyes, for the concept of unemployment, or indeed of retirement, is a relatively modern one; nineteenth-century censuses do not normally describe men as either 'unemployed' or 'retired' but, instead, give them the occupational title which they would have had if in work. This reflected the fact that unemployment was considered to be short-term, the product of seasonal or cyclical downturns in demand, rather than a permanent or semi-permanent state. There is no reason to believe that the Army and Marine authorities did other than follow common practice; they presumably asked the recruit to describe his normal occupation and recorded his answer.

But is that answer likely to have been accurate? Some men, for example apprentices who had run away from their masters, did have an incentive to conceal their true occupation, since such apprentices, seamen and other occupational groups were, in theory, debarred from joining the Army. In other cases, the recruiting sergeant may have taken little care to record the answer correctly; Alexander Alexander, a runaway son, enlisted in 1801 and reported that (McGuffie 1964: 15):

The serjeant entered me as a day-labourer. At this I remonstrated, but he silenced me by saying that it was his instruction, for all those who had no trade, to be entered as labourers.

There was, indeed, little reason for the sergeant to take great care since the Army apparently made little or no use of the occupational description once the recruit had been approved. Yet, for the same reason, unless the recruit was in one of the prohibited categories, there was also little or no cause for him to lie about his occupation. He may, of course, have attempted to inflate his standing or have chosen only one of a variety of unskilled jobs which he had held, but it seems unlikely that either motive would lead to a systematic bias in the sample data. Lack of accuracy is not, therefore, a serious problem in the use of this evidence.

Much more serious is the problem of analysis. The very large number of recorded occupations makes it essential that they should be grouped together for the purposes of analysis, but the choice of groups is extremely difficult. Indeed, similar problems of the grouping of occupations and their mapping into socio-economic categories have been a major focus of sociological and economic enquiry for many years. Nineteenth-century social enquirers, notably Charles Booth, produced classifications of occupations, while most analysis in the twentieth century has been based on the Registrar-General's scheme first published in the report on the census of 1911 (Szreter 1986). The problem is compounded in the present analysis by the long time-span of the enquiry since it is certain that some occupations changed markedly over the period, in the content of the work, in the pay relative to other occupations, or in the prestige accorded to the occupation by the rest of the community; the sad decline of handloom weaving from high pay and high status in the eighteenth century to derided poverty in the nineteenth is but one example.

In the light of these problems, the analysis of occupations in this and subsequent chapters is based upon a relatively small number of broad occupational categories.[7] These are shown in appendix 3.1. The categorisation is based on a classification of the skill attached to a particular occupation, further categorised where possible on an industrial basis. Thus the classification incorporates a hierarchy of occupations from unskilled to white-collar. The unskilled and labourers are not further distinguished (by necessity since labourers were not normally assigned to a particular industry in the original records), but those occupations incorporating some element of skill or training are further grouped as shown in appendix 3.1; the number of such subdivisions was partly determined by the wish to group together congruent occupations, as in the case of the building trades, partly by the need to maintain reasonable sample sizes. The purpose of this twofold classification is to attempt to incorporate into the analysis some reflection of both the likely relative income of the recruit and the working conditions which he would have experienced before joining the armed forces.

It will be recalled that discussion of the geographical composition of the samples was complicated by the difference in recruiting patterns between the Army and Marines. It is of great interest, therefore, that the differences between the civilian occupations of Army and Marine recruits were extremely small. Throughout the period covered by the samples, the largest civilian occupation of recruits was that of labourer (including manual and unskilled), followed by the apprenticed non-building trades category, followed by textiles (although this had a marked downward trend), then by work with animals and the apprenticed building trades, and concluded by commerce, domestic service and white-collar occupations. The full pattern is shown in table 3.8 and, for selected major occupations, in figures 3.3, 3.4 and 3.5. The congruence between Army and Marine patterns is particularly interesting because it suggests that both types of units were drawing on essentially the same population, mediated only by the geographical differences in their recruiting areas. Thus the excess proportion of textile workers among the Army, particularly among the birth cohorts

---

[7] Although the occupations have been grouped into categories, this grouping was not carried out until a late stage in the analysis. During data recording, each occupational title was recorded in full. Then, as a second stage, each occupation was assigned a unique number based on the classification scheme developed by Michael Anderson in his study of the machine-readable sample of the 1851 census (1987); this was itself based on Charles Booth's classification as modified by W. A. Armstrong (1972). Only as a third stage were the occupations grouped into the categories used in analysis. Data-sets containing the full occupations and the codes are available from the ESRC Data Archive.

Table 3.8. *The occupations of Army and Marine recruits: 1747–1862 (percentage of total recruits to each service).*

Birthdate	Apprentice non-building		Labourers		White collar		Commerce		Domestic service		Unskilled		Working with animals		Textiles		Apprentice building	
	Army	Marines	Army	Marines	Army	Marines	Army	Marines	Army	Marines	Army	Marines	Army	Marines	Army	Marines	Army	Marines
1747.5	28.40	36.30	15.90	32.10	0.40	0.80	2.30	1.20	1.10	0.10	0.00	0.40	6.80	4.00	13.10	12.90	9.10	5.90
1752.5	28.10	30.80	16.40	40.00	1.50	1.20	2.80	1.70	1.40	0.10	18.00	0.50	5.80	1.80	12.40	12.00	8.70	6.80
1757.5	26.10	27.30	21.70	43.80	1.20	0.80	2.20	1.40	0.50	0.20	0.00	0.70	5.70	1.90	16.40	9.90	8.60	6.40
1762.5	26.70	26.60	26.00	48.00	1.30	0.30	1.00	0.80	1.10	0.30	0.00	1.20	6.40	1.60	18.40	11.00	8.70	4.00
1767.5	28.70	28.30	26.30	42.40	0.60	0.40	0.90	1.60	1.20	0.50	0.00	0.50	3.80	1.40	20.80	12.50	6.50	6.80
1772.5	25.90	29.00	19.10	44.10	0.50	0.70	1.40	1.00	0.50	1.00	0.10	0.20	2.00	1.70	24.40	13.00	8.40	4.90
1777.5	23.80	26.40	23.50	42.90	0.50	0.50	0.80	0.80	0.70	1.70	0.10	0.50	1.50	1.40	22.00	14.20	11.00	6.30
1782.5	23.20	24.80	29.80	48.70	0.60	1.00	1.10	0.90	0.60	1.20	0.10	0.80	1.40	1.20	24.30	10.90	8.80	5.30
1787.5	20.50	23.20	38.50	50.20	1.10	0.60	0.70	1.40	0.80	1.50	0.20	0.80	1.80	1.00	24.40	9.90	5.60	6.70
1792.5	19.30	19.30	47.30	50.50	0.90	0.60	0.70	0.60	1.50	1.50	0.10	0.60	1.60	0.70	17.00	15.30	4.90	4.40
1797.5	19.80	23.90	53.50	44.90	1.40	2.50	0.70	1.10	1.30	1.90	0.10	0.00	1.10	3.10	13.80	10.40	3.50	6.10
1802.5	18.40	23.40	55.10	52.50	1.10	1.30	0.80	0.80	1.50	0.90	0.00	0.00	1.30	2.20	14.00	8.40	3.40	5.60
1807.5	17.60	24.20	52.70	48.60	0.70	1.10	0.70	1.00	1.80	1.10	0.10	0.00	1.00	3.40	18.00	8.70	3.90	7.50
1812.5	25.30	24.10	47.40	51.30	1.60	2.00	1.20	1.20	2.30	1.90	0.30	0.00	2.60	4.60	8.90	4.90	6.70	7.10
1817.5	26.10	20.20	47.60	60.30	2.30	0.90	1.50	1.10	2.60	2.40	0.10	0.20	2.30	3.10	8.30	3.00	4.80	6.20
1822.5	25.80	20.30	41.40	60.20	2.20	0.70	1.10	1.00	3.30	1.90	0.20	0.10	4.40	4.20	10.10	3.20	6.90	5.40
1827.5	18.30	20.30	52.10	57.30	2.10	0.50	1.40	1.10	3.20	1.80	0.50	0.50	5.40	7.10	9.00	3.60	4.10	4.50
1832.5	20.60	22.10	54.00	54.50	1.50	1.90	1.00	1.20	1.60	1.50	0.70	0.40	5.50	5.00	5.20	3.60	5.50	5.80
1837.5	21.20	22.20	52.00	52.50	2.30	3.30	1.00	0.40	2.60	1.60	0.40	0.80	3.90	4.60	7.70	3.30	4.50	6.20
1842.5	23.60	22.80	47.50	50.40	3.80	3.50	1.30	1.80	2.70	1.40	0.60	1.00	5.00	6.40	4.70	2.70	5.50	6.00
1847.5	21.90	21.40	45.00	47.90	6.40	3.50	1.80	1.80	2.20	2.00	1.10	1.90	9.00	7.60	1.20	1.70	6.60	7.40
1852.5	20.10	19.50	48.10	43.90	3.90	4.60	2.20	2.00	1.40	2.00	1.40	2.70	7.00	8.80	2.30	0.90	7.80	11.20
1857.5	20.80	18.00	43.90	45.80	3.50	5.10	2.50	2.10	0.90	1.90	2.20	3.30	4.50	7.30	4.50	1.90	5.40	6.50
1862.5	13.30	18.70	46.50	44.40	1.70	4.60	3.10	4.40	2.10	2.50	0.70	4.00	5.60	7.60	4.50	1.10	9.80	7.90

Source: Samples of Description Books.

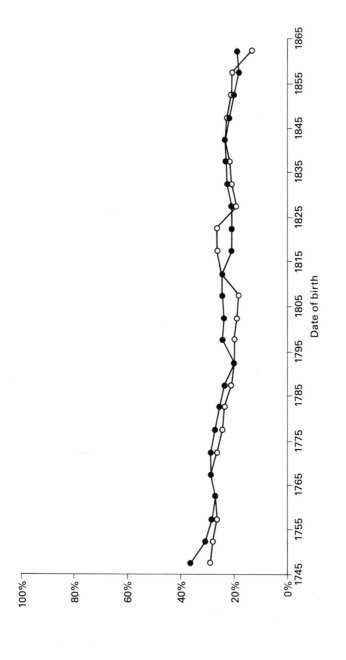

Figure 3.3. Men from apprenticed non-building trades as proportions of recruits to the Army and Marines, 1747–1862. Source: table 3.8.

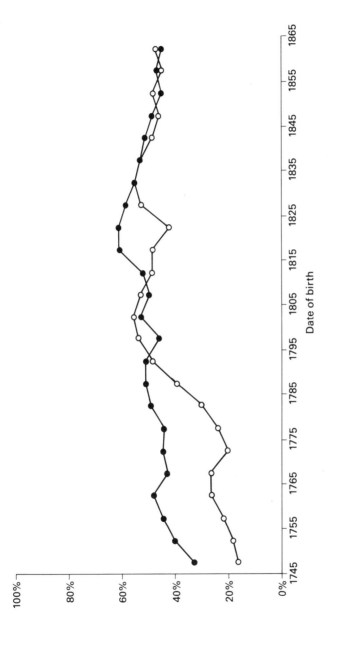

Figure 3.4. Labourers as proportions of recruits to the Army and Marines, 1747–1862. Source: table 3.8.

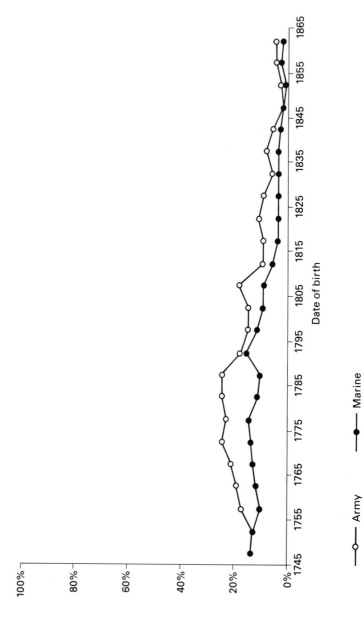

Figure 3.5. Textile workers as proportions of recruits to the Army and Marines, 1747–1862. Source: table 3.8.

of the eighteenth century, is largely accounted for by the relatively large numbers of Scottish and Irish among Army recruits.

The evidence of military samples can be supplemented, for the late nineteenth century, by the published reports of the Army Medical Department, which recorded the civilian occupations of the men it had inspected. Data calculated from these reports are shown in table 3.9. Although the categories which were used cannot be compared directly with those used in analysing the samples, these data confirm the preponderance of labourers among recruits and otherwise closely match the sample evidence.

Further evidence about the occupational background of military recruits can be gathered from the records of the Marine Society and of the Royal Military Academy at Sandhurst. As might be expected from the description of the recruits to the Marine Society which was quoted in chapter 2, the boys helped by the Society seem to have come exclusively from the working class and predominantly from unskilled or semi-skilled occupations. Table 3.10 sets out the occupations of boys and their fathers taken from samples of the Marine Society records.[8] There is no guarantee, of course, that the occupational descriptions are either accurate or comparable to those of military recruits, but the data show that, as would be expected, the occupations of a group of poor London children and their parents differed very substantially from the national pattern of recruits.[9] It is particularly interesting that a very small proportion, either of boys or of their fathers, is described as labourers, although this category predominates in the military data. It is possible, of course, that many of the fathers for whom no occupation is recorded – or who were dead or no longer responsible for their boys – came from the labouring group, but this seems unlikely; it is more reasonable to infer that, in London at least, there was a relative paucity of labouring jobs or, alternatively, that most of the Army and Marine recruits referred to as labourers were, in fact, agricultural workers.

The last sample, that from Sandhurst, does not provide any systematic occupational data, since the occupations neither of the boys and young men nor of their parents were recorded. On the other hand,

---

[8] While the heights and ages of all boys recruited by the Society were recorded, occupational and other background information was recorded only for samples from the records.

[9] Throughout the period, almost all the Marine Society children came from London; the proportion from London in the samples were: 1755–84: 71.7 per cent; 1785–96: 86.5 per cent; 1797–1806: 87.8 per cent; 1807–18: 85.4 per cent; 1819–48: 88.9 per cent.

Table 3.9. *The occupations of recruits at medical inspection, 1860–1903 (percentages).*

1 Date	2 Lab. etc.	3 Art. etc.	4 Mech. etc.	5 Shop etc.	6 Prof. etc.	7 Boys	8 Number
1860	50.3	14.2	25.6	9.1	0.4	1.0	27 853
1861	48.5	15.1	24.3	9.7	0.6	2.0	12 191
1862	49.0	16.6	20.6	8.9	0.7	4.3	7 684
1863							
1864	59.2	14.2	17.4	6.5	0.7	2.1	27 096
1865	61.0	14.9	15.1	6.3	1.0	1.8	24 891
1866	61.6	14.5	15.8	6.4	0.5	1.2	20 201
1867	59.1	15.8	16.4	6.4	0.7	1.6	26 646
1868	57.2	14.0	18.6	7.1	0.9	2.3	23 543
1869	58.3	13.7	17.7	7.1	1.2	2.1	17 749
1870	64.7	7.5	19.5	6.5	0.7	1.2	38 408
1871	63.8	8.0	18.2	7.8	0.8	1.5	36 212
1872	61.6	8.8	19.7	6.6	0.8	2.5	28 390
1873	59.9	10.5	20.0	6.0	0.7	2.9	24 895
1874	61.9	11.6	17.6	5.8	0.8	2.2	30 557
1875	59.1	11.8	17.6	7.5	1.1	3.1	25 878
1876	61.0	12.0	17.5	6.8	0.8	1.9	41 809
1877	62.0	10.8	17.7	6.9	1.0	1.6	43 803
1878	60.5	9.8	18.0	8.6	1.2	1.9	43 867
1879	59.4	10.1	19.5	8.1	0.9	2.0	42 658
1880	60.5	12.8	16.7	6.7	1.0	2.2	46 064
1881	64.0	11.7	15.5	5.6	0.8	2.3	47 403
1882	59.5	13.8	15.9	6.7	1.3	2.8	45 400
1883	60.5	14.5	15.8	5.4	1.1	2.7	59 423
1884	63.3	12.6	14.5	6.3	1.0	2.3	66 878
1885	64.1	14.5	13.4	5.4	0.8	1.8	72 248
1886	63.4	15.6	12.1	5.7	1.2	2.0	74 979
1887	63.5	15.6	11.6	6.2	1.4	2.2	60 964
1888	61.7	15.7	12.0	6.6	1.2	2.9	49 163
1889	61.8	16.2	11.6	6.5	1.3	2.7	53 890
1890	62.1	16.7	10.8	6.4	1.2	2.8	55 348
1891	64.0	15.8	10.8	5.7	1.0	2.7	61 322
1892	65.7	14.1	10.9	5.8	1.0	2.6	68 761
1893	67.3	14.3	9.4	5.7	1.0	2.4	64 110
1894	65.0	14.7	9.9	6.4	1.2	2.7	61 985
1895	67.9	13.1	9.4	5.8	1.1	2.9	55 698
1896	66.2	12.0	10.4	7.3	1.1	3.0	54 574
1897	64.0	14.8	10.2	7.3	1.0	2.8	59 986
1898	65.7	13.9	9.2	7.2	0.9	3.1	66 502
1899	64.9	14.1	10.3	6.8	1.0	3.0	68 087
1900	61.6	14.2	13.3	7.1	1.0	2.9	84 402
1901	64.0	12.2	13.1	6.3	1.1	3.2	76 750
1902	66.9	11.7	11.7	6.0	0.9	2.9	87 609
1903	67.9	11.4	11.2	4.9	0.7	4.0	69 553

histories of the Royal Military Academy and the very large number of civil, military, naval and clerical titles which can be observed in the records make it clear that Sandhurst recruited exclusively from the ranks of the upper and upper-middle classes (Smyth 1961; Thomas 1961).

Both sample and Army Medical Department data show that recruits were not representative in occupational terms of the British and Irish populations as a whole, but how far do they represent the occupations of the working class? This is an extremely difficult question to answer in detail, not because of any deficiencies in the sample data but because of the paucity of evidence with which they can be compared.

National data on the distribution of occupations among the population was not collected by the state, except in a rudimentary fashion, before the census of 1841. Before that date, historians of occupations have had to rely upon the estimates made by Gregory King in 1688, by Joseph Massie in 1759 and by Patrick Colquhoun in 1801–3, as well as on the highly aggregated returns from the censuses of 1811, 1821 and 1831. Apart from these data, there exist only listings of inhabitants for a small number of towns and villages, collected at the whim of local clergy or gentry and, for a larger number of parishes, records of baptisms, marriages and burials which happened to record – there was no compulsion so to do – the occupations of those involved in these life events. Peter Lindert has surveyed such data, collected a sample of burial records and, with their aid, attempted estimates of the occupational distribution of the population for 1688, 1700, 1740,

Notes to Table 3.9

Source: Calculated from annual reports of the Army Medical Department.

Notes:
Col. 1. Date of inspection.
Col. 2. 'Labourers, Servants, Husbandmen, etc.'
Col. 3. 'Manufacturing Artisans (as Clothworkers, Weavers, Lace Makers etc.)'
Col. 4. 'Mechanics employed in Occupations favourable to physical development (as Smiths, Carpenters, Masons etc.)'
Col. 5. 'Shopmen and Clerks.'
Col. 6. 'Professional Occupations, Students etc.'
Col. 7. 'Boys under 17 years of age.'
Col. 8. Total number inspected and with stated occupations. A very small number, in addition, had no stated occupation – in 1866 there were 209 such recruits, otherwise no more than 44 in any year.
Before 1864 recruits who were rejected by civilian medical officers at primary inspection were not included in the tables.

Table 3.10. *The occupations of recruits to the Marine Society and of their fathers, 1755–1848 (percentages).*

	1755–84 N = 1072	1785–96 N = 288	1797–1806 N = 913	1807–18 N = 1415	1819–48 N = 1640
Boys' occupations					
Manual	5.4	8.0	3.7	9.0	7.3
Animals, domestic, commerce	20.1	18.1	4.9	17.7	19.3
Unskilled	43.6	43.4	59.7	36.0	41.6
Labourer	1.7	1.0	0.9	1.4	3.4
Pauper	3.5	1.0	1.1	1.0	0.9
Home	11.5	8.0	8.8	3.1	1.9
Apprenticed	8.9	19.1	8.1	29.0	23.2
Blank	5.3	1.4	12.8	2.9	2.4
Fathers' occupations					
Manual	10.3	8.7	3.8	10.2	10.0
Animals, domestic, commerce	16.0	8.7	6.1	25.7	24.3
Unskilled	4.0	2.4	6.0	7.4	7.3
Labourer	2.5	2.4	7.2	5.8	10.2
Pauper	1.1	0.7	1.8	1.3	2.1
Apprenticed	20.5	26.0	25.3	27.3	30.4
Blank	45.6	51.0	49.7	22.4	15.7

Source: Samples from the records of the Marine Society.

1755, 1801–3 and 1811 (Lindert 1980: 702–3; Lindert and Williamson 1982, 1983a).

Lindert is careful to warn his readers about the possible errors in his estimates, but a more serious bar to adequate comparison of the occupations of recruits with his estimates lies in his choice of dates, designed to allow a check to be made on the estimates of Massie and Colquhoun. 1755 is somewhat before the date at which recruitment data is available in sufficient quantity, but a more serious problem is that in both 1801–3 and 1811 a very high proportion of the male population, 14.3 per cent in 1801–3 and 17.3 per cent in 1811, is shown as engaged in maritime or army occupations; this proportion of course contains 100 per cent of all recruits whose occupations we have recorded. To compare the occupations of recruits with the occupations of civilians, at those dates, is to make the implicit assumption that the men engaged in maritime and army occupations were drawn at random from all civilian occupations. But since the whole purpose of comparing the occupations of recruits with that of the population

Table 3.11. *A comparison of the occupational distribution of recruits with Lindert's 'roughly estimated occupations' in England and Wales in the middle of the eighteenth century.*

Occupational category[a]	Lindert estimate for 1755 (%)	Recruitment data for birth cohort of 1755–59[b]	
		Army (%)	Marines (%)
Agriculture	25.8[c]	5.2[d]	2.1[d]
Professions and white-collar	0.6	1.0	0.5
Commerce	13.0	2.0	1.1
Building trades	7.6[c]	8.5	6.4
Manufacturing	16.4[c]	37.9	38.5
of which textiles	2.7	9.0	10.4
Labourers	13.0	23.7	42.8
Servants and other services	3.3	0.6	0.2

Sources: Lindert estimates from 1980: Table 3, pp. 702–3. Recruitment data from samples of Description Books.

Notes:
[a] A number of categories from Lindert's table have been omitted.
[b] Data are drawn only from those born in England and Wales, giving sample sizes of 1083 for Army and 2240 for Marine recruits.
[c] These percentages are said to exclude labourers in these occupations.
[d] Recruitment category is 'working with animals'.

as a whole is to check whether such is the case, it is logically impossible to make the implicit assumption. Comparison with Lindert's data for these time periods is therefore ruled out.

The problem still exists, but in a much reduced form because of the smaller size of the armed forces, for Lindert's computations for 1755. A comparison with this estimate is shown in table 3.11. Labourers and workers in manufacturing trades generally are over-represented in the recruiting data as compared to the data drawn from parish registers and lists of inhabitants which Lindert used, and agriculture and commerce correspondingly under-represented. There is also a notable absence of servants from the recruiting data. There is a multiplicity of possible causes of such discrepancies; recruiting data represent young men rather than the whole male population, the classification of labourer is very indeterminate and the overall classification schemes do not match well. But if they are to be taken seriously, they suggest that in the middle of the eighteenth century

Army and Marine recruits came less from agricultural than from urban or industrial occupations than was true of the population as a whole. The recruits are, however, unambiguously from the working class.

Similar comparisons with later data, for example from the nineteenth-century censuses, is fraught with difficulty since classification schemes differ from those used in the published census, notably in the omission from the latter of a separate category of labourer. It would in principle be possible to compare the recruitment data with the sample of the 1851 census drawn by Michael Anderson (1987), particularly since we have adopted his classification scheme, but that has not yet been possible.

3.2.3 Other indicators

Both the geographical origins and the occupations of the military recruits suggest that they were drawn widely from the working class and did not constitute a particularly deprived group from among that class. This impression is confirmed by an examination of evidence about the literacy of recruits, drawn from the annual reports of the Army Medical Department; unfortunately, data on literacy were only sporadically collected by Army recruiters and entered into the Description Books during earlier periods. Table 3.12 sets out the results of a comparison between Army literacy rates and those of the male population as a whole.[10] It must be remembered first that the male population included the middle and upper classes, second that the criterion of illiteracy is crude in the extreme and third that the criterion probably differed between recruits and civilians; the literacy of recruits was assessed by the medical officer and it is not clear whether any test was involved. For the civilian, on the other hand, the criterion was that of the inability to sign his name in the marriage register. Comparison of the two rates is made more reasonable, however, by the fact that the average age of recruits and of bridegrooms cannot have differed by more than a few years.

Bearing these differences in mind, table 3.12 shows that the illiteracy of recruits was higher than that of the civilian population until the late 1880s, with both rates following a downward trend; thereafter, the downward trend continued, with Army recruits being somewhat more literate than the population as a whole, although by that time both illiteracy rates were very low indeed. The overall impression

---

[10] A brief discussion of earlier literacy rates in London, on the basis of the records of the Marine Society, can be found in Floud and Wachter (1982).

is that of convergence between the national and the Army illiteracy rates, although they were never far apart. It is interesting to remember that universal primary education was provided for, in England and Wales at least, by the Education Act of 1870, enacted some 19 years before, according to table 3.12, the literacy of 19-year-old recruits became similar to that of the population as a whole. This suggests that table 3.12 is recording not a bias in Army recruits as a sample of the working class but a genuine decline in the illiteracy of the British working class.[11] It is impossible to tell, of course, whether the literacy of recruits had been significantly worse in earlier periods than that of the population as a whole, or at least of the working class.

3.3 CHANGES IN THE POOL OF RECRUITS: INFERENCE FROM MILITARY SAMPLES TO THE BRITISH WORKING CLASS

This study of British heights rests heavily, if not quite exclusively, upon evidence drawn from volunteers to the armed forces. This and the last chapter have shown that, while those volunteer soldiers were predominantly drawn from the working classes, they do not seem to have been drawn from a particularly unusual section of that class. There is certainly little reason, on the basis of the evidence which has just been presented, to suspect any systematic bias in the samples.

Soldiers were, it is clear, drawn from the ranks of the unemployed, of the casual trades and of men who had little or no other means of subsistence. Whatever the appeal of the uniform, of travel and adventure or of martial music, it was necessity which drove most men to enlist. But necessity could press upon many men in eighteenth- and nineteenth-century Britain, the product of cyclical depression, technological change or even, as in the case of so many Irish recruits, of land-hunger and famine. Even in late twentieth-century Britain, unemployment has proved a potent recruiting officer, and in the past two centuries there was no social-security system to provide even a bare subsistence to a young and able-bodied man.

In one respect, it is true, the samples which we have drawn differ markedly from the population of Description Books from which they were drawn. As appendix 3.1 makes clear, the sample consists of

---

[11] It should be noted that the change in the late 1880s may have another explanation. In the years up to and including 1886, the Army Medical Department recorded the literacy of all recruits who were inspected, while from 1887 they recorded literacy only for those finally approved. If literacy itself played a part in the approval of recruits, then the rising literacy rates of the late 1880s might be spurious. However, the fact that the Army rates mimic the downward trend in the population rates, both before and after 1886, suggests that comparable forces are at work.

Table 3.12. *The illiteracy of Army recruits, 1864–1905.*

1 Date	2 Average weighted male illiteracy rate Britain and Ireland (per 1000)	3 Illiteracy rate of Army recruits (per 1000)	4 Col. 3 as % of col. 2
1864	268.7	333.9	124.2
1865	258.5	356.6	138.0
1866	245.1	217.4	88.7
1867	227.7	329.1	144.5
1868	218.1	300.8	137.9
1869	229.4	261.1	113.8
1870	210.6	291.1	138.2
1871	207.9	243.1	116.9
1872	195.9	263.8	134.6
1873	200.8	236	117.5
1874	194.5	281	144.5
1875	185.7	245.4	132.2
1876	182.6	271.2	148.5
1877	175.1	240.3	137.3
1878	166.5	255.4	153.4
1879	161.8	238.5	147.4
1880	159.2	233.1	146.4
1881	151.0	263.3	174.3
1882	143.3	239.7	167.3
1883	136.0	202	148.6
1884	129.7	184	141.8
1885	118.9	176	148.0
1886	110.7	134	121.1
1887	103.5	122	117.9
1888	94.5	97	102.6
1889	90.1	74	82.2
1890	85.9	66	76.8
1891	76.6	56	73.1
1892	70.3	55	78.2
1893	64.2	48	74.8
1894	58.5	39	66.7
1895	54.5	35	64.2
1896	50.5	32	63.3
1897	47.3	31	65.6
1898	43.7	29	66.3
1899	40.2	29	72.1
1900	38.2	27	70.6
1901	35.7	Not given	—
1902	33.2	20	60.3
1903	30.1	24	79.8
1904	27.7	18	65.0
1905	25.6	14	54.6

approximately 5000 Army and 5000 Marine recruits from each decade of recruitment; the Army was in reality much larger throughout the period than was the Marines. In addition, the Army consisted of many different units, from the Guards to the men of the Military Train who carried the baggage and from the specialised units such as the Royal Engineers to the general infantry of the Line regiments. No attempt was made in the sampling procedure to ensure that a correct representation was achieved of these different types of unit. This was despite the fact that it was known that different units had different criteria for entry; some demanded specialist knowledge and training but, in addition, different units had different standards of height.

These sampling procedures would have been a serious handicap if the object of the analysis had been to estimate the average height of the British Army or Royal Marines or of individual units within them.[12] It would then have been necessary either to ensure that the sample represented the different units in their correct proportion or to have weighted the sample results to achieve such proportions. But our purpose is different; it is to estimate the average height of the population of Britain and Ireland and of various geographical and occupational groups within it. For this purpose, we are treating Army recruits as a sample from the population as a whole and comparing

Notes to Table 3.12
Notes and sources:
Col. 1: Date of recruitment of soldiers and date of marriages. It would be possible to lag the marriage date by some years to take account of marriage age being, on average, later than age of recruitment. This has not been done in this table.
Col. 2: Average weighted male illiteracy rate. This was calculated by applying to the Registrar-General's illiteracy rates for each country weights which were calculated from the proportions of English and Welsh, Scottish and Irish recruits in each year. Soldiers from other nations who were counted as English and Welsh country proportions in census years are shown in table 3.4.
Col. 3: Illiteracy rate of Army recruits from annual reports of the Army Medical Department.
Col. 4: Col. 3 as a percentage of Col. 2.

[12] In fact, the regular musters of the Army provide this information in the muster books kept in the Public Record Office. It is not entirely clear how the height distributions which are given in the muster books were derived, but it seems unlikely that the whole regiment was remeasured every year and more likely, therefore, that the information was taken from the Description Books and that the height of each man was that at the time of recruitment.

that sample, as we have done in the first part of this chapter, with that population.

This procedure would be suspect if there was evidence that the process of recruitment or the sampling which we have undertaken biassed the selection of recruits within any of the occupational or regional groups and thus led to a mis-estimation of the heights of that group. But there is no evidence that this was so. The recruitment process meant that, for most of the eighteenth and nineteenth centuries, recruiting parties vied for recruits wherever they could be obtained and distributed potential recruits between the units. It was certainly true that some units such as the Guards were more attractive to potential recruits than were others, but age and height standards operated to distribute recruits between units; the tallest and those between 18 and 25 could, if they wished, enter the elite regiments while shorter, older or younger men were forced into the regiments of the Line or the Marines. In 1802–1806, for example, men seeking to enter the Heavy Cavalry had to be 5 ft 8 in (172.7 cm) or more and those joining the Light Cavalry between 5 ft 7 in and 5 ft 9 in (170.2–175.3 cm) – the upper limit being to protect the horses – while the Infantry of the Line had a minimum height limit of 5 ft 6 in (167.6 cm), and the Infantry (General Service) a limit of 5 ft 5 in (165.1 cm); even lower limits were applied to recruits to the Marines and to the army of the East India Company.

For such reasons, as well as the fact that they were unlikely to be able to travel far to join a particular unit, it seems that many men ended up in units which they had not originally intended. Many were indifferent even about whether they were joining the Army or Marines, and the recruiting process did not emphasise the difference; William Cobbett intended to join the Marines but found himself in the Army (see McGuffie 1964) while, nearly a century later, a member of the Inter-Departmental Committee on Physical Deterioration refuted the view that the Marines 'attract a higher class of men' by stating that 'I do not suppose that one man in ten entering the Marines but thinks he is going to be a soldier' (PP 1904 xxxii: Q72–3).

In other words, although there was certainly a hierarchy of units within the Army, and although the taller a man the more choice he might have, there is no evidence that the recruitment process vitiates the use of recruitment data as a sample of the population as a whole. It acted to sort men between units, rather than to bias the selection as a whole. Since this is so, there is no reason to believe that our sampling process – though it definitely over-represents some units at the expense of others – biasses the sample as a whole. It is important, of course, that we should take note of such differences as exist between the proportions of different socio-economic or geographical groups in the sample and in the population and weight our results accordingly; this is done, wherever it is relevant, in the estimates which are presented in chapters 4 and 5.

A second possible source of bias in the use of recruitment data applies to the source as a whole, rather than to the distribution of recruits between units or to the sampling process. It has sometimes been argued that changes in the nature of the labour market over time make it impossible to draw conclusions from military recruits about the whole population, or even the working-class population, of Britain. At the beginning of this century, for example, the Inter-Departmental Committee on Physical Deterioration examined the allegations made by General Frederick Maurice and others that the quality of the race was deteriorating and that this was demonstrated by Army recruiting statistics.

The Committee found itself in difficulty, in interpreting the statistics of medical inspection of recruits, for two reasons. First, it recognised that the changing military height standard made it impossible to compare the mean heights of recruits at times when the standard differed; the Committee did not possess the statistical methods which are used to solve this problem in the next chapter. Second, however, the Committee accepted the view of some of its witnesses that vicissitudes in the labour market made it impossible to draw conclusions from recruiting statistics about the population as a whole.

As described in the last chapter, some witnesses felt that recruits were a fair sample of the working class, but others had no doubt that the recruits were a biassed sample. Cunningham's view was that the recruits varied with the condition of trade, over the course of the trade cycle, but other witnesses saw a trend. Dr Alfred Eichholz, one of His Majesty's Inspectors of Schools and a medical doctor, had examined the height and physique of schoolchildren and was committed to the view that physical degeneracy was 'decidedly decreasing' but that much still needed to be done to improve health (PP 1904 xxxii: Q428). He had looked at the trend of Army recruitment over time and commented on it in a passage which was quoted in full and with approval in the Committee's report:

The apparent deterioration in army recruiting material seems to be associated with the demand for youthful labour in unskilled occupations, which pay well, and absorb adolescent populations more and more completely each year. Moreover, owing to the peculiar circumstances of apprenticeship which are coming to prevail in this country, clever boys are often unable to take up skilled work on leaving school. This circumstance puts additional pressure on the field of unskilled labour, and, coupled with the high rate of wages for unskilled labour, tends to force out of competition the aimless wastrel population at the bottom of the intellectual scale and this, unfortunately, becomes more and more the material available for army recruiting purposes.

Eichholz was supported by the Royal College of Surgeons, who believed that (PP 1904 xxxii: 105):

There are reasons for believing that, compared with former times, most of the men who now offer themselves as recruits are drawn from a class physically inferior, and that a general statistical statement may be, therefore, misleading ... [various factors] have altered the conditions of labour and raised at once the comparative standard of efficiency of the workmen, the standard of living, and the rate of wages. In the struggle for employment the better educated, the more intelligent and the more active and industrious are attracted to the better paid and more coveted occupations. The result is a large, and probably growing, *remainder* of those who, more or less unfit, fail to obtain regular employment. And it is apparently from this residue that the Army has to obtain the larger proportion of its recruits.

It must be remembered that Eichholz, the Royal College and the Committee were arguing from a false premise; as we shall show in the next chapter, correction of the statistics to allow for the changing height standard shows that the mean height of recruits was in fact gradually improving during this period. In addition, it is clear that there are logical flaws in their description of the labour market which is, in any case, not buttressed by evidence (Floud, Gregory and Wachter 1985: 11–13). Finally, there is very little sign from the recruiting statistics themselves, which give the proportion of recruits from different occupational groups, of any systematic change; table 3.9 shows that between 1863 and 1903, for example, the proportion of recruits drawn from 'labourers, servants, husbandmen, etc.' was never lower than 57.2 per cent nor higher than 67.9 per cent of those recruited and there was no consistent trend (Floud, Gregory and Wachter 1985: 23).

It is true that in theory periods of substantial change in labour markets might, just because Army recruitment was so intimately bound up with the condition of the labour market, cause changes in measured mean heights which do not reflect a true change in the heights of the working-class population. On the other hand, the evidence drawn from samples which has been presented in this chapter does not suggest that there was any major or systematic difference between military recruits and the population as a whole. It is, nevertheless, a possibility which must be borne constantly in mind when, in subsequent chapters, we describe the course of height changes.

A third possibility we have named 'offer bias'. This is the possibility that, particularly in wartime, the propensity of men or boys to offer themselves as recruits was partially determined by their height. Imagine that relatively tall men of each age were more attractive to civilian employers than relatively short men of that age; this might be due to their greater robustness or good health. Since such taller men were attractive to employers, they could command higher civilian wages than could the relatively short, while military wages were unrelated to height once the height standard had been attained. Particularly in times of heavy demand for both military and civilian labour – such as in the time of a major war – the pool of those who offered themselves to military recruiters would for this reason have been denuded of the relatively tall, while at the same time the military authorities were forced to lower the height standard to get men. This process would have the effect of under-representing the relatively tall and over-representing the relatively short in the Army or Marines and thus in our samples.

We call this possibility 'offer bias' because it is a distortion due to self-selection of recruits for a volunteer Army who did not offer themselves for recruitment because of the competing attractions of civilian employment. If it occurred, the result would be an underestimation of working-class heights in wartime and, as the process reversed itself at the end of the war when demand for labour fell, an overestimation of working-class heights in peacetime. The effect would be particularly troublesome since it would be unlikely, except in the most extreme circumstances, to be visible in the height distributions of recruits on which we base the estimates of average height which are reported in the next chapter.

We return to 'offer bias' in the next chapter, when we consider it as a possible explanation for the observed changes in heights. For the moment, it can simply be said that there is no independent evidence that eighteenth- or nineteenth-century labour markets operated in the way that the hypothesis would imply. It is important to note that, for offer bias to affect height distributions, an employer preference for taller men would have to operate *within* each age; a general preference for taller men would express itself most obviously in a preference for older men and such a preference would not necessarily lead to biassed recruitment *within* a given age. In addition, it is not clear how many civilian occupations had physical and therefore height requirements akin to those of the Army or whether civilian employers took height into account when hiring men. There is, it is true, convincing evidence that such preferences affected the demand for slaves in the United States, since the price of field hands was related to their height, but similar evidence is not available in Britain.

It is not fruitful at this stage to speculate further. It is clear that hypotheses can be advanced which would vitiate any attempt, either as a whole or at specific periods, to make inferences from military recruits to the British working class as a whole. It is also clear that there is no independent evidence which would enable us to decide whether these hypotheses are correct. In the light of this, and of the fact that this and the last chapter have demonstrated the many links which exist between Army recruits and the class from which they were drawn, we now turn to the evidence; we will keep the hypotheses in mind and examine them again wherever they might provide an alternative explanation for the trends and variations which we will observe.

3.4 ESTIMATION OF AVERAGE HEIGHTS FROM THE MILITARY SAMPLES

As we have explained, the primary reason why samples of military recruits are not representative of the whole population is that recruits had to pass a minimum height standard. We now explain the statistical methods of estimation which have been used to overcome this problem, to produce measures of average height for given age-groups in different periods, and in some cases to break these measures down by occupational and regional groups for the analyses in chapters 4 and 5. Two methods have been used, called 'quantile bend estimation' and 'reduced sample maximum likelihood estimation'. Technical details of these methods and their application to samples of heights are given elsewhere, in Wachter and Trussell (1982), and Trussell and Wachter (1984). The purpose here is to explain what they do in intuitive terms, so as to make comprehensible the statistical basis for our substantive conclusions.

The quantile bend estimator, used primarily with Marine Society and Army Medical Department data, is the easier one to explain, and a presentation designed for historians is already available in Wachter (1981). It is motivated by a straightforward graphical display called a 'quantile – quantile plot'. 'Quantile' is a general word for a level like a quintile or decile or percentile, the level above which some given fraction of a statistical distribution is to be found. For example, the median is the 0.50-quantile of a distribution. We can plot selected quantiles of a sample, say the levels above which 10 per cent, 20 per cent, 30 per cent, etc. of the points fall, against the corresponding quantiles of a theoretical distribution, say the levels above which 10 per cent, 20 per cent, 30 per cent, etc. of the area under the standard normal curve falls. The result is a quantile – quantile plot of the sample against the standard normal model. If the sample fits the normal model, the plotted points fall along a straight line. The intercept and slope of the line measure the mean and variance of the sample compared to the mean (zero) and variance (one) of the standard normal distribution.

If observations at low heights are systematically missing from the sample because of the minimum height standards, quantiles for the sample will no longer match quantiles for the normal curve. Not only is the agreement spoiled for heights below the height standard; the absence of the missing observations also deflates the denominator of the ratio of sample points above a given level to total sample points. By deflating the denominator, it bends the quantile – quantile plot away from a straight line even at tall height levels. For these tall height levels, however, we can try augmenting the count of observations in the denominator, to make up for the missing observations. We eventually reach a denominator which straightens out the bend, provided the underlying distribution is really a good approximation to the normal. Adult heights are remarkably close to normally distributed, as Wachter and Trussell (1982) argue. Adolescent heights do deviate from normality because of the adolescent growth spurt, but experimentation shows that the estimator performs reasonably well under such violations of the assumptions. This idea is incorporated into an automatic procedure which tests for bends with a numerical criterion. It does not depend on knowing beforehand where the minimum height standard falls. Like all our methods, however, it does depend on observations being under-represented primarily at the short end and not at the tall end of the distribution.

The reduced sample maximum likelihood estimators are slightly more complicated. They make greater demands on historical information, requiring reasonably accurate records of what the minimum height standards were for a given group at a given time. They also yield richer information, providing estimates of differentials in average heights for sample subgroups too small to sustain separate estimates group by group. Were it not for the minimum height standards, we could use ordinary least squares regression procedures, which are relatively familiar to historians. Adjusting for the minimum height standards, we actually use a procedure, reduced sample maximum likelihood, which can be regarded as a direct generalisation of least squares regression.

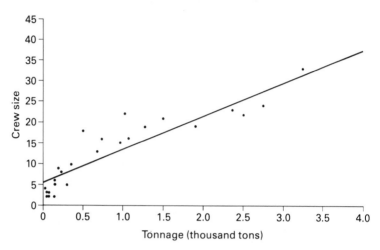

Figure 3.6. A scatter diagram of ships by crew size and tonnage, for cargo ships only. Source: see text.

A word first about regression itself, a technique whose name actually results from its first use with height data by Francis Galton. A more detailed explanation intended for historians may be found in Floud (1984: 19–25). Regression analysis is a statistical technique for specifying, in simple cases, the form of relationship between two or more sets of data. To take an elementary example from Floud (1979), it is a matter of common observation that the larger a ship, the larger will be its crew. Over some range of normal cases, the relationship may be a simple one. Perhaps for many kinds of ship every increase of 10 tons in the tonnage of the ship calls for one extra crew member. Such a simple relationship will not, of course, cover all cases. There must be a minimum size of crew. On ships that are very large, the number of crew members may not increase commensurately with size. The relationship between tonnage and crew size is also likely to be different for bulk carriers compared to passenger liners. But, if we restrict our attention appropriately, the relationship may be a simple one.

Imagine that we have collected a number of observations of reasonably similar ships and their crews and wish to make sense of the average relationship between tonnage and crew size by regression analysis. We begin by displaying the data in a scatter diagram such as figure 3.6 in which each point on the graph represents a ship. We first take only cargo ships. We can represent the average relationship between tonnage and crew size by the single straight line, drawn on the graph, which passes as close as possible to each and every one of the points; 'as close as possible' is defined in a particular way. There are many straight lines which could be drawn through the scatter of points. We stipulate that the line which gives the 'best' fit to the points and thus best represents the average relationship between tonnage and crew size is the so-called 'least squares' line in which the sum of the squared deviations of each point from the line is at a minimum. A computer program for regression analysis can be thought of – although it does not actually work in this way – as trying every possible line, calculating the squared deviations of each point from it, adding them for each line, and selecting the line giving the smallest total.

We can, thus, imagine least squares as a kind of shouting match, in which each point shouts the louder, the larger is its squared distance from the line. A point twice as far from the line as another is four times as vociferous. The least squares method chooses the line which minimises the sound of protest.

The chosen line, like any straight line, can be described fully in terms of two numbers, its intercept and its slope. In figure 3.6, the intercept is the point at which the line crosses the vertical axis, while the slope describes the angle at which it does so; since the line is straight, that slope is also the slope of the line at every point on it. In figure 3.6, regression calculation of the least squares line shows that it crosses the vertical axis at the point 5.4481, and for every subsequent increase of one ton the line climbs by 0.0082 crew members. The intercept is thus 5.4481 and the slope 0.0082 and we can describe the line – and thus the average relationship between crew size and tonnage – by the equation:

$$Y = 5.4481 + 0.0082X$$

where Y is the crew size and X the tonnage. In general, we can describe any straight line graph by the formula:

$$Y = a + bX$$

where a is the intercept, b is the slope and X and Y are the two variables whose relationship we are exploring. Y is called the dependent variable, X the independent or 'carrier' variable and b the coefficient of the independent variable.

If we now return to our height data, we can see that it differs from this elementary example in three ways. First, we know that data about short people are missing because of the height standards which were mentioned in chapter 2 and earlier in chapter 3. Thus we have only a partial set of observations of the relationship between height and its determinants, biassed in a particular way. Second, we believe that average height is related not simply to one determining factor (as crew size might be to tonnage) but to several, such as age, place of birth and occupation. Third, some of those possible determinants, such as place of birth and occupation, cannot be measured in the same way as age or crew size; they are discrete categories, not values on a scale.

Let us take these problems in turn, beginning with the effects of the military height standard. Our likelihood maximisation procedure maintains the basic structure of least squares regression but enhances it with an extra feature to accommodate the effects of the height standards. Because of the height standards, the distribution of recruits of a given unit, age, occupation, region, and time, which might have been a good facsimile of a normal distribution had there been no height standards, instead resembles a truncated normal distribution, with observations missing, generally from the lower end. If we plot observations of height on the Y-axis against some variable like age or year or the indicator of membership in some subgroup on the X-axis, just as we plotted crew size against tonnage, the observations for recruits close to a given age or belonging to a given group will spread out along each vertical line like a truncated normal distribution; points are missing from the whole lower portion of the graph.

Recall the comparison of least squares to a shouting match. We are selecting a line through the scatter of points. Points shout to have the chosen line run close to them. With truncation of shorter heights from the distribution, some points on the short side are being prevented from taking part in the shouting, while the points on the tall side keep asking to have the line placed close to them. Assuming this happens to some extent in all subgroups (along all portions of the X-axis), the whole line is shifted toward higher heights, and least squares gives an overestimate of the intercept. The exclusion of points on the short side from the shouting is most serious in a subgroup whose average is low relative to its truncation point. If the same or similar truncation points apply to most subgroups, the exclusion is worst where the line ought otherwise to reach the shorter heights. Without these points, the line does not reach so far towards shorter heights, and the result is that least squares underestimates the magnitude of the slope.

Fairness can be restored to the least squares shouting match by giving the missing points an independent voice. We know (if we are using this method at all) approximately where the truncation level falls. If we also knew that a particular line were the right one, we would have a good guess at how loud a group of shouters must be missing. Imagine trying each possible line, supplementing the shouts from the points we do hear with the missing voices that there would have to be if that line were the true one. The line that minimises the noise of protest is the line that makes it most likely, in a statistical sense, that we see the points we do see. It is the line that maximises the so-called likelihood function, and also maximises its logarithm, which is more convenient for calculation than the likelihood function itself.

For any data, truncated or not, that follows the normal distribution, the logarithm of the likelihood function already includes, with a minus sign, the sum of squares that serves as the least squares criterion. For truncated normal distributions, it also includes another term which represents, also with a minus sign, the independent voice of the missing points. Maximising with a minus sign is the same as minimising with a plus sign. Maximum likelihood and least squares are the same thing for fully normal data, but maximum likelihood offers a correction to least squares for truncated normal data.

Intuitions based on least squares are still relevant to the outputs of maximum likelihood calculations with truncated data, as long as the missing points are imagined back into the match. In other words, we can still interpret the relationship between variables in the same way as with regression estimates. Just as, in our simple example, we can say that on average crew size increases for each increase of 0.0082 in tonnage, so we can say that on average height increases by so many inches for every extra year of age.

For our applications, the standard deviation of heights around their mean is also estimated by the maximum likelihood program. It is estimated as a value common to all subgroups in a given period. The method makes it necessary to specify beforehand the truncation height for the unit of each recruit, and to discard all data points below this height, so as to create sharp truncation in the sample, even if enforcement was loose in practice. This discarding has the effect of reducing the sample, lending the name 'reduced sample maximum likelihood' to the procedure. The need for prespecified truncation levels makes the procedure less general than the quantile bend methods, but allows within-sample analysis of differentials as quantile bend methods do not.

The second difference which we identified between our simple example and that of the estimation of the determinants of height is more straightforward. Instead of only one independent variable such as tonnage, we want to think of height as being determined by several factors, among them age, birthplace and civilian occupation. This can be done by multiple regression or its maximum likelihood equivalent, in which the dependent variable (Y) is thought of as being determined by a series of independent variables $(X_1, X_2, \ldots X_N)$ such that:

$$Y = a + bX_1 + cX_2 + \ldots + nX_N$$

The interpretation of this equation is exactly the same as that of the simple regression equation, although the actual estimation procedure is necessarily more complex; b is the estimate of the extent to which change in X_1 produces change in Y (holding everything else equal) and c is the estimate of the extent to which change in X_2 produces change in Y (again holding everything else equal). There is thus no difficulty in incorporating multiple determinants of height into our analysis.

The third difference from our simple example was that some of those hypothesised determinants of height were not measurable on a scale such as age or height; technically they are nominal rather than interval scale variables (Floud 1979: ch. 1). To understand how we can cope with this difficulty we need to return to our simple example. We mentioned that the relationship between crew size and tonnage might well be different for cargo and for passenger ships. Let us imagine that we plotted some passenger ships on our graph (figure 3.7). We see that they uniformly need more crew than do the original cargo ships; this is represented by the fact that, if we plot a line through the new points, it has a greater intercept than the first line, though the same slope. If we were to estimate a regression equation on all the points in the graph, without taking account of whether they were from cargo or passenger ships, we would estimate a line somewhere in the middle with different slope and intercept from either line we have drawn. In doing so, we would miss a vital feature of the data; crew size is determined not just by tonnage but by the type of ship.

The statistical technique which allows us to estimate the effect on crew size of the type of ship as well as the tonnage is known as regression with dummy variables. We take our familiar regression equation and add a second independent variable Z to represent type of ship, so that:

$$Y = a + bX + cZ$$

Instead of having two pieces of information about each ship (tonnage and crew size) we now have a third, Z, a 'dummy variable' which takes the value zero when the ship is a cargo ship and one when it is a passenger ship. When we estimate the regression, passenger

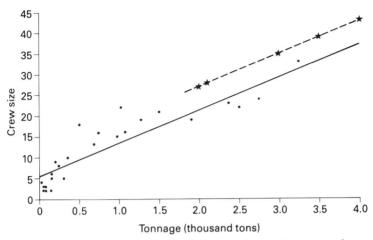

Figure 3.7. A scatter diagram of ships by crew size and tonnage, for cargo and passenger ships. Source: see text.

ships but not cargo ships will affect the value of c, the coefficient of Z, since cZ will (by simple arithmetic) be zero whenever Z is zero. The final estimated value of c thus gives the change attributable to the passenger ships. In practice, when using dummy variables we normally dispense with the separate intercept (by subtracting the mean of the dependent variable from each value):

$$Y = bX + cZ$$

In this equation, b represents the overall change in Y brought about by a change in X, while c is the change attributable to passenger ships. It takes the place of the intercept, shifting the line up or down but retaining the slope given by b. Z in this case is known as the 'base variable'.

In our simple example, we have used both an interval scale independent variable (tonnage) and a dummy variable (type of ship), but it is possible to work entirely with dummy variables and, in our analysis of heights using the analogous maximum likelihood technique, that is exactly what we have done. For flexibility, in fact, we have treated age, an interval scale variable, as if it were a dummy variable with discrete categories and have worked, therefore, with three sets of dummy variables representing respectively ages, places of birth and occupations. Table 3.13 shows a specimen set of results from 1806–1809, one of the 24 quinquennial estimates. In this more complex example of the use of dummy variables, we have a multiple baseline

Table 3.13. *A comparison of results from the reduced sample maximum likelihood (MLE) and the ordinary least squares (OLS) estimation procedures, for the birth cohort of recruits, 1806–1809.*

Birth cohort of 1806–1809
Truncation at 65 inches
2099 recruits
Baseline category: English urban 18-year-olds in trades outside building requiring apprenticeship.

Variable	MLE	OLS	*t* for MLE	*t* for OLS
Baseline	66.02	66.68	—	—
Standard deviation	2.17	1.61	—	—
Professional	—	0.43	—	1.17
Apprenticed builders	−0.68	−0.34	−2.41	−2.36
Manual	0.19	0.12	0.48	0.55
Textile workers	0.15	0.09	0.74	0.87
Workers with animals	0.73	0.48	1.75	1.91
Domestic servants	−0.33	−0.18	−0.45	−0.47
Workers in commerce	−0.74	−0.36	−1.19	−1.19
Labourers	−0.08	−0.03	−0.48	−0.40
Blank occupation	0.45	0.26	1.25	1.31
Unskilled	—	−0.25	—	−0.66
London	−1.19	−0.62	−3.54	−3.83
English, rural	−0.78	−0.41	−3.99	−4.07
Scottish, urban	0.98	0.55	2.85	2.73
Scottish, rural	1.15	0.68	4.54	4.61
Irish	−0.27	−0.15	−1.43	−1.50
Foreign	−1.02	−0.53	−5.53	−3.69
Age 15	1.30	0.72	0.68	0.63
Age 16	−1.34	−0.58	−2.01	−1.99
Age 17	−0.72	−0.29	−1.79	−1.54
Age 19	0.69	0.35	2.53	2.51
Age 20	1.06	0.56	3.88	3.92
Age 21	0.95	0.47	3.29	3.17
Age 22	1.14	0.61	3.82	3.90
Age 23	1.13	0.64	3.66	3.90
Age 24–29	1.29	0.68	5.78	5.99
Age 30–up	0.96	0.55	3.39	3.81

category – men aged 18 from English urban counties and from the apprenticed trades excluding building – and each of the coefficients can be read as a difference from that baseline. Thus the coefficient -1.19 for London shows that, holding all else constant, a soldier or Marine from London was 1.19 inches (3.02 cm) shorter than one from the English urban counties. The coefficients for different sets of dummy variables are additive, so that one can add the coefficients for age 23, Scots rural and workers with animals to conclude that a person with those characteristics would have been on average:

$$1.13 + 1.15 + 0.73 = 3.01 \text{ inches } (7.65 \text{ cm})$$

taller than the average person with the base characteristics.

The average height levels and differentials that we estimate, either from the quantile bend or from the reduced sample maximum likelihood procedures are analysed in the following chapters from a number of points of view. There is always a margin of error associated with our estimates, some of it from sampling, but most of it from the uncertainties of our adjustments for the height standards. For this reason, it is frequently advantageous to smooth the estimates that we obtain for a given group as a function of time. For most of our smoothing, we have used a special variety of moving average, using the 'lowess' or 'locally weighted scatterplot smoother' of Cleveland (1979: 830).

The computation of moving averages is a common smoothing technique, in which a point on a graph is replaced by an average of itself and the points before and after it. The moving average we use is 'robust' in the sense that apparently wilder points are given less weight. Furthermore, the smoothed value for a given time is not a simple average of surrounding times. Instead, closer surrounding times are given more weight than further ones. In our uses, the lowess method tends to give very smooth curves, capturing the general tendency while downplaying the decade-by-decade detail. In chapter 4, we also use a popular 'Tukey' smoother (Tukey 1977: chs. 7 and 16), which performs several operations on medians of successive groups of points and which preserves the abruptness of changes, although at some cost in a more jagged summary.

This concludes our discussion of our main statistical tools. A great deal depends on these estimation procedures. They have been tested on many sets of artificial data, as described in Wachter and Trussell (1982), as well as tried on many subsamples and with many specifications besides those reported in this book. But no methods are perfect. We should always keep in mind some picture of a real-life recruiting sergeant, cajoling some bright-eyed youngster into taking the King's shilling, without regard for the effect his impromptu decisions would have on our manipulations with normal distributions centuries afterward. All kinds of things go wrong with historical reconstructions, and what we hope for, at best, is that they do not go too far wrong on average in unforeseen directions too much of the time.

Appendix 3.1

The collection and processing of data

The primary sources used in this study were the various series of Description Books of the British Army and Royal Marines held in the Public Record Office, Kew (PRO series W025, W054, W067, W069, ADM158), the records of the Marine Society of London held at the National Maritime Museum, Greenwich, and the Description Books of the Royal Military Academy, Sandhurst, held at the Academy itself. These are not the only records which contain information about the height of men in the eighteenth and nineteenth centuries; other sources include the Description Books of the East India Company army from 1801 to 1860 (India Office Library L/MIL/9/29–46), the Description Books of the Royal Navy from 1825 to 1875 (PRO series ADM37, ADM38, ADM139), records of the men of the merchant navy in 1844–1856 (PRO series BT113–116), numerous records of prisons (PRO series PrCom2) and records of transported prisoners held in Australia and Tasmania (Nicholas and Shergold 1982, 1988). However, the British Army and Royal Marine records used in this study are the longest and most consistent series available for Britain and Ireland and among the longest in the world (Fogel 1986b).

THE ARMY AND MARINE RECORDS

The Army and Marine records begin with recruitment in the 1750s, and thus with men born from the 1720s onwards, but the numbers of surviving Description Books before the 1760s are not large enough to give reliable estimates. At the end of the period, in the 1880s, there was a change in Army practice, after which time the records describe not all recruits – the previous practice – but only those who survived to draw a pension. The published annual reports of the Army Medical Department (e.g. PP 1862 xxxiii: 1) provide aggregate information from that time but do not give individual details. Aggregate analysis thus covers the period from 1760 to 1914 – based first on samples of individuals from the Description Books and second from the published aggregate data – but the detailed occupational and geographical correlates of height variation could be analysed only for the recruitment years between 1760 and 1880 and thus for men born between 1745 and 1865.

It was initially intended to draw a cluster sample of 13 000 recruits from each quinquennium between 1760 and 1880, on the basis of which, it was calculated, it would be possible accurately to estimate mean heights within each of 17 British wage regions. In retrospect, this calculation was flawed in several ways: first, it took no account of the possibility of estimating the heights of occupational as well as geographical groups within the British population; second, it took no account of the need to make separate estimates for different age-groups. Both these omissions illustrate the naivety typical of initial exploration of an uncharted field; it was not realised that it would be so valuable to explore socio-occupational correlates of height variation, nor that the age at which growth ceases is an indicator of nutritional status, making it necessary to secure data which delineates the tempo of growth as well as final heights. Third, it was assumed that it would be necessary to make separate estimates for each univariate distribution of heights, using the quantile – quantile plot or similar methods (Wachter 1981, and chapter 4 below). Fourth, it was assumed that it would be possible to manipulate a data-set containing more than 400 000 observations, each with at least six variables. Fifth, it was assumed that it would be possible to collect consistent data up to recruitment in 1914.

Exploration of pilot samples made it possible to correct some of these misconceptions. In addition, the development of methods for multivariate rather than univariate estimation of the covariates of the height distribution (Wachter and Trussell 1982, and chapter 5 below) made it possible simultaneously to estimate the effects of age, socio-occupational status and geography upon heights, without producing a data-set which was unmanageably large.

The process of drawing the sample was as follows (the process was carried out separately but identically for Army and Royal Marine recruits):

1 Lists were made of the Description Books which contained information about recruitment in each decade from 1750 to 1880; many books span more than one decade and therefore were included in successive decadal lists.

2 The Description Books were numbered and a random sample of them was drawn within each decade list.

3 Starting with the book drawn first in the random sample, the books were searched for recruits who had joined during the decade and particulars of each recruit were recorded; successive books drawn by the sample were searched in this way until particulars of approximately 5000 recruits had been recorded.

4 The following details of each recruit were recorded: age, height, occupation, place of birth, place of recruitment, date of recruitment, military unit and, for some decades, colour of hair, eyes and complexion, literacy, height at age 24 and reason for death or discharge.

The total data-set used in the analyses in this book consists of 108 171 complete observations, each with at least seven variables. It was not possible, in some earlier decades, to secure 5000 observations for Army and 5000 for Marine recruits. Despite this, substantially more observations were collected but not used in the analysis because some information was missing. There is no sign that these omissions were anything but accidental, caused either by failures by the recruiting officers or by omissions by the data collection staff. In view of the large size of the remaining data-set, no interpolation or estimation of missing data was carried out.

The data were initially recorded in a format which duplicated that of the original records; the format differed between one military unit and another. The variables were then reordered into a consistent format. The details of occupation and of place of birth and recruitment were then machine-coded with unique codes for each occupation but place-names were coded only by the county in which they fell. The occupational codes were based on the work of W. A. Armstrong (1972) as extended by Professor Michael Anderson (1987) when he drew a machine-readable sample of the 1851 census. The coding scheme results in a unique eight-digit code for each occupation, incorporating codes for the industry and different aspects of the work such as its place within the hierarchy of skill. It was necessary, however, to extend Professor Anderson's directory considerably to cover occupations not met in the 1851 census sample and the final directory consists of 5889 occupation codes. This directory, together with the place-name directory of 8182 codes, has been deposited in the ESRC data archive at the University of Essex, together with uncoded and coded versions of the full data-set. All are available for use by other scholars.

For the purposes of most analyses, both occupations and place-names were grouped into categories, which are given below together with the short titles or mnemonics used in tables and figures below.

Occupational categories

The occupational classification is intended primarily to reflect the degree of skill or training brought to the occupation, with subcategories for particular industrial groups.

1 *Professional or white-collar*: Occupations which required literacy or university/chartered examinations' qualification.
2 *Apprenticed building*: Occupations in the building trades which required training or experience over a period of years.
3 *Apprenticed non-building*: Occupations, not in the building trades, which required training or experience over a period of years.
4 *Manual non-textile*: Occupations, not in the textile trades, which required training or experience over months, weeks or days.
5 *Textile*: Occupations in the textile trades which required training or experience over months, weeks or days.
6 *Animals*: Occupations which involved work with animals or plants, including agriculture.
7 *Domestic service*: Occupations involving personal service.
8 *Commerce*: Occupations in trade or commerce.
9 *Unskilled*: Occupations which required minimal or no special qualifications.
10 *Labourer*: General labourers not otherwise specified.
11 *Blank*: No occupation given.

Geographical categories

These are the counties included in each category. The numbers in brackets refer to the wage areas identified by Hunt (1973).

1 *London*: London, Surrey, Kent, Middlesex, Essex (1).
2 *English rural*: Wiltshire, Dorset, Devon, Cornwall, Somerset, Gloucestershire, Sussex, Hampshire, Berkshire, Hertfordshire, Buckinghamshire, Oxfordshire, Northamptonshire, Bedfordshire, Cambridgeshire, Suffolk, Norfolk, Hereford, Cardigan, Brecknock, Radnor, Montgomery, Flint, Denbigh, Merioneth, Caernarvon, Anglesey, Rutland, Lincoln, Yorkshire (East Riding), Yorkshire (North Riding), Cumberland, Westmorland (2, 3, 5, 7, 9).
3 *English urban*: Monmouth, Glamorgan, Carmarthen, Pembroke,

Shropshire, Staffordshire, Worcestershire, Warwickshire, Leices-
tershire, Nottinghamshire, Derbyshire, Cheshire, Lancashire, York
(West Riding), Durham, Northumberland (4, 6, 8, 10).
4 *Scottish urban*: Ayr, Renfrew, Dumbarton, Lanark, Stirling, Midlo-
thian, East Lothian, West Lothian, Fife, Clackmannan (12).
5 *Scottish rural*: Bute, Kinross, Perth, Forfar, Kincardine, Aberdeen,
Banff, Elgin, Nairn, Inverness, Argyll, Ross and Cromarty, Suther-
land, Caithness, Orkney, Shetland, Dumfries, Kirkcudbright, Gal-
loway, Wigtownshire, Peebles, Selkirk, Roxburgh, Berwick (11, 13).
6 *Ireland*.
7 *Foreign*.

These categories are inevitably arbitrary, even at one moment in
time. Over the course of the period from 1760 to 1880, in addition,
the character of many areas and even of occupations was changed
by the Industrial Revolution. A county such as Warwickshire, seat
of the Midlands metal industries, was transformed by industrialisation, as were many jobs in the engineering, metal working and textile
trades. It would have been possible to adjust the categories over the
period to reflect such changes – and it is still possible for other scholars
to undertake this work – but it was decided instead to hold the categories constant and to attempt to explain changes in the covariates
of height by reference to the economic and social changes which we
know to have occurred.

A further stage of processing was to reorganise the data so that
it was ordered by the date of birth of the recruit rather than by his
date of recruitment and then to base analysis on what we have called
'quinquennial birth cohorts', groups of recruits born within a five-year
period. This was undertaken so as to bring together recruits who
would have been brought up in similar periods, so as to minimise
the variation for that reason and make it possible to examine other
causes of variation. In addition, analysis of the tempo of growth
demands data of this type.

In a further stage of processing, another piece of information was
added to the record of each individual recruit. The maximum likelihood estimation procedure which is discussed in section 3.4
demanded information about the height standard which each recruit
had satisfied on entrance to the Army or Marines. This information
was assembled in two ways. First, the *Annual Regulations* and *Orders
of the Day* of the Army specified the height standards in force at any
one time and in each type of unit; guards, cavalry, infantry, artillery
all had their own requirements. These standards were collected with

the invaluable help of the Librarian of the Ministry of Defence and a height standard was assigned to each unit at each period. This understates the complexity of the task, since there were often multiple height standards, differing for 'growing lads', boys under 18, men between 18 and 25 and older men; in addition, the standards were changed frequently. Taking these complexities into account, a height standard relevant to each individual, given his age, unit and date of recruitment, was then assigned to him.

The second method was applied to the Marines. It does not appear that height standards for the Marines were ever published, nor are there any documents relating to Marine recruiting which give such information. The assignment of a height standard to each Marine recruit was therefore based on inspection of the height distributions of each quinquennial recruitment cohort of Marines, taking each age-group separately, and on the results of quantile bend estimates of the degree and extent of the lower-tail shortfall in those distributions. Once these estimates had been made, each Marine recruit was assigned the relevant standard.

Other data

Two further sets of data about individuals were collected, both dealing with adolescent boys. These data stemmed from the records of the Marine Society of London and of the Royal Military Academy at Sandhurst. In each case, data about age and height were recorded about each boy recruited to the Marine Society or the RMA, a total of about 50 000 observations for the former and 20 000 for the latter. In addition, a sample of Marine Society recruits was gathered and information collected for the members of that sample about the occupation and address of the boy and his parents, about his literacy, about whether he had had smallpox and about the relationship to him of the person who brought him to the Society. These data were coded in an analogous way to that used for the Army and Marine records, and coded and uncoded data-sets have been deposited in the ESRC data archive at the University of Essex.

4

Long-term trends in
nutritional status

4.0 INTRODUCTION

For many years, discussion of long-term trends in the height of populations was dominated by the concept of the 'secular trend' which was contrasted with other short-term causes of variation, such as those associated with famines and with wars. As Tanner puts it (1978: 150–1):

During approximately the last hundred years in industrialized countries, and recently in some developing ones, children have been getting larger and growing to maturity more rapidly. This is known as the 'secular trend' in growth. Its magnitude is such that in Europe, America and Japan it has dwarfed the differences between occupational groups . . . From about 1900 to the present, children in average economic circumstances have increased in height at ages 5 to 7 years by about 1–2 cm per decade. The trend starts early in childhood, as pre-school data make clear. At least in Britain it began a considerable time ago . . . During the same period there has been an upward trend in adult height but only to the lesser degree of about 1 cm per decade since 1880.

'Secular' is used here in the sense of 'continuing through long ages' and, although Tanner was careful to limit his statements to what was then known from various sources about heights in the past, less cautious commentators tended to envisage an upward trend from some far distant time to the present. Popular experience of rising heights in the twentieth century, together with evidence of the size of clothing, shoes and armour in the past, all contributed to such a view.

It is obvious, however, that the growth in the height of populations which has been so marked in recent years must have begun quite recently in human history; archaeological evidence from the classical and medieval periods shows that, although men and women of those periods were probably short by modern standards, they were not dwarfs. At some point in the relatively recent past, therefore, increase in human height must have begun or, at least, accelerated.

If this occurred, it must have done so for some reason; Tanner states

134

that 'The causes of the trend are probably multiple' and cites better nutrition and a lessening of disease along with a number of more speculative causes, including 'the rather fanciful idea [of] increased psychosexual stimulation consequent on modern urban living', climatic changes and heterosis or the effects of outbreeding (1978: 153). Meredith (1976: 322) cites 15 such suggested causes including the increase in athletic participation and the effects of lighter and less restrictive clothing.[1] Many of these environmental causes can be expected to have operated differentially on different social classes or occupational or geographical groups; indeed, it is often observed that class differences in height have lessened in recent years and in some countries, most notably Sweden, have disappeared altogether.

The coincidence of a rising trend and diminishing social and geographical variation in heights in so many countries, indeed throughout the world, suggests that a social phenomenon of major significance has been at work. In this chapter, we shall describe the evolution of heights in Britain since the beginning of the eighteenth century and begin to try to identify the causes and correlates of that evolution.

4.1 ADULT HEIGHTS

We look first at adult heights, for adult data supply the most nearly comparable and least ambiguous indicators of well-being. They are not so much affected as are adolescent heights by the changing tempo of growth which has accompanied earlier maturation and which is both difficult to measure and difficult to interpret from cross-sectional surveys taken at different times. Adult heights, reached after longer or shorter periods of growth in childhood and adolescence, have, as Tanner pointed out, changed much less dramatically during the past hundred years than have childhood heights. But their less dramatic changes provide the historian with a sure guide and what is, in the jargon of economists, a 'lower bound' on the change which has occurred.

---

[1] The full list cited by Meredity is: decline in the frequency of illnesses that retard growth; population changes due to immigration; the effects of urbanisation; increase in athletic participation; reduction in child labour; improvement in housing and community hygiene; changes to less restricting and lighter clothing; increase in nutritional content of diets; effects of assortative and selective mating; improvement in medical care and personal health habits; changes in world temperature and humidity; reversal of a prior biological adaptation to hard labour and crowded conditions; manifestation of an evolutionary tendency for organisms of a phylum to increase in size; cumulative expression of heterosis; and decrease in family size. Another explanation is that of the effects of vaccination in infancy (Landauer and Whiting 1964: Landauer 1973).

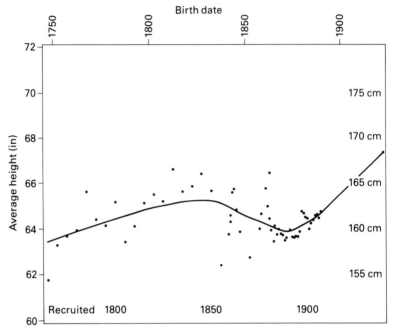

Figure 4.1. The mean height of 18-year-old military recruits, 1750–1916.
Source: see text.

4.1.1 Military samples from 1740 to 1914

The military samples which have been discussed in chapters 2 and 3 supply a basis for estimating the height of the male working class of Britain and Ireland between the 1740s and the end of the nineteenth century. It is first wise to examine the overall trend before, in the next chapter, considering any adjustments that should be made for the social and geographical composition of the recruits. Figures 4.1, 4.2 and 4.3 show, respectively, the mean heights of recruits to the British Army and Royal Marines aged 18, 21–23 and 24–29. The underlying data are given in table 4.1.

These mean height estimates originate from three different sources. Those marked RDB in table 4.1, primarily for recruits born between 1745 and 1845, are based on the samples of Army and Royal Marine Description Books described in appendix 3.1. Those marked AMD, primarily for recruits born after 1841 and before 1890, are derived from tabulations of height by age of Army recruits found in the annual reports of the Army Medical Department, as described in Floud,

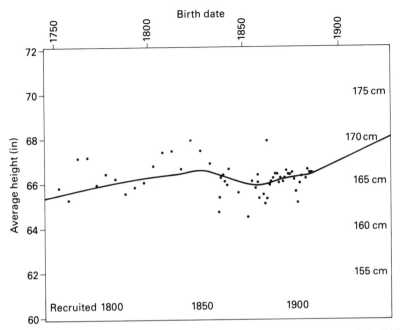

Figure 4.2. The mean height of 21- to 23-year-old military recruits, 1750–1916.
Source: see text.

Wachter and Gregory (1985) and at the end of section 3.4. The points
for 1916, 1922.5 and 1957.5 are from modern sample survey data,
described below.

In all cases, one estimated value relates to all members of a given
birth cohort, that is to all individuals having the same specified age
at time of recruitment. For instance, the first point on figure 4.1 is
the mean height estimate based on the 186 recruits born between
1745 and 1750 (as inferred from their reported ages) and 18 years
old at the time of their recruitment between 1763 and 1768. The points
centred on 1747.5 in figures 4.1, 4.2 and 4.3 derive from recruits born
in the same interval, but recruited in different periods, at the various
ages to which the graphs apply. The sample material is arranged in
quinquennial birth cohorts, while the Army Medical Department
material is annual. The sample sizes for each age in the Army and
Royal Marine samples range from about 150 to 500. The Army Medical
Department data report the experience of several thousand men at
any given age. The total numbers of men measured by the Army
Medical Department are given in table 3.9.

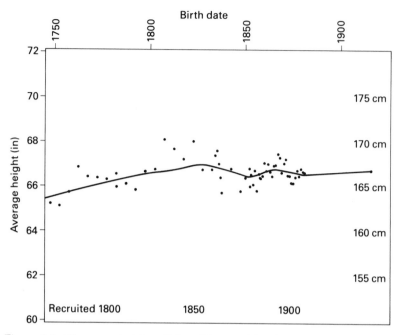

Figure 4.3. The mean height of 24- to 29-year-old military recruits, 1750–1916.
Source: see text.

The principal step in deriving both sets of estimates is the correction for the effects of minimum height standards which we have already mentioned at the end of section 3.4. This is a complicated statistical problem and dealing with it has been the main technical challenge of the present work. It must be recognised that the problem has no perfect solution. The recruiting process was too haphazard and the information about it is too limited to allow for precise adjustments. Since long-term trends as well as short-term differentials are all of interest, it is important to maintain consistency of procedures, and to avoid adjustment of 'special cases' and *ad-hoc* judgements, even though in particular years and at particular ages in particular series some estimates could certainly be improved using detailed inspection of the particular raw distributions. The fact that some cohorts' ages and series fit the assumptions behind the analysis better than others shows itself in haphazard scatter on the graphs, much greater than can be ascribed to sampling error. The scatter, in other words, reflects more than anything else the uncertainties in the size of correction for under-representation of short recruits due to minimum height standards, as they affected different service units, birth cohort by birth cohort and age by age.

The true story of changing heights in the pool from which recruits were drawn is better represented by a smooth curve through the quinquennial and annual estimates than by the estimates themselves. For this reason, figures 4.1 to 4.3 show, superimposed on the points themselves, smooth curves derived by a form of moving average, the 'lowess' procedure which is described in detail in section 3.4. Our confidence in the main trends shown by the estimates is grounded on our experiments with a number of alternative forms of correction for the minimum height standards, forms which make different assumptions about the operation of the standards, but which lead, on the whole, to the same main trends. For the estimates shown in figures 4.1 to 4.3, half-a-dozen variants of the estimation methods developed in Wachter and Trussell (1982) have been applied to these data series.

The estimates shown in table 4.1 for the RDB samples were obtained from the maximum likelihood calculations described in chapter 3. The estimates for the AMD series were obtained from the quantile bend procedures explained in Wachter and Trussell (1982: 282). For the RDB estimates, the recruits to the Royal Marines and the Royal Army have been pooled in a single estimation for each quinquennial cohort. Each recruit's height has been linked to a minimum height standard which applied to his unit at his time of recruitment; the information on which this was based is described in appendix 3.1. The procedure then works by discarding all observations below a selected cut-off for each unit, after which a truncated normal distribution with a fixed lower truncation level at that point of cut-off is fitted by the method of maximum likelihood. This produces an estimate of the mean and standard deviation of the full normal distribution that would be expected if the minimum height standard had not removed recruits from the sample. There is a trade-off in the method, since higher cut-offs lead to more variable estimates but to less chance of bias in the corrections.

The most important issue in this procedure is the decision to pool the recruits from the different branches of military service. The historical logic behind this procedure was explained in chapter 3; it was that many recruits were apparently indifferent between units and that the height standards essentially operated to sort men to units dependent upon their height and the height demanded by the units. In other words, the higher minimum standards of some parts of the Army served not to exclude men shorter than those standards from

Long-term trends in nutritional status

Table 4.1. *Mean heights of military recruits by age and date of birth.*

Date of birth	Mean height in	Mean height cm	Source
Age 18			
1747.5	61.75	156.85	RDB
1752.5	63.29	160.76	RDB
1757.5	63.68	161.75	RDB
1762.5	63.91	162.33	RDB
1767.5	65.62	166.67	RDB
1772.5	64.42	163.63	RDB
1777.5	64.16	162.97	RDB
1782.5	65.16	165.51	RDB
1787.5	63.44	161.14	RDB
1792.5	64.11	162.84	RDB
1797.5	65.11	165.38	RDB
1802.5	65.49	166.34	RDB
1807.5	65.19	165.58	RDB
1812.5	66.59	169.14	RDB
1817.5	65.63	166.70	RDB
1822.5	65.84	167.23	RDB
1827.5	66.40	168.66	RDB
1832.5	65.65	166.75	RDB
1837.5	62.39	158.47	RDB
1841.5	63.76	161.95	AMD
1842.5	64.30	163.32	RDB
1842.5	64.59	164.05	AMD
1843.5	65.59	166.60	AMD
1844.5	65.75	167.00	AMD
1845.5	64.81	164.61	AMD
1847.5	63.89	162.28	RDB
1852.5	62.74	159.36	RDB
1857.5	64.01	162.59	RDB
1858.5	64.66	164.23	AMD
1860.5	65.76	167.03	AMD
1861.5	64.98	165.05	AMD
1862.5	66.44	168.76	RDB
1862.5	64.44	163.67	AMD
1863.5	63.94	162.41	AMD
1864.5	63.45	161.17	AMD
1865.5	64.13	162.89	AMD
1866.5	63.75	161.93	AMD
1867.5	63.97	162.49	AMD
1868.5	63.77	161.98	AMD
1869.5	63.72	161.85	AMD
1870.5	63.51	161.31	AMD
1871.5	63.62	161.59	AMD
1872.5	63.89	162.27	AMD

Table 4.1. (*cont.*)

| Date of birth | Mean height | | Source |
	in	cm	
1873.5	63.95	162.43	AMD
1874.5	63.64	161.65	AMD
1875.5	63.62	161.59	AMD
1876.5	63.66	161.70	AMD
1877.5	63.66	161.70	AMD
1878.5	63.88	162.26	AMD
1879.5	64.76	164.50	AMD
1880.5	64.67	164.26	AMD
1881.5	64.50	163.83	AMD
1882.5	64.44	163.69	AMD
1883.5	63.98	162.52	AMD
1884.5	64.25	163.18	AMD
1885.5	64.39	163.56	AMD
1886.5	64.57	164.01	AMD
1887.5	64.61	164.11	AMD
1888.5	64.45	163.69	AMD
1889.5	64.70	164.34	AMD
Age 19			
1742.5	61.22	155.50	RDB
1747.5	63.53	161.37	RDB
1752.5	64.49	163.80	RDB
1757.5	64.59	164.06	RDB
1762.5	64.70	164.34	RDB
1767.5	66.59	169.14	RDB
1772.5	65.78	167.08	RDB
1777.5	65.53	166.45	RDB
1782.5	65.52	166.42	RDB
1787.5	64.67	164.26	RDB
1792.5	64.96	165.00	RDB
1797.5	66.00	167.64	RDB
1802.5	66.02	167.69	RDB
1807.5	66.12	167.94	RDB
1812.5	67.20	170.69	RDB
1817.5	66.02	167.69	RDB
1822.5	67.45	171.32	RDB
1827.5	66.35	168.53	RDB
1832.5	66.23	168.22	RDB
1837.5	63.80	162.05	AMD
1840.5	64.50	163.83	AMD
1841.5	66.26	168.30	AMD
1842.5	64.72	164.39	RDB
1842.5	65.75	166.99	AMD
1843.5	65.84	167.22	AMD

Table 4.1. (*cont.*)

Date of birth	Mean height		Source
	in	cm	
1844.5	64.82	164.65	AMD
1847.5	65.06	165.25	RDB
1852.5	63.38	160.99	RDB
1857.5	64.64	164.18	AMD
1857.5	64.76	164.49	RDB
1859.5	65.35	165.98	AMD
1860.5	65.46	166.27	AMD
1861.5	64.13	162.89	AMD
1862.5	66.69	169.39	RDB
1862.5	64.84	164.69	AMD
1863.5	64.83	164.68	AMD
1864.5	65.12	165.39	AMD
1865.5	64.71	164.37	AMD
1865.5	65.70	166.87	AMD
1866.5	65.01	165.13	AMD
1867.5	64.91	164.87	AMD
1868.5	64.50	163.83	AMD
1869.5	65.32	165.91	AMD
1870.5	65.24	165.71	AMD
1871.5	65.22	165.65	AMD
1872.5	65.58	166.58	AMD
1873.5	65.57	166.54	AMD
1874.5	64.96	165.00	AMD
1875.5	65.52	166.42	AMD
1876.5	65.26	165.75	AMD
1877.5	65.62	166.67	AMD
1878.5	65.32	165.91	AMD
1879.5	65.14	165.45	AMD
1880.5	65.41	166.13	AMD
1881.5	65.38	166.06	AMD
1882.5	65.02	165.16	AMD
1883.5	65.36	166.02	AMD
1884.5	65.69	166.84	AMD
1885.5	65.72	166.92	AMD
1887.5	65.46	166.26	AMD
1888.5	65.63	166.69	AMD
Age 20			
1742.5	64.88	164.80	RDB
1747.5	63.50	161.29	RDB
1752.5	64.53	163.91	RDB
1757.5	65.09	165.33	RDB
1762.5	65.25	165.74	RDB
1767.5	67.47	171.37	RDB

Table 4.1. (*cont.*)

Date of birth	Mean height		Source
	in	cm	
1772.5	65.95	167.51	RDB
1777.5	65.67	166.80	RDB
1782.5	66.07	167.82	RDB
1787.5	65.17	165.53	RDB
1792.5	65.73	166.95	RDB
1797.5	66.65	169.29	RDB
1802.5	66.33	168.48	RDB
1807.5	66.00	167.64	RDB
1812.5	67.49	171.42	RDB
1817.5	66.18	168.10	RDB
1822.5	67.45	171.32	RDB
1827.5	67.32	170.99	RDB
1832.5	66.63	169.24	RDB
1837.5	65.10	165.35	RDB
1839.5	64.69	164.31	AMD
1840.5	66.66	169.31	AMD
1841.5	66.48	168.86	AMD
1842.5	65.83	167.21	RDB
1842.5	65.75	166.99	AMD
1843.5	64.87	164.77	AMD
1847.5	65.51	166.40	RDB
1852.5	64.36	163.47	RDB
1856.5	65.72	166.94	AMD
1857.5	65.78	167.08	RDB
1858.5	65.74	166.97	AMD
1859.5	65.32	165.91	AMD
1860.5	64.83	164.66	AMD
1861.5	65.70	166.87	AMD
1862.5	67.66	171.86	RDB
1862.5	65.30	165.86	AMD
1863.5	65.62	166.67	AMD
1864.5	65.00	165.09	AMD
1865.5	65.55	166.50	AMD
1866.5	65.36	166.01	AMD
1868.5	65.76	167.04	AMD
1869.5	65.85	167.26	AMD
1870.5	65.50	166.38	AMD
1871.5	65.75	167.01	AMD
1872.5	65.73	166.95	AMD
1873.5	65.63	166.69	AMD
1874.5	65.76	167.03	AMD
1875.5	65.92	167.45	AMD
1876.5	66.09	167.87	AMD
1877.5	65.97	167.57	AMD

Table 4.1. (*cont.*)

Date of birth	Mean height in	Mean height cm	Source
1878.5	65.68	166.82	AMD
1879.5	65.47	166.30	AMD
1880.5	66.07	167.82	AMD
1881.5	65.62	166.68	AMD
1882.5	65.74	166.98	AMD
1883.5	65.94	167.49	AMD
1884.5	66.37	168.57	AMD
1885.5	66.01	167.68	AMD
1886.5	66.31	168.43	AMD
1887.5	66.19	168.13	AMD
Age 21			
1742.5	65.32	165.91	RDB
1747.5	64.16	162.97	RDB
1752.5	65.39	166.09	RDB
1757.5	65.33	165.94	RDB
1762.5	66.33	168.48	RDB
1767.5	67.56	171.60	RDB
1772.5	66.59	169.14	RDB
1777.5	65.82	167.18	RDB
1782.5	66.11	167.92	RDB
1787.5	65.41	166.14	RDB
1792.5	65.64	166.73	RDB
1797.5	66.24	168.25	RDB
1802.5	66.58	169.11	RDB
1807.5	67.22	170.74	RDB
1812.5	67.69	171.93	RDB
1817.5	66.64	169.27	RDB
1822.5	67.66	171.86	RDB
1827.5	67.58	171.65	RDB
1832.5	66.92	169.98	RDB
1837.5	65.07	165.28	RDB
1838.5	65.52	166.43	AMD
1839.5	66.79	169.65	AMD
1840.5	66.44	168.76	AMD
1841.5	65.74	166.97	AMD
1842.5	66.85	169.80	RDB
1842.5	65.38	166.07	AMD
1847.5	65.12	165.40	RDB
1852.5	65.07	165.28	RDB
1855.5	66.15	168.02	AMD
1857.5	65.96	167.53	AMD
1857.5	66.27	168.33	RDB
1858.5	65.59	166.60	AMD

Table 4.1. (*cont.*)

Date of birth	Mean height		Source
	in	cm	
1859.5	65.32	165.92	AMD
1860.5	65.81	167.16	AMD
1861.5	64.22	163.11	AMD
1862.5	68.00	172.72	RDB
1862.5	65.32	165.90	AMD
1863.5	65.54	166.48	AMD
1864.5	65.83	167.22	AMD
1865.5	65.73	166.96	AMD
1866.5	65.58	166.58	AMD
1867.5	66.33	168.48	AMD
1868.5	66.36	168.54	AMD
1869.5	65.78	167.08	AMD
1870.5	65.98	167.59	AMD
1871.5	65.66	166.77	AMD
1872.5	66.05	167.77	AMD
1872.5	65.98	167.60	AMD
1873.5	65.95	167.52	AMD
1874.5	66.15	168.01	AMD
1875.5	66.03	167.71	AMD
1876.5	65.94	167.48	AMD
1878.5	65.75	167.02	AMD
1879.5	65.44	166.21	AMD
1880.5	65.70	166.89	AMD
1881.5	65.87	167.30	AMD
1882.5	66.28	168.36	AMD
1883.5	66.41	168.68	AMD
1884.5	66.37	168.57	AMD
1885.5	66.24	168.25	AMD
1886.5	66.35	168.53	AMD
Age 22			
1742.5	64.25	163.20	RDB
1747.5	65.41	166.14	RDB
1752.5	65.82	167.18	RDB
1757.5	65.27	165.79	RDB
1762.5	67.15	170.56	RDB
1767.5	67.17	170.61	RDB
1772.5	65.94	167.49	RDB
1777.5	66.43	168.73	RDB
1782.5	66.21	168.17	RDB
1787.5	65.55	166.50	RDB
1792.5	65.84	167.23	RDB
1797.5	66.05	167.77	RDB
1802.5	66.78	169.62	RDB

Table 4.1. (*cont.*)

| Date of birth | Mean height | | Source |
	in	cm	
1807.5	67.41	171.22	RDB
1812.5	67.46	171.35	RDB
1817.5	66.66	169.32	RDB
1822.5	67.91	172.49	RDB
1827.5	67.48	171.40	RDB
1832.5	66.88	169.88	RDB
1837.5	65.36	166.02	AMD
1837.5	64.72	164.39	RDB
1838.5	66.31	168.42	AMD
1839.5	66.37	168.58	AMD
1840.5	66.07	167.82	AMD
1841.5	65.95	167.52	AMD
1842.5	66.64	169.27	RDB
1847.5	65.58	166.57	RDB
1852.5	64.48	163.78	RDB
1854.5	66.11	167.93	AMD
1856.5	65.81	167.16	AMD
1857.5	66.05	167.78	AMD
1857.5	66.38	168.61	RDB
1858.5	65.37	166.04	AMD
1860.5	65.51	166.39	AMD
1861.5	65.09	165.34	AMD
1862.5	67.92	172.52	RDB
1862.5	65.31	165.89	AMD
1863.5	65.94	167.50	AMD
1864.5	66.09	167.87	AMD
1865.5	66.24	168.24	AMD
1866.5	66.42	168.72	AMD
1867.5	66.41	168.68	AMD
1868.5	66.03	167.71	AMD
1869.5	66.24	168.25	AMD
1870.5	66.09	167.86	AMD
1871.5	66.21	168.18	AMD
1872.5	66.56	169.07	AMD
1873.5	66.44	168.75	AMD
1874.5	66.41	168.67	AMD
1875.5	66.49	168.87	AMD
1876.5	66.21	168.16	AMD
1877.5	65.63	166.69	AMD
1878.5	65.13	165.42	AMD
1879.5	66.00	167.63	AMD
1880.5	66.28	168.36	AMD
1881.5	66.33	168.48	AMD
1882.5	66.22	168.19	AMD

Table 4.1. (*cont.*)

Date of birth	Mean height		Source
	in	cm	
1883.5	66.59	169.14	AMD
1884.5	66.47	168.82	AMD
1885.5	66.47	168.82	AMD
Age 23			
1742.5	64.03	162.64	RDB
1747.5	65.88	167.34	RDB
1752.5	65.48	166.32	RDB
1757.5	65.66	166.78	RDB
1762.5	67.05	170.31	RDB
1767.5	67.07	170.36	RDB
1772.5	65.86	167.28	RDB
1777.5	66.47	168.83	RDB
1782.5	66.24	168.25	RDB
1787.5	65.77	167.06	RDB
1792.5	65.73	166.95	RDB
1797.5	66.14	168.00	RDB
1802.5	67.05	170.31	RDB
1807.5	67.40	171.20	RDB
1812.5	67.53	171.53	RDB
1817.5	67.03	170.26	RDB
1822.5	68.07	172.90	RDB
1827.5	68.06	172.87	RDB
1832.5	66.84	169.77	RDB
1836.5	66.12	167.94	AMD
1837.5	66.83	169.75	AMD
1837.5	64.86	164.74	RDB
1838.5	67.25	170.80	AMD
1839.5	65.90	167.38	AMD
1840.5	66.14	167.99	AMD
1842.5	66.49	168.88	RDB
1847.5	64.83	164.67	RDB
1852.5	65.79	167.11	RDB
1853.5	66.25	168.28	AMD
1855.5	66.54	169.00	AMD
1856.5	66.67	169.33	AMD
1857.5	65.25	165.74	AMD
1857.5	66.51	168.94	RDB
1859.5	65.96	167.54	AMD
1860.5	66.13	167.98	AMD
1861.5	66.01	167.66	AMD
1862.5	66.96	170.08	RDB
1862.5	66.28	168.34	AMD

Table 4.1. (*cont.*)

Date of birth	Mean height		Source
	in	cm	
1863.5	66.45	168.78	AMD
1864.5	66.45	168.78	AMD
1865.5	66.69	169.40	AMD
1866.5	66.37	168.57	AMD
1867.5	66.33	168.48	AMD
1868.5	66.43	168.74	AMD
1869.5	66.28	168.36	AMD
1870.5	66.37	168.59	AMD
1871.5	66.76	169.58	AMD
1872.5	66.80	169.67	AMD
1872.5	66.31	168.44	AMD
1873.5	66.86	169.81	AMD
1874.5	66.77	169.61	AMD
1875.5	66.36	168.55	AMD
1876.5	65.85	167.25	AMD
1878.5	66.04	167.74	AMD
1879.5	66.19	168.13	AMD
1880.5	66.42	168.71	AMD
1882.5	66.58	169.12	AMD
1883.5	66.47	168.82	AMD
1884.5	66.77	169.60	AMD
Age 24–29			
1742.5	65.39	166.09	RDB
1747.5	65.22	165.66	RDB
1752.5	65.12	165.40	RDB
1757.5	65.74	166.98	RDB
1762.5	66.84	169.77	RDB
1767.5	66.42	168.71	RDB
1772.5	66.37	168.58	RDB
1777.5	66.30	168.40	RDB
1782.5	65.97	167.56	RDB
1787.5	66.11	167.92	RDB
1792.5	65.84	167.23	RDB
1797.5	66.66	169.32	RDB
1802.5	66.76	169.57	RDB
1807.5	68.09	172.95	RDB
1812.5	67.67	171.88	RDB
1817.5	67.22	170.74	RDB
1822.5	68.02	172.77	RDB
1827.5	66.73	169.49	RDB
1832.5	66.74	169.52	AMD
1834	67.40	171.18	AMD
1835	67.61	171.72	AMD

Table 4.1. (*cont.*)

| Date of birth | Mean height | | Source |
	in	cm	
1836	67.00	170.19	AMD
1837	66.39	168.63	AMD
1837.5	65.71	166.90	RDB
1842.5	66.78	169.62	RDB
1847.5	65.78	167.08	RDB
1850	66.38	168.61	AMD
1852	66.80	169.67	AMD
1852.5	66.00	167.64	RDB
1853	66.53	168.98	AMD
1854	66.10	167.88	AMD
1855	66.71	169.44	AMD
1856	65.81	167.15	AMD
1857	66.57	169.10	AMD
1857.5	66.40	168.66	RDB
1858	66.38	168.60	AMD
1859	66.48	168.86	AMD
1860	67.06	170.32	AMD
1861	66.70	169.41	AMD
1862	67.02	170.23	AMD
1863	66.68	169.36	AMD
1864	66.48	168.86	AMD
1865	66.95	170.05	AMD
1866	66.97	170.10	AMD
1867	67.48	171.40	AMD
1868	67.31	170.96	AMD
1869	66.62	169.21	AMD
1870	67.04	170.29	AMD
1871	67.24	170.79	AMD
1872	66.51	168.94	AMD
1873	66.49	168.88	AMD
1874	66.18	168.10	AMD
1875	66.16	168.06	AMD
1876	66.43	168.73	AMD
1877	66.74	169.51	AMD
1878	66.47	168.84	AMD
1879	66.81	169.69	AMD
1880	66.67	169.34	AMD
1881	66.63	169.23	AMD

Source: see text.

military service altogether, but rather to direct them to military units
with lower standards, such as the Marines for much of the eighteenth
and early nineteenth centuries. In addition, as chapter 3 showed,
the occupational distribution of Marine recruits was very similar to
that of Army recruits, the geographical distribution differing mainly
because the Marines did not recruit in Scotland.

The statistical basis for the decision stems from the fact that examination of the distributions of the heights of Marines alone showed that
there were very few Marines with the taller heights which were fully
represented in the Army height distributions. Thus the Marine height
distributions would seem to under-represent taller heights as well
as being subject to truncation from minimum height standards. The
under-representation seems to operate in a progressive way rather
than as a sharp cut-off, and leaves the appearance of a normal distribution for Marine heights at the taller end of the distribution; the mean
of the distribution cannot, however, reflect the true distribution of
heights in the working class as a whole, since taller recruits appear
in large numbers in other services. The other services, by contrast,
often had minimum standards high enough to exclude 40 to 50 per
cent or even more of the whole distribution; under-representation
of this order leaves the estimates extremely variable. The distributions
of the Marines and of the Army complement each other, and it was
therefore advisable to combine them in some way.

A number of methods of combination were tried. An attempt was
made to estimate the correct weightings of the different services as
part of the same form of maximum likelihood procedure, but this
led to estimates so unstable as to be useless. A second attempt was
made to reweight the services on the basis of somewhat inadequate
information about their relative size in each year, but these procedures
led to distributions of implausible shapes, suggesting that the information was not leading to realistic weights. In the end, the sampling
fractions reflected in the data collection, described in appendix 3.1,
have been taken to be the best available relative weights for the services
and the observations were therefore combined with equal weights.

Support for this decision is found in the observed histograms, cohort
by cohort and age by age. If the balance of the services in the sample
were far out of line with the truth, the histogram would be expected
to show multiple modes and irregular wavy forms or else under-
representation far above the minimum height standards. All of the
hundreds of distributions have been individually scrutinised and,
although aberrant cases are certainly not absent, they are relatively
rare. For recruitment cohorts, where there is less problem of varying

height standards, the maximum likelihood estimates have been compared with estimates made by the quantile bend procedure (Wachter and Trussell 1982: 283) and a general similarity of results was observed.

The quantile bend procedure was used to estimate the mean heights of the Army Medical Department data; these are based exclusively on Army data, with no Marines. Since the population of recruits as a whole, rather than a small sample of them, was measured, the contribution of sampling error to variability is much reduced. The minimum height standards, sometimes reaching far up into the distributions, leave the correction for under-representation somewhat variable, but it is comforting that about the same variability is found in the latter series as in the former, although annual rather than quinquennial estimates can be made.[2]

We turn now to the interpretation of figures 4.1 to 4.3. The dominant pattern in all three is not a steady upward trend, but rather a great cyclical swing from slow increase to moderate decrease to rapid increase. The net trend is upward, but it is broken by downward tendencies among those born after the mid-1840s. The nadir is not very sharply defined but seems to have been reached for those born in the early 1850s or possibly slightly earlier for the older recruits. The reversal in trend occurs just in the period when the AMD data start to replace the RDB samples. Fortunately, there is a little overlap in the estimates from the two sources and we see the beginnings of decrease in the RDB samples for birth cohorts centred on 1852.5, 1857.5 and 1862.5. It therefore seems that the downward trend is not simply an artefact of the transition from one source to another; the series from the two sources mesh very well with each other.

This evidence for a period of decrease in heights is interesting for several reasons, some of which we shall return to in chapter 7. First, it contradicts the popular view of a steady upward 'secular trend' in heights. Second, it is evidence against the view that the third quarter of the nineteenth century was a time of gain for the bulk of the British population; by contrast, the figures suggest that height gains in the late eighteenth and early nineteenth centuries were lost, not to be regained until the twentieth century. Thus the era of the early Industrial Revolution seems on this evidence to have led to an improving standard of living for the working population, while the years of further industrialisation and urbanisation, after the Irish famine

---

[2] It is comforting also that estimates made independently from the same data by S. Rosenbaum (1988), using the method of Cohen (1959) to correct for truncation, give very similar results.

and the repeal of the Corn Laws, stand out as years of retrogression. We discuss why this may have been so in chapter 7.

The decrease in heights is also interesting because it parallels a similar trend in the United States. Fogel (1986) finds a downward trend in US heights for those born after 1830, reaching a nadir for those born sometime after 1870. This decrease is seen in the heights of native-born white males; for the whole population, the decrease was more substantial, due to the shorter heights of most new immigrants.

The smoothed curves shown in the diagrams average several decades, with appropriate weights, and indicate sustained swings in average height levels. It will be observed that there is some evidence for consistent short-term oscillations. For all ages, in particular, there are three or more points well above the smoothed line for quinquennial birth cohorts born around the 1820s and 1830s. There is also a suggestion of points above the smoothed curve for cohorts born in the 1760s and some dipping below the smoothed curve for those born around 1800. There is a great deal of variability in the estimates and it would be a mistake to build too much on such short-term patterns, particularly as they are not wholly consistent throughout the age-groups. Nevertheless, the data may be suggesting the presence of an early cycle in heights, an increase, decrease and increase again with the nadir for those born in the hungry decade of the 1790s and recruited at the end of the Napoleonic Wars.

If we do give credence to the lower points for those born in the 1790s and the higher points for those born in the 1820s and 1830s, then the increase between those periods is much more dramatic than that shown by the smoothed series. For 21-year-olds, the increase was about two inches (5 cm) in three decades, reaching a sustained plateau before the drop in the 1850s. Such an increase matches very well the evidence from the Marine Society discussed below, which suggests a 'great height leap' among the poorest of London boys following the end of the Napoleonic Wars and is even reflected in the heights of the rich boys of Sandhurst.

It is wise, however, to be cautious. The period spanning the Napoleonic Wars was one of extremely rapid change in the demand for recruits. It is not difficult to construct an imaginary scenario which would explain away the short-term oscillations in the series, in line with the discussion of offer bias in the labour market in section 3.3 above. In brief, it is possible that the interplay of military recruitment with the civilian labour market could have produced such an oscillation. If it did, then the drop in heights for those born in the 1790s might be an artefact of such a process, as might the rapidity of the increase thereafter. It might similarly be argued that the data from the third quarter of the nineteenth century might be affected by the Crimean War and that from the 1890s and 1900s by the Boer War.

We do not know that such effects did or did not occur, since there is no independent evidence to which we can turn. The fact of an overall increase in the early period is, however, hard to doubt, since the levels characteristic of the third quarter of the eighteenth century, before the effects of war, are uniformly lower than those of the second quarter of the nineteenth century, after the effects of war. This is true also of the Marine Society data. Similarly, the declining heights of the third quarter of the nineteenth century are sustained through many changes in the labour market so that, although the pace of change may be in doubt, the fact of the decrease is hard to question.

If the rapidity of the decreases and increases is not explained away by the operation of offer bias, then the timing of changes is quite sharply defined. In particular, the effects of the immiseration of the later 1790s is clearly seen among those born and passing through childhood at the time. The rapid increase comes very soon after the war; it appears in the heights of cohorts born after the war as well as in those already into or just past childhood at the time of Waterloo.

All the changes are most dramatic for the 18-year-olds, raising the possibility that the movements have been amplified by mis-statements of age. A varying proportion of younger men may have posed as 18-year-olds in order to join up during wartime. But it is also possible that the effects of nutrition on tempo of growth are responsible, shifting the tempo and age of attainment of final height more than the final height itself.

Figure 4.4 shows the smoothed series for each of the ages from 18 to 23 and for those aged 24–30 on a single plot. The consistency of the different curves is reassuring, especially as the later estimates for different ages are statistically entirely independent. These smoothed curves suggest that substantial growth was still occurring between ages 18 and 19, tapering to about half of that rate between 19 and 21. During the period of decrease in the third quarter of the nineteenth century, growth was postponed to later ages and the majority of the decline is seen in tempo rather than in absolute levels of adult height. As we shall see in chapter 6, this makes good physiological sense. The most dramatic increases in height are seen among 18-year-olds at the onset of the twentieth century, suggesting that the ages of rapid growth were then shifting well below the age of 18 and that differentials in height by age above that age were disappearing, as they have now almost entirely done.

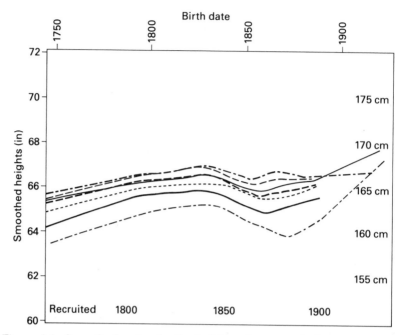

Figure 4.4. Smoothed series for the heights of men aged 18, 19, 20, 21, 22, 23 and 24–30, 1747–1916. Source: see text.

These findings have profound implications for the study of the changing standard of living of the British population in the eighteenth and nineteenth centuries. They suggest that conventional measures of living standards such as real wages or the level of gross domestic product per capita, which show relatively steady upward trend movements, have misled scholars concerned with the impact of industrialisation and economic development on the British people. We return to these findings later in the chapter, but first consider how they relate to other evidence about the height of the British.

4.1.2 Surveys of height in the nineteenth century

The evidence of military height samples can be supplemented from a number of other sources and studies. It is important, however, to make sure that the evidence of such sources is comparable with that provided by the military data and that it is indicative of the national population.

As part of the growth of interest in physical anthropology and anthropometry during the nineteenth century, a number of enquiries were made into heights and other physical characteristics; these are usefully summarised by Boyne and Leitch (1954). The first attempt to arrive at the average height of the entire British population and of that of geographical groups within it was made by Beddoe in 1870, on the basis of evidence supplied to him by friends and others, many of them general practitioners and Army doctors; the majority of the data related to the general population in rural areas, to criminals, to the inhabitants of asylums and to military recruits. Although his was a careful and extensive enquiry, its results suffer from the fact that they are based on non-random samples and, to a large extent, upon military data which had not been adjusted for the effects of the lower height limit. Naturally, since the concept of the secular upward trend in heights had not, at that time, been expressed, Beddoe also took no account of the possible effects of such a trend on his data; for example, he grouped together all those aged between 23 and 50, without examining carefully the profile of heights arranged by the date of birth of the subjects.

Beddoe found that there were differences between different regions and, within them, between different occupations and he speculated about the effect on such differences of the military height standard. His overall conclusion was (1870: 545):

What may be the average stature of adult Englishmen is a matter of speculation and curiosity, on which one cannot give any but a cautious and guarded opinion. Without doubt it lies somewhere between 5 feet 6 inches and 5 feet 7 inches (1.676 and 1.702 metres). The mean of my private returns (excluding those which consist mainly or wholly of picked men) would occur somewhere about 5 feet 6⅔ inches (1.693 metres) . . . The mean of the English lunatic reports would be somewhere about 5 feet 5¾ inches . . . Recruits over 23 years, including rejected men, average . . . about 5 feet 7 inches . . . On the whole, my estimate would be 5 feet 6.6 inches or 1.690 metres.

The average for Scotland must certainly be very much higher, perhaps as high as 5 feet 7½ inches; but this can be little more than a mere guess. That for Ireland cannot differ much from that for England.

Beddoe's conclusions are remarkably close to our own estimates, both in the average height of older recruits and in the contrast between the Scots and their southern compatriots, as will be seen in chapter 5.

Beddoe's enquiry was followed, a decade later, by the work of the Anthropometric Committee of the British Association for the Advancement of Science, whose most influential members were Charles Roberts and Francis Galton. The Committee produced a number of interim reports in which they investigated the anthropometry of various groups and a final report, in 1883, in which they brought together a mass of measurements into summary tables of heights, weights and other characteristics of the British population. This procedure makes it extremely difficult to discover the exact sources of the data which appear in the summary tables, but it is clear that a significant proportion of the evidence came from military recruitment sources, again without any correction for the effects of the military standard. The labouring class in towns was also seriously under-represented in their data and does not appear in the summary tables.

As Boyne and Leitch point out (1954: 259), the British Association report makes a number of estimates of adult height, some of which adjust for discrepancies between the composition of its samples and the geographical and social composition of the national population. The resultant estimates vary between 67.21 and 67.66 inches (170.7 and 171.9 cm). It seems likely that all these estimates were biassed upwards by the use of military height data without adjustment.

Beddoe, Roberts, Galton and others were anxious that there should be a national anthropometric survey and pressure to this end continued throughout the late nineteenth and early twentieth centuries. Such a survey was recommended by the Inter-Departmental Committee on Physical Deterioration which, for the reasons set out above, poured scorn on the use of military data. No survey was held, although the institution of the regular medical inspection of schoolchildren provided some relevant data. Between then and 1980, however, five anthropometric surveys took place which provide evidence approximating to that of a national sample, although each with its own significant differences.

4.1.3 Sample surveys and the evidence of military recruits in the twentieth century

Five large surveys in the twentieth century, together with other material on military recruits, might be thought to put the study of British height on a secure footing. But in fact the interpretation of the material before the 1980s is almost as problematic as is the case with nineteenth-century data. There are at least four reasons. First, the four earlier surveys are clustered in a narrow period between 1935 and 1943, so the observations are poorly spaced for estimating trends. Second, problems of coverage make the series hard to compare; the much-publicised data on military conscripts after 1916, for example, relate to men who were conscripted *after* many of the fittest had enlisted during the first two years of war (Winter 1980). Third, the data are entirely cross-sectional, so that historical trends and ageing effects are confounded in the measurement of height by age. Fourth, many authors have happily averaged changes over long periods, instead of looking critically at the period-by-period changes out of which the larger overall net change in heights has been composed.

Of the four twentieth-century surveys before 1945, the first was published by Cathcart, Hughes and Chalmers in 1935. They reported the results of a survey, taken in 1929–32, of 10 593 male industrial workers aged from 14 to 65 and over. Agricultural and fisheries workers were not represented, but additional samples were taken of undergraduates and of unemployed men. On this basis, they estimated the mean maximum (i.e. at the attainment of full stature) height of the general population as 67.3 inches (170.9 cm).

The other three surveys were all related to the Second World War. Martin (1949) studied the medical examinations of men aged 20–21 conducted under the Military Training Act of 1939; a sample of 91 163 men from all over the country gave a mean of 67.5 inches (171.45 cm). Once war began, a much larger number of men were examined by the medical boards of the Ministry of Labour and National Service, and the records of these examinations were subsequently examined by Clements and Pickett (1952, 1957). They based their findings on samples of 3692 Scotsmen and 21 296 men from England and Wales, all of whom were examined in 1941. These showed that Scotsmen aged 20–26 had a mean height of 66.99 inches (170.15 cm), while men from England and Wales averaged 67.27 inches (170.87 cm); men aged 30–39 were approximately 0.5 inches (1.27 cm) shorter in each case. If the two geographical samples are combined, the mean height for the whole of Britain was 67.23 inches (170.76 cm).

The third wartime sample was analysed by Kemsley (1950). Unlike the two other samples, this survey by the Ministry of Food covered the civilian population and was based essentially on volunteers or on the selection of a 'representative sample' from workplaces, although samples of industrial workers in small firms and of housewives were collected by a commercial survey organisation (1950: 165). 27 515 men and 33 562 women were measured in 1943. As Boyne and Leitch argue (1954: 260–2), the exclusion of men in the armed services is likely to have biassed the results downwards, and it is likely that not all geographical areas were fully represented; nevertheless, the survey showed a maximum mean height (the mean height of the tallest age-group) of 67.34 inches (171.04 cm) for men aged 22, with heights diminishing with age thereafter.

The only direct evidence of trends in the post-war period comes from military records, specifically the heights of Army recruits between 1951 and 1974 reported by Rosenbaum (1988). Table 4.2 reproduces his results. These data are, unfortunately, difficult to compare with other evidence and even lack internal consistency because of changes in military recruitment practice. Recruitment before 1960 was both to the Regular Army, made up of volunteers, and for National Service – the British name for conscription; thereafter, only volunteers were recruited apart from a number of older conscripts who had deferred entry, typically while completing higher education. This practice biasses the age profile of heights of National Servicemen. The records do not, in addition, take account of any truncation by height limits or of the rejection of unhealthy and possibly shorter recruits. At the same time, they give clear evidence of increased average heights since the Second World War. Taking recruits to the Regular Army aged 20–24, for example, heights rose from 172.6 cm (67.95 in) for those recruited in 1951–54, and thus born between 1927 and 1934 in the depths of the economic depression, to 174.1 cm (68.54 in) for those recruited in 1970–74 and thus drawn from the immediate post-war generation, born between 1946 and 1954.

This increase is confirmed by the most recent survey of *Adult Heights and Weights*, the only one to have been based on a properly designed and drawn sample of the entire British population. It was conducted by the Office of Population Censuses and Surveys (Knight and Eldridge 1984) and covered 10 018 men and women aged between 16 and 64. The maximum mean height recorded for any age-group of males was that of 176 cm (69.29 inches) for 20–24-year-olds, with height declining with age thereafter.

In summary, for males in their early twenties, Beddoe's height estimate of 66.7 inches (169.4 cm) may be set beside the four estimates of the 1930–43 period around 67.3 inches (170.9 cm) and beside the good 1983 estimate by Knight and Eldridge of 69.3 inches (176.0 cm). Between 1870 and the 1930s, therefore, growth in average adult height averaged a little less than an inch per century. From the 1930s to the 1980s, growth accelerated to over four-and-a-half inches per century for a net gain of two inches between the Second World War and the early 1980s. Secular change there has certainly been, but whether there has been a secular *trend*, in the sense of a reasonably uniform and enduring pace of change, is a matter of more doubt if the intermediate estimates of the 1930s and 1940s are to be believed.

Are they to be believed? One problem faced both by those who analysed these survey data and by those who, like Boyne and Leitch

Table 4.2. *The heights of recruits to the British Army, 1951–1974 (cm).*

Date of recruitment	Age							
	18		19		20–24		25	
	Regular	National Service	Regular	National Service	Regular	National Service	Regular	National Service
1951–54	172.4	172.3	172.7	172.5	172.6	173.9	171.8	175.3
1955–59	172.1	172.6	172.5	172.6	172.7	173.7	172.0	173.5
1960–64	172.5		172.9		173.0	173.0	172.5	
1965–69	172.9		173.2		173.5		173.3	
1970–74	173.8		174.2		174.1		173.9	

Source: Adapted from Rosenbaum (1988).

(1954) and Morant (1950), attempted to summarise the results, was that all the samples were essentially cross-sectional; that is, they measured a number of men and women, usually of different ages, at a single point in time. There have been no large-scale longitudinal surveys, in which adult individuals were followed and measured throughout their lifetimes, although some children have been measured in this way. Cross-sectional data essentially give a snapshot view of the community at one time, but they inevitably aggregate individuals who, because of their age as well as their economic and social circumstances, have had very different life experiences.

The interpretation of series of mean heights for age, drawn from cross-sectional data, is also a complex task. Figure 4.5, taken from the study by Kemsley of civilians in 1943, shows a typical arrangement of such data, in which heights are shown to be at a maximum for men aged 20, rising to that level from men aged 15 and falling away again until the end of the series, men with a mean age of 72. The problem with such an arrangement, which is certainly a correct representation of heights by age as they were for this population in 1943, is that such a pattern could be produced by at least three distinct phenomena. First, there is growth in height in adolescence (and, for data-sets containing earlier ages, in childhood); second, there is shrinking in height in middle and old age; third, there is change in the environment which alters the nutritional status of the people con-cerned and increases (or possibly decreases) the mean height attained at a given age. If nutritional status in childhood and adulthood has affected mean heights, then it is almost certain that different age-groups within a population such as that in figure 4.5 will have been differentially affected. The men of mean age 72 were born, on average, in 1871 and grew to full height between then and about 1891, during the so-called 'Great Depression' of the late nineteenth century, while the men aged 15 were born in 1928 and grew up during the depression of the 1930s and the early years of the Second World War.

The position is complicated yet more by the fact that the tempo of growth and the age at which final height is attained are also affected by nutritional status. We cannot therefore partition the process under-lying figure 4.5 into two endogenous components, reflecting the innate processes of human maturation, and an exogenous component reflect-ing environmental influences. It is even possible, although there does not appear to have been any study of this, that the rate of shrinkage with middle and old age is also affected by nutritional status; since we know that expectation of life in middle and old age is correlated with height, such a link is a reasonable supposition.

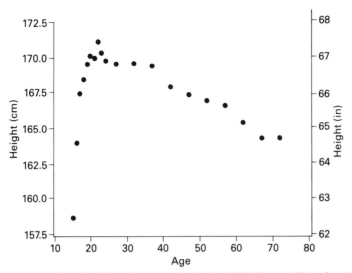

Figure 4.5. The height of a civilian population in 1943. Source: Kemsley (1950).

It is possible to attempt to disentangle some of these complicated relationships and, at the same time, to make it easier to link different cross-sectional studies, by presenting data in an alternative form which is also more suited to historical analysis. Figure 4.6 shows a rearrangement, essentially a mirror-image, of the Kemsley data arranged by the mean dates of birth of the subjects and suggests a substantial increase over time in the mean height of the adults measured in the survey, from a mean height of under 165 cm (63.8 in) for those born in the 1870s to one of over 170 cm (66.9 in) for those born in the 1920s. This latter figure is, however, somewhat problematical because of the puzzling estimate for 21-year-olds, which is much higher than for those slightly older or slightly younger. It seems likely, in fact, that this is an aberration and that the true figure is somewhat lower than 170 cm.

Unfortunately, this increase in the height of adults, which looks so large in figure 4.5, is produced by at least two distinct factors. As Miall *et al.* (1967: 445) put it:

Surveys of adult stature usually show young adults to be taller than their elders. It is generally believed that part of this trend is due to individuals becoming shorter as a result of age changes in the skeleton and in posture and part is due to succeeding generations attaining progressively greater adult statures consequent on secular improvements in living standards.

But how much of the apparent rise in adult height data such as that

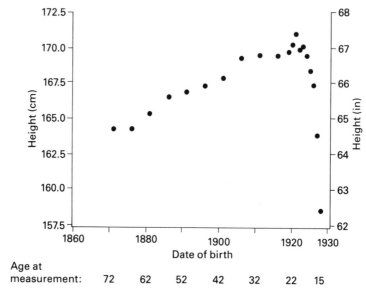

Figure 4.6. The data of figure 4.5 rearranged by the date of birth of the subjects.

analysed by Kemsley is likely to be due to each of these factors? Miall *et al.* measured men and women in two Welsh communities at intervals of six or eight years, and estimated that (1967: 454):

by 70 years of age Vale men would be 1.7 cm, Rhondda men 3.6 cm ... shorter than they had been at age 25. Cross-sectional data ... showed differences in height between subjects aged 25 and 70 to be about 7 cm [and] 6.2 cm ... respectively. The difference between these figures may be largely attributable to secular changes in living standards

although they suggest that disproportionate migration by taller people may also have played a part. Miall *et al.* also speculate that excess mortality of taller people might complicate the picture, but, as they recognise, there is no evidence for this phenomenon; the later work of Waaler (1984) and others suggests instead that shorter people have the higher mortality.[3] In other words, most of the apparent increase in height can be put down to factors other than shrinking by age and, if one is prepared to use the study of Miall *et al.* as typical, it is possible to adjust series such as that of Kemsley to remove the likely effects of shrinking by age. A safer procedure, however, is to make use of another of the findings of Miall *et al.*, that 'estimated

[3] See chapter 6 below.

changes in height from 25 to 45 years were small' although it should be noted that, even within that age-range, there were slight changes: men continued to gain in height between 25 and 35, by 0.3 cm in the Rhondda and 0.7 cm in the Vale of Glamorgan, while men in the Rhondda began to decline in height at 35, men in the Vale only at 40. It makes sense, nevertheless, to concentrate attention, in making comparisons between cross-sectional studies, on that age-range. This procedure will be followed later in this chapter.

4.2 THE HEIGHTS OF CHILDREN AND ADOLESCENTS

While there have been very significant changes in the heights of adults during the past two hundred years, they are dwarfed in absolute size by the changes which have occurred in the heights of children and adolescents. This is not surprising; environmental conditions exert their maximum effect in infancy, childhood and adolescence, while changes in the length of the growing period dampen these effects on adult heights. It is unfortunate, therefore, that it is not possible, through lack of data, to compile series of child or adolescent heights that are as long or as comprehensive as the series for adults. In fact, we know very little indeed about the heights of pre-adolescent children before the latter part of the nineteenth century. In some compensation, the series of adolescent heights which are available for the eighteenth and nineteenth centuries provide contrasts which illustrate dramatically the effects of the environment on growth. We look first, however, at the long-run movements of adolescent heights.

4.2.1 *The heights of adolescents in the eighteenth and nineteenth centuries*

As is the case with data about the heights of adults, information about the heights of children and adolescents is of two kinds. First, there were a number of contemporary studies of the height, weight and health of children, conducted either as part of enquiries into the conditions of factory children or as part of the interest in anthropometry in the latter part of the nineteenth century. Second, information has been collected as part of this study which makes it possible to compile long-run series of the heights of particular groups of adolescents.

The first such series is drawn from the records of the Marine Society of London, whose recruits were briefly described in chapter 3. Founded in 1756 by Jonas Hanway, the Society has since devoted itself to the welfare of seamen, particularly young men joining ships for the first time. Hanway and his City friends had two main objects, to help to man the Navy and to help poor boys from the London slums who would be willing to join the Royal or Merchant Navy but could not afford the sea clothing which they would need.

It is likely that the quasi-military character of its work led to the Society recording the heights of its boys, a practice begun in 1770. It found that naval captains were unwilling to take very short boys, believing that they would be unable to stand up to the naval life, and the Society was therefore forced to institute its own height standards.

Like military height standards, those of the Marine Society were altered over time to control the flow of recruits. In August 1814, for example, it was resolved that, since 'the demands for boys are too small', the height standard should be raised to 4' 6" (137.2 cm) from 4' 3" (129.5 cm), but in May 1815 the standard was lowered again to 4' 4" (132.1 cm) 'as the Society had not got a sufficient number of boys to supply the demands'. The height standards, and the years in which they came into effect, were: 1770 – 51" (129.5 cm); 1786 – 54" (137.2 cm); 1792 – 52" (132.1 cm); 1798 – 54" or 52"; 1809 – 50" (127 cm) or 51"; 1812 – 51"; 1814 – 54" (but 52" for one month in 1815); 1818 – 55" (139.7 cm); 1821 – 56" (142.2 cm); 1824 – 57" (144.8 cm); 1854 – 59" (149.9 cm); 1857 – 57". It does not seem that the age of the boy was of much importance; the height standard was applied irrespective of age and the Society was prepared to accept boys from the age of 12 to 17 or sometimes older.

Like military recruiters, the Society sometimes gave in to requests to admit boys below the official standard. In December 1812, a sub-committee found that a number of boys had been admitted below the height standard of 4' 3" (129.5 cm) which was then in force; they attributed this to the fact that 'the recital of the miseries of suffering humanity has too powerful an influence on the minds' of the committee in charge of admissions (Marine Society 1812). As the sub-committee pointed out, the admission of under-standard boys was ultimately self-defeating, since naval officers would not accept them and, if sent successive boys whom they thought too short, would cease to ask the Marine Society to supply recruits. In addition, the Society would be feeding and housing, on its training ship in the Thames, boys who had no prospect of employment. It was therefore recommended that no boy under the height standard should even be admitted to the offices of the Society, and a rule was set up outside the door so that boys could measure themselves.

The existence of a varying height standard made it necessary, as with regimental recruits, to adjust the observed data for under-representation of short heights. For this purpose, the quantile bend estimator of Wachter (1981) and Wachter and Trussell (1982) was used. This estimator, discussed in chapter 3, differs from the maximum likelihood estimator employed for the Army samples primarily by inferring the extent of under-representation from the shape of the observed distribution rather than by relying on reported minimum height standards. Although height standards are reported in Marine Society minute books, they appear to have been so haphazardly enforced at some periods as to be misleading. The quantile bend estimates are obtained separately for each age-group and birth cohort, so the curves for different ages are statistically independent, an advantage over the regimental estimates. The quantile bend procedures do not permit adjustment for covariates like region or occupation, but the boys were almost all Londoners, and table 3.10 in section 3.2.2 has shown that changes over time in the mix of occupations of boys or of their parents or guardians was slight.

Figure 4.7 shows the estimates of average height for birth cohorts for Marine Society boys aged 13, 14, 15, and 16 from 1755 to 1859. Some suggestive observations from other sources are also included to indicate later trends. These observations will be discussed later in this section, as will the smoothed curves superimposed on the scatter of readings over time for each age. The series for 13-year-olds ends with those born in 1819, because the Society stopped accepting such boys after 1832. A few boys 12 or younger and 17 or older were admitted, but the numbers were too small for analysis. The number of 16-year-olds recruited after 1850 dropped to very low levels, so the later portion of the trend shown for 16-year-olds is uncertain.

The estimates plotted in figure 4.7 are tabulated in table 4.3. In times of heavy recruitment, each cohort spans only a year or so, while in times of lighter recruitment, the cohort spans up to five years. Since the same height standard applied to all ages, the shortfall at low heights is most pronounced for 13-year-olds and least for 16-year-olds. Thus the estimated average heights differ most from the raw mean heights for the youngest group.

Three principal features are apparent in figure 4.7: first, the low overall levels of height; second, the amplification of trends already visible in the adult military data; third, the unprecedented rapidity of the increase in heights among boys born after 1800. The first feature is the most striking and most sobering.

The boys of the Marine Society were extraordinarily short, particularly in the eighteenth century. Thirteen-year-olds born in 1753–1780 average 51.4in (130.6cm), a full 10 inches (25.4cm) less than the children of London measured by Tanner and others in the 1960s. The

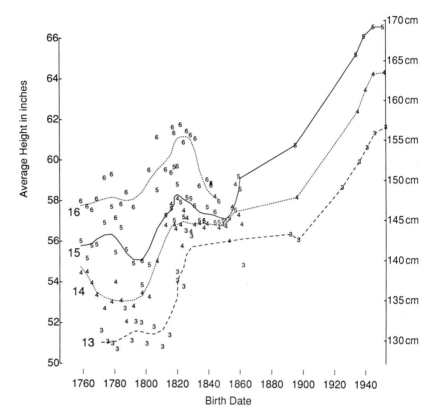

Figure 4.7. The mean height of working-class children since 1758. Source: see text and table 4.3.

full contrast, in both the eighteenth and the early nineteenth centuries, is brought out vividly by figure 4.8, which plots two birth cohorts against the modern British standard growth chart; if a Marine Society boy of 1787 were miraculously transported into a doctor's surgery in 1987, his next step would be into hospital as a sufferer from under-nutrition or child abuse.

The second feature worth noting from figure 4.7 is the accentuation of the dips and rises present in the regimental data, namely the dip for those recruited during the 'Great Immiseration' of the turn of the nineteenth century, the rise after the Treaty of Vienna, and the dip for those recruited after the mid-1840s. The first dip, only hinted at among Army recruits, is conspicuous among these charity boys, especially among 14- and 15-year-olds. Changes in nutrition might be expected to exercise more leverage over heights at ages of rapid

Table 4.3. *The estimated heights of Marine Society recruits, 1758–1859.*

	Estimated height	
Date of birth	in	cm
Age 13		
1771.5	51.59	131.04
1775.5	51.05	129.66
1778.5	50.97	129.45
1781.5	50.67	128.71
1786.5	52.67	133.79
1791	51.09	129.78
1793.5	52.04	132.17
1797	51.98	132.04
1800.5	50.95	129.41
1805	51.78	131.51
1810.5	50.80	129.03
1815	51.38	130.49
1820	54.05	137.29
1825.5	56.50	143.50
1829	56.24	142.84
Age 14		
1758.5	54.43	138.24
1762.5	54.48	138.37
1765.5	53.93	136.98
1768.5	53.33	135.46
1773.5	52.68	133.81
1778	53.00	134.62
1780.5	53.97	137.08
1784	53.07	134.79
1787.5	52.03	132.16
1792	52.79	134.09
1797.5	53.43	135.72
1802	53.25	135.26
1807	55.01	139.72
1812.5	56.77	144.20
1816	57.82	146.87
1818	56.79	144.24
1820	58.09	147.55
1822	56.79	144.25
1824	57.49	146.02
1826	57.13	145.11
1828.5	56.47	143.42
1831	56.80	144.27
1834	56.87	144.44
1837	56.65	143.89
1839	56.85	144.39
1841.5	58.84	149.45
1844	58.20	147.82
1846.5	56.65	143.89

Table 4.3. (*contd.*)

Date of birth	Estimated height	
	in	cm
1849	56.81	144.30
1851	56.72	144.07
1853	56.00	142.25
1855	57.69	146.52
1857	58.80	149.35
1859	57.29	145.50
Age 15		
1758.5	55.98	142.20
1762.5	55.13	140.03
1765.5	55.76	141.63
1768.5	55.81	141.75
1773.5	56.88	144.48
1778	57.67	146.48
1780.5	55.43	140.79
1784	56.64	143.87
1787.5	55.56	141.12
1792	54.90	139.44
1797.5	53.83	136.73
1802	54.82	139.25
1807	58.50	148.58
1812.5	57.25	145.42
1816	57.59	146.28
1818	57.00	144.77
1820	58.78	149.30
1822	57.90	147.07
1824	57.17	145.22
1826	58.14	147.67
1828.5	58.09	147.55
1831	57.73	146.64
1834	57.00	144.79
1837	56.97	144.71
1839	57.66	146.46
1841.5	58.83	149.43
1844	56.90	144.53
1846.5	56.91	144.55
1849	57.02	144.83
1851	56.97	144.70
1853	57.11	145.07
1855	57.62	146.35
1857	57.51	146.07
1859	59.18	150.33
Age 16		
1758.5	57.95	147.19

Table 4.3. (*contd.*)

Date of birth	Estimated height	
	in	cm
1762.5	57.68	146.50
1765.5	57.51	146.08
1768.5	58.05	147.45
1773.5	59.09	150.09
1778	59.27	150.54
1780.5	57.12	145.08
1784	57.80	146.82
1787.5	58.38	148.29
1792	57.65	146.43
1797.5	55.01	139.73
1802	59.48	151.08
1807	61.10	155.19
1812.5	59.50	151.13
1816	59.36	150.77
1818	61.31	155.74
1820	59.67	151.56
1822	61.72	156.77
1824	60.85	154.56
1826	61.41	155.99
1828.5	61.22	155.49
1831.5	61.04	155.04
1834	58.70	149.10
1837	57.00	144.78
1839	59.01	149.89
1841.5	58.74	149.19
1844	57.42	145.84
1846.5	57.94	147.18

Source: Marine Society records.

Note: The heights have been adjusted for truncation, as described in the text.

growth by affecting tempo as well as level, postponing or accelerating whatever part of the adolescent growth spurt boys still experienced under such conditions of overall deprivation. For this reason, it is not surprising that trends should show more clearly among the young, unless one is committed to the view that prenatal or perinatal nutrition must altogether eclipse nutrition during adolescence as a determinant of height by age. As with the regimental data, the Marine Society data are easier to relate to the chronology of historical events if influences near age of recruitment are important and not just influences during gestation and infancy.

Along with the early dip, a sharp rise after the Napoleonic Wars in figure 4.7 agrees with the regimental and Army Medical Department

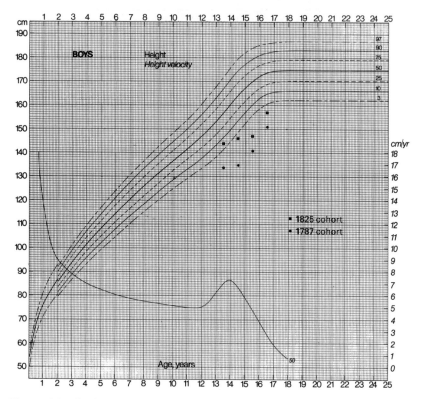

Figure 4.8. The heights of Marine Society recruits plotted against the modern standard. Source: see text. Means estimated by the quantile bend estimator.

estimates in figures 4.1, 4.2 and 4.3. There is also a suggestion of agreement in a drop in height for those admitted after 1845, although it is most pronounced among 16-year-olds and only after the samples become too small to be reliable. The later data points from other sources suggest an eventual rise in heights at the end of the period. These trends are all indicated by the smoothed curves superimposed on the actual estimates. The estimates themselves, as usual, show considerable scatter reflecting the inevitable uncertainties of the adjustment process. The smoothing procedure used here is one developed by Tukey (1977) based on running medians, which gives a clearer picture of transitions here than the lowess procedure used elsewhere in this book. After the Marine Society data end, the curves are simply extended through the occasional later points from other sources to present to the eye an overall sense of trend.

The third striking feature of figure 4.7 is the rapidity of the rise in heights for those born after 1800 and recruited after about 1815. Heights rise to levels three to five inches (7.6 to 12.7 cm) above previous levels. This 'great height leap' among poor London boys is, to our knowledge, the largest and most abrupt change in the cross-sectional profile of height by age for any large group yet reported. Taken at face value, it suggests that the poorest of the London poor were major and immediate beneficiaries of the fall in prices, especially in prices of foodstuffs, that followed the end of the Napoleonic Wars. As we shall discuss in chapter 7, this fall in prices propelled a rise in real wages that is one of the few movements on which all the alternative estimates of real wage series agree.

There is, however, some question as to whether the rapidity of the great height leap should be taken at face value, for the same reasons as have been mentioned in section 4.1.1 in connection with regimental recruits. Rapidly changing labour demand at the start and end of the war might have created 'offer bias' in the group of boys actually presenting themselves to the Marine Society for aid. In the case of the Marine Society, the greater part of the leap in heights at each age is concentrated between one pair or two pairs of birth cohorts, over less than a decade, and it is found precisely at a period when the numbers of boys accepted at these ages also changed abruptly. As before, it is the rapidity of the change that is at issue, for the higher levels are sustained for three decades or more, through many further changes in labour markets, and so cannot easily be ascribed to short-term mechanisms of this kind. With a change as dramatic as this one, the question also arises as to whether improvements in general nutrition, say protein and calorie intake, are most likely to be responsible, or whether there is a need to appeal to other proximate determinants of height. These are delicate scientific questions, on which we do not wish to be dogmatic; they deserve further study.

An important reason for believing the overall trends shown by the Marine Society data is the close agreement of the later estimates with a handful of other samples of children's heights in other areas of Britain. The earliest contemporary survey of the heights of working-class children dates from the 1830s. Three more were made before the 1880s. All stem from enquiries into the condition of children in factories and are described at length by Tanner, who reprints their statistical findings (1981: 147–61, 168–72).

The first, by Samuel Stanway and J. W. Cowell, appeared in the report of the Factory Commission of 1833 and related to the heights of 1933 children aged 9 to 18 in Manchester and Stockport (PP 1833 xx: 697). The second, by Lionel Horner, one of the early Factory Inspectors, reported the results of examinations of 8469 boys and 7633 girls aged 8 to 14 in a number of towns and contiguous rural areas in Lancashire and Yorkshire (Horner 1837: 270–2). The third, by J. H. Bridges and T. Holmes, examined just under 10 000 children aged between 8 and 12 in Yorkshire, Cheshire and Lancashire (PP 1873 xv: 847–53). In addition, the results of the enquiries by Bridges and Holmes were used by Charles Roberts, who added to them 'all the statistics of the absolute heights (without shoes) of males in this country which I have been able to collect' (1874–76: 19). Many of these results, together with others collected by the Committee, were used again in the report of the Anthropometric Committee of the British Association (1883).

None of the surveys related to London; a direct comparison with the Marine Society is therefore impossible, but table 4.4 shows that the heights of Marine Society children in the 1830s were very close to those found by Cowell, Stanway and Horner. The Marine Society heights do not, however, rise significantly between the 1830s and the conclusion of the series with children born in the 1850s, whereas the Bridges and Holmes sample of the 1870s does suggest an increase, although the difference remains small. Larger differences exist between the Marine Society data and the Bridges and Holmes sample, on the one hand, and the results for urban artisans reported by the Anthropometric Committee of the British Association for the Advancement of Science in 1883 (BAAS 1883), although it seems likely that, for the older age-groups at least, the problem of the military height standard is a serious one.[4] Such comparisons are, however, too sparse and too distant in space to do more than allay fears that one or the other group is highly aberrant.

It must always be remembered that both the Marine Society and the factory children were drawn from the manual working class and that those who sought help from the Marine Society were among the most deprived of that class. It would be illegitimate, therefore, to regard the evidence of these children as providing in any sense a random sample of the children of Britain and Ireland in the eighteenth and nineteenth centuries, even to the extent that, as we argued in chapters 2 and 3, the military recruits can be so regarded as a

---

[4] A substantial part of the data collected and published by the British Association came from recruitment records or the observations of Army medical officers; there is no reason to believe that any correction was applied to this material to take account of the operation of the height standard. Nor, unfortunately, it is possible to isolate data of this kind from the other material collected by the British Association.

Table 4.4. The heights (in inches) of adolescent working-class boys in the mid nineteenth century.

Age	1 1833	2 1833	3 1833	4 1837	5 1873	6 1873	7 1873	8 1873	9 1873	10 1873
9		48.14	48.56	47.88		48.05	49.21	49.37	48.35	48.30
10		49.79	50.65	49.44		49.77	51.00	51.02	49.63	50.41
11		51.26	51.01	50.72		51.44	52.87	52.57	51.36	51.76
12		53.38	52.96	52.00		52.82	54.05	53.56	52.64	53.18
13	54.05	54.48	54.97	53.76						
14	56.79	56.59	56.63	55.75						
15	57.00	59.64	58.02		57.29					
16	59.36	61.60	63.20		57.51					
17		62.67	64.07							
18		63.32	69.89							

Sources:

Column 1: Recruits to the Marine Society. Taken from the records of the Society. Estimated mean height, after correction for truncation, for the relevant recruitment cohort.

Column 2: Factory Commission. Boys employed in factories (Cowell 1833).

Column 3: Factory Commission. Boys not employed in factories (Cowell 1833).

Column 4: Children from Manchester, Bolton, Stockport, Preston, Leeds, Halifax, Rochdale, Huddersfield, Skipton and neighbouring rural districts (Horner 1837).

Column 5: As column 1.

Column 6: Children in schools in Lancashire, Cheshire and West Riding: factory children of factory parents (urban and suburban) (Bridges and Holmes 1873).

Column 7: Children from schools as in column 6: children in non-factory districts (urban and rural).

Column 8: Children from schools as in column 6: non-factory children of non-factory parents in factory districts (urban and suburban).

Column 9: Children from schools as in column 6: urban factory children.

Column 10: Children from schools as in column 6: suburban factory children.

sample of the working class. The interest of the Marine Society and factory children lies, instead, in the picture that they provide of the nutritional status of children under some of the most difficult conditions of growth in urban areas during the period of British industrialisation.

It is particularly fortunate, therefore, that the only other sources of evidence about the heights of adolescents in the nineteenth century come from institutions which were far distant in social terms from the Marine Society. The Royal Military Academy at Sandhurst was established in 1806 as a school and training establishment for future Army officers. For the first years of its existence it catered for boys of 12–16, but from the 1850s it specialised instead in young men of 16–20. Almost all were the sons of members of the British upper classes; the names of the fathers of the recruits are entered in the Description Books and provide a catalogue of peers, clergymen and army and naval officers. While there was some differentiation in the fees which were paid, based on the income of the parents, the cadets came from a narrow segment at the top of the British class and income distribution.

Figure 4.9 displays the heights of the Sandhurst cadets and table 4.5 gives the underlying data. It was not necessary to adjust the observed data to take account of the Army height standard; it seems that upper-class boys could pass the standard with ease and the observed distributions are very close to normal. Figure 4.9 has two striking features. First, the cadets were very tall by the standards of the Marine Society, though still short by comparison with upper-class adolescents of today; this is also made clear by figure 4.10, on which a Sandhurst cohort has been plotted next both to the modern standard and to cohorts from the Marine Society. Second, there exist substantial movements in the heights of the recruits over time.

Further evidence about the heights of the upper classes was gathered later in the century by a number of observers, often inspired and guided by Francis Galton. An example is the set of cross-sectional measurements made at Marlborough College by Fergus and Rodwell (1874–75), but Galton himself reported shortly afterwards the results of measurements at a number of other public schools. He found that boys at the country schools, Marlborough, Clifton, Haileybury, Wellington and Eton, were significantly taller than those at town schools; the boys from country schools also seem close in heights to the slightly older boys at Sandhurst. Galton also collected data on the heights of the upper and professional classes at his Anthropological Laboratory in South Kensington; some of these data are described in the

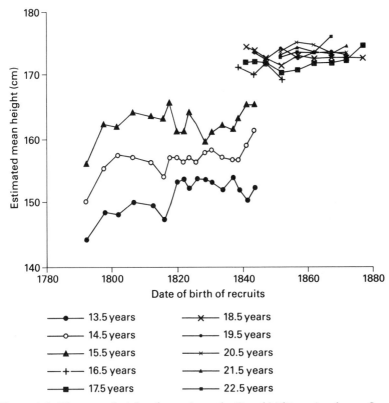

Figure 4.9. The mean height of recruits to the Royal Military Academy, Sandhurst, by age and date of birth, 1792–1877. Source: table 4.5.

British Association report of 1883. As Rosenbaum (1988) points out,
the report of 1879 also contains information on the heights of boys
at Christ's Hospital.

4.2.2 Children and adolescents in the twentieth century

One of the few tangible results of the work of the Inter-Departmental
Committee on Physical Deterioration was the passage, in 1907, of
the Education (Administrative Provisions) Act which laid upon the
local education authorities in England and Wales the duty of providing
for the medical inspection of children in the public (i.e. state) elementary schools. In setting out these duties, the Board of Education made
it clear that the recording of the heights and weights of children was
to form part of the routine of medical inspection, while, in August

Table 4.5. *The estimated heights of Sandhurst recruits.*

	Mean height	
Date of birth	in	cm
Age 13		
1792	56.73	144.09
1797.5	58.36	148.24
1802	58.36	148.24
1807	59.12	150.15
1812.5	58.87	149.52
1816	58.00	147.32
1818	58.97	149.79
1820	60.23	152.98
1822	60.45	153.54
1824	59.81	151.91
1826	60.46	153.58
1828.5	60.39	153.40
1831	60.28	153.11
1834	59.89	152.11
1837	60.65	154.04
1839	59.79	151.87
1841.5	59.25	150.50
1844	59.91	152.18
Age 14		
1792	59.06	150.02
1797.5	61.25	155.58
1802	62.05	157.61
1807	61.79	156.94
1812.5	61.50	156.22
1816	60.64	154.03
1818	61.76	156.87
1820	61.88	157.17
1822	61.57	156.39
1824	61.78	156.92
1826	61.59	156.44
1828.5	62.19	157.97
1831	62.27	158.16
1834	61.80	156.97
1837	61.71	156.73
1839	61.74	156.81
1841.5	62.60	159.01
1844	63.61	161.56
Age 15		
1792	61.38	155.89
1797.5	63.77	161.97
1802	63.67	161.71
1807	64.61	164.12

Table 4.5. (*contd.*)

Date of birth	Mean height	
	in	cm
1812.5	64.38	163.52
1816	64.15	162.95
1818	65.00	165.10
1820	63.36	160.93
1822	63.33	160.87
1824	64.46	163.73
1826	63.92	162.35
1828.5	62.79	159.48
1831	63.43	161.11
1834	63.82	162.10
1837	63.54	161.38
1839	64.22	163.12
1841.5	65.00	165.10
1844	65.11	165.38
Age 16		
1839	67.33	171.03
1844	66.93	170.00
1847.5	67.65	171.84
1852.5	66.65	169.29
Age 17		
1841.5	67.66	171.86
1844	67.76	172.12
1847.5	67.70	171.95
1852.5	67.14	170.54
1857.5	67.21	170.71
1862.5	67.77	172.13
1867.5	67.68	171.90
1872.5	67.88	172.41
1877.5	68.71	174.53
Age 18		
1841.5	68.59	174.21
1844	68.38	173.68
1847.5	68.04	172.82
1852.5	67.57	171.62
1857.5	68.11	173.00
1862.5	67.93	172.53
1868	67.96	172.63
1872.5	68.09	172.94
1877.5	68.00	172.72
Age 19		
1844	68.44	173.83
1847.5	67.91	172.49

Table 4.5. (*contd.*)

Date of birth	Mean height	
	in	cm
1852.5	68.64	174.34
1857.5	67.94	172.57
1862.5	68.32	173.54
1867.5	68.36	173.63
1872.5	68.20	173.22
Age 20		
1852.5	68.44	173.85
1857.5	68.93	175.07
1862.5	68.75	174.63
1867.5	68.25	173.36
1872.5	68.28	173.44
Age 21		
1852.5	68.23	173.31
1857.5	68.71	174.53
1862.5	68.33	173.55
1867.5	67.81	172.23
1872.5	68.72	174.56
Age 22		
1852.5	68.07	172.90
1857.5	68.39	173.71
1862.5	68.35	173.60
1867.5	69.36	176.18

Source: Records of the Royal Military Academy, Sandhurst.
Note: No adjustment has been made for truncation; inspection of the height distributions indicated that no truncation operated.

1908, it was further stated that the annual reports of School Medical Officers should include 'tables showing the height and weight of children inspected (according to age at date of inspection and sex)' (Greenwood 1913: 2).

The 1907 Act thus began the ritual of medical inspection remembered by all English schoolchildren educated between then and 1974, when the School Medical Service disappeared and routine medical inspection ceased. During that period, weighing and measuring – normally at the ages of 5, 8 and 13 – formed part of the process of identifying those children who required medical or social work attention. The Act was much less successful in ensuring that the statistical results of the inspections should be put to the use which the Inter-Departmental Committee had envisaged, that of providing a means for constantly monitoring the state of the nation's physical health. Not all School

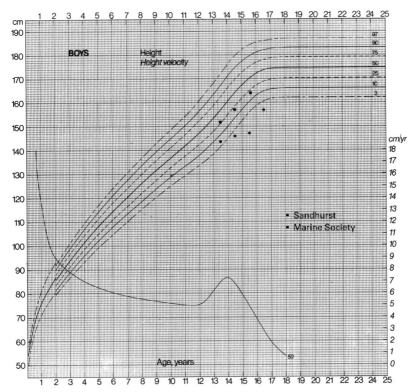

Figure 4.10. The heights of Sandhurst and Marine Society recruits plotted against the modern standard. Source: see text. Marine Society heights are estimated by the quantile bend estimator.

Medical Officers published their results and only sporadic attempts were made to collate them on a national basis. It follows that, despite the millions of man-hours which must have been devoted to this part of medical inspection, there are still major difficulties in discovering what happened to the heights of British children and adolescents in the twentieth century. It is especially unfortunate that the published results of the only attempt to collate these records, the article by Boyne, Aitken and Leitch (1957), gives the results only in graphical form. Worse still, the records of this survey of data from 12 cities, 73 county boroughs and 61 counties over the period 1911 to 1953 were destroyed by the Rowett Research Institute in the 1980s.

Immediately after the onset of medical inspection, the results of the new process were used in two studies, by Tuxford and Glegg (1911) and by Greenwood (1913), using essentially the same material and with very similar results. Greenwood, for example, gathered together the results of medical inspections in 1908, 1909, and 1910, with a few from 1911, a total of over 800000 children aged between 3 and 15. Although Greenwood does not comment on the fact, it is clear from the results which he presents that the bulk of inspections were of children aged 5, 7, 10, 12 and 13, while much smaller numbers were inspected at other ages. There must be some suspicion that only selected children, presumably those with some obvious signs of ill-health, were inspected at the other ages. The growth profile is, however, quite smooth and consistent with the results of the British Association a generation earlier. As Tanner comments:

The means are slightly below those of the Anthropometric Committee of the British Association of 1883, by about 2.5cm at all ages in boys, and 2cm in girls at ages 13–15; in girls of 3–12 there is no difference. Greenwood explains that the Anthropometric Committee was able to include rich children in private schools, excluded from his data, and in contrast failed to obtain adequate representation of social class V (the lowest) which he thinks better represented in his survey. (Tanner 1981: 215)

The next systematic attempt to use the records of school medical inspection for a nationwide assessment and for comparison over time was not made until 1957, when Boyne, Aitken and Leitch published their survey of secular change in the height of children.[5] Their published report is unfortunately abbreviated, but they concluded, on the basis of the records of over 1180000 measurements of schoolchildren, that:

The analysis shows clear upward trends of height and weight, and of the weight : height ratio over the time under review (1911–1953), with acceleration since 1945. The same trends are found in measurements from such individual centres as provide long series, and so are not artefacts due to the representation of different centres in the several annual samples. (1957: 15)

More recently, Bernard Harris (1989) has collected together all the published reports of the School Medical Officers in order to examine the statistics of height and weight compiled during the inter-war period.

School medical reports of various kinds do not exhaust the twentieth-century studies of child growth, many of which are described in Tanner (1981: ch. 14). The London County Council was particularly active in the field of child health and, between 1904 and 1966, conducted 11 surveys of schoolchildren; the results have been collated

---

[5] There had, of course, been a number of earlier studies of parts of the country; see, for example, Keddie (1956).

and analysed by Cameron (1979). The height of London children rose between 1904 and 1949 and, with 'a considerable post-war acceleration' between 1949 and 1954, before slower growth for the remainder of the 1950s and, Cameron suggests, little if any upward movement between 1959 and 1966. Outside London, however, the National Study of Health and Growth has been used by Chinn and Rona to suggest that the upward secular trend in height may have continued between 1972 and 1979 (1984: 1) though at a slow rate. In comparing their figures with those of Cameron they conclude that (1984: 13):

> the secular trend in height was continuing during the 1970s ... Cameron (1979) calculated secular trends for several periods covering the years 1905–1966, using the LCC survey data. He reported trends by age-group, and mean trends for the age range 5.0–16.0 years, so that comparison with the NSHG estimates is a little difficult. However, the NSHG estimates for English children of 0.77 cm/decade for boys and 0.46 cm/decade for girls are certainly less than those reported by Cameron for any period during 1905 to 1954, and probably comparable to those reported for 1954 to 1959.

while, they suggest, the onset of mass unemployment during the 1970s may mean that the upward trend has ceased or, possibly, been reversed.

The school medical data, relating as it does initially to elementary schools and, later, to primary and secondary schools within the state system, provides an approximate basis for comparison with data on the working classes during the nineteenth century. For data to compare with the measurements from Sandhurst and the nineteenth-century public schools, it is necessary to turn to measurements in those schools during this century. Early in the century Mumford (1912) reported on the physique of boys at Manchester Grammar School, while much later, in 1960, Leitch and Boyne surveyed data from Eton, Marlborough and Mill Hill School (1960). Of these groups, only the boys of Eton, presumably at the peak of the class structure, showed no increase in height between 1937 and 1957. The data are, however, extremely limited in coverage, even of the private sector of education, and the results must be treated with caution. The same applies to studies of university students, some of which also show limited growth in average height during the twentieth century (Bailey 1951).

Rosenbaum has recently (1988) drawn attention to a series of measurements from a school which occupies an intermediate position between the state and public schools, independent of the state system but admitting only boys of parents of moderate means. Christ's Hospital, which had figured in the reports of the Anthropometric Committee of the British Association, continued to measure its boys between

1905 and 1933 and the results were reported by its medical officer (Friend 1935). Rosenbaum has republished these figures, with some corrections and additions, and has added to them measurements of children who had left the school in the four years before 1986. Table 4.6 reproduces the resultant changes between the 1870s and the 1980s for boys aged 10–18.[6] As the table shows, there was an increase for 14-year-old boys from an average height of 146.6 cm (57.72 in) in the 1870s to 149.9 cm (59.02 in) just before the First World War, to 155.6 cm (61.25 in) in the early 1930s and to 161.6 cm (63.62 in) in the mid-1980s; this is an overall increase of 15 cm (5.9 in) over 110 years.

4.3 TRENDS IN BRITISH HEIGHTS

A full picture of the changes which have occurred in average British heights over the last 250 years requires piecing together all the disparate sources mentioned in the previous two sections. When all the estimates are set beside each other, as in figures 4.11 and 4.12, a surprisingly consistent picture emerges. The consistency is all the more surprising when one considers that few of the surveys or sources are exactly comparable. There are many dangers in using the data which have been described in the first two sections of this chapter to draw a picture of long-term change in British heights. Few of the surveys or sources of height information are exactly comparable one with another, many rely on statistical adjustment of imperfect data and many sources are deficient in their descriptions of the populations from which samples were drawn, of the sampling methods that were used and of the methods of measurement. All these factors are reasons for caution in drawing inferences, especially about short-term changes. But the diversity of sources which all lead to a single general picture of long-term changes gives ground for some confidence in the results.

The figures mentioned above show that, over a period of nearly 250 years, British adult heights estimated from military records have risen from a mean of just over 165 cm (64.97 in) during the middle of the eighteenth century to a mean of just over 175 cm (68.90 in) for men born at the end of the 1950s. During the same period, the heights of working-class adolescents, aged 14, rose from approximately 135 cm (53.15 in) to just under 164 cm (64.57 in), while the

---

[6] We are most grateful to Mr Rosenbaum for allowing us to see these statistics in advance of publication.

Table 4.6. *The heights of boys at Christ's Hospital from the 1870s to the 1980s (cm).*

Date of Measurement	10	11	12	13	Age 14	15	16	17	18
1870s	130.1	133.5	137.8	141.8	146.6	151.3	160.1	168.3	172.2
1906–18	132.7	136.0	140.4	145.1	149.9	156.3	163.1	169.8	172.5
1919–22	132.4	136.7	142.4	146.8	152.0	158.5	165.0	170.8	173.4
1923–26	135.2	139.3	143.5	148.1	154.0	160.7	166.7	171.2	173.8
1927–30	135.7	139.5	143.6	148.7	154.7	161.2	166.8	172.1	174.1
1931–33	136.0	141.0	145.3	149.5	155.6	162.2	168.2	176.1	
1986		143.7	148.1	154.2	161.6	168.9	173.5		

Source: Adapted from Rosenbaum (1988).

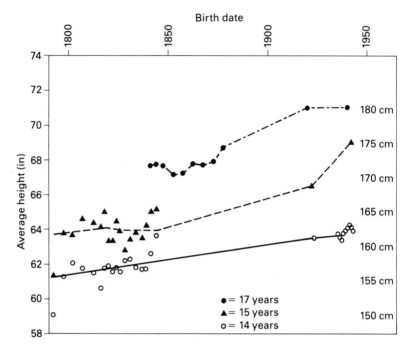

Figure 4.11 The heights of upper-class adolescents, 1790–1950. Source: see text.

heights of upper-class boys of the same age rose from approximately 150 cm (59.06 in) at the beginning of the nineteenth century to approximately 169 cm (66.54 in), although the latter figure is particularly tentative.

In other words, British adult male heights have risen on average by about 10 cm (3.94 in) during 250 years, while over the same period the heights of working-class 14-year-olds have increased by about 29 cm (11.42 in) and the heights of upper-class 14-year-olds by about 19 cm (7.48 in). A working-class boy of 14 is now almost as tall as a working-class adult male of the mid-eighteenth century.

A very large number of qualifications need to be attached to these statements. The boys of the Marine Society were drawn from the London slums, while the modern standard of Tanner and Whitehouse relies on measurements of children from the whole range of London state schools in the 1960s; similarly, the soldiers of the mid-eighteenth century represent a segment of the population which does not exactly correspond to the OPCS sample of British male adults in 1980. These

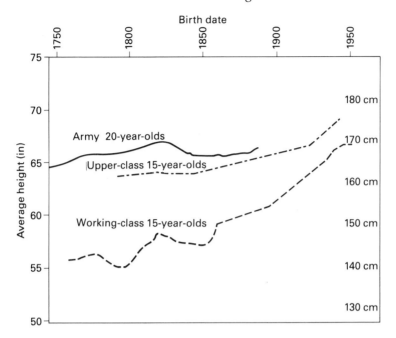

Figure 4.12. Heights in Britain, 1750–1950. Source: see text.

qualifications must always be emphasised and borne in mind; but the overall pattern is clear.

Caution becomes even more imperative as shorter periods become the subject for study. It is possible, however, to discern some features of the data which are common to all three sets of figures and thus to different sources of data and different social groups. First, all show substantial increases in height for boys and men born at and immediately after the end of the eighteenth century. Second, after that growth came a period of stability or, certainly in the case of the adult series and possibly in the case of the working-class teenagers, a downward movement lasting for about a quarter of a century. Third, there has been a period of sustained long-term growth during the twentieth century, perhaps ending with the 1960s or 1970s.

Modern evidence suggests that improvements in nutritional status will be reflected both in absolute increases in heights and in earlier maturation; in other words, as nutritional status improves, people will achieve both a given level of height at an earlier age and ultimately a greater final height. It is conventional to examine the tempo of growth particularly by discovering both the age at peak height velocity in adolescence and the age at which final height is achieved; both can be clearly seen in growth charts.

Tanner (1982: 575) suggests that, while increases in tempo and in absolute height are positively correlated, the correlation is not perfect; some groups of people, for example, grow faster than others but do not achieve a greater final height. Other groups grow slowly but continue growing longer to reach a greater final height:

A population which is short at age 14 may be so either because its children are delayed in growth (in which case they may reach a considerable height as adults) or because they are simply short – before, then, and later with average tempo. As for trends within a single population, in historical data increasing mature size usually is accompanied by increasing tempo of growth. But the two should certainly not be regarded as inseparable; at least in theory a trend in tempo might continue beyond the point at which a trend in mature size finished, or even vice versa. Until we know more about the physiological determinants of each of the processes an open mind should be kept on this question.

In general (although this topic is further examined in chapter 6), it seems likely that substantial increases in heights in the past would have been accompanied by increases in the tempo of growth.

It is of interest, therefore, to examine the military and associated height data for evidence of the tempo of growth. Unfortunately, no one set of the data permits us to observe both the age of maximum mean increment of height in adolescence (the equivalent for a population of the age of peak height velocity for an individual) and the age at final height for the same group of men. We are forced to examine adolescents using data from the Marine Society and Sandhurst, but can look at adults only by using military data.

It must first be asked whether the Marine Society evidence on maximum mean increment can be believed. After all, height velocity is calculated as the difference between two observations of mean height, which in the case of the Marine Society evidence are themselves estimated from truncated distributions; any errors in the estimation procedures and any sample biasses will be magnified in the calculation of velocities. This question was considered at some length in Floud and Wachter (1982: 440–3) where the Marine Society patterns of growth were compared with evidence from 81 modern samples tabulated by Eveleth and Tanner (1976) to show that the Marine Society data do not seem out of line with modern experience. In addition, as Tanner comments, the implied age at maximum mean increment, of about 14.5 years:

would not be out of line with values obtained from studies of factory children and adolescents in the 1830s (Tanner 1981: 116, 149) and from studies of boys transported to Australia as convicts at a similar date (Tanner 1981: 116, 149, 159). (1982: 576)

It does not seem that the tempo of growth of the Marine Society children altered very much during the period of observation. Table 4.7 is based on the heights of children at the age of 14 and at the age of 16 and compares those heights with 18-year-old and adult heights for the same birthdates; these are taken from the military samples, making an adjustment for London origin and occupation of labourer (from the results of the maximum likelihood estimations), to give the best comparator possible. The table also shows similar statistics drawn from the British Association collections of the 1880s and from the United Kingdom in the modern period (Eveleth and Tanner 1976: 277 ff). The table shows that Marine Society birth cohorts were consistently short by modern standards and that they had a slower tempo of growth, but that there are some signs that tempo increased, between the late eighteenth and the early nineteenth centuries, at the time of the marked increase in absolute height which we have called the great height leap. The speeding up is relatively slight, however, which suggests that there may have been some feature of the malnutrition experienced by the Marine Society children in the 1700s which was particularly adverse to growth in size but had less effect on the timing and relative contribution to final height of the growth spurt. Tanner, in fact, suggests that (1982: 576):

The Marine Society children, therefore, were stunted, but without having their growth tempo slowed down in the way that Guarinoni describes for children living in the countryside in the seventeenth century. At least in modern data, such marked stunting with only a minor degree of delay characterises children who have suffered some sort of privation very early in their growth period.

We shall return to possible causes in chapter 6.

The evidence of military records also fails to suggest that there were any striking changes in the tempo of growth; although a comparison of 18-year-old and final heights in table 4.7 shows a small increase, this is not statistically significant. However, there is some evidence of a slight change in tempo, not in the eighteenth century at all, but in the second half of the nineteenth century. The modern evidence discussed by Tanner suggests that there should be a positive correlation, though imperfect, between tempo and absolute height, and this can be tested by regressing the proportion of adult height which has been achieved at a particular age on adult height itself. Such a procedure shows no significant relationship at all in the

Table 4.7. *Evidence on the tempo of growth; height during growth as a percentage of final height (aged 24–29), Marine Society, Army and Marines, 1756–1960s.*

Birth cohort	Marine Society		Army and Marines
	Height at age 14 (%)	Height at age 16 (%)	Height at age 18 (%)
1756	83	89	97
1761	83	87	96
1764	81	85	99
1767	81	88	99
1770	80	89	97
1777	81	90	97
1779	82	88	99
1782	81	88	99
1786	79	89	96
1789	81	89	98
1795	81	84	98
1800	80	89	98
1804	82	91	97
1810	84	88	99
1815	86	88	98
1817	83	91	98
1819	84	88	97
1821	84	91	97
1823	84	90	97
1825	86	92	100
1827	85	92	100
1830	85	91	100
1883	85	94	99
1960s	88	92	98

Sources:
1756–1830 Marine Society birth cohorts compared with Army/Royal Marine RDB sample estimates, adjusted for London birth and occupation as labourer.
1883 British Association for the Advancement of Science: Town Artisans.
1960s Eveleth and Tanner (1976: 277).

eighteenth century, but between 1861 and 1890 the relationship has the form

$$x = 221.3 - 1.84\,y \qquad R^2 = 0.76$$

where x = height at age 20 as a percentage of height at age 24–29

and y = height at age 24–29

Contrary to expectation, the coefficient has a negative sign. The same relationship is found for other ages, suggesting that there was a slight reduction in tempo in this period, when absolute height was showing either a slight overall increase or, as in the case of height at age 24–29, no overall trend against time. It seems clear, however, that there have been changes in tempo during the nineteenth and twentieth centuries, although there is still a paucity of data covering both adolescent and adult heights.

It is clear that the evidence of tempo, such as it is, does not conflict with the evidence of absolute height. Taken as a whole, the data suggest a substantial increase in nutritional status in the period, with most of the improvement occurring in the eighteenth and the beginning of the nineteenth century and in a longer period during the twentieth century. This growth was accompanied, in the latter period, by substantial increases in the tempo of growth. Last, the fact that the heights of working-class children have risen at almost 150% of the rate of increase of the heights of upper-class children suggests that there has been a substantial narrowing of class differentials in height.

Can we believe these findings? This question can be answered in at least three ways. First, we can examine the statistical properties of the estimates. Second, we can compare the apparent pattern of British and Irish heights with that found in other countries. Third, we can compare the height data with other indicators of nutritional status and the standard of living.

4.3.1 Statistical issues

We discussed, in the last chapter, the need to make substantial adjustments to the original recruitment data in order to compensate for the effects of the height standards imposed by the Army and Marines. Figures 4.1–4.3 were based on such adjustments, carried out for birth cohorts up to the 1860s by the reduced sample maximum likelihood estimator described in chapter 3. This procedure estimates both the mean and the standard deviation of a distribution of heights from a particular group of recruits; the means were given in table 4.1. Note that the means shown in table 4.1 do not exactly correspond with the estimated mean heights shown in figures 4.1–4.3. Table 4.1 shows the estimated mean of the excluded categories in the maximum likeli-

Table 4.8. *Reduced sample maximum likelihood estimates of British military heights (inches).*

| Birth cohort | 'Best estimate' | | Estimate of mean when SD fixed at 2.3 in |
	Mean	Standard deviation (SD)	
1750–54	63.04	2.62	
1755–59	63.80	2.61	
1760–64	64.18	2.54	
1765–69	65.65	2.18	
1770–74	64.17	2.47	
1775–79	64.26	2.36	
1780–84	65.07	2.31	
1785–89	63.63	2.61	
1790–94	63.97	2.51	
1795–99	65.02	2.24	64.94
1800–04	65.14	1.93	64.20
1805–09	64.94	2.05	64.21
1810–14	66.78	1.82	66.18
1815–19	65.50	2.02	64.70
1820–24	65.97	1.80	64.74
1825–29	66.74	1.82	65.83
1830–34	66.06	2.15	65.91
1835–39	62.32	2.72	
1840–44	64.25	2.25	64.17
1845–49	63.58	2.33	
1850–54	61.98	2.47	
1855–59	63.45	2.11	
1860–64	66.23	1.41	63.96

Source: RDB samples.

hood estimation (English urban, apprenticed non-building trades, 18-year-old) while figures 4.1–4.3 are weighted to estimate the mean height of the whole sample. The difference is small.

There is considerable variation over time both in mean and in standard deviation and an inverse relationship between the two, a feature which is also apparent in the quantile bend estimates used on the Army Medical Department data for birth cohorts from the 1860s. Mistakes in the estimation of the proportion of the population missing from the observed counts would distort the mean and standard deviation in opposite directions, so this relationship probably reflects the imperfections of the adjustments for truncation.

Most modern distributions of adult heights show standard deviations in the range 2.3–2.7 inches (5.8–6.9 cm), although lower values

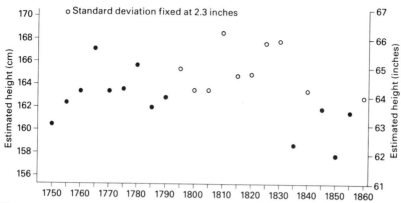

Figure 4.13. The estimated heights of British military recruits, on the assumption of a fixed standard deviation of 2.3 inches for the height distributions. Source: table 4.9.

may exist for populations subject to high mortality. In the light of this, it is sensible to ask whether the cyclical pattern of height change is entirely, or largely, a feature of the difficulty of the estimating procedure in arriving at good estimates of the shape of the underlying distributions. As some check on this possibility, the maximum likelihood estimators were re-computed with the standard deviation constrained to be 2.3 inches (5.8 cm), and table 4.8 shows the results, while the heights of 21- to 23-year-olds, estimated on this basis, are shown in figure 4.13. The most substantial change occurs, as might be expected, in the estimated height of birth cohorts around 1815 but it can be seen that, although the amplitude of the cycle at this period is reduced, the overall shape remains. It would be possible to carry out the same process for the quantile bend estimator, but the range of standard deviations is much smaller and, for reasons of economy, the computations were not carried out. It should be stressed that there is no reason to believe, on the basis of modern data, that the standard deviation should be so rigidly fixed as this procedure implies and, because they make full use of all the available information, the original estimates remain in the statistical sense the best estimates of the underlying parameters.

4.3.2 Comparisons with other data

Two types of comparison are possible. First, we can seek evidence from other sources, particularly in other countries, about the British heights which we have estimated. Second, we can examine data from other countries, in order to see whether the changes which we have observed in British heights are in any way replicated or paralleled by changes in those countries.

The first type of comparison relies on evidence of the heights of British natives who were measured overseas. Three major sources of such information are available for the eighteenth and nineteenth centuries. First, many American military sources state the country of birth of the recruit and it is therefore possible to extract and analyse the heights of British-born soldiers in the American armies, both before and after the American Revolution. Table 4.9 shows the results of such a comparison, together with some estimates from Sokoloff (1984) of the heights of American native-born soldiers recruited at the same periods. It is clear that there is a close correspondence between the heights of British-born recruits to the two armies. A similar correspondence emerges, as might be expected, between the heights of men recruited to the British Army and Royal Marines and those who joined the forces of the East India Company, whose recruitment records have been studied by Mokyr and O'Grada (1986).

In some ways, the close correspondence which emerges between the heights of migrants and of those who stayed at home is surprising. It is often argued that those who migrate are more adventurous, perhaps stronger and healthier, than those who stay at home, although Robert Louis Stevenson disputed this view hotly in his account of his voyage on an emigrant ship in 1879 (1984: 14):

Comparatively few of the men were below thirty; many were married and encumbered with families; not a few were already up in years; and this itself was out of tune with my imaginations, for the ideal emigrant should certainly be young. Again, I thought he should offer to the eye some bold type of humanity, with bluff or hawk-like features, and the stamp of an eager and pushing disposition. Now those around me were for the most part quiet, orderly, obedient citizens, family men broken by adversity, elderly youths who had failed to place themselves in life, and people who had seen better days. Mildness was the prevailing character; mild mirth and mild endurance.

Migrants, in other words, were much like those whom they left behind.

The same is probably true of the other group of British emigrants whose heights were measured, the involuntary migrants transported as convicted criminals to Australia. Evidence of the heights of transported children was first collected by Gandevia (1976, 1977), who argued that their heights were low by comparison with those of the British population, but recently Nicholas and Shergold (1988) have

Table 4.9. *Comparisons of the heights (in inches) of British recruits to the British Army and Royal Marines and to the armies in America.*

Time period	US recruits (native-born)	US recruits born in			Birth cohort	British recruits
		England	Scotland	Ireland		
French and Indian wars	67.7	65.2	67.0	67.1	(1740–49)	65.39
					(1744–49)	65.22
American Revolution	68.1	65.5	66.6		(1755–59)	65.74
					(1760–64)	66.84
1820s	68.1	66.1	66.9	65.9	(1795–99)	66.66
					(1800–04)	66.76
1850s	68.1	67.3	67.6	68.0	(1825–29)	66.73
					(1830–34)	66.74
Civil War	68.5	67.6	67.3	67.6	(1830–34)	66.74
					(1835–39)	65.71
1880s		66.1	67.0	67.5	(1855–59)	66.40

Source: British recruits from RDB and AMD samples.
American recruits from samples described in Fogel (1986).

Table 4.10. *Comparison of the heights (in inches) of British military recruits with the heights of convicts transported to Australia.*

Date of birth	Convicts (aged > 23)	British recruits (aged 24–9)	
1724–89	66.00	65.95	(Mean of birth cohorts 1740–89)
1790–99	65.75	65.84	(Birth cohort 1790–94)
		66.66	(Birth cohort 1795–99)
1800–09	65.75	66.76	(Birth cohort 1800–04)
		68.09	(Birth cohort 1805–09)
1810–19	65.75	67.67	(Birth cohort 1810–14)
		67.22	(Birth cohort 1815–19)

Source: Convicts from Nicholas and Shergold (1988).
British recruits from RDB samples.

collected the heights and other details of 19711 men, women and children; they find mean heights very similar to those of British Army recruits. Table 4.10 sets out the comparison.

While most such comparisons can be made only for single instances or short periods of time, the evidence of these three independent sets of data does suggest that the level of British mean heights drawn from our data sources is approximately correct. But are these British sources believable in the light of what is known of height change in other countries, such as the material presented in chapter 1? First, although British mean heights were above those of any other European country for most of the eighteenth and nineteenth centuries, they were at the same time below those of the American colonies and the United States; in other words, British heights were not so high that they should thereby be disbelieved, particularly in the light of the general belief that Britain was among the richest, if not the richest country in the world at that time.

Second, the path of British mean heights does differ from those characteristic of other European countries in that the pattern is less smooth and appears to contain cycles in which mean heights have actually fallen. It is clear that the nature of the British evidence of heights, and the statistical adjustments which are necessary, does impart some irregularity to the series, which is absent from the unproblematical and regular results of the examinations of conscripts. However, the evidence from study of recruits in the United States – where statistical adjustments are much less necessary – is that there too are cycles in movements of final heights. It seems likely, therefore, that the apparent contrast between the irregularity of British height change and the regularity of that in other European countries is, to some extent, an illusion; we observe height change in Europe, from the late nineteenth century, at a time at which it was regular and upward. At earlier periods the irregularity might have existed in those countries as well.

4.4 CONCLUSION

This chapter has presented and discussed a great deal of material about the changing heights of the British and Irish since the eighteenth century. It has not, however, sought to explain those changing heights in the context of what else is known about the social and economic history of the period. This is the task of chapter 7; before we attempt it, we need to examine the current state of knowledge about the relationship between height growth and the environment, much of it based on present-day experience in the less-developed countries of the world, and to consider the relevance of that knowledge to the developing economy and society of Britain and Ireland in the eighteenth and nineteenth centuries.

5

Regional and occupational differentials in British heights

5.0 INTRODUCTION

The long-term trends in the average height of the British population tell only half the story. Just as, in conventional studies of the economic welfare of populations, descriptions of changes in average income are paralleled by analysis of its distribution among different groups in the population, so we can also use height statistics to explore the differences between the experiences of different groups. Indeed, it is such differences which, because they are immediately apparent to even the casual observer, have stimulated much interest and enquiry into the phenomenon of height; differences between groups within European populations gave rise to the enquiries of Villermé, stimulated the comments of Chadwick and the factory inspectors, impelled the European recruitment officials to record the average heights of men from different districts or social classes and, most recently, have been a focus of interest in modern sample surveys.

There are four sets of data that make it possible for us directly to observe differences in height between social or geographical groups within Britain and Ireland. These are: first, the records of Sandhurst and the Marine Society in the first part of the nineteenth century; second, the enquiries of the British Association for the Advancement of Science in the 1870s and 1880s; third, the sample survey of adult heights and weights conducted in the 1980s; last, the evidence of the samples of British Army and Marine recruits. The last set of data is the primary focus of this chapter, but we begin by surveying briefly the first three sources.

We discussed in the last chapter the heights of the boys of the Marine Society and of the Royal Military Academy, but did not explicitly contrast them. Yet the contrast between them is dramatic. It spans the whole class structure of early nineteenth-century Britain; the children of the Marine Society were the children of the London slums. Their addresses read like a roll-call of the rookeries of the city so graphically

196

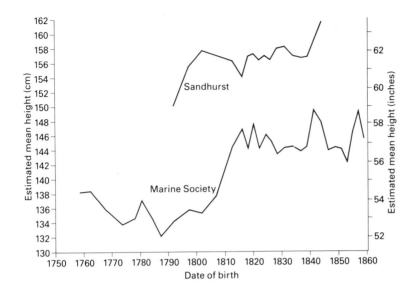

Figure 5.1. Height by social class: a comparison of the heights of recruits aged 14 to the Marine Society and Sandhurst, 1760–1860.

depicted by Hogarth, Doré and Dickens; many had no parents or guardians; many had no occupation and most only unskilled jobs. Their appearance and their life-stories were so pitiful that even the Trustees of the Marine Society, presumably inured to the social conditions of London, had to be prevented from seeing their fellows who could not meet the height standard. By contrast, the parents of Sandhurst boys were drawn from the aristocracy, the professions and the higher ranks of the Army and Navy. They had presumably not suffered material deprivation – though some were exempted from all or part of the fees – and they can, therefore, be taken as good examples of the healthy middle and upper classes of nineteenth-century Britain.

The difference between the heights of 14-year-old boys of the Marine Society and of Sandhurst is shown in figure 5.1. It may be that well-nourished Sandhurst boys had already passed into or even through the adolescent growth spurt, while the stunted London boys had not yet reached that stage of growth. We do not, of course, know the final heights of either group and it is highly likely that the London boys would have continued growing longer than those of Sandhurst, significantly reducing the gap between them by the time final height was attained. Last, almost all the Marine Society boys came from

London, while the Sandhurst boys were drawn from the whole country.

Despite the caveats, the gap is still a real one. It is so large that almost all the Sandhurst boys would have been taller than almost all the London boys, so visible a difference that it becomes clear why contemporary observers could see it in the streets around them.[1] Although a comparison of the time trends in the two sets of data suggests that the gap between them was narrowing towards the middle of the nineteenth century, it still remained large.

The work of the Anthropometric Committee of the British Association for the Advancement of Science (BAAS), under the leadership of Charles Roberts and Francis Galton, has frequently been described (Tanner 1981: 481–2). They amassed a large quantity of data, drawn from miscellaneous sources, which was drawn together in the final report of the Committee in 1883, and produced a number of summary tables in which they calculated the height and weight of children and adults from different social classes and different parts of the country (Szreter 1986a). Some of the late adolescent and adult data came from military sources and may have been biassed by the height standard.

Nevertheless, the BAAS data suggest that the most extreme differentials of the early nineteenth century had diminished. The Committee found, for example, that 14-year-old boys from the professional classes averaged 61.29 inches (155.68 cm) against a national average for Great Britain of 59.33 inches (150.70 cm). Boys from the commercial classes in towns averaged 59.47 inches (151.05 cm), the children of town artisans 58.61 inches (148.87 cm) and the children of the labouring classes in the countryside 57.94 inches (147.17 cm). The Committee were unable to measure enough people from the labouring classes in towns to produce a meaningful average, but they did report on the height of a number of children in industrial schools, described as 'illustrating the physique of children bred under the most unfavourable conditions of life' (BAAS 1883: 44). The average height of 102 such 14-year-old boys was 54.46 inches (138.33 cm). The gap between these deprived boys and those of the professional classes was thus 6.83 inches (17.35 cm), smaller than that between the Marine Society and Sandhurst boys sixty years earlier. It seems likely, also, that the children in industrial schools were somewhat more deprived than most of the children of the Marine Society.

---

[1] It is impossible to resist quoting the words of Mrs C. F. Alexander in the children's hymn *All Things Bright and Beautiful*:

The rich man in his castle,
the poor man at the gate,
God made them high and lowly
and ordered their estate.

Table 5.1 *Average height of males (in cm) by age and social class in Britain in the 1980s.*

| | Age | | | | |
Social class	16–19	20–24	25–29	30–34	All ages (16–64)
I and II	176.5	178	177.1	176.2	175.5
III (non-manual)	174.8	178.3	176.1	176.2	174.9
III (manual)	174.7	175.1	174.7	174.2	173.4
IV and V	173	174.9	173.9	173.7	172.3

Source: Knight and Eldridge (1984).

The Anthropometric Committee also reported on adult heights, finding, as would be expected, that class differences were much smaller in final heights. Thus, heights at age 24 ranged from 68.82 inches (174.80 cm) among the professional classes to 66.55 inches (169.04 cm) among urban artisans, a gap of 2.27 inches (5.77 cm), although it is possible that the artisan figure was inflated by the operation of the military height standard.

Last, the committee was greatly interested in the existence of the differences between the populations of different regions within Britain and reported mean height by county within each nation (BAAS 1883: 10–11). They found that, among adult men aged 23—50 arranged by their place of birth, the Scots were the tallest at 68.71 inches (174.6 cm), followed by the Irish at 67.90 inches (172.6 cm), the English at 67.36 inches (171.2 cm) and the Welsh at 66.66 inches (169.4 cm). The counties with the greatest average height were Kirkcudbright, Ayrshire and Wigton at 70.14 inches (1.782 cm), the shortest Glamorgan, Caermarthen and Pembroke at 66.47 inches (168.9 cm).

Nearly one hundred years later, the Office of Population, Censuses and Surveys sample of adult heights and weights also examined the social and geographical distribution of heights (Knight and Eldridge 1984). The geographical distribution is considered below, but it is important to remember here, as a background to the rest of this chapter, that the social distribution still demonstrated, in late twentieth-century Britain, a clear relationship between height and social class. This is reproduced from the OPCS report in table 5.1. Although the gross differentials of the nineteenth century have disappeared, and the overall gap between social classes I and II and social classes IV and V is only 3.2 cm, the pattern of class differentials can still clearly be seen; we return to why this should be so in chapter 7.

Our primary purpose in this chapter, however, is to consider the evidence of differences in the heights of different occupational and geographical groups in Britain which we can derive from the records of individual soldiers and marines. In the late nineteenth century, the published records of the Army Medical Department provide some evidence on regional differences but none on occupational differences in height. This chapter is mainly concerned, therefore, with the results of the samples of the heights of soldiers and marines born between the middle of the eighteenth and the middle of the nineteenth century; these heights are considered in relation to their birthplace and in relation to their last civilian occupation, both of which are recorded in the Description Books.

5.1 REGIONAL DIFFERENTIALS IN HEIGHTS

In a moment of fancy, it is pleasing to imagine the people of the British Isles towards the start of Queen Victoria's reign as standing up to form an enormous living bar-graph. Imagine their heights from toe to crown as a graphical display of well-being round the kingdom. Of course, as we have stressed in chapter 1 and will stress again in chapter 6, individual heights reflect factors in addition to nutrition and net physical condition. But the many random influences apparent at the individual level average out over large groups or regions. Genetic differences can have accounted for little or nothing of the average differences among English, Welsh, Scots and Irish or among other large groups in historical Britain. What counted, more than anything else, were environmental influences on net nutritional status. These influences would have made the average East Anglian in the great living bar-graph taller than his average London neighbour, the average rural Scot taller than the average Irishman; from our data on height by age we can therefore build an imitation of the living bar-graph and reconstruct, in a rough way, the auxological geography of Britain.

What goes for places is true also for occupations. Controlling for regional differences, we can take relative average heights in different occupational categories as indicators of relative conditions among different segments of the working class. For both regions and occupations, we can further trace the general patterns of changes over time in each of the categories and the differences between them.

Regional differences in average heights as we reconstruct them from our data are shown in figure 5.2. They apply to male military recruits born around the time of the Treaty of Vienna and reaching adulthood around Queen Victoria's accession. The levels behind this display are shown on the left of figure 5.3. These differentials have been stan-

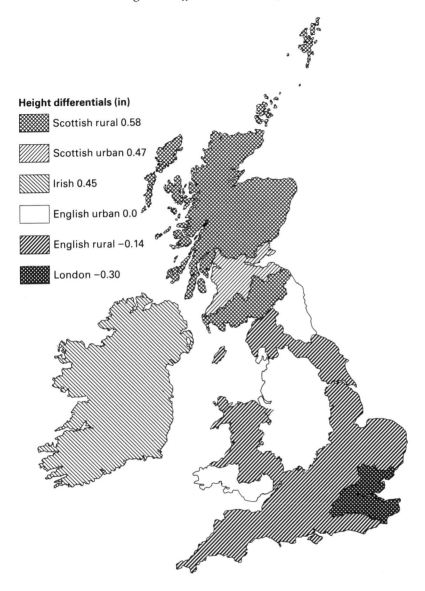

Height differentials (in)

Scottish rural 0.58

Scottish urban 0.47

Irish 0.45

English urban 0.0

English rural −0.14

London −0.30

Figure 5.2. Regional height differentials in Britain and Ireland, around 1815.

dardised for the mix of ages and occupations in the samples and are the product of a chain of calculations which we shall shortly describe.

Even with a sample size of over 120000 soldiers and marines, it was necessary to group counties and occupations together to secure subsamples large enough for accurate statistical estimation. The regions themselves, therefore, are made up of groups of counties. The English urban region, for instance, consists of 16 whole counties, largely in the north and the Midlands. These were counties where the bulk of the population increasingly lived in urban areas, the growing manufacturing areas of the Industrial Revolution. Both the urban and the rural portions of these 'urban' counties are classed in the urban region. Similarly the rural English region includes towns within predominantly rural counties, while the London region includes the surrounding rural counties. The separate category for foreigners is too meagre to be displayed. The selection of counties for each group is based on aggregating between one and four of the wage areas which E. H. Hunt (1973) defined on the basis of similarity in wage patterns between 1850 and 1914. Hunt (1986) carries the analysis of wages back as far as 1767. In the 1700s, distinctions between the 'urban' and 'rural' counties of our classification were less systematic, but distinctions in wage levels between England and Scotland were much more pronounced. The assignment of counties to regions can be read off figure 5.2 and is shown in detail in appendix 3.1.

At the time of the accession of Queen Victoria, young Scotsmen were taller than young Englishmen. If we compare rural counties, we find that the Scots were taller than the Irish who in turn were taller than the English. In comparing urban counties, we find the Scots again on top, the English outside London in the middle, and the Londoners at the bottom. These gradients are most unlikely to have a genetic origin, for they are reversed from what is found in the 1980s. The 1982 Survey of Adult Heights and Weights (Knight and Eldridge 1984) found Scots shorter than any of the English groups, and northern English, today's inhabitants of most of the counties we classify as urban, shorter than the English from the south; their data for selected age-groups are reproduced in table 5.2. Instead the gradients of the early nineteenth century, like those of the 1980s, are most likely to have had their origin in systematic differences in nutritional status.

The apparently disadvantageous condition of the London working class compared with everyone else is no surprise. It does run counter to the relatively high level of nominal wages Hunt (1986) estimates for London, but urban disamenities, disease, unemployment, crowding and high costs of living would be expected to take their toll. Londoners in our sample were, after all, young men who were born in London and had mostly lived there throughout their lives, rather than the immigrants to London whom we know made up a large part of the capital's popula-

Table 5.2. *Geographical differences in height of adult males in Britain in the 1980s.*

Region	Mean height [cm]
South West	175.1
East Anglia	174.8
South East	174.7
East Midlands	174.4
Yorkshire and Humberside	174.1
London (GLC area)[a]	173.7
West Midlands	173.5
North	173.3
North West	173.1
Scotland	173.0
Wales	171.9

Source: Knight and Eldridge (1984).
[a] Area covered by the Greater London Council, as it was in 1984.

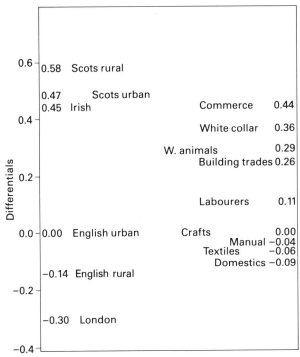

Figure 5.3. Regional and occupational differentials in height in Britain and Ireland, 1815.

tion, lured by wage levels and the city whose streets were paved with gold. The younger counterparts of the Londoners in our sample were the children of the Marine Society, whose bodies are sufficient evidence of the impact of a London working-class childhood on health and growth.

The advantage of the Scots, on the other hand, would not perhaps have been predicted. It is especially thought-provoking because, as we shall see, it is no less pronounced before 1800. Hunt (1986) sees substantial Scottish disadvantage in nominal wages before 1800 which is not overcome until around 1850. Imaginative recreations from Samuel Johnson to Sir Walter Scott certainly portray the Scots as poorer than their neighbours south of the Tweed. But that bleak picture should have some brighter lines to it, not only in respect of the high literacy rates in Scotland which Schofield (1972–73) and others have noticed, but also, according to our indicators, in respect of net nutritional status. Some scholars, notably Maisie Steven (1985), have claimed nutritional superiority for the much-maligned Scots diet including oats, pulses and dairy products. Steven, for example, quotes writers of the Statistical Account of Scotland in the 1790s as speaking of the people as being 'remarkably healthy' and argues herself that 'the diet of the Scots rural workers was in most respects a highly nourishing one' (1985: 23). Perhaps the money spent on food, though less in total, was better spent.

Among these men born around 1815, those from the counties we classify as urban were much on a par with those from the counties we classify as rural. It may be that urbanisation and the generally higher wages which it brought had not yet touched the lives of many residents in these 'urban' counties. Perhaps, also, the heyday of cottage industry had not yet altogether passed. In England, this regional parity would prove quite temporary, as we shall shortly show. Compared to the English, the Irish appear to have been doing well before the famine, as most historians have believed (Mokyr 1985b).

The height differentials serve as indicators of relative nutritional status, and their absolute size is not at present so important to us as their ordering. Their statistical significance, which does depend on their absolute size, is a matter for later discussion. Still, one cannot help being curious about the absolute size of the differences, and about whether they were sufficient to be visible to contemporaries or at least sufficient to be ferreted out without modern samples and statistical machinery. Here it is useful to remember that typical standard deviations of adult male height in general and in all our samples are between two and three inches, and that heights are nearly normally distributed. Ignoring the extreme 5 per cent of a distribution, the height of a subgroup ranges therefore from about five inches above to about five inches below its average. Thus the heights of all our groups overlap. At the extremes, however, the differences begin to be visible. Our average rural Scotsman turning 20 around 1837 is nine-tenths of an inch taller than our average Londoner. The occupational differentials, which we shall discuss later on, add further contrast; such differences persist, though with some important changes, through the century. If Sherlock Holmes had been forced to guess, at the start of his career, which of two suspects was a Scots husband-man and which a London hodcarrier, he would have had a two-to-one chance of guessing right on the basis of height alone.

We can now turn from a static picture of those recruited in the late 1830s to look at change over time. Patterns of gradual change are shown in figure 5.4 for the mainly rural regions and in figure 5.5 for the mainly urban regions. These figures show trajectories which have been smoothed by the lowess procedure described in section 3.4. The differentials are shown relative to a standardised national average which was computed using fixed weights for the relative size of geographical regions which were obtained from the 1831 Census.

The outstanding feature of these figures is the contrast between the regions in overall trend. Relative to the rural regions, the urban counties of Scotland and England show a pattern of decline. This decline is unmistakable, and adds valuable information to the discussion of long-term trends in nutritional status in chapter 4. It suggests that the lack of any sustained rise in average heights during much of the nineteenth century was partially a product of the effects of urban living. There is a convergence between heights in these areas and those in London, in line with the view that other cities were taking on the problems for which London had already long been notorious.

Our indicators are sufficiently sensitive to track a strong negative impact of the Irish famine. Because the figures show smoothed estimates, the drop on the curve is not as sudden as it is in unsmoothed data. It is also interesting how strong a rebound is evident among Irish families who survived and stayed. Londoners born after Waterloo, for their part, enjoyed a period of relative advantage which parallels the 'great height leap' of those born immediately after the end of the War, which is so dramatic a feature of the Marine Society evidence.

Taking trends into account, we must modify our picture of regional differentials if we focus not on young Victorians, but instead on those born at the time of the Treaty of Paris in 1763, who reached adulthood near the time of the rebellion of the American colonies. As an easy

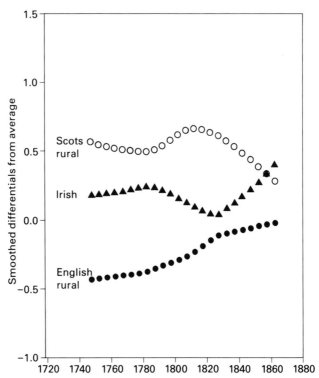

Figure 5.4. Differentials over time between heights in rural regions. Source: see text.

mnemonic, we may think of relative height in these early years as following latitude. London and the largely southern English rural counties come together, about 0.6 inch below Ireland and the English soon-to-be urban counties, themselves between 0.3 and 0.6 inch shorter than the Scots. By the end of our period, on the other hand, among men born around 1860, the long decline of urban counties had left English urban counties just 0.3 inch above London at the bottom. The decline had left Scottish urban counties in the middle with the English rural counties 0.3 inch above the London and English urban counties and about 0.3 inch below the Irish and rural Scots.

5.2 THE CALCULATION OF HEIGHT DIFFERENTIALS

How did we secure these results? So far, we have confined ourselves to discussing features of the data whose statistical significance is assured by the tests with strict levels that we have performed. We

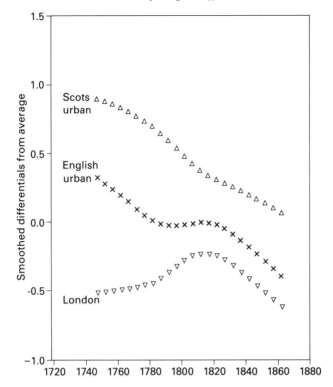

Figure 5.5. Differentials over time between heights in urban regions. Source: see text.

shall now explain what these tests are and how the estimates of differentials have been obtained. This explanation entails delving into statistical matters more complicated than is usual in historical studies. But the difficulty in drawing inferences from these rich but problematic data is also greater than usual, and sceptical readers have a right to expect full disclosure of the basis on which our generalisations rest.

The levels and trends that we have been discussing are based on three stages of statistical processing. First, there is the generation by maximum likelihood methods and the inspection, quinquennium by quinquennium, of estimates of differentials at each point of time. Second, there is an exploratory non-parametric analysis, making particular use of robust moving averages, which suggests features for confirmation and interpretation. Third, there is a confirmatory parametric analysis, using weighted regression and normal theory. We shall now explain each of these stages.

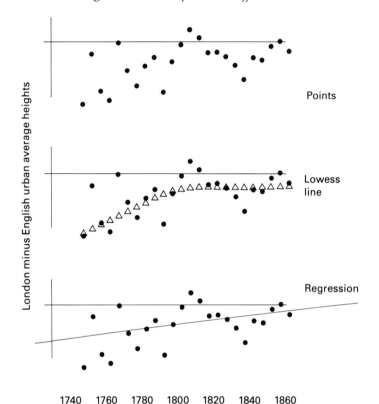

Figure 5.6. An example of the calculation of estimates, lowess line and trend.
Source: see text.

5.2.1 Point estimates of differentials

Our main calculations can be followed step by step with the example
shown in figure 5.6. The top of this figure shows a series of differentials
between average heights in London and in English urban counties
over time. We will concentrate on the heights of Londoners but will
also refer to other geographical groups while discussing statistical
issues; the substantive results will be summarised in section 5.2.5.

Each point on the graph comes from a separate computation by an
estimation program which operated on data about the heights and
characteristics of recruits who were born during a particular five-year
period. These points were obtained from the reduced sample maximum
likelihood procedures described in section 3.4. Each point is the estimated coefficient of a dummy variable (cf. section 3.4) indicating London
origin. The omitted dummy variable, the baseline geographical cate-

gory, is the English urban county category; the points therefore show differentials between Londoners and men from English urban counties. Other dummy variables control for age and occupational category.

5.2.2 *Smoothing the differentials over time*

We turn now to the next stages of the analysis. A point in the top part of figure 5.6 for a given quinquennium is estimated with much random error, because of the sampling process and the uncertainty of adjustments for truncation. But inspection of the overall tendency of the points suggests that they rise slightly with time. To obtain a clearer view of this tendency we now, in the second exploratory stage of analysis, smooth the series using the lowess procedure of Cleveland (1979: 830) described in section 3.4. In the middle part of figure 5.6, the points from the top part are repeated together with the estimated smooth curve through them. The curve certainly rises over time. It is fairly straight, but there is some hint of the rise tapering off. This tapering suggests that when regression methods are used in the later stage of parametric analysis, it would be well to use them to fit a bending line, say a quadratic or cubic polynomial, rather than a straight line. Our simple example above used a straight line, and the technique used was therefore formally 'linear regression', but it is equally possible to fit a curved line such as:

$$Y = a + bX + cX^2$$

The curves in figures 5.4 and 5.5 have been obtained in the same way as in our example of figure 5.6 but with differentials measured from the standardised national average instead of from the baseline category. This standardised national average reference line was chosen after much experimentation because it shows the relative movements of rural and urban categories so clearly, and this feature is the most salient one in these series. The tapering of the differential between London and English urban counties in figure 5.6 corresponds to the parallel drop in both London and English urban counties together, to be seen on the right of figure 5.5. Most of the lowess lines for regional differentials appear rather straight. But we note for further checking possible S-bends for both Scottish series, a pause in the English urban county decline, and a trough for Irish born around 1830. Of all of these suggested non-linearities, only the Irish trough proves statistically significant in the later confirmatory analysis.

The smoothing process shown in figures 5.4–5.6 can be used in another way. It supplies an opportunity for some checks on statistical significance of the ordering of the categories to which we have been devoting so much attention.[2] Consider, for example, the ranking of Londoners as shorter than English urban residents for the birth cohort of 1815, which is reflected in the negative sign on the smoothed value plotted with a triangle over 1815 in the middle part of figure 5.6. How firmly rooted in the data is this negative sign? One rough way to tell is to pick out at random a subset of the points in the top part which determine the middle-part values, then re-calculate the smoothed value for 1815, and see if the sign stays negative. The more often the sign stays negative when this random selection is repeated, the more firmly rooted is the sign. This reasoning, needless to say, relies on the hope that the points we do see are typical, in their variability, of the points we might have seen had the chance mechanisms at work in the real world presented us with samples other than the one sample that we have. That hope itself may be too bold, but it is much less bold than the kind of hopes for normal error distributions and trends of a specific form that are common in statistical analysis and which motivate the parametric tests in the later stage of our analysis.

The procedure of subset selection and re-calculation that we have carried out is called a 'bootstrap' experiment. It was invented by Efron (1979). Different variants exist, but we used the 'simple bootstrap' recommended by Efron and Gong (1983: 43) and recently defended by Efron against criticisms by Wu. When there are many more points than the 24 we have, the bootstrap can be shown to generate valid statistical confidence intervals of the familiar kind in applications somewhat similar but not identical to ours, as in Freedman (1981). We use outcomes of the experiment as less formal indicators. Each random subset of points we select is drawn 'with replacement' so that the same point may be selected two or more times and count twice as heavily, or more, while other points are left out entirely. Counting duplicates, each subset has 24 points like the original collection. We repeat the process 1000 times, each time calculating new smoothed lines for all six regions with the same subset, and tallying results of key comparisons.

The 1000 bootstrap repetitions produced reassuring outcomes for 1815. Both Scottish regions exceeded all three English regions in height in all but 24 of the 1000 cases. The ordering of rural county Scots before Irish before rural county English was violated again in only 2.4 per cent of the cases. Urban Scots were taller than urban English and the latter taller than Londoners in all but 2.5 per cent of the

---

[2] For an introduction to the concept of statistical significance see Floud (1979: ch. 8).

cases. Thus the generalisations we have drawn from the smoothed differentials appear firmly rooted in the data in a statistical sense.

5.2.3 Regression estimates of trends over time

The third stage of analysis, a parametric stage, incorporates some further information from the likelihood maximisations which the smoothing ignored. Parametric tests assume some knowledge of the structure of the process or variable which is being analysed, while non-parametric tests and methods do not. The extra information from the likelihood estimations consists of the estimated standard errors of the point estimates of average heights. These are indicators of the possible sampling errors in the point estimates. At this third stage, these standard errors are used to weight the contributions of the points to weighted linear or curvilinear regression. The main effect of this weighting is to take into account, first, the differing size of samples in the various categories over different quinquennia and, second, the less precarious estimation in quinquennia which had lower minimum height standards and more modest amounts of shortfall. For convenience, the intercept of the regression is calculated for 1815, roughly at the centre period.

The weighted linear regression line for the differential between London and English urban counties is shown in the bottom part of figure 5.6. The intercept equals − 0.30 inch with a standard error of 0.061 inch. The slope is positive, estimated at 0.44 inch per century, with a standard error of 0.175 inch per century, and a *t*-test would show it significantly positive at levels as strict as 0.009. The residual standard error of the weighted linear regression is 1.39, which is close enough to unity to indicate that variability from period to period is mostly due to the sources of randomness that are already measured within each period in the course of the likelihood maximisation calculations. There is some excess residual error over unity, as is to be expected. There are bound to be some biasses in each quinquennial estimation that cannot be eliminated by the regression procedure and which show up as excess random error from period to period. They can be ignored so long as they are not systematically related to time. These residual errors for this example are typical of the residual errors for all the geographical and occupational categories in the analysis.

Unweighted curvilinear cubic regressions were also computed for all differentials from the English urban baseline, both by least squares and by a robust regression criterion. The robust criterion made no difference, nor did the non-linear terms increase the regression *R*-square by more than random amounts in any case except Ireland, as judged by *F*-statistics whose *p*-values on 2 and 22 degrees of freedom, for Scots, rural and urban, Irish, English rural and London, were 0.92, 0.89, 0.07, 0.81 and 0.55. For Ireland, the cubic regression line is a good fit to the lowess line, but neither captures the abruptness of the drop for those born between 1815 and 1839. Since the abnormal experience of these particular birth cohorts has such an obvious historical explanation in the Irish famine of the 1840s, the most sensible representation of the data (when we take our reference year, 1815, before the famine) seems to be to treat these cohorts as outliers, and calculate a linear trend omitting them from the regression. These linear regressions provide the intercepts for the regions on the left of figure 5.3.

The differentials have been calculated as differentials between each category and the baseline category of English urban county origin, but for practical purposes differentials between other pairs can be obtained by subtraction. Strictly speaking, differentials calculated with a different baseline category would be slightly different, both because of the weights in the weighted regression, which change a little with baseline category, and because some time periods are missing for some occupational categories; there were too few such recruits at certain times for stable estimates. But an exploratory analysis with recruitment cohort data, in which each pair of categories was checked separately, revealed no differences of any consequence. The recruitment cohorts were ten years wide, and the estimates were much more variable, but robust regressions agreed closely with ordinary least squares regressions. Most important, the recruitment cohort regressions provided almost exactly the same ordering of categories by average height and gave trends in the same direction as the birth cohort regressions reported here. That agreement in final estimates is very heartening. The original data are the same in the recruitment cohort and the birth cohort analysis, but they have been carved up into very different subsets, subjected to different corrections for shortfall in different likelihood maximisation runs, and entered at last into different regressions. That the results agree helps one to believe that the results are produced primarily by the data and not by the procedures applied to them.

In the context of the regression analysis, we can test the statistical significance of differentials with familiar parametric tests. These tests are more efficient than the indications of significance we have drawn from the bootstrap experiments, but they also make more rigid and less certain assumptions about the data. The most familiar, though not, as we shall see, the most appropriate, tests of significance with regressions are separate *t*-tests of the coefficients. In such separate *t*-tests, the regional differences in average height revealed by the regressions centred on 1815 would all be judged statistically significant at levels as strict or stricter than 6 per cent, with the exception of the difference between rural and urban Scots, whose *t*-test *p*-value is 20 per cent. These tests ignore the presumed weak positive correlations between the separate regressions due to the shared baseline category, an effect which would make the tests slightly conservative. For rural and urban Scots, including the correlation (without weighting) strengthens the significance level of that separate *t*-test merely from 20 to 19 per cent.

Since we are interested in the whole pattern of differentials, however, and not in some one contrast in isolation, none of these separate *t*-tests in isolation is an appropriate guide. It is more informative to compute an overall significance level. As it turns out, these data would allow us to reject any null hypothesis whose ordering of regions differed by more than one transposition from that in figure 5.3, at an overall significance level stricter than 1.37 per cent. In other words, the pattern of regional differences around 1815 is pinned down by the data that we have.

Our precise characterisation of regional differentials depends on using together the data on all the time periods, in the belief that real changes in differentials are mainly gradual ones. No short period yields enough data spread across ages and across nine occupational groups as well as across the six main regions to give statistically precise contrasts. For instance, for the 1810–1815 birth cohort, the differential between Scots urban county and English urban county origin is negative at − 0.06 inch rather than positive at + 0.47 inch, and the estimated standard error from the likelihood maximisation is 0.21 inch. For the smaller categories, estimated standard errors approaching half an inch are not uncommon, and many of the contrasts within individual quinquennial cohorts would on their own appear to have poor statistical significance, especially when occupations rather than regions are in question. Despite the large estimated standard errors for single quinquennia, however, there is a rough consistency from quinquennium to quinquennium, on which the regressions capitalise to tease out the patterns we have been discussing here.

The labour of analysis might have been shortened had estimation quinquennium by quinquennium been omitted altogether and had the whole data-set been fed to a supercomputer in a single vast likelihood maximisation run with level and trend parameters for all the contrasts. In such a run, categories of geography, occupation and period might have been slightly refined. But inspection of output from separate runs, quinquennium by quinquennium for the birth cohorts and decade by decade for recruitment cohorts, provides a safety check against specification errors, for instance in truncation levels for military units, which one would be loath to do without.

5.2.4 *Standard errors estimated by maximum likelihood methods*

The analysis of differentials and estimates of standard errors from the quinquennial likelihood maximisations reveals an interesting statistical phenomenon. While the description of this phenomenon and of the solution to the problem that underlies it is complex, it is discussed here because the problem delayed our analysis for many months and might do so again for others using our methods.

Ours is a case where the usual formulae for the sizes of tests of simple null hypotheses from likelihood calculations seem to perform badly, exaggerating the sizes of tests and leading to excessively conservative inferences. The evidence of this behaviour can be found in a comparison of the likelihood statistics with statistics from ordinary least squares regressions of height on the same batch of covariates. The role of the likelihood maximisations is to adjust the effects of the minimum height standards, working with the family of truncated normal distributions in place of the family of full normal distributions. Categories with different true mean heights are affected differently by the same minimum height standard, for shortfall will intrude deeper into the distribution of the category with the lower true mean, leaving the observed raw mean higher than the true mean and thereby reducing the observed raw differences between categories. For this reason, comparison of raw means (or its multivariate counterpart, comparison of coefficients on dummy variables in an ordinary least squares regression) typically produces underestimates of height differentials. The likelihood maximisation, by reckoning in the effects of truncation should increase the estimates of differentials, restoring them to something closer to their true magnitude.

It is easy to observe this effect in our data. Differentials from the likelihood maximisations, whenever they are sizable, generally have the same sign and about twice the magnitude of differentials from the ordinary least squares regression with the same data and the same specifications. This effect can be seen in table 3.13, which reproduces least squares and maximum likelihood estimates for the same quinquennium, 1806–1809. Although the truncations should and do affect the magnitude of the coefficients, they should not affect the significance level for testing a null hypothesis of no difference between categories. This is because, under the null hypothesis, the categories which share the same mean should suffer the same amount of shortfall from the same truncation level. In Table 3.13, the t-statistics are indeed comparable, but very often this is not the case. For many cohorts and many pairs of categories, we would reject the null hypothesis of no difference at much stricter significance levels with the least squares statistics than with the likelihood statistics. Many differences for particular cohorts appear significant at a 5 per cent level with least squares that do not with likelihood calculations.

For our substantive purposes, this effect is of no consequence, since our assessments of statistical significance have been based on our time series regressions with all 24 cohorts together and not on tests within some one cohort or another. But it is still a puzzle why the two kinds of single-cohort statistics fail to agree. The key to the answer is to be found in the inferiority of one of the approximations involved in the likelihood-based theory. Both kinds of statistics have their significance levels computed using approximations valid for large samples. Our samples are certainly large by any reasonable standard, with a minimum of 2132 and a maximum of 5800 recruits in any quinquennial birth cohort. But for our family of underlying models, each a truncated normal distribution, the likelihood calculations turn out to demand markedly larger 'large samples' than the calculations with least squares, because with truncated normal models with 30 to 50 per cent shortfall, the standard errors are themselves highly sensitive to the position of the means. If the true means of the categories are near their maximum likelihood estimates, then the approximated standard errors should be near their true values. But if the null hypothesis of no difference in means between two apparently quite different categories were a true hypothesis, then the approximated standard errors could be much larger than the standard errors under the null hypothesis, and this error in approximation would vitiate the significance level. In that situation, the least squares calculations which use standard error estimates independent of the assumption about the means would give more trustworthy significance levels.

This phenomenon, an example of practical failure on the part of maximum likelihood methods, can be documented with artificial examples with two subgroups and the algebraic formulae for likelihood solutions with truncated normals given by Cohen and Woodward (1953). Here the sufficient statistics for maximum likelihood and for least squares are the same, so the discrepancy in distributions of test statistics can be observed directly. The discrepancies hold both for likelihood ratio calculations and for Fisher-information calculations and can be visualised by plotting the likelihood surface and noting on one side a precipitous asymmetric drop. Sample sizes sufficient to impose *t*-distributions for least squares are insufficient to banish this drop from the relevant neighbourhood of the maximum. Still larger samples or third-order calculations would remedy the problem, but for a large data-analytic project like ours, these are not practical alternatives. The general superiority of likelihood methods is so much a part of statistical folklore that it is disconcerting to find this example where faith in likelihood theory leads to trouble.

The theoretical problem with likelihoods just described might not be the only source of discrepancy between maximum likelihood and least-squares based tests in our large data analyses. Any strong tendency for taller subgroups to be more heavily represented in military units with lower minimum height standards (a counter-intuitive but conceivable state of affairs) would cause least-squares based tests to exaggerate differentials, while likelihood-based tests, which adjust for truncation, would then yield sounder inferences. In fact, while geography and unit membership are correlated, occupation and unit membership are not much correlated, whereas the test-statistic problem occurs as much for occupations as for regions. Thus the theoretical problem seems the more likely source of trouble, and this example offers a cautionary lesson against routine application of textbook statistical procedures.

5.2.5 *Regional differentials in heights: a summary of results*

The exposition of statistical details, mandatory though it is, should not divert attention from the results. At the beginning of our period, men born in the 1760s differed by as much as 1.5 inches (3.81 cm) in their adult heights, depending on their place of birth. The Scots were on average significantly taller than the Irish, who were themselves taller than the English and Welsh, with men born in London and the home counties trailing in last. But this pattern soon began to change, until today it is very nearly reversed. Within the hundred years to the 1860s, the urbanising counties of both England and Wales and Scotland experienced declining average heights, falling towards but not quite reaching the depths of London. This fall in urban heights was most marked in the middle of the nineteenth century, when it contributed markedly to the overall decline in heights which we observed in chapter 4. For most of the period, by contrast, the rural areas of England and Wales experienced stable or rising heights relative to the national average, but both the Irish and the Scots rural populations experienced deterioration, temporary in the case of the Irish but more prolonged in the case of the Scots.

5.3 OCCUPATIONAL DIFFERENTIALS IN HEIGHTS

We now match our account of the spatial geography of average height with an account of its social geography. Highly specific occupations – such as 'apple vendor' or 'needle hardener and temperer' or 'Spanish leather dresser' – were recorded for recruits and have been coded. The directory of occupational titles, compiled during the coding of the data, contains just over 5900 such job descriptions, although a substantial part of the directory is made up of variant spellings.[3] The titles have been grouped into ten categories based on the classification first set out by W. A. Armstrong (1972) and later modified by M. Anderson (1987), subdivided according to sectors of the economy. Descriptions and typical members of each category are to be found in appendix 3.1.

The relative heights of all categories but one are displayed on the right-hand side of figure 5.3, across from their counterparts by region. The baseline category is that of men in apprenticed trades excluding building. A category missing from figure 5.3 is the 'unskilled' who as such were too sparsely represented, since jobs demanding little skill such as 'labourer' were placed in other categories. The relative average heights in figure 5.3 again refer to men born in 1815 and recruited on the eve of Queen Victoria's accession. The occupational estimates in figure 5.3 derive, just as the regional estimates did, from weighted regressions performed in a third, parametric stage of analysis with specifications suggested by robust smoothings in a second, exploratory stage of analysis, with points originating in the first stage of likelihood maximisation.

The occupational differentials have a smaller range than the regional differentials. We must recall, however, that we are dealing not with the whole spectrum of occupations in the population but with distinctions within the working class. Our occupational classification draws relatively fine distinctions within a broadly homogeneous group, so it is gratifying to be able to pick up as much variation as we do.

Tallest in the table, not surprisingly, we find workers in commerce like shopkeepers and self-employed small vendors, along with the rare white-collar recruits in this working-class population. These 'white-collar' workers are mostly clerks, policemen and the like, rather than trained professionals. Members of these comparatively high-status groups loom a third of an inch (0.8 cm) over the baseline category of workers in trades with apprenticeship requirements outside

---

[3] The directory is deposited, with the data, in the ESRC Data Archive at Essex University and may be copied and used by anyone interested.

the building industry. Next in average height come those working with animals, mainly husbandmen, and workers in the building trades with apprenticeship requirements. They are followed closely by labourers, whom we presume to be mainly agricultural labourers. Workers in the large baseline category of trades requiring apprenticeship outside the building industry, labelled 'crafts' in the figure, are slightly shorter on average, in a group with manual workers, textile workers and domestic servants.

The interest of this ordering of occupations by average height is that it is so natural. The occupations sort themselves out by height very much in line with intuitive expectations. Workers with animals and labourers enjoy an advantage that might easily reflect agricultural diets. Although the effects of occupations are estimated while controlling for the effects of geography, the geographical groupings are so broad that local distinctions between more urban and more rural places probably remain to express themselves in these occupational variables. As described in Floud and Wachter (1982: 424–5), Victorian reformers like Chadwick, as well as those who late in the century raised a hue and cry about the physical degeneration of the population, commonly assumed that country-born Britons were stronger and healthier than town-born ones. But on a regional level, as one may recall from figure 5.3, English rural counties show shorter heights than English urban counties, so the effects picked up by the occupational variables seem to reflect decidedly local differences.

Those with no listed occupation, not shown in figure 5.3, turn out to have been relatively tall, so they are probably not those without occupation, but rather those whose occupations happened to be omitted. At the bottom of the ordering we find the small number in our sample of domestic servants. This placement is an interesting one. On the one hand, there are several reasons for expecting it. Domestic service might attract workers not robust enough for heavier physical labour. Census data indicate that by the middle of our period the number of living-in servants was relatively small, so that many recruits in the domestic-service category may have been living-out servants, whose low wages were not even supplemented by board and lodging. Domestic service was a predominantly urban occupation, with the attendant disadvantages. Those domestic servants who left or lost their positions to join the military may have been the less well-off, possibly so much as to make them less typical of servants in general than other recruits were of other occupations. Or perhaps they were typical. There is no lack of Victorian literature describing atrocious living and working conditions for living-in servants, albeit mainly females. On the other hand, those negative accounts must be set beside the countervailing body of Victorian literature – *The Moonstone* and *Wuthering Heights* are examples – which contain unselfconscious portrayals of domestic servants whose occupations offered much protection and advantage. So it is interesting to find the evidence of our sample of heights, as far as it goes, running contrary to the favourable picture surviving from such works.

The occupational differentials in figure 5.3 are derived by the same three-stage procedure as the regional differentials. In terms of statistical significance, since there are more categories, the ordering of them all is less precisely pinned down. With a single *t*-test in isolation, we could reject the hypothesis of no difference between workers with animals and labourers with a significance level of 5 per cent, or an hypothesis of no difference between labourers and those in the apprenticed non-building trades with a significance level of just under 2 per cent. But we could not reject an hypothesis of no difference between those in the apprenticed trades outside building and workers in textiles with significance levels as lax as 24 per cent. In other words, we can distinguish the top and middle of the hierarchy from the bottom, but we cannot draw statistically significant distinctions between many adjacent pairs of occupations.

Smoothed trajectories of the occupational differentials are shown in figure 5.7, the companion to figures 5.4 and 5.5. Three of the occupations are omitted from the graph, because they are represented in sufficient numbers only over part of the period. Our non-linear analysis is forced to concentrate on the six occupations which are represented in all 24 quinquennia. Unlike the regional differentials, whose bends suggested cubic regression, the occupational differentials appear to converge along fairly linear trajectories up to the early 1800s and then settle down to levels with only minor further change over time. These patterns suggest piecewise linear regression. Separate regressions for the second half of the period show no slopes significantly different from zero, so a composite specification with a linear trend up to the early 1800s and constant levels thereafter seems appropriate. The transition point is not precisely determined, and we have used 1815, which gives smaller residual errors than 1805.

The three categories represented in sufficient numbers for analysis only in a subset of quinquennia are more problematic. Only one data point for white-collar workers is available before 1800, at 0.3 inch (0.7 cm) above baseline. Births between 1800 and 1820 supply three low and widely scattered points, and thereafter all points fall more than 0.7 inch (1.8 cm) above baseline, among the highest that we shall

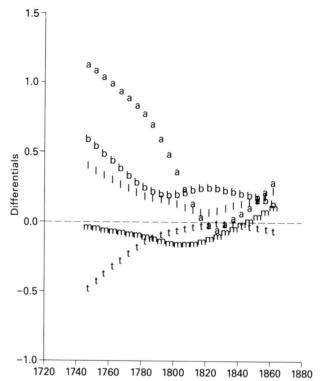

Figure 5.7. Differentials over time between heights of various occupations. Source: see text. Notes: a = workers with animals; b = building trades; l = labourers; m = manual; t = workers in textiles.

see. With so few points, no model could claim much priority over others, but differentials seem clearly to be widening, and we have fitted an unweighted quadratic regression to the points to obtain the estimate of figure 5.3. For workers in commerce, the results are, unlike other categories, sensitive to the weights. The weighted regression shows a negative slope as big as half an inch per century, significantly negative at a level as strict as 0.055. The unweighted regression shows no significant slope at all. The weights do have a statistical basis in the data, and we have used the weighted estimate for 1815, but it would be foolish to make much of the trend.

For domestic servants, all varieties of regression, weighted and unweighted, robust and otherwise, show substantial positive slopes but with very weak statistical significance. The estimate for those born in 1815 does not depend much on the choice of model, with or without slope, and we have used the weighted regression results with positive slope. Were the evidence for an upward trend on a solider footing, it would be a very interesting finding, but as it stands we cannot put much faith in it.

The major pattern in figure 5.7 is one of convergence over time. Occupations which are well separated in average heights when we scrutinise those born around 1780 are only barely distinguishable among those born after 1815. A lowess bootstrap experiment for 1780 showed only one case in a hundred violating the ordering in which workers with animals were taller than those in building trades with apprenticeship requirements and labourers, who were taller than those in trades with apprenticeship requirements outside building, than manual workers, and than workers in textiles. For 1815, the parallel experiment showed at best that one would reject a null hypothesis of merely random differences in average heights. For instance, apprenticed building trades came above apprenticed non-building trades in 92 out of 100 cases and the latter came above manual workers in 90 cases out of 100, but on the whole there was a great dispersion in ranks in the experiment, reflecting weak statistical significance of the ordering in and after 1815.

One might be tempted to recognise in the rapid progressive disappearance of the height advantage of workers with animals (and the small decline among labourers) a reflection of economic transition in agriculture. Certainly the eighteenth century saw great increases in agricultural productivity, which could have buoyed up the rewards of workers, while after 1815 English agriculture suffered sharp depression and for several decades – if not for the whole century – there was great poverty in many rural areas in southern England. The decline in the height advantage is a steady one. Perhaps the onset of troubles in the agricultural sector was more gradual than the usual focus on the post-war collapse would suggest. There is even a hint of recovery of part of the height advantage of workers with animals for those growing up after 1845, but this hint does not reflect a statistically significant trend.

It is fascinating to find the average height of textile workers rising relative to those in other semi-skilled or skilled trades, despite the famous immiseration of the handloom weavers. However, our category of workers in textiles includes workers in mills as well as in cottage industry, and many workers in textiles were engaged in spinning and other preparatory or finishing trades. But average heights in the urbanising northern counties where most of the mills were to be found were falling relative to the rural English counties. One might argue that the effect of immiseration should be found among the children of handloom weavers, whom we cannot identify, rather than among young men who had tried employment in the textile industry before joining the Army, the men whom we can identify. Still, our positive slope for heights of textile workers cannot help but brighten, in respect of the whole industry, the dismal picture that testimony to the conditions in one part of it has left.

The pattern of convergence that we have seen means that the worse-off were doing better relative to the bulk of the working class. At the same time, the small amount of data we have for minor white-collar professionals does suggest that the better-off extreme of the working class were pulling away from the rest. The worst-off are doing better and the best-off are doing better, even more so.

How do these conclusions on the basis of the evidence of heights compare with existing knowledge about the relative well-being of different groups within English society in the eighteenth and nineteenth centuries? While many historians have assumed that income inequality and, within it, skill differentials, changed little during this period, Williamson has presented a radically different interpretation. His account of inequality (1985: 72–3) reaches the following conclusions:

> there was a rise in inequality across the century following 1760. The inequality drift was universal, since the income shares at the top rose, the shares at the bottom fell, the relative pay of the unskilled deteriorated, and the earnings distribution widened . . .
>
> [It] follows that the inequality evidence traces out a Kuznets curve over the century and a half from 1760 to World War I . . . [It] appears that the upswing of the Kuznets curve was interrupted by the French Wars. The pay ratio and earnings distribution data clearly document an egalitarian levelling across the Napoleonic period, perhaps starting as early as the 1780s. These trends are reversed following the Wars, with a surge in wage inequality from the 1820s to mid-century. These trends are also apparent in the tax assessment data. In addition, the tax assessment data suggest that the wartime trends from the 1780s to the 1820s reflect offsetting movements: improvements took place at both the bottom and the top of the distribution – the middle being squeezed – but net egalitarian trends are apparent in all the summary statistics. The post-Waterloo period, by contrast, was one of consistent inequality movements.[4]

Williamson bases his conclusions on data which relate only to the period after 1781. These show, however, that increasing equality began somewhat before the Napoleonic period, however elastic that time period is thought to be. He suggests, for example, that the per-

---

[4] The Kuznets curve, named after the American economist Simon Kuznets who first propounded it, describes the process by which, during the course of economic development, there is initially an increase in economic inequality before overall rising incomes are reflected later in narrowing inequality (Kuznets 1955).

centage differential by which urban unskilled wages exceeded farm wages fell from 36.8 per cent in 1781 to 30.7 per cent in 1810, before rising to 42.0 per cent in 1827 and to a nineteenth-century peak in 1851 of 47.0 per cent (1985: 49, table 3.8). Similarly, both non-farm and economy-wide pay ratios (the ratios of average skilled to average unskilled wages) are thought to have fallen from 1781 to 1805 before rising to 1819 (1985: 47, tables 3.4 and 3.5).

Our data suggest that Williamson may be mistaken in seeing the period of the Napoleonic Wars as reversing previous trends to rising inequality and, by extension, also mistaken in his view that the war produced such trends. It seems on the basis of the height data that occupational differentials in nutritional status were narrowing significantly from the beginning of our period – men born in the 1750s – until the period marked by men born at the end of the war and reaching final heights in the 1830s and 1840s. In other words, there was a much more long-standing movement towards equality within the working class than Williamson's data suggest and this movement was significantly reversed only some years after the end of the French Wars. Thereafter, the height data suggest that inequality remained relatively stable, although there are some signs that white-collar workers were improving relative to the rest of the working class during the second and third quarters of the nineteenth century. This latter trend, if confirmed, would provide the only support from nutritional status data for Williamson in his identification of this period as one of an upswing in the Kuznets curve.

Just as it was necessary in chapter 4 to emphasise the distinction between measures of welfare based on real incomes or wages and those based on height and net nutritional status, so it is necessary here to emphasise that there is no necessary correspondence between measures of inequality based on wage data and those based on the height of different occupational groups. The two methods measure different things, with the measurement of height giving much more weight to such factors as the quality of the environment and the disease pattern. It appears, however, that just as in chapter 4 it was possible to identify an approximate correspondence between the two measures in the period before the 1820s, when both measures suggest an improvement, the correspondence becomes less good after the 1820s, with the height data once again showing a stable pattern while wage data – or at least those analysed by Williamson – suggest considerable changes. C. H. Feinstein (1988) has thrown very considerable doubt on the conclusions which Williamson reached; whether or not Williamson is right to identify so substantial an improvement in real wages, and so substantial a movement to inequality, after the 1820s, the height data give him little support.

It is important, at this point, to recall the first section of this chapter and the analysis of geographical differences. These suggested that there were marked downward trends in the heights of those born in English and Scots urban counties in the eighteenth century, counterbalanced by slight improvements in the heights of men born in English and Scots rural areas and in London. In the second quarter of the nineteenth century, the relative downward trend of the urban areas – now including London – is consistent and even more pronounced and is now accompanied by a relative fall for Scots rural areas. In other words, the pattern of geographical height differentials suggests a strong negative effect of urbanisation in the nineteenth century, counterbalancing the improvements in occupational differentials which have just been discussed and leading, once those improvements ceased, to the overall stability or slight fall in the overall height of the population which was observed – in chapter 4 – to have occurred in the period between the 1820s and the 1850s or 1860s.

It seems as if the pattern of occupational and geographical differentials suggests that the early phases of the Industrial Revolution brought substantial improvements for the working class in Britain and a significant reduction in inequality within the working class. After the 1820s, however, this improvement ceased and was succeeded by a long period in which, even if real wages were rising, the nutritional status and welfare of the working class bore the marks of the decline in the urban environment which is so marked a feature of the popular perception of Britain in the middle of the nineteenth century.

6

Height, nutritional status and the environment

6.0 INTRODUCTION

The discussion in earlier chapters has demonstrated the existence of consistent height differentials between adults in different occupational groups in Britain in the nineteenth century, and of some dramatic differences between the mean heights of adolescents among the poorest and richest classes. This pattern has been related in general terms to living standards in this period, but we need to consider whether it is possible to be more specific about what these height differentials measure and about the conditions which produced them. What type of explanation could account for a difference of eight inches (20 cm) between the heights of 14-year-old boys sent to the Marine Society and cadets at Sandhurst?

Such contrasts are today found only among peoples in the third world, where many researchers have investigated the relation between health and growth. In this chapter we will therefore consider to what extent these studies, together with some from early twentieth-century Britain, can help us to interpret height differences in the last century. We will also consider how modern evidence can help us to explore the relationship between nutritional status in childhood and adolescence, on the one hand, and health and productivity in adult life on the other.

6.1 PATTERNS OF GROWTH IN CHILDHOOD

The normal pattern of growth in childhood and adolescence was described in chapter 1. Here we are concerned principally with environmental factors which disturb that pattern or cause groups of children to adopt one growth path rather than another. Such factors, together with ethnic origin, cause differences in mean heights between

225

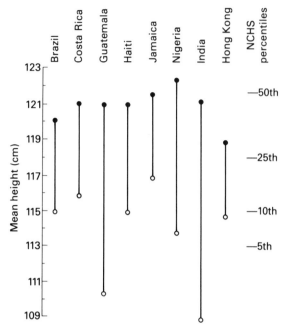

Figure 6.1. Mean heights of 7-year-old boys of high (•) and low (○) socio-economic status in various developing countries. Source: Martorell and Habicht 1986, p. 244.

different countries and between different social groups within those countries. Even by the age of 7 there are large variations between the mean heights of children in different socio-economic groups in developing countries. Figure 6.1 demonstrates this and incidentally provides a means of comparing (Martorell and Habicht 1986: 244):

the variation in height that may be attributed to ethnic origin (i.e. the genetic effect) to that which reflects the influence of environmental factors. ... The differences that could be attributed to genetics (ascertained by looking at the differences among the dark circles) are small and amount to no more than a few centimeters. The differences associated with social class, on the other hand, are very large.

This accords with our conclusions in chapter 1 on the relative importance of genetic and environmental factors in determining population variation in height.

The diagram is informative, however, because it shows not only the magnitude of environmental effects on height, but also that these are already evident at such a young age. This is such a consistent finding in both developed and underdeveloped countries that we will begin by examining the characteristics of the age-pattern of 'stunting'. This term is used by human biologists to denote retardation in height growth relative to the standard for well-nourished people, and may be contrasted with 'wasting', which is used to denote low weight-for-height (Martorell and Habicht 1986: 245).

In their recent summary of the results of third-world studies, Martorell and Habicht note that it is uncommon for babies in the first 2 or 3 months of life to be stunted, relative to the standards for length in developed countries (1986: 245):

> The length of children from developing countries is generally near the fiftieth percentile of the NCHS growth charts during the first few months of life. Somewhere between the second and sixth months, the length begins to fall precipitously relative to the NCHS charts as rate of growth becomes affected.

As an example, figure 6.2 illustrates the decline in height growth which occurs between 6 and 12 months among some Honduran infants. A similar pattern is found in the mean weights of infants from low socio-economic groups in developing countries (Eveleth and Tanner 1976: 241–2; see also Mata *et al.* 1972: 1268; Malcolm 1970: 19, 46).

Growth rates in height in most developing countries remain low during the second year of life but become closer to normal by about 3 years of age. After early childhood, however, it is rare for the rate of growth to be fast enough for children to regain the centile position in height which they had in early infancy, and this period of restricted growth therefore leaves a permanent legacy (Martorell and Habicht 1986: 248):

(1) growth impairment during the first few years of life largely determines the small stature exhibited by adults from developing countries; and
(2) within a malnourished population, those who exhibit a greater degree of stunting as young children are those who are shortest as adults.

Figure 6.3 and table 6.1 illustrate the degree of stunting which occurs in low socio-economic groups in two urban areas in Nigeria.

Why should the pattern be so consistent? Not only are differences in mean height established by the age of 5, but different groups remain on roughly the same centile throughout childhood. This suggests, first, that the influence of environmental factors before about the age of 5 is crucial, and, second, that the demands on nutrition for body maintenance and growth in later childhood are still heavy enough that, under normal circumstances, full catch-up in growth cannot take place later. 'Catch-up' growth is the phrase used by human biologists to describe the much faster rate of growth which occurs (assuming

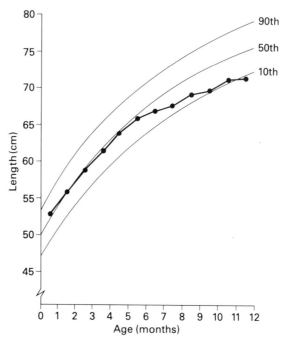

Figure 6.2. Mean length of 459 Honduran male infants relative to NCHS
percentiles. Source: Martorell and Habicht 1986, p. 246.

an adequate diet) after a period of restricted growth, whether the
latter was caused by lack of food, illness, or other factors (Tanner
1978: 154-60). The reason why stunted children in low socio-economic
groups do not have adequate catch-up would therefore appear to lie
in environmental factors, since, according to a recent FAO report on
energy and protein requirements, the capacity for catch-up in height
is probably retained until the end of the adolescent growth spurt (FAO/
WHO/UNU 1985: 143).

A striking example of catch-up growth taking place in later childhood and adolescence after earlier deprivation is the experience of
slave children in the United States. Steckel (1988) has shown that
such children were extremely stunted during early childhood, remaining below the second centile of the modern distribution until the age
of eleven. During adolescence, however, the children grew very
rapidly. This improvement occurred at the age when the children
were beginning to be used for field-labour, at which time their diet
was 'adequate, if not exceptional, for the tasks performed by slaves'
(Steckel 1988: 130).

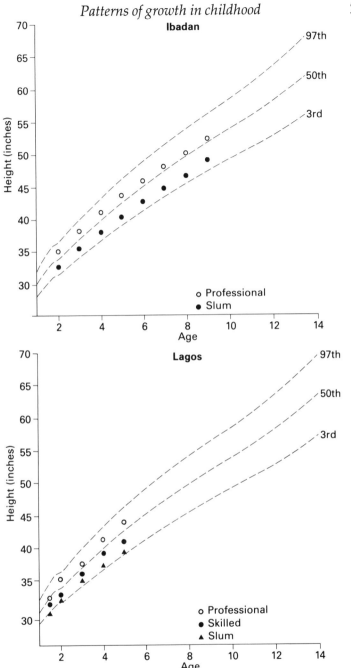

Figure 6.3. Stunting among low socio-economic groups in Ibadan and Lagos, Nigeria. Source: Eveleth and Tanner 1976; Rea 1971.

Table 6.1. *Stunting among different socio-economic groups in Nigeria.*

Age	Height (inches)	Centile	Frequency
Ibadan – professional			
1.00	30.55	32.587	N.A.
2.00	35.12	84.099	N.A.
3.00	38.31	78.988	N.A.
4.00	41.06	73.532	N.A.
5.00	43.74	72.184	N.A.
6.00	45.94	65.849	N.A.
7.00	48.15	63.289	N.A.
8.00	50.16	58.194	N.A.
9.00	52.40	59.938	N.A.
Ibadan – slum			
1.00	28.66	31.667	N.A.
2.00	32.68	18.967	N.A.
3.00	35.51	14.797	N.A.
4.00	38.03	12.205	N.A.
5.00	40.39	11.483	N.A.
6.00	42.64	10.957	N.A.
7.00	44.76	10.019	N.A.
8.00	46.69	9.240	N.A.
9.00	49.17	13.092	N.A.
Lagos – professional			
0.08	21.65	69.081	5
0.25	24.92	88.522	7
0.50	26.57	38.242	10
1.00	30.08	51.458	13
1.50	32.32	50.095	15
2.00	35.20	85.523	8
3.00	37.56	62.196	9
4.00	41.34	78.584	8
5.00	44.06	77.540	8
Lagos – skilled			
0.08	21.30	51.979	9
0.25	23.94	51.736	18
0.50	25.79	12.405	17
1.00	29.13	19.632	25
1.50	31.30	19.550	23
2.00	32.76	20.653	22
3.00	36.06	24.821	11
4.00	39.17	31.235	17
5.00	40.94	18.234	13

Table 6.1. (*cont.*)

Age	Height (inches)	Centile	Frequency
Lagos – slum			
0.08	20.63	21.256	11
0.25	23.46	30.423	13
0.50	25.39	5.672	15
1.00	28.66	9.671	16
1.50	29.80	1.721	18
2.00	32.09	9.120	25
3.00	35.04	8.723	19
4.00	37.52	7.110	13
5.00	39.37	4.018	11

Sources: Rea 1971: 52; Eveleth and Tanner 1976: 330–1.

This example certainly illustrates the plasticity of growth with respect to the environment, although it is probably more significant as an illustration of the abnormality of such change and its association with the highly unusual circumstances of a command economy, where the diet is controlled by a superior authority.

What pattern of stunting is likely to have been found in the particular circumstances of industrialising Britain? The earliest period for which data about the heights of young children are available in sufficient quantity for sensible discussion of this problem is the early twentieth century. Some examples are shown in figure 6.4 and table 6.2. It is apparent that, in these examples, differences in mean heights between children from different socio-economic groups were established by the time the children went to school, and that the children remained on roughly the same centile position until at least early adolescence. Rona, Swan and Altman reached the same conclusion in a study of primary schoolchildren in Britain in the 1970s (1978), while Smith, Chinn and Rona (1980: 113) found that height differences by class were 'established before the age of five and do not alter appreciably during the primary school years'. If, as these examples suggest, stunting occurs before the age of 5 in both the third world and in early and late twentieth-century Britain under normal circumstances, it seems unlikely that the pattern in eighteenth- and nineteenth-century Britain would have been different.

In the next two sections we will consider why environmental factors should have such severe and permanent effects on height growth in early childhood. The first section examines the main environmental factor which is essential for height growth – nutrition – and the second will focus on the main environmental factor which depletes nutrition – infection. This will be followed by a discussion of the relevance of studies of less-developed countries to industrialising Britain.

6.2 NUTRITION AND GROWTH

No-one disputes that undernourished children are shorter and/or lighter than those who are well-nourished, but when we consider the mechanisms by which undernutrition affects height growth, many questions confront us. We might consider why children are more likely to become stunted in very early childhood than later on, whether certain degrees of stunting can be related to corresponding levels of undernutrition, and whether particular nutrients affect height growth more than others.

If these questions concerned weight rather than height, we would be able to suggest some answers from common experience. In a society where slimness is highly valued and obesity is a common problem, most people have a rough idea of the ways in which a restricted food intake can reduce weight, and of the types of food which contribute most to weight gain.

People are generally less interested in the nutritional factors which influence height growth, and consequently know less about them. Perhaps this lack of commonsense knowledge partly explains why some idiosyncratic explanations for increases in mean height within a population have been put forward, such as the introduction of electric light, or other forms of sensory stimulation (see Hiernaux 1982: 64; Tanner and Eveleth 1976: 145). Stunting is, however, a familiar phenomenon in the third world, and the literature on this subject suggests that the effects of environmental factors on height are no more mysterious than those which affect weight.

If we relate the age-pattern of stunting to nutritional requirements at different ages, it is apparent that it is at the age when stunting is most likely to occur that growth makes particularly heavy demands on nutrition. Children in modern England achieve half of their adult height by about the age of 2, and the same proportion of adult weight by about the age of 11 (calculated from Tanner, Whitehouse and Takaishi 1966: 626-7). Small children need a much larger quantity of food per unit of body weight than do adults, and the qualitative needs are also slightly different because of the requirements for growth; in particular, they need a much larger quantity of protein at this age, possibly five times as much per kilogram of body weight at 6 months as in adulthood (Martorell and Habicht 1986: 251).

There is therefore no doubt that growth makes particularly heavy demands on nutrition in early childhood, but it would be helpful if we could be more specific – is it possible to relate particular degrees of stunting to corresponding levels of undernutrition? In order to make such a comparison the researcher requires a measure of undernutrition which is independent of anthropometric measures, but unfortunately nutritionists have become increasingly sceptical of the utility of the various measures used earlier this century. The identification of under-nutrition is itself, in consequence, becoming more and more elusive. Let us review the different measures which might be used.

One apparently obvious method of measuring undernutrition is to measure food intake and to relate this to food requirements, but there are two sources of difficulty with this method. First (Acheson *et al.* 1980: 1147):

The measurement of habitual food and energy intake in man has been said to be one of the hardest tasks a physiologist can undertake. The two basic problems are the accurate determination of the subject's customary food intake, and the conversion of this information to energy and nutrient intakes. Any technique has to be accurate but, however, should not be so intensely applied as to interfere with the subject's dietary habits and thus alter the parameter being measured.

Since the method is time-consuming, Acheson and his colleagues recommend a week as the most practicable time period in which to conduct a household consumption survey. In developing countries it is also necessary to take into account often large seasonal variations in the availability of different foods (Acheson *et al.* 1980: 1151-2; Pacey and Payne 1985: 78-9; Payne 1987: 5, 8, 31-2).

The second source of difficulty concerns the application of standards for food requirements. Nutritionists increasingly emphasise the varia-bility in food requirements between different ecological contexts, depending on the customary claims against food intake – such as work, growth and illness (these will be discussed further below). The geographical and social variations in these conditions of existence therefore multiply the possible sources of disagreement between

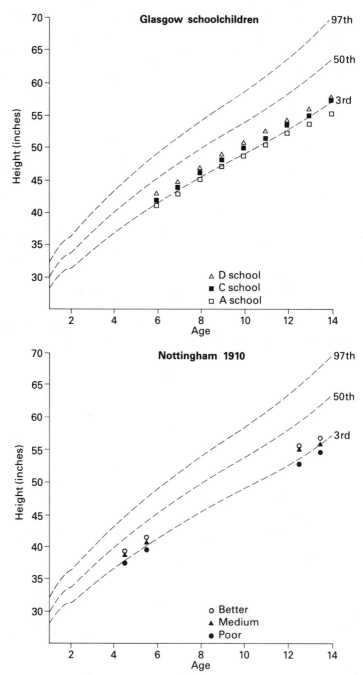

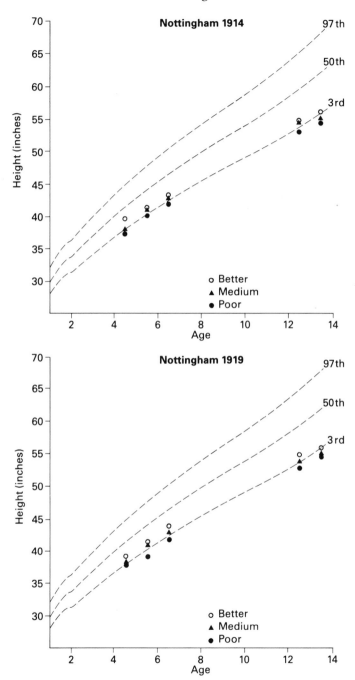

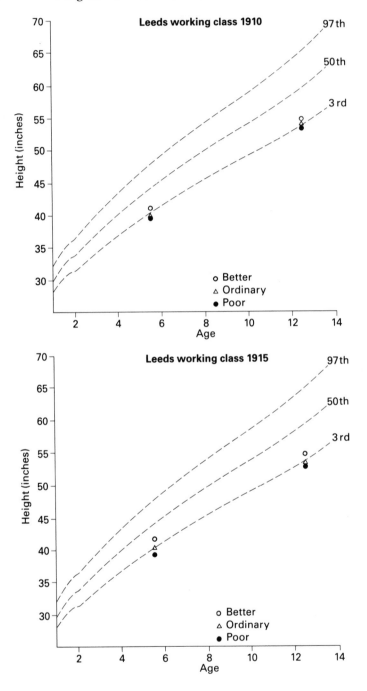

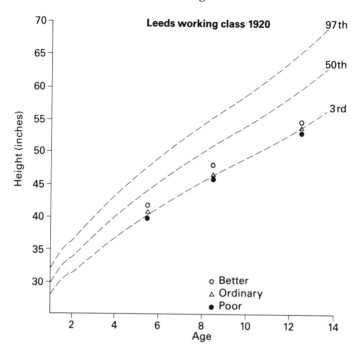

Figure 6.4. Heights of young children in early twentieth-century Britain. *Sources*: Elderton 1914 (Glasgow); Harris 1989 (Nottingham and Leeds).

nutritionists (Pacey and Payne 1985: 51–72). Philip Payne concluded that (1987: 31):

of all the possible ways that might be used to assess nutritional problems, direct measurement of intakes is in fact the most difficult and in practice the least satisfactory.

A further familiar method of measuring malnutrition is to look for clinical signs. Some types of undernutrition, such as mineral or vitamin deficiency, can of course be identified by clinical signs, but these deficiencies are largely specific to certain geographical regions and are often associated with mono-cropping. They consequently cannot be used as a universal measure of undernutrition.

Very severe deficiency – once thought to be primarily of protein – is also identifiable by clinical signs, the most characteristic of which is oedema (swollen tissues). It is an acute condition which is most commonly found among children between the ages of 2 and 4 (when it is referred to as 'kwashiorkor'), and death is a frequent outcome within a few weeks of the onset of symptoms if the condition is not

Table 6.2. *Stunting in early twentieth-century Britain.*

Age	Height (inches)	Centile	Frequency
Glasgow 1914			
D school			
6.00	43.00	14.697	417
7.00	44.80	10.327	506
8.00	46.90	10.851	581
9.00	49.00	11.590	528
10.00	50.90	11.444	558
11.00	52.60	10.687	594
12.00	54.20	9.179	571
13.00	55.90	7.245	611
14.00	57.70	4.425	383
C school			
6.00	42.10	6.745	500
7.00	44.00	4.989	649
8.00	46.20	6.126	642
9.00	48.10	5.720	630
10.00	49.90	5.373	616
11.00	51.50	4.830	568
12.00	53.50	5.758	601
13.00	55.00	4.006	582
14.00	57.20	3.171	259
A school (in the poorest district)			
6.00	41.30	2.931	1244
7.00	43.00	1.682	1354
8.00	45.10	2.113	1535
9.00	47.00	2.034	1402
10.00	48.80	1.985	1379
11.00	50.60	2.255	1278
12.00	52.30	2.294	1178
13.00	53.80	1.619	1202
14.00	55.20	0.680	428
Nottingham 1910			
Better			
4.50	39.40	13.788	30
5.50	41.60	11.790	134
12.50	55.63	11.428	35
13.50	56.72	5.815	413
Medium			
4.50	38.90	8.522	245
5.50	40.80	5.503	636
12.50	55.00	7.804	244
13.50	55.80	3.152	1220

Table 6.2. (*cont.*)

Age	Height (inches)	Centile	Frequency
Poor			
4.50	37.60	1.782	79
5.50	39.70	1.520	201
12.50	53.00	1.792	71
13.50	54.67	1.344	344
Nottingham 1914			
Better			
4.50	39.56	15.866	41
5.50	41.28	8.843	119
6.50	43.30	8.146	83
12.50	54.80	6.859	185
13.50	56.13	3.959	30
Medium			
4.50	37.84	2.463	174
5.50	40.91	6.163	921
6.50	42.66	4.523	447
12.50	54.52	5.687	1200
13.50	55.14	1.942	459
Poor			
4.50	37.23	1.047	65
5.50	40.08	2.447	227
6.50	41.99	2.250	91
12.50	53.14	2.013	417
13.50	54.45	1.124	154
Nottingham 1919			
Better			
4.50	39.12	10.616	41
5.50	41.42	10.056	186
6.50	43.89	13.116	63
12.50	55.00	7.804	200
13.50	56.01	3.648	139
Medium			
4.50	38.01	3.069	190
5.50	40.98	6.614	964
6.50	42.95	5.960	268
12.50	54.12	4.293	800
13.50	55.12	1.913	498
Poor			
4.50	37.89	2.630	99
5.50	39.13	0.697	298
6.50	41.84	1.902	68
12.50	52.98	1.763	201
13.50	54.65	1.323	203

Table 6.2. (*cont.*)

Age	Height (inches)	Centile	Frequency
Leeds working class 1910			
Better			
5.50	40.90	6.100	N.A.
12.50	54.70	6.420	N.A.
Ordinary			
5.50	39.60	1.333	N.A.
12.50	53.90	3.653	N.A.
Poor			
5.50	39.40	1.018	N.A.
12.50	53.40	2.485	N.A.
Leeds working class 1915			
Better			
5.50	41.80	13.952	N.A.
12.50	54.80	6.859	N.A.
Ordinary			
5.50	40.30	3.175	N.A.
12.50	53.50	2.689	N.A.
Poor			
5.50	39.30	0.887	N.A.
12.50	52.90	1.648	N.A.
Leeds working class 1920			
Better			
5.50	41.80	13.952	N.A.
8.50	48.00	11.592	N.A.
12.50	54.60	6.004	N.A.
Ordinary			
5.50	40.70	4.952	N.A.
8.50	46.60	3.559	N.A.
12.50	53.70	3.140	N.A.
Poor			
5.50	39.80	1.728	N.A.
8.50	45.90	1.749	N.A.
12.50	52.90	1.648	N.A.

Sources: Glasgow: Elderton 1914: 296, 304–21.
Nottingham, Leeds: Annual Reports of School Medical Officers; see Harris 1989: 177.

treated. Hunger oedema is usually precipitated by infectious disease (Bengoa 1974: 5; Gurney 1979: 189; Feigin 1981: 17; Golden 1985: 174–83). It is not a common occurrence unless the diet is near starvation level – for example, during the Dutch Hunger Winter of 1944–45, hunger oedema affected only 10 per cent of the city populations by May 1945, when over a quarter of working-class deaths in the Hague in the first quarter of 1945 were caused by undernutrition. The Jewish physicians in the Warsaw Ghetto described the symptoms of hunger oedema in detail in 1940–42, noting that it principally affected children under the age of 5. By the end of 1941 there were few surviving under-fives to attend the hospital (Stein *et al.* 1975: 45; Winick 1979: 59, 47; Pacey and Payne 1985: 65–6).

The other category of severe undernutrition – marasmus, or calorie deficiency – is characterised by emaciation, and differs from mild-to-moderate calorie deficiency only in the degree of thinness. Clinical signs are less often referred to than in the case of kwashiorkor – for example, health workers in the Punjab identified those suffering from marasmus by the presence of wrinkled skin on the buttocks and little or no subcutaneous fat (Kielmann *et al.* 1983: 149). The second type of 'hunger disease' described by the physicians in the Warsaw Ghetto is identifiable as marasmus, which they distinguished from kwashiorkor as 'dry' and 'wet' hunger disease respectively (Winick 1979: 57–9).

Measures of severe undernutrition of this kind are clearly not useful as a means of comparing the nutritional status of different groups in a society, and it may be concluded from our review that there are no universal measures of mild-to-moderate undernutrition apart from anthropometric indices.

The commonest method of assessing how stunting reflects under-nutrition consequently does not involve using indices which are independent of anthropometry. Instead, the normal diet is supplemented with added nutrients, and the subsequent rate of growth is then compared with that of a control group (Kielmann, Ajello and Kielmann 1982). For example, in a study of the effects of supplementation in four Guatemalan villages carried out by INCAP (the Institute of Nutrition of Central America and Panama), it was found that 3-year-old children in a control group were about 12 centimetres shorter than the 50th centile of the NCHS standard. Those whose diet had been supplemented with a high-protein energy drink of over 200 kilocalories per day during the first 3 years of life were only 7.5 centimetres shorter than the 50th centile (Martorell and Habicht 1986: 253).

As in this study, supplements are most commonly measured in

terms of their energy content, since nutritionists emphasise that the quantity of food consumed by an individual is a more crucial factor than quality in developing countries. People who receive adequate calories are unlikely to suffer from serious deficiencies of protein, vitamins or minerals, at least if they rely on more than one staple food. It is therefore thought to be misguided to focus, for example, on signs of vitamin deficiency such as are manifested in a case of pellagra, since the root cause is lack of food. The common use of the term 'protein–energy malnutrition' indicates that both protein and calories have the greatest importance, but since in terms of quantity much more energy is required than protein, the emphasis on quantity of food in practice involves a focus on number of calories. Protein can also be utilised by the body to produce energy when there is a low intake of other foods, but it is a less efficient source of calories than fat or carbohydrate (FAO 1987: 17–18; Pacey and Payne 1985: 25, 67, 69, 98–100; Passmore *et al.* 1974: 19; Jelliffe 1975).

It may be questioned whether this emphasis on the energy content of the diet is as appropriate in studies of industrialised societies as in those of the third world, and this is an issue which we will return to in section 6.4. Another issue which we will return to in the same section, but which should be mentioned here, is the question of which anthropometric measures should be used – in particular, whether weight or height provides the 'best' index of nutritional status. This is important because in practice health workers find that weight, or weight-for-height, is the most useful measure, since it reflects the balance between recent food intake and claims against that intake, and it responds more quickly to dietary restriction than does height. In a historical study, however, height is more useful since it measures the cumulative effect of these factors in early childhood. Many nutritionists believe that, apart from differences in timing, stunting and wasting reflect the same causes, and we will discuss this issue further below (Martorell and Habicht 1986: 245).

We began this section by noting that the period of early childhood when growth makes particularly heavy demands on nutrition is also the age when stunting is most likely to occur. Height velocity does not, however, decline steadily until adulthood, and it might be thought that the time of the adolescent growth spurt would be another 'sensitive period' when stunting could occur. There are unfortunately not many studies of growth in adolescence, but what there are suggest that a decline in food intake during this period may delay the timing of a growth spurt, but is unlikely to have an appreciable effect on final height (Tanner 1962: 121–3).

If we consider possible reasons for this, it is apparent that the nutritional demands for height growth are much less than in early childhood. The height spurt appears dramatic because it occurs after a period of relatively low growth and is followed by a rapid falling off in growth, but it is a relatively short period of increased velocity and, in the event of dearth, can be delayed somewhat until more prosperous times. In early childhood, on the other hand, high rates of growth in height have to be maintained for several years if the child is not to end up stunted. A British boy of 12 who has not entered the height spurt still has on average only 15 per cent more to grow before he reaches adult height, although he will still be short on adult weight by about 40 per cent (Heald 1979: 240; figures calculated from Tanner, Whitehouse and Takaishi 1966). The adolescent is also not affected by the high frequency of infection which is characteristic of early childhood.

Growth makes heavy demands on nutrition before birth and in the early months of infancy as well as in early childhood, and it might therefore be asked whether stunting in early childhood could be a legacy from earlier insults. One way to look at this question is to relate birth weight to height in childhood (birth weight is more commonly used than birth length since the latter is difficult to measure). Some relationship between birth weight and height at age 7 among British children born in 1958 was demonstrated in the National Child Development Study, but the importance of this relationship is modified when we consider the much stronger relationship between birth order and height at age 7 (see figure 6.5). Since the 'effect of birth order on height is opposite to its effect on birth weight, where the later born children are heavier' at birth but shorter in childhood, this suggests that some factors in the post-natal environment must have a relatively greater effect on height in childhood than intra-uterine factors (Davie, Butler and Goldstein 1972: 83). L. A. Malcolm found a slightly different pattern among the Bundi of Papua New Guinea, but referred to the same factors to explain it – competition between siblings for food, and whether or not an older person was available to feed toddlers or help them collect food (Malcolm 1970: 39). A more recent explanation would relate greater stunting among younger siblings to the higher rate of infection in larger families. In these circumstances young children would be more likely to come into contact with infection through their older siblings than in smaller families, and the severity of the illness would be worse, and its effect on growth greater, at young ages (Reves 1985). It should be noted that the birth-order effect usually disappears by adulthood in well-nourished

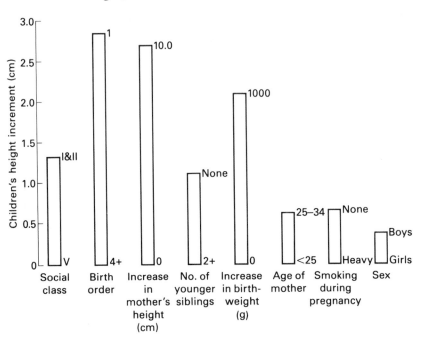

Figure 6.5. Effects of different social and biological factors on the height of 7-year-olds in the National Child Development Study. Source: Davie *et al.* 1972, p. 82.

populations, although it was still evident in the heights of French army recruits in the nineteenth century (Tanner 1962: 142).

Let us now consider why children are less likely to become stunted in the early months of infancy than later on. Nutritionists consider that it is when breast milk needs to be supplemented with other foods that infants are most likely to become undernourished. This is also a time when young children require frequent meals, and are dependent on other people to feed them (Pacey and Payne 1985: 100–2; Gurney 1979: 195–8). The other main factor, however, is the protection from infection which breast-fed babies gain from the anti-infective property of breast milk, and from their relative lack of contact, in comparison with toddlers, with substances which can spread infection. It is therefore to the interactions between infection, nutrition and growth that we must now turn (Martorell and Habicht 1986: 252).

6.3 INTERACTIONS BETWEEN INFECTION, .
GROWTH

A wide range of factors which are peculiar to the
conditions and physical constitution of an individu
his or her health in both positive and negative w
a farmer living in an isolated area might avoid the in.
in urban areas and benefit from clear air and unpolluted water, ᴜᴜ.
suffer from a restricted diet and damp housing. An urban artisan,
on the other hand, might have quite different problems and benefits.
To distinguish the effects of these different factors on height growth
would be impossible, but we can make some general statements about
the effects of infection on nutritional status, and at the end of this
section we will consider whether in some circumstances it is possible
to disentangle the effects of undernutrition from those of infection.

Lack of food is only one of the two main causes of undernutrition,
and indeed in a recent FAO World Food Survey it is noted that (1987:
35):

Many studies suggest that a closely paced series of common childhood infections is the most important cause of malnutrition, retarded growth, and child
mortality.

The interactions between infection, nutrition and growth are complex, and it is therefore useful to consider the effects of infection on
nutritional status, and of undernutrition on resistance to infection,
before considering the effects of infection on growth.

Infection affects nutritional status by a number of different mechanisms. These include loss of appetite, energy lost as heat during fever
and loss of other nutrients in sweat, vomiting, decreased absorption
of nutrients, protein catabolism,[1] and reduced food intake resulting
from cultural factors. Malabsorption can result from infestation with
intestinal parasites, but the most common and severe cause is diarrhoea, which causes food to pass through the intestine too quickly
to be absorbed (Martorell 1980: 95–6; Martorell and Habicht 1986: 251;
Scrimshaw 1977; Kielmann, Taylor and De Sweemer 1983: 5–7;
Chandra 1980: 3–5).

---

[1] The mechanism causing protein catabolism is hormonal; in response to a stress such
as infectious disease, or even psychological stress, the body increases the excretion
rate of urinary nitrogen, which is broken down from the protein which constitutes
lean tissue. The effect of infectious disease is to cause some of this protein to be
catabolised for energy use and end-products then excreted as urinary nitrogen (Tanner
1978: 25; Scrimshaw, Taylor and Gordon 1968: 37; Passmore *et al.* 1974: 16; Jackson
1985: 115–18).

Infection causes nutritional status to deteriorate, but at the same time undernutrition decreases resistance to infection – a 'synergistic' relationship. Most aspects of the immune system are impaired by undernutrition, although the production of antibodies in the blood is an exception, as evidenced by the effectiveness of vaccination in the third world. Cell-mediated immunity is most impaired by under-nutrition, and this is particularly important in providing resistance against viral and intra-cellular bacterial diseases. Some studies show that it is the severity rather than the incidence of infection that is affected (Martorell 1980: 96–99; Chandra 1980: 8–14; Chen and Scrimshaw 1983: 12; Kielmann, Taylor and De Sweemer 1983: 173).

Measles is the classic example of a viral disease which is exacerbated by undernutrition – most children catch it, but only among malnour-ished populations is it a major cause of death. In Glasgow in the early twentieth century, for example, there was a sixfold difference in the fatality rate for measles, depending on the socio-economic status of the parents (Morley 1976: 66). The secondary complications – usually diarrhoea and bronchopneumonia – may be more important than the illness itself in causing fatalities (Cecil 1947: 23). Mortality rates in the 1960s from measles in Latin America as a multiple of the USA rate were (Scrimshaw, Taylor and Gordon 1968: 15):

Mexico (1961)	83
El Salvador (1962)	128
Guatemala (1962)	268
Ecuador (1960)	274

Finally, let us consider the effects of infection on height growth. It can be seen that since illness has a dramatic effect on nutrition, this will be reflected in restricted growth. We can also see that nutritional problems which are associated with the weaning period will be particularly exacerbated by illness, first because the child no longer enjoys passive immunity from the mother and has to build up anti-bodies of its own, and second because it is more likely to come into contact with substances which can carry infection. It is particularly unfortunate for the infant that it is not well protected by antibodies in the blood, since this appears to be the only form of immunity which is little affected by undernutrition. The demands which growth and illness make on food intake, and the effects of undernutrition in increasing the severity and length of disease episodes, thus conspire to make this a critical period for stunting.

The degree of stunting, however, depends on the extent to which catch-up growth is possible after the episode of illness. In this respect the severity of the illness is relatively less important than the availability of an adequate diet during convalescence, and whether or not another period of illness starts before catch-up can be completed after the earlier episode (Whitehead 1977; FAO/WHO/UNU 1985: 145–6).

The importance of frequency of illness is emphasised, for example, by Whitehead in an article on the nutrients required for catch-up growth after infections. He refers to one village in Guatemala, where 'children are infected with one illness or another for around 35 per cent of the time or ... Keneba, the Gambia, where at some times of the year the average child has diarrhoeal disease for 20 per cent of the time' in spite of the presence of a full-time paediatrician (Whitehead 1977: 1545). Whitehead and colleagues found that in spite of the very low average growth rate between the ages of 0.6 and 3 years in different villages in Uganda and the Gambia, there was a wide range in growth at different times. They concluded that the children were capable of very rapid rates of growth when they were not suffering from disease and had sufficient food to support catch-up (1977: 1546–7):

> if the concentration of nutrients in the diet relative to energy content is insufficient to cover the whole range of growth rates a child is trying to achieve, he will take longer to reach maximum size ... If we limit the relative concentration of protein, for example, to allow only for an average rate of growth, the ability of the child to catch up is going to be very impaired. Before very long the child will be hit by another infection and this is why for long periods of time the children in our villages do not appear to grow at all.

Some nutritionists emphasise the importance of protein in promoting catch-up growth, whether after a period of infection or of low food intake (FAO/WHO/UNU 1985: 143–4).

Martorell has summarised some studies of the effects of infection on growth in developing countries, many of which showed a significant relationship between growth retardation and incidence of diarrhoea, but not of respiratory infections. For example, Guatemalan children who were relatively free of diarrhoea from birth to 7 years were on average 3.5 centimetres taller and 1.5 kilograms heavier than children who had suffered much more from diarrhoea (Martorell 1980: 92–95; Martorell and Habicht 1986: 250–51).

Studies of the effects of infection on growth in developed countries have not shown such significant results as those in developing countries (Baumgartner and Mueller 1984; Martorell and Habicht 1986: 250–1; Martorell 1980: 90). One study which did was the Oxford Child Health Survey, which investigated the growth and health of a group of 650 children of relatively low socio-economic status in the 1940s and 1950s. Children who had no illness from 1 to 5 years were on average one inch (2.54 cm) taller than those who had experienced a severe illness in each of the four years. In a similar study of 614 children in Newcastle-upon-Tyne in the same period, those who had had four or more attacks of pneumonia or bronchitis before their third birthday were about one inch (2.54 cm) shorter than those with no attacks (Tanner 1962: 131–2).

Tanner points out that it is difficult to distinguish between the effects of infection and of underlying undernutrition, though he suggests that the lack of catch-up growth among the children in the Oxford Study indicates that an inadequate diet may be at least a contributory factor. Even if we look at the effects of disease on the weight of individuals, it is often not possible to isolate the effects of one episode of illness from another if they are frequent, as can be seen from the longitudinal weight curves of some Guatemalan children (see figure 6.6).

It is apparent that undernutrition and infection each make the other worse, but it is also useful to consider whether the effects of each can be disentangled. We will take as an example a well-designed study from Punjab – the Narangwal project – in which the effects on nutritional status of food supplements and medical services were compared (Kielmann, Taylor and De Sweemer 1983; Beaton and Ghassemi 1982: 887–8).

The villages were divided into four groups, each with different service inputs: (1) food supplements only (NUT), (2) health care only (HC), (3) both (NUTHC), and (4) control. The NUTHC villages were given only half the inputs of each of the other service villages, in order to make costs equivalent, and because the researchers expected the combined care to have a greater effect on the synergistic interaction between infection and nutritional status than either of the other services on their own. The normal diet of villagers was relatively high in protein and low in energy, and the diseases from which the children suffered were in general common childhood complaints – diarrhoea and lower respiratory infections accounted for more than 60 per cent of deaths in children aged 0–5, and there were no tropical or parasitic diseases (Kielmann, Taylor and De Sweemer 1983: 146, 207).

It was found that NUT inputs had the greatest effect on height between the ages of 18 months and 3 years, but in the first year of life health care alone was more important than nutrition. The synergistic effect was less than expected, and the NUTHC inputs had an intermediate effect between the NUT and HC inputs (see figure 6.7). There are not enough well-designed studies of this kind for us to judge whether these findings may be generalised, but it is worth bearing in mind that health care may be more important than nutrition in the first year of life in improving nutritional status, whereas in early childhood after the first year nutrition may be more important than health care.

Finally, we will consider a problem that is not an important issue in third-world studies – whether infection can affect the growth of children who are well-nourished. It is important in an historical context, however, since the mean heights of even those in the highest social class in the nineteenth century were lower than those in the same social class today. Since this was unlikely to have been caused by undernutrition, could it have been caused by infection? This question was not addressed in the study discussed below, and the comments presented here are therefore only intended to be suggestive.

As part of a study of growth in Lagos in the 1960s, Rea measured the heights of children from the equivalent of British social classes I and II, living on a freehold housing estate. The measurements were a mixture of cross-sectional and longitudinal, with one child contributing up to eight points. Between the ages of 2 and 5 years, these children were above the 60th centile of the British standard for height, whereas children from the lowest socio-economic group were below the 10th centile at the same ages. All groups, however, had experienced a sharp retardation in growth in the middle months of infancy, which proved to be temporary for the elite group but not for the poorest group. Between the ages of 3 and 6 months, those in the poorest group declined from the 30th to the 6th centile, those in the middle group from the 52nd to the 12th centile, and those in the elite group from the 89th to the 38th centile. The children in two of the groups achieved some catch-up in the following couple of years – those in the elite group caught up to about the 70th centile by the age of 2, and those in the middle group to the 21st centile, but children in the poorest group remained below the 10th centile until at least the age of 5. We should not place too much emphasis on the individual figures since the number of observations is very small, particularly for the elite group, but there appears to be a consistent pattern in all three groups (see figures 6.3 and 6.8; Rea 1971: 47, 52). Children of African stock are more advanced in growth at all ages than European children unless their growth has been restricted by environmental factors, and it therefore seems likely that infection would have been the main factor responsible for this slowing down in height growth (Eveleth and Tanner 1976: 274).

Tropical diseases are prevalent in this region of Nigeria, and

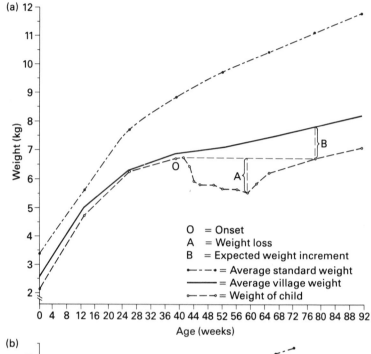

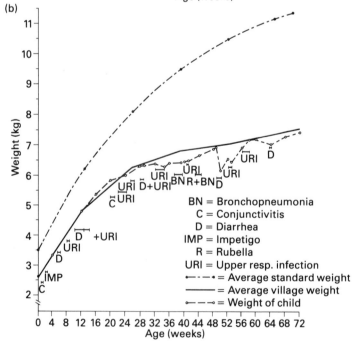

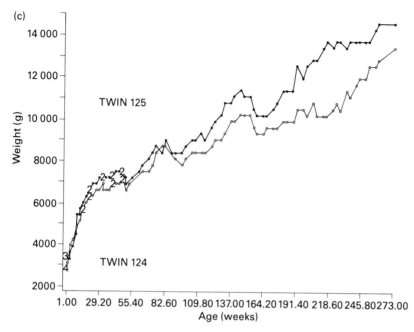

Figure 6.6. Weight curves and infectious diseases for children from the village of Santa María Cauqué. (a) Girl's loss of weight after onset of whooping cough (Mata 1978, p. 284). (b) Boy's weight curve and infectious diseases (Mata *et al.* 1972, p. 1272). (c) Weight curves of monozygotic twins in the first five years of life; the infectious diseases suffered by these children in the first three years are shown in table 6.3 (Mata 1978, p. 288).

sanitation was very deficient at the time when these children were measured – the water supply was inadequate, and there was no centralised sewage-disposal system (in a city with a population density of nearly 10 thousand per square kilometre). The consequences of these factors for health are reflected in the fact that diarrhoea and dysentery were the third highest cause of death in Lagos at this time (Williams and Walsh 1968: 9, 99–101; Sofola and Lawal 1983). This suggests that infections can cause stunting even with an adequate diet, but that after a critical period in the first year these children were well enough fed to be able to catch up in growth to above the 60th centile by the age of 2 years.

We can conclude that the early years of childhood are a critical time for stunting in developing countries because both growth and infection make large claims on nutrition at this age (FAO/WHO/UNU 1985: 145):

Table 6.3. *Infectious diseases suffered by monozygotic twins from Santa María Cauqué in the first three years of life. Their weight curves are shown in figure 6.6(c).*

Age (weeks)	Twin 124	Twin 125
First year		
0–12	Conj.	Conj.
	Impetigo	Impetigo
	Diarrhea	Diarrhea
	URI	URI
	Diarrhea with mucus, URI[a]	Diarrhea
13–25	Conj.	Conj.
	Conj.	URI
	URI	Conj.
	Diarrhea and vomiting	Diarrhea
26–38	URI, Conj.	URI, Conj.
	Diarrhea with mucus, URI, Conj.[a]	Bronchitis, Conj., Diarrhea[a]
	URI, Conj.[a]	
	Exanthem	
	Bronchopeneumonia	
39–51	URI	Rubella
	Rubella, Bronchopneumonia[a]	URI
	Diarrhea with mucus, Exanthem[a]	Diarrhea, dehydration, URTI, URI[a]
Second year		
52–64	URI	URI
	URI	Diarrhea with mucus
	Diarrhea	
65–77	Herpes simplex oralis	URI
	URI, Conj.[a]	
	Uri	
78–90	Whooping cough, Bronchopneumonia, Stomatitis, URI, Diarrhea[a]	Dysentery Whooping cough, Bronchopneumonia, Diarrhea[a]
91–103	None	URI
		Vomiting
Third year		
104–116	URI	URI, Diarrhea[a]
	Diarrhea	
	Vomiting	
117–129	Bronchitis, Impetigo, Conj.[a]	URI, Conj.[a]
		Diarrhea and Vomiting

Table 6.3. (*cont.*)

Age (weeks)	Twin 124	Twin 125
130–142	Dysentery, Conj.[a] Impetigo, URI[a] Diarrhea	Impetigo Diarrhea
143–155	Impetigo Varicella Bronchitis Laryngotracheobronchitis	Bronchitis Varicella

Source: Mata 1978: 255–56.

Note: Conj. = conjunctivitis; URI = upper respiratory illness; URTI = urinary tract illness.

[a] Two or more overlapping illnesses.

Children under 3 years of age, who have the highest protein and energy needs per kg of body weight, are the group most frequently affected by infections and most severely ill.

6.4 THE APPLICATION OF THE RESULTS OF STUDIES OF THE DEVELOPING WORLD TO GROWTH IN INDUSTRIALISING BRITAIN

In the first part of this chapter we saw that the age-pattern of stunting in the third world and in industrialised countries is similar. There are two possible areas of difficulty, however, and some speculations on these problems are presented below.

First, we need to consider whether differences in types of disease between developed and less-developed countries should influence our interpretation of height as an index of nutritional status. In some third-world countries tropical diseases are of course prevalent, but it is the common childhood diseases – diarrhoea and respiratory infections – which are most discussed in the literature (Martorell 1980: 92–4; FAO/WHO/UNU 1985: 140; Martorell and Habicht 1986: 250–1; Scrimshaw 1977: 1539). Intestinal parasites only have a severe effect if there is a high rate of infestation; malaria has a large effect on growth, but because it occurs relatively infrequently compared to diarrhoea, the overall effect is less (Scrimshaw 1977: 1537; Chen and Scrimshaw 1983: 5). One consequence of this emphasis on diarrhoea and respira-

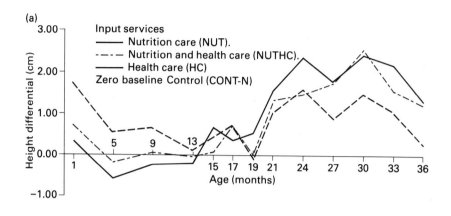

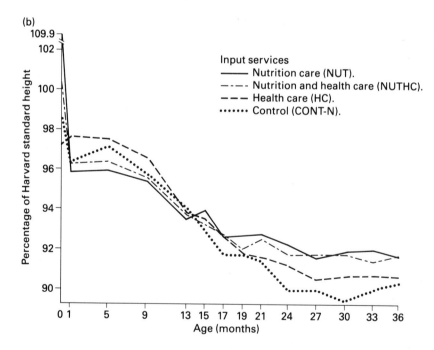

Figure 6.7. (a) Effects of different types of input services on the mean heights of children from the Narangwal project in the first three years of life (adjusted for sex, birth order, mother's age, caste, year and season of observation). (b) Mean heights of the same children relative to the Harvard height standard (adjusted for caste and sex). Source: Kielmann *et al.* 1983, pp. 104, 106.

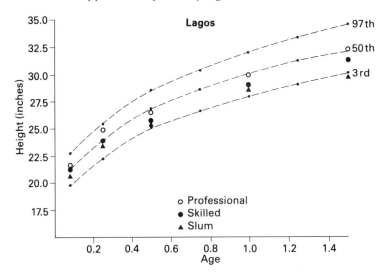

Figure 6.8. Growth in different socio-economic groups in Lagos. Source: Rea 1971.

tory infections is that there is little concern in the literature about causative agents, possibly because it is difficult to attempt to identify all of these (Scrimshaw, Taylor and Gordon 1968: 12). We may therefore conclude that differences in types of disease between developed and less-developed countries are not a major cause for concern.

This was certainly the conclusion reached in one explicit study of this subject. Aykroyd (1971) relied on Newman's study of *Infant Mortality, a Social Problem* (1906) for his information on late nineteenth-century England and Wales and thus on observations of the situation *after* the major decline in mortality. Nevertheless, he emphasises the similarity of mortality patterns at the time and in the current developing world, in particular the high mortality in the second year of life, together with the prevalence of mortality from diarrhoea and enteritis.

The second area of difficulty is more complex, and concerns the question of whether weight and height measure the same aspects of nutritional status. As mentioned above, researchers in the third world usually consider that stunting and wasting are caused by similar factors, if on a different time-scale. In studies of developed countries, however, more consideration has to be given to the question of whether height and weight always respond in similar ways to different environmental factors, because these anthropometric indices often do not appear to tell the same story. Children in lower socio-economic groups in developed countries always have lower heights than those in higher socio-economic groups, but they also usually have higher weight-for-height than their better-off peers (Martorell and Habicht 1986: 259). Obesity is not uncommon among these children, and it is therefore inappropriate to use weight-for-height as a means of distinguishing between the standard of living of different social groups (Eveleth and Tanner 1976: 251). As Martorell and Habicht point out (1986: 259): 'the question of whether conditions that allow for maximal growth in height also predispose to obesity is complex'.

As was mentioned above, weight and weight-for-height are the most commonly used indices of nutritional status in developing countries, where weight-for-height increases with income level, and obesity is rare except among well-off urban groups (Eveleth and Tanner 1976: 251–6). It is perhaps a mistake to consider weight-for-height or weight-for-age as synonymous with nutritional status, as is sometimes implied (e.g. Kielmann *et al.* 1976: 479). Pacey and Payne refer to a useful analogy for the difficulties in defining nutritional status (1985: 49):

In discussing the interpretation of anthropometric data, Trowbridge . . . recalls the story of the blind men who encounter an elephant and have to identify it from the shapes they can feel. Each man touches a different part of the elephant and comes to a different conclusion about the nature of the beast. Similarly, weight-for-age, weight-for-height and arm circumference each touch upon 'different aspects of the vague entity called malnutrition'; none gives us a view of the whole condition.

Let us consider an example of the problems involved in interpreting anthropometric indices in industrialised societies. In the early twentieth century British school medical officers took annual measurements of the heights of school entrants (and of children at other ages) which indicate that those in urban areas were very short but also rather fat. For example, 5-year-olds (midpoint 5.5 years) from Nottingham and Leeds who were described as 'poor' and 'poor working class' respectively were below the 3rd centile of the British height standard in all years between 1910 and 1920, but well above the third centile in weight, if we allow 2 lb (0.91 kg) for indoor clothing (see figure 6.4 and table 6.2 for heights; Harris 1989 and personal communication). These children were very short even by third-world standards, if we compare them with Eveleth and Tanner's survey of modern height studies. Of the four broadly defined racial groups which Eveleth and Tanner distinguish in the less-developed world (excluding those of European stock), none of the mean heights of African 5-year-olds (midpoint 5.0) were below the 3rd centile (the studies do not include pygmy children), and only 27 per cent of the Asiatics, 29 per cent of the Indo-Mediterraneans, and 43 per cent of the Aborigines and Pacific Islanders (number of studies 9, 11, 7 and 7 respectively; studies of people referred to as 'well-off', or living in industrialised countries, have been excluded; figures calculated from Eveleth and Tanner 1976: 330, 358, 388, 406).

Few figures are available for the heights and weights of children in the nineteenth century, and it is possible that weight-for-height was lower in the early nineteenth century than a century later. It is clear, however, that we have to confront the problem of why children in developed countries are often both short and fat.

If we compare the factors that detract from nutritional status in developed and less-developed countries, it is evident that there may be important differences, and it is possible that these differences may be reflected in anthropometric indices. Let us begin with less-developed countries, since more is known about the interpretation of anthropometric indices of nutritional status in this context than in developed countries. One factor which may be important is seasonality of food supply, particularly among those cultivators in tropical countries who have only one harvest per year. It is noted in a recent FAO world food survey that problems associated with seasonality are particularly emphasised in current research (FAO 1987: 27; see also FAO/WHO/UNU 1985: 146, 148).

In a survey of this issue, Chambers, Longhurst and Pacey note that 'most of the very poor people in the world live in tropical areas with marked wet and dry seasons' (1981: xv), and that the importance of seasonality is often underperceived by western observers. In these areas people often expect to lose weight during a pre-harvest 'hungry season'. The effects are magnified in areas where this is also the season when agricultural work is heaviest, and sometimes disease is also prevalent at this time. Young children are particularly likely to suffer if, at the most critical time of the agricultural year, mothers spend long hours in agricultural work and do not have the time to prepare the frequent meals which they require. For example, the mean body weight of 205 mothers in one area of Bangladesh dropped by over 1 kg (3 per cent of body weight) between August and September, and seasonal weight fluctuations among men and women in a Gambian village are shown in figure 6.9 (Pacey and Payne 1985: 39; Chambers, Longhurst and Pacey 1981: xv, 5, 11, 59).

Seasonal effects are often exacerbated when financial necessity causes people to sell their labour or crops, or to grow cash crops at the expense of food for the family. A vicious circle arises if lack

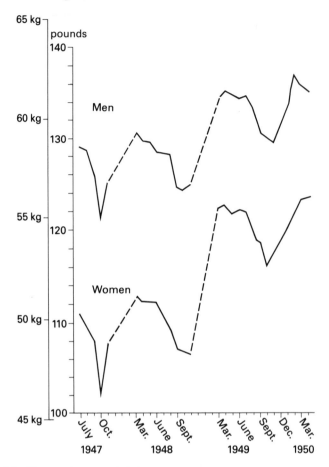

Figure 6.9. Fluctuations in adult body weight by season in a Gambian village.
Source: Fox 1953: 58v.

of food before the harvest forces cultivators to sell their labour when they need it for their own crops, and to buy food when prices are high, and then to sell their own crops when prices are low after the harvest in order to pay off debts. Part of the problem associated with seasonality arises as a result of imperfect markets – seasonal and regional price fluctuations are not levelled out as they are in developed countries, because of inadequate marketing, transport and storage facilities. These problems are exacerbated if, as is often the case, local merchants or landlords control the transport, marketing and credit facilities, and often also the opportunities for employment (Pacey and

Payne 1985: 155–76; Jones 1972; Pottier 1985; Harriss 1984). Seasonality is therefore a critical factor in immiseration (Chambers, Longhurst and Pacey 1981: xv):

> This is a time of year marked by loss of body weight, low birth weights, high neonatal mortality, malnutrition, and indebtedness. It is the hungry season and the sick season. It is the time of year when poor people are at their poorest and most vulnerable to becoming poorer.

Seasonality is therefore responsible for periodic hunger and weight loss, and it also contributes to overall impoverishment. How is this reflected in anthropometric indices? There is no doubt that seasonal hunger depletes the fat stores that are laid up in more prosperous times, and this would be likely to keep adults on a low centile for weight, relative to the standards for developed countries. It is not so clear whether young children would be equally affected in both weight and height, or if, instead, seasonal hunger would result in greater wasting than stunting.

If we turn to nineteenth-century Britain, seasonality may still have exacerbated the insecurity of working-class life, but this degree of periodic hunger would not have been a common experience among people living in an industrialising society and in a temperate climate. It would be more appropriate to emphasise other factors which would have detracted from nutritional status, such as bad housing and working conditions, a high rate of infection, or a low quality diet. It might, therefore, be argued that children in low socio-economic groups in developed countries are fatter than those in rural areas in much of the third world because they have a more constant supply of food and consume a greater quality overall, but this still does not resolve the question of why their degree of stunting is comparable to that found in low socio-economic groups in less-developed countries. One possibility is that the type of factors which most commonly detract from nutritional status in developed countries are reflected more in height than in weight (and we should also allow for the fact that stunted people require less food to make them obese than those who are not stunted).

This question can be further explored – if not answered – by an examination of a pioneering study of the relation between height growth and nutrition which was undertaken in Scotland in the 1920s. In a very simple but effective experiment, Boyd Orr compared the effects on the heights of children in three age-groups (5–6, 8–9 and 13–14) of additions to the school diet of (1) fresh milk, (2) skimmed milk, and (3) biscuits which contained the same quantity of calories as the other diets but lacked the protein and some vitamins and minerals which the others included. A control group was included which did not receive supplements. It was found that after 7 months those in the first two groups grew 20 per cent more than the control group (at all ages), and the group fed on biscuits grew no more than the control group. In a follow-up study, Leighton and Clark found that those who received milk supplements in the second as well as the first year continued to grow at the faster rate, and those taken off the milk supplements returned to the slower growth rate. There are some methodological problems with this experiment, but the calculations were confirmed by several other studies. It is probable that the nutrient in the milk which encouraged height growth was protein (Orr 1928; Leighton and Clark 1929; Tanner 1962: 124–5; Golden 1985: 171, 174).

What kind of explanation would account for this importance of protein? Two possibilities can be suggested. First, high-protein foods may have been more of a limiting factor in the diet if they were more difficult to obtain, more expensive, harder to keep, or more likely to be contaminated (thus reducing demand) than low-protein foods. Since protein cannot be stored in the body as energy can in the form of fat, it is more important to have a regular intake (Passmore *et al.* 1974: 3).

More dramatic results than those of Boyd Orr were produced with a similar supplementation programme among children who lived on a very low-protein diet in Bundi, highland New Guinea. L.A. Malcolm found that the rate of height growth doubled with an additional supplement of skimmed milk, administered over a 13-week period, whereas additional energy (margarine) with the same calorie content as the milk had no effect on height growth (Malcolm 1970: 67–9; see also Lampl, Johnston and Malcolm 1978). The Bundi have a reliable supply of food throughout the year from their two staple root crops, although the diet is unusually low in calories derived from protein. Bundi children in this area were below the first centile of the British height standard after the age of 2, although they were well within the British range early in infancy in the 1960s (see figure 6.10 and table 6.4). Children below the age of 12 were on a higher centile, which suggests that the health clinic established in 1959–60 may have benefited these children in infancy. Another supplementation experiment which differentiated between the effects of high-energy and high-protein supplements on the growth of upper-class Iowa infants demonstrated similar contrasts between the effects of the two types of supplements to those observed among the Bundi (Golden 1985: 173–4).

Second, if, as some authors suggest, illness has a particularly severe effect on protein (nitrogen balance), it may have been a high rate of infection which caused children to be deficient in protein. At the 1977 conference on the effects of infection on nutritional status (*American Journal of Clinical Nutrition* 30), the participants agreed that the nutritional requirements recommended by the then current FAO/ WHO standards for healthy children should be increased as follows to allow for stress or infection: double the calorie allowance for infants, and treble the protein allowance at all ages (calculated from Feigin 1977: 1549–50; and Passmore *et al.* 1974: table 1).

In an attempt to quantify the effects of infectious disease on nutritional status, Scrimshaw has estimated that 0.6–1.2 g/kg body weight of protein is lost per day as a result of infectious disease, depending on the nature of the infection, and that the recovery phase may take three times as long as the catabolic phase to replace the lost nutrients in an undernourished adult (Scrimshaw 1977: 1540; for a more recent discussion of the effects of infection on nitrogen balance, see Jackson 1985).

In the above discussion we have tried not to prejudge the issue as to whether a low protein intake (relative to the standard for healthy populations), or a high rate of infection, was the most likely explanation for Boyd Orr's results, and indeed both may have been important. The first explanation is the one that is most intuitively obvious, and we therefore discussed it first, but for this reason it is easy to give undue emphasis to it. The example of the Narangwal villages (discussed above) is instructive on this point, where most children had a protein intake from wheat, milk and lentils which would have been adequate for healthy populations (according to the FAO recommendations which were current then). The researchers, however, considered that this was inadequate to cope with the 'staggering' disease burden – even in the relatively healthy climate of the Punjab – suffered by these children, since a third of them had depressed immune capacity. A low energy intake was, however, also an important factor (Kielmann *et al.* 1983: 18, 140–1, 205).

Finally, it has also been suggested that additional protein may encourage height growth more than additional energy, if energy intake is adequate. It is therefore possible that a high level of stunting and low level of wasting may be compatible with inadequate protein, either in the form of low intake or high claims against that intake (Malcolm 1978: 363–4; Golden 1985: 170–4). As a recent survey puts it (FAO/WHO/UNU 1985: 173):

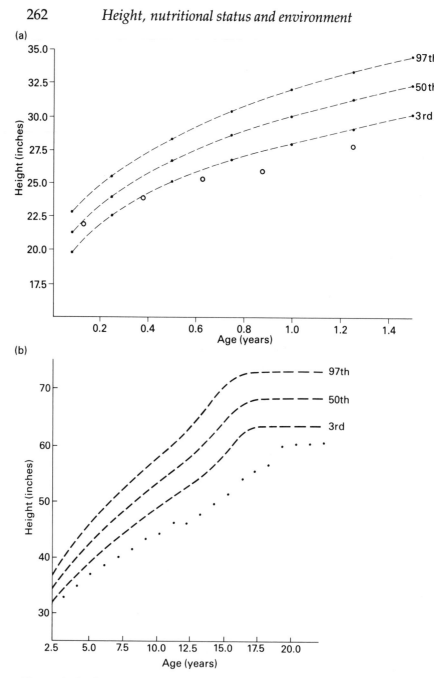

Figure 6.10. Growth profiles of Bundi children and adults. Source: Malcolm 1970.

Table 6.4 *Growth profile of Bundi children and adults.*

Age	Height (inches)	Centile	Frequency
0.13	21.89	—	12
0.38	23.94	—	10
0.63	25.35	—	7
0.88	25.98	—	10
1.25	27.83	0.111	31
2.00	30.20	0.266	57
3.00	32.95	0.307	48
4.00	34.92	0.133	48
5.00	37.05	0.139	42
6.00	38.62	0.065	78
7.00	40.08	0.021	62
8.00	41.46	0.013	68
9.00	43.27	0.014	47
10.00	44.17	0.004	34
11.00	46.26	0.013	20
12.00	46.14	0.002	32
13.00	47.76	0.002	36
14.00	49.72	0.002	28
15.00	51.57	0.000	35
16.00	54.25	0.000	23
17.00	55.71	0.000	40
18.00	56.85	0.000	15
19.00	60.20	0.053	8
20.00	60.55	0.084	21
21.00	60.59	0.089	17
22.00	60.87	0.126	12
25.00	61.14	0.178	75
35.00	61.61	0.312	214
45.00	61.73	0.357	183
55.00	61.34	0.225	108

Source: Malcolm 1970: 90–99.

the widespread prevalence of stunting in linear growth raises the question whether the protein requirements for growth in height may be greater than those for weight gain, which has hitherto been regarded as an adequate criterion.

It is important, however, not to make too strong a distinction between energy and protein, since the body will utilise protein in the form of calories if the intake of energy is inadequate.

In this section we have drawn contrasts between the types of claims made against nutritional status in developed and less-developed countries, and there is clearly a danger in taking this argument too far.

All the data relating to developed countries concerns children in urban areas in the early twentieth century, and we cannot assume that the factors operated in the same way a century earlier. We would also need to make distinctions between urban and rural areas, since many studies show that children in urban areas in both less-developed and the less-industrialised developed countries are fatter (in terms of skin-fold thickness) than those in rural areas (Tanner and Eveleth 1976: 159). Our discussion of less-developed countries has also focussed on only one type of economic context (apart from the references to the New Guinea Highlands and Punjab) – cultivators in tropical areas, in particular those who rely on one annual harvest. It is also necessary to note that in some areas in the less-developed world stunted children are not necessarily wasted (FAO/WHO/UNU 1985: 142; see also Malcolm 1970: 62–3; Adrianzen, Baertl and Graham 1973: 927–9). We may nevertheless conclude that even if weight is not a reliable means of distinguishing between the nutritional status of different socio-economic groups, height is more likely to be a good indicator of factors such as undernutrition, infection and stress which together detracted so much from nutritional status in nineteenth- and early twentieth-century Britain.

6.5 HEIGHT AND NUTRITIONAL STATUS AFTER THE CESSATION OF GROWTH

As previous sections of this chapter have shown, there is a complex series of interactions between growth and the environment during the foetal period and in infancy, childhood and adolescence. It might be thought that these interactions would cease to be of interest once adult height has been achieved and that, thereafter, the interaction between the human body and the environment would be expressed in terms of changes in other anthropometric indicators, such as weight, or in the impact on the health of the human body of nutrient intakes, pollutants, cold or warmth. In other words, heights would be of interest for what they can tell us about the past of a person or group of people, but not about their future.

This was not, of course, the view that British Army recruiters took. To them, height was a potent source of information about the likely ability of a recruit to stand up to Army life. While the medical examination of a recruit was designed to reveal current ailments or defects, it is certain that the majority of rejected recruits were turned away simply because they were too short. It was even believed that tall men would be more resistant to disease. In 1588, following the failure of the Armada, Lord Admiral Howard reported that he had fumigated a ship after an outbreak of infection, but that in spite of getting 'new men, very tall and able as ever I saw' to replace the former crew, the infection had broken out again (Wernham 1984: 3–4).

On the other side of the Atlantic, slave-owners exhibited the same preferences. They were prepared to pay more for tall slaves and selected relatively tall slaves for elite tasks on the plantation (Fogel 1988):

other things being equal, a male who was three inches taller than the typical adult male was 62 per cent more likely to be a driver than one who was three inches shorter than the typical male. On average, drivers were an inch-and-a-half taller than the men (and five inches taller than the women) who laboured in the gangs.

Advantage in height also increased the likelihood that men would be selected as craftsmen and that women would be chosen as domestics.

Even within modern industrialised societies, it is clear that choices are made which appear to exhibit preference by height. A number of studies have shown that relatively tall men and women are more likely to be upwardly socially mobile, whether by occupational mobility or through marriage. This relationship has been shown by Illsley (1955) in his studies of pregnancy and childbirth in Aberdeen and by Knight and Eldridge (1984) in their survey of British adults. It has also recently been demonstrated in an analysis of the British National Child Development Study by Power, Fogelman and Fox; they show that there is a clear class gradient in height at age 23 and that this persists even after controlling for the social class of the parents (1986: 409):

Thus, social mobility between birth and 23 was selective with respect to height, but mobility did not account for the social class gradients in height; indeed, there was some suggestion that the differences in the proportions short might be wider by social class at birth than by social class at 23.

It is easy to see why such preferences should arise, and be expressed in choice of marriage partners or employees, in a society where social classes are differentiated by height. The biological mechanisms which we have just explored are likely to reinforce such preferences; healthier children, who are probably richer, have had a better start in life and thus have a better chance of achieving upward social mobility than their poorer and iller peers, because relative poverty and ill-health detract from education and affect appearance. It has even been suggested that such poverty affects brain development and thus intelligence, although such a connection is highly speculative at the income levels which are achieved in the more-developed countries.

But is there any evidence which suggests that the views of Army recruiters or American slave-owners about the potential benefits of greater height have any basis? Are height preferences really height prejudices, perhaps to be called 'sizeism', or does the cumulated nutritional status which is summed up by adult height actually confer economic or biological advantage?

There are several ways in which such advantage, if it existed or exists, might be manifest.[2] All imply a possible correlation between biology and economic productivity. First, greater height might imply greater strength and therefore an enhanced ability to perform economic tasks involving manual labour; this could be reflected in greater strength, in greater endurance or in some combination of the two. Second, greater height might imply an enhanced ability to resist disease which would otherwise diminish work effort. Third, greater height might imply an enhanced expectation of life. Last, it is feasible and even obvious that severe undernutrition can cause all three: debility, disease and death. It is convenient, however, to begin with disease and death.

6.5.1 Height, disease and death

It may seem bizarre to suggest that cumulated nutritional status in childhood and adolescence could affect the expectation of life of adults. But a number of recent studies have shown that, after controlling for other variables, height has an independent effect on life expectation even in middle age and after. Marmot, Shipley and Rose (1984) found in a study of the British civil service that height was a significant predictor of cardiovascular mortality, even after controlling for social class, work status, smoking behaviour and other variables.

The most striking evidence of a link between nutritional status and expectation of life comes from a study by Waaler (1984) which linked information from a mass radiography programme in Norway with mortality records. This made it possible with a sample of 1.8 million individuals to examine the relationship between height, weight and the body mass index, on the one hand, and expectation of life on the other; figure 6.11 shows the relationships for height. Short Norwegian men aged 40–59 at risk between 1963 and 1979 were much more

---

[2] An excellent survey of the relationship between nutrition and physical and mental capacity, education and work capacity in the modern world can be found in Correa (1975).

likely to die than tall men; the risk of mortality for men with heights of 165 cm (65.0 in) was on average 71 per cent greater than that of men of 182.5 cm (71.9 ins). The relationship between height and mortality is smooth and well-defined across the height distribution, with mortality levels reaching a minimum at heights of about 187.5 cm (73.8 in) for that age-group; other age-groups show a very similar pattern. Waaler also shows that the same relationship exists for a number of specific causes of death, in particular for cardiovascular and respiratory diseases, though not for accidents and many cancers; this appears to rule out any suggestion that the relationship is accidental or systematically related to some other factor such as occupation or social class, although this possibility was not explicitly explored.

The interest of this finding is greatly enhanced by a study carried out on a nineteenth-century population, that of recruits to the Union Army at the time of the American Civil War. Fogel *et al.* (1986) show that the pattern of rejection for chronic disease shown in the Army records and plotted in figure 6.12 is related to height in exactly the same way as Waaler found in modern Norway;

Both the Norwegian curve and the US all-causes curve have relative risks that reach a minimum of between 0.6 and 0.7 (where 1.0 is the average risk) at a height of about 187.5 cm. Both reach a relative risk of about 2 at about 152.5 cm (60.0 ins). (Fogel 1987: 14).

The importance of the Union Army evidence is not just that it confirms the existence of a significant relationship between height, morbidity and mortality. It might be argued on the basis of the Waaler curves – though Waaler himself implicitly rejected this view – that mortality levels are systematically linked to an individual's height relative to the current national average, rather than to the absolute height which was achieved. It is, after all, relative rather than absolute heights that presumably play a part in social preferences in such fields as marriage and employment. But the coincidence between the Norwegian and the American evidence, despite the difference in mean heights, in genetic factors and in other aspects of the environment, suggests that it is indeed absolute height which is important. As Fogel puts it, the evidence suggests that (1987: 14):

the relative risk of morbidity and mortality depends not on the deviation of height from the current mean, but from an ideal mean: the mean associated with full genetic potential.

If this is so, and Fogel rightly points to many pitfalls and gaps in evidence, then it is possible to argue that the higher mortality levels

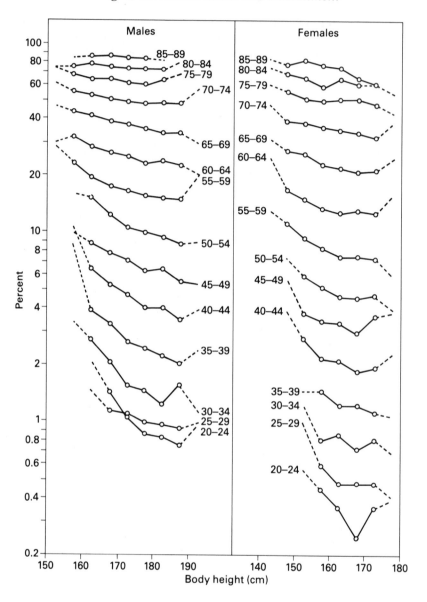

Figure 6.11. The association in modern Norway between body height and mortality by sex and age. Source: Waaler 1984.

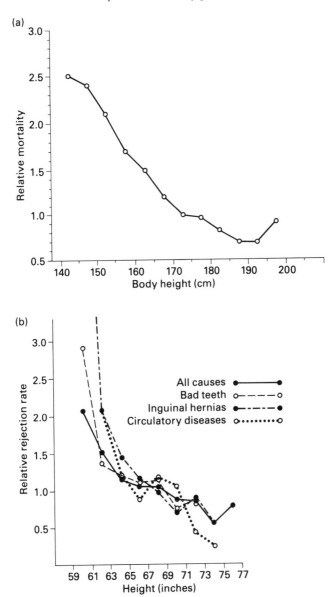

Figure 6.12. A comparison of the relationship between body height and relative risk of morbidity or mortality in two populations. (a) Relative mortality
rates among Norwegian men aged 40–59, between 1963 and 1979 (Waaler
1984). (b) Relative rejection rates for chronic conditions in a sample of 4245
men aged 23–49 examined for the Union Army (Fogel *et al.* 1986).

of populations in the past were directly associated with their lower nutritional status as measured by their lower mean height.

Such an argument is potentially of great importance in establishing a link between nutritional improvements and mortality change in the nineteenth and early twentieth centuries, because it corresponds with other evidence which suggests that people carry with them, throughout life, an endowment which is acquired during childhood and adolescence but which affects their later health. It is over fifty years since Kermack, McKendrick and McKinlay pointed to 'certain regularities in the vital statistics of Great Britain' (1934: 698). They argued on the basis of studies of mortality in England and Wales since 1845 and in Scotland since 1860 that 'each generation is characterised by its own relative mortality-rate', in the sense that, compared to the period which they took as a standard (1934: 698–9):

apart from more or less random deviations, the relative mortality is approximately constant for each generation at all periods of life . . . It would seem that the actual calendar year is of relatively little importance in determining the improvement in the specific death-rates. What is of importance is the year of birth of the generation or group of individuals under consideration. Each generation after the age of 5 years seems to carry along with it the same relative mortality rate throughout adult life, and even into extreme old age.

Kermack, McKendrick and McKinlay were not able to suggest a specific biological explanation of the pattern that they had observed, but they argued strongly that (1934: 699–700):

the health of the child is determined by the environmental conditions existing during the years 0–15, and that the health of the man is determined preponderately by the physical constitution which the child has built up . . . If the above hypothesis is correct it would be implied that the decreased death-rates were in fact largely the result of the improved physique of the population.

A more specific connection between health status in childhood and adult mortality has been suggested by recent studies of the relationship between geographical distributions of infant mortality in the early part of this century in Britain and current distributions of adult mortality. Barker and Osmond (1986a, 1986b) have investigated the relationship between infant mortality, childhood nutrition and adult mortality from bronchitis and from ischaemic heart disease. They concluded that there was (1986b: 1275):

strong support for the hypothesis that pulmonary infection during infancy may have persisting effects and cause chronic bronchitis in adult life . . . We now conclude that the high mortality from chronic bronchitis in England and Wales, especially in the towns, is another legacy of poor social conditions which led to high rates of respiratory infection in young children.

A similar geographical relationship between current mortality rates for ischaemic heart disease and past infant mortality rates led to the same conclusion, that 'childhood influences increase the risk of adult heart disease' (1986a: 1080), while work in progress demonstrates a similarly close relationship between current death rates from stroke and maternal mortality from causes other than puerperal fever 75 years ago.

These disparate pieces of evidence, which have not yet been integrated into a comprehensive theory, strongly suggest that some endowment bearing on mortality in adult life is carried forward from childhood. The exact biological mechanisms remain unclear; Barker and Osmond suggest, for example, that rates of ischaemic heart disease may be linked to infant nutrition and in particular to levels of breast-feeding. It is suggested that bottle-feeding and the ingestion of animal fats may lead to higher levels of serum cholesterol (1986a: 1080). Forsdahl, however, was inclined to attribute a similar relationship, which he had observed in Scandinavia, to living conditions which were markedly better in adult than in child life. Mortality from bronchitis may be linked, on the other hand, so Barker and Osmond suggest, to abnormalities of lung function brought about by acute lower respiratory tract infection during the period of rapid growth in infancy (1986b: 1274). A direct link between respiratory disease and delayed growth was found by Rona and Florey (1980). Since respiratory infections are associated with low nutritional status in infancy, the link of both types of disease with nutritional status must be explored further, particularly because of the suggested link between stroke and maternal mortality, itself often linked to the nutritional status of the mother. If this is itself linked to the nutritional status of the mother during her own childhood, then the very long-period effects of improved nutritional status can clearly be seen.

Not all the associations between nutritional status in childhood and later mortality have suggested an inverse relationship; Micozzi (1985) has argued that larger adult body size and earlier maturation may be related to increased risk of breast cancer. But such findings, while fascinating, merely reinforce the need for further research which will incorporate the skills of human biologists, epidemiologists and historians.

Because all the studies which have been reported have relied on mortality as an index of ill-health, none bears explicitly on the issue of whether poor nutritional status in childhood is linked with an increased risk of disease in adulthood. There are, however, two indirect inferences which can be made to suggest that this is so. First, many of the causes of death which are linked to nutritional status are also causes of long-term morbidity; people do not typically die of respiratory diseases without warning or a period, often lengthy, of ill-health and physical debility. Similarly, although some deaths from cardiovascular diseases occur suddenly to men and women who previously appeared healthy, the vast majority are preceded by symptoms such as high blood pressure or angina which are likely, at the least, to lead to a reduction in physical activity and a feeling of ill-health. Second, a great deal of investigation has demonstrated a clear relationship between social class and levels of morbidity; since, as we have seen, nutritional status as measured by height is correlated with social class, it is clear that nutritional status will similarly be inversely correlated with measures of ill-health.

This argument makes an important point with which we should end this section. At present, the evidence presented by epidemiologists and human biologists about the relationship between nutritional status and morbidity and mortality in adult life remains evidence only of correlation. We do not know exactly why or by what mechanisms nutritional status in early life can affect chances of mortality sixty or more years later. We cannot, therefore, with confidence make causal statements to the effect that nutritional status determines mortality either in whole or in part. Such statements must await further research by human biologists. What we can say is that the correlation is well attested and that we should take it into account in our account of historical trends.

6.5.2 Height, nutritional status and work

There are a number of ways in which nutritional status might affect the amount of work done by an individual. First, poor nutritional status might simply lead to physical weakness, as was believed by the army recruiters. This might be manifested either as an inability to carry out physically demanding short-term tasks or as an inability to endure long periods of effort. Second, poor nutritional status might lead to high levels of disease which inhibited or entirely prevented work effort. Third, poor nutritional status might lead to death.

The second and third of these possibilities were considered, though from a slightly different perspective, in the last section. Here we should simply note that the potential consequences, in terms of improvements to labour productivity, of improved work effort through the reduction of levels of morbidity and mortality, are very large. Calculations with model life tables suggest that an increase in male life expectation from 40 to 60 years (such as in fact occurred in Britain between the cohort born in the 1840s and that born in the 1930s) could imply nearly a 20 per cent increase in expected working life (between 15 and 70) for those who survived to age 15. This is very much an illustrative calculation, and the result will be much influenced, for example, by the age-structure of mortality, but it is indicative of the large scale of potential benefits to improved mortality levels. Similarly, a reduction in levels of chronic disease, for example by a drop in the number of those suffering from tuberculosis, will also have dramatic consequences in a reduction in days of work lost through disease. A number of studies have demonstrated the effects of ill-health on earnings (Luft 1975; Cropper 1981; Chirikos and Nestel 1985), although it is important to note that it has been suggested that there may be an inverse relationship between morbidity and mortality, such that declining mortality levels have been associated with rising ill-health (Verbrugge 1984: Riley and Alter 1986).

The benefits of improved life expectancy, which essentially reflect changes in the number of days or years during which a person was at work, seem likely to have been much more substantial than benefits of improved nutritional status in the form of increases in work effort on a given day. Development economists have recently paid a great deal of attention to the question of whether work output can be significantly affected by improvements in nutrition (Rodgers 1975; Johnston 1977; Bliss and Stern 1978; Correa 1975; Biswas and Pinstrup-Andersen 1985; Dasgupta and Ray 1985); they were anticipated by many years in this research effort by physiologists and nutritionists (FAO 1962; Belavady 1966; Morrison and Blake 1974; Spurr 1983). Many of the former studies have found difficulty in modelling all the factors which may affect labour productivity, while many of the latter were conducted in artificial conditions involving, for example, the systematic starving of previously well-nourished subjects. Nevertheless, this work has essentially been inconclusive. There is some evidence that low levels of nutritional status reduce the endurance of workers, so that they are incapable of sustaining heavy physical work over long periods. There is, by contrast, little evidence that even quite malnourished individuals cannot summon up energy for short bursts of work effort.

The significance of these findings therefore rests heavily on the type of work which is, or was, involved and in the strategies which individuals have evolved to cope with the physical demands which their work places on them. It seems likely on the basis of these findings that the Army were right to be concerned about nutritional status since, in an age before motorised transport, most soldiers had to be capable of enduring long marches while carrying large loads; this is exactly the type of work effort which may have been difficult if not impossible for malnourished men. Plantation work in the cultivation of cotton may have had the similar characteristic of a forced pace which had to be maintained for long periods. But other forms of agricultural work and many other tasks in the manufacturing and service industries do not require such sustained effort. The total effect of improvements in labour productivity through improvements in the ability of the population to undertake intensive and strenuous work thus depends on the structure of industry and the exact energy demands of each task, which is difficult to establish. It seems sensible, however, to conclude that such effects are unlikely to have been as important as improvements to the overall levels of morbidity and mortality.

6.6 CONCLUSION

This chapter has considered many aspects of the relationship between humans and the environment within which they live. Its purpose has not been to present this material, summarising the work of many scholars in many fields of study, for its own sake – although it certainly deserves such presentation – but to assist in the analysis of historical evidence about changing height in Britain. It is to that evidence and task that we now return.

7

Nutritional status and physical growth in Britain, 1750–1980

The overall course of change in heights in Britain is fascinating in its historical context. Average male height by birth cohort rose from the middle of the eighteenth century and into the late 1820s, though with a possible check for those born just before and thus growing up in the Napoleonic Wars. Average male heights then began to fall for those born and experiencing childhood in the hungry thirties and continued to fall for the birth cohorts of the 1840s and early 1850s. For those born after the 1860s, reaching adulthood in the 1870s and 1880s, a modest rise occurred, regaining earlier levels only with those born at the start of the twentieth century and then rising more rapidly, especially after the Second World War.

At the same time, there were very substantial changes in the geographical distribution of height. The significant Scottish advantage in height over the rest of the United Kingdom, so apparent in the eighteenth century, was eroded during the nineteenth century and has disappeared entirely in the twentieth. Conversely, the markedly lower heights of Londoners in the eighteenth and nineteenth centuries were replaced by a height advantage which London now shares with the rest of south-east England. Over the period as a whole, the urban areas, led by London, first showed declining heights in relation to rural areas, before demonstrating an increase which has now led, in Britain as in other developed countries, to an urban height advantage.

Socio-economic differences in height have been pervasive, both between and within social classes. Between the classes, the extreme differences which characterised English society early in the nineteenth century, particularly seen in the heights of adolescents, were substantially diminished, but clear and consistent height differences still characterised the social classes in the 1980s. Within those classes, the evidence is much sparser, but the eighteenth- and nineteenth-century data described in chapter 5 certainly demonstrate a clear connection between height and occupation, with differentials altering over time consistently with the probable socio-economic position of the different occupational groups.

Within a wider context, average height in Britain has also varied in relation to the heights of other nations. As was shown briefly in chapters 1 and 4, in the eighteenth century Britain and its American colonies appear to have had average male heights greater than those of any other country, with the Americans of European origin somewhat taller than the British. The American advantage was, however, eroded by the second quarter of the nineteenth century and, thereafter, British and white American heights followed a similar course, first falling, then rising gradually and then more rapidly in the present century. Meanwhile, there was substantial growth in average heights in a number of northern European countries, who matched Britain and the United States at the beginning of the twentieth century and have since grown significantly taller. Last, several southern European countries have lagged noticeably behind and, despite recent rapid increases in average heights, their male citizens remain significantly shorter than those of Britain, the United States and many countries of northern Europe.

But why have all these changes occurred and what do they tell us about the health and welfare of these peoples? In the last chapter, we set out the modern evidence about the relationship between the environment, human nutritional status and physical growth. That evidence is a constant reminder of the multivariate and synergistic relationships which characterise human growth and health, and a warning against simplification. Many of the studies are concerned with infant and child health and the literature on growth constantly emphasises the importance of the early years of life in setting a pattern for later life. That message is reinforced by studies in the developed world which demonstrate relationships between nutritional status in childhood and mortality many years later. But it is also clear that severe deprivation or, conversely, substantial improvements in nutritional status at later childhood ages can cause growth patterns to diverge substantially from those set in infancy (Steckel 1987). Although the literature suggests that we should pay particular attention to influences which affect growth in the early years, experiences in childhood and adolescence may have been important too.

In this chapter we shall examine the evidence of changing heights in Britain in relation to our knowledge of the environment – of changes in real wages and incomes, in morbidity and mortality, in diet and in housing – during the periods of birth, adolescence and early adulthood of the members of our samples. In the process, we shall sketch out an interpretation of the causes and correlates of changing nutritional status as measured by height.

7.1 POVERTY IN THE EIGHTEENTH AND NINETEENTH CENTURIES AND THE 'STANDARD OF LIVING DEBATE'

What, then, do we know about factors in the economy and society of Britain during the past 250 years which could have contributed to the nutritional status of the population and produced the patterns of changes in mean height which we have described? In essence, because nutritional status can be affected by so many features of the environment, this question can be replaced by another: what is the current state of knowledge about the standard of living of the British people since the middle of the eighteenth century? And the circle can be completed by asking: what does the evidence of heights add to our knowledge of the standard of living?

This is not the place for an extended account of the 'standard of living debate', as the most sustained controversy in British economic history has normally been called.[1] Under such names as 'the condition of England question', the question of the effect of industrialisation upon the working class preoccupied mid-Victorian commentators as diverse as Engels, Disraeli, Marx and Macaulay. At the end of the nineteenth century, fears of German competition and of the deterioration of the British race revived the controversy, though in a slightly different form, while in the twentieth century the standard of living debate, now largely the province of historians, has engaged the attention of such distinguished scholars as Clapham, Ashton, Chambers, Hartwell, Hobsbawm and Thompson. As Cannadine (1984) suggests, the course of the debate has been much influenced by the contemporary state of politics and the economy; although the main focus of the debate has been on the classical period of the Industrial Revolution between 1780 and 1850, other controversies have raged about the so-

---

[1] Brief accounts from different perspectives can be found in O'Brien and Engerman (1981), Crafts (1985) and Lindert and Williamson (1983), all of which draw on an earlier summary of the debate by Taylor (1975). The most up-to-date, though often technical, summaries of the debate can be found in *Explorations in Economic History* (1987) with articles by Crafts (1987), Williamson (1987) and Mokyr (1987). A historiographical treatment, by a social historian, can be found in Cannadine (1984).

called 'Great Depression' of the late nineteenth century and about the impact of depression and unemployment between the two World Wars.

Part of the reason for the lengthy and sustained nature of the political and scholarly debate has been that the 'standard of living' is so amorphous a concept. At its narrowest, it has been taken to be identical to real per capita national income; at its broadest, it has embraced the contrast between an overcrowded urban hovel and a country cottage with roses blooming round the kitchen door. The narrow definitions are sometimes thought to be easier to measure, although this has not always proved to be the case, while the broadest are almost by definition immeasurable, selected precisely because they attempt to convey the smell or feel of life in the past. In between, measures of mortality and morbidity, measures of the consumption of bread, meat, tea or beer and measures of urbanisation jostle with accounts of life in the slums or of the horrors of the sewers of Victorian London. Even the subject of measurement, the 'working class', remains itself elusive and ill-defined.

What is not in doubt is the extent and the depth of poverty among the working class of the eighteenth and nineteenth centuries in Britain. There are in essence two aspects of poverty in the past which concern us; they are closely inter-related but it is helpful to distinguish them. The first is what may be called the absolute level of income at a point in time and the extent to which that income was insufficient to maintain physical growth. The second is the changing levels of income over time and the effect that those changes may have had on the nutritional status of the population.

As an example, no amount of change in the standard of living can remove the impression left by one of the most impressive of nineteenth-century studies of the life of the working class, Seebohm Rowntree's *Poverty: a study of Town Life*, first published in 1901. Rowntree's study is important to us because it was the first careful attempt to arrive at a definition of an absolute level of poverty. This had been done implicitly by the Poor Law authorities for several centuries when they set levels of assistance, but Rowntree's work in York was directed to a slightly different aim, that of establishing the extent of poverty by reference to an absolute standard. To do so, he was forced to define poverty in two precise ways.

Rowntree asserted that families living in poverty should be divided into two groups (1901: 86–7):

(1) Families whose total earnings are insufficient to obtain the minimum necessaries for the maintenance of merely physical efficiency.

Poverty falling under this head may be described as 'primary' poverty.

(2) Families whose total earnings would be sufficient for the maintenance of merely physical efficiency were it not that some portion of it is absorbed by other expenditure, either useful or wasteful. Poverty falling under this head may be described as 'secondary' poverty.

Using these definitions, Rowntree found that about 13 per cent of the population lived in primary poverty and approximately a further 14 per cent in secondary poverty, giving rise to the famous and much-quoted figure of 27 per cent in poverty. This matched closely with the figure of 30 per cent in poverty which was derived from Charles Booth's survey of London (1902), while the estimate of numbers in primary poverty was close to those arrived at in Bowley's surveys of a number of other English towns (Hennock 1987: 219–26).

These figures of numbers in poverty related to the whole urban population, but Rowntree and others also observed what has come to be called, in the tradition of Chayanov, the life-cycle of poverty; that is:

families were most prone to severe poverty when they had young children or when the head of the household was aged, than in the period of relative ease before the first child was born, or when the children were old enough to earn. (Thane 1981: 226)

As one survey of urban poverty puts it (Treble 1979: 152):

Where ... the husband, working in an unskilled or sweated occupation, was the sole breadwinner, undernourishment was invariably a feature of the family's diet. As one observer of Huddersfield's woollen handloom weavers proclaimed in 1849, 'if they have young families ..., that is, families over young to help them by working in the mills, they don't get half enough to eat.' That verdict, of much wider application than this relatively restricted group of outworkers, was endorsed fifty years later when Rowntree in York and Cadbury, Matheson and Shann in Birmingham examined the socio-economic position of labourer's households in which there were no supplementary wage-earners. Labourer's children, it was concluded, 'fare worse during infancy than at any other time, unless indeed they grow up to marry labourers and try to bring up families on an irregular 18/- to 20/- a week [in 1906]. These children often live for weeks or even months at a time chiefly on bread and tea, and it is no uncommon occurrence for the supply to run out.'

Such impressions received statistical confirmation in the work of Bowley and Burnett-Hurst in 1913 (Bowley and Burnett-Hurst 1915).

They found that, while 23.3 per cent of working-class families in Reading lived below the primary poverty line, 45 per cent of children under 5 did so; the comparable figures for Warrington were 13.4 and 22.5 per cent, for Northampton 8.9 and 17 per cent and for Stanley 6.0 and 5.5 per cent (Treble 1979: 171; Hennock 1987: 225). In other words, where poverty was greatest, it bore much more heavily on children. In addition, as Treble and others have pointed out, families in poverty with children were also most likely to suffer bad housing conditions, in particular overcrowding, and to be inadequately clothed (Treble 1979: 171–83).

In such circumstances, the health of the male breadwinner had to be protected, even at the expense of the wife and children; as Rowntree put it (1901: 135):

We *see* that many a labourer, who has a wife and three or four children, is healthy and a good worker, although he only earns a pound a week. What we do not *see* is that in order to give him enough food, mother and children habitually go short, for the mother knows that all depends upon the wages of her husband.

Rowntree's work is of particular interest for two reasons. First, he was using a definition of poverty which relates it closely to nutritional status; poverty is a level of income which gives rise to poor nutritional status, a level of food intake insufficient to maintain health in the face of the other demands made on the body. Second, his observations and those of his contemporaries provide a description of poverty and a standard, however impressionistic, against which we can measure poverty and the standard of living of the working class at other periods.

We lack statistical evidence, comparable to that provided by Rowntree and his contemporaries, of the extent and implications of poverty earlier in the nineteenth and in the eighteenth century; in particular, it is not clear how far the experience of the larger urban areas was shared in small towns and rural areas where, in earlier periods, the bulk of the population had lived. But there seems no reason to believe that conditions for the poor, and particularly for their children, were significantly easier earlier in the nineteenth century. It is probable, in other words, that the absolute level of income of a large section – at least 30 per cent – of the population was then insufficient to support health and growth.

But to emphasise the extent of urban poverty as late as 1900 and its pervasiveness among the working class is not enough; to go further, and to chart the movements of living standards in the preceding two centuries, we need to return to the classic standard of living debate and to the evidence which it has mustered.

7.1.1 The measurement of living standards

Living standards have been measured in many different ways. In recent years, most of the focus of historical research in this area has been on the measurement of real income and real wages, but other indicators which have been intensively studied include the course of mortality, the incidence of disease, housing patterns and the evidence of surveys of working-class diets. Meanwhile, social historians have directed attention to the changes which have occurred in the structure of the family and in support networks within the community. There is a natural tendency for each historian to claim precedence for his or her own method of measurement, rather than to accept that each method can provide a different view of a complex reality. In addition, concentration on one or other method of measurement tends to obscure the extent to which each measurement interlocks with others.

This is best illustrated by considering the estimates of real income and real wages which have been the primary focus of most recent research within the standard of living debate. Accounts of movements in real income spring from estimates of the national income of the country, themselves based on estimates of the output of industry, agriculture and services or on estimates of the income of those employed in those activities. Although such estimates have been made at various times since the invention of systematic national income analysis in the 1930s, most recent British estimates derive from the work of C. H. Feinstein (1972, 1981). Estimates of income and of the proportion of income devoted to personal consumption are then confronted with evidence of the changing prices of consumption goods to derive indices of real consumption or real consumption per head.

The calculation of real wages, by contrast, relies on the accumulation of information about the incomes of groups of workers and about the cost of the goods which they consumed. This information is then used to construct indices of wages and of prices which are contrasted with each other to provide a final index of real wages.[2] That final index is only as good as the materials which have been used to construct it and the procedures used; despite decades of historical

---

[2] Early indices are surveyed in Flinn (1974) and von Tunzelmann (1979).

research, some information – for example, that about the rent of hous-ing – remains obstinately elusive. In addition, the indices are extremely sensitive to assumptions which must be made about the relative weight of particular items within consumption expenditures and about the relative importance of particular groups of consumers.

In a recent exchange of views on this subject, for example, Crafts (1985a) has criticised Lindert and Williamson (1983b) for their treat-ment of the cost of clothing in their new cost of living index. In their reply, Lindert and Williamson (1985) admit the need to revise their index, and do so, while claiming that the main conclusions of their original article still hold; yet the revisions increase the rate of growth of real wages between 1810 and 1819 by 59 per cent while reducing the rate of growth between 1819 and 1851 by nearly 20 per cent. The situation has not greatly improved since von Tunzelmann concluded his survey of earlier indices with the remark that they showed gains in real wages between 1750 and 1850 of anything between zero and 150 per cent (1979) and, continuing the latest round of debate, Mokyr (1987) has recently questioned the conclusions both of Crafts and of Williamson.

These difficulties in the measurement of real income, real wages or real consumption per head, by whatever method, are not confined to the period of the Industrial Revolution. Feinstein's (1972) estimates of national income for the latter part of the nineteenth and the early part of the twentieth century are, the author emphasises, subject to wide margins of error; while the increasing availability of production statistics, culminating in the Census of Production of 1907, makes it easier to measure manufacturing output, great difficulties are encountered in the measurement of the output of the growing service sector. The measurement of real wages in that period is also problem-atical; historians have relied for many years on the estimates of Bowley (1900), but Gazeley and Feinstein have recently shown in unpublished work that these estimates need to be significantly altered. The course of real wages before 1914 is thus undergoing considerable revision.

For most historical periods, it has proved to be remarkably difficult to obtain appropriate price series which reflect what the consumer actually paid, rather than bulk import prices or wholesale prices within the home market. Another major problem has been that of taking account of the fact that incomes are typically earned and consumed within the framework of a family. Not only is it extremely difficult to link together the income of different family members to compute total family income, but it is also virtually impossible to know how consumption was distributed within the household. Moreover, the question of distribution within the household is a special case of a wider problem; measures of income per capita based on national income take no account of inequalities in the distribution of income and wealth, either across classes or occupational groups, among members of the household, or across regions within the nation. Even measures of real wages for specific occupational groups, where they can be obtained, require careful adjustment to yield estimates of aggregate changes in the welfare of the community as a whole.

Difficulties and errors of measurement, acute though they are, are not the only problems which historians have encountered in measuring consumption and real income or wages in the past. As Dan Usher among others has argued, we measure economic growth to discover something about the welfare of people within the community (1980: 1–2):

economic growth to a country is like a raise in salary to an individual . . . For without such a translation, measures of real income and economic growth are mere numbers with no apparent effect upon our lives and no status as indicators of progress towards goals that people might want the economy to achieve. Without the possibility of such a translation, the measurement of economic growth is nonsense. Why, after all, would we want to measure economic growth, why is public policy directed to the promotion of economic growth, if we are not better off after economic growth than we were before?

But if this is indeed the purpose of measuring economic growth, then the traditional measures have serious deficiencies. For economic growth has had many more dimensions and consequences than those which appear to be measured by traditional computations of real income per capita.

For example, modern European societies are certainly much richer today than they were a century ago, in terms of income per capita, but in addition the average citizen of those countries also enjoys that higher income for half again as long, because of the great increase that has occurred in expectation of life not only from birth but from adulthood. Most of us would probably regard that reduction in mortality as a major improvement in our welfare, but it is one that is largely ignored by conventional measures. Similarly, those longer lives are, in most cases, lived within environments that are notably less polluted than the towns and cities of nineteenth-century Britain, themselves notably more polluted than those of eighteenth-century Britain and before. Neither direction of change is reflected in measures of real income.

While Usher speaks in terms of measures of national income per capita, exactly the same criticisms apply to the use of conventional measures of real wages (Crafts 1985b: 108). Longevity gains and changes in conditions of work need to be integrated with such measures. Similarly, conventional measures fail to take account of the amount of work effort required to produce a given level of income. Not only have hours of work within the working day, and weeks of work within the year, fallen drastically in the past century, but in many occupations work is now easier, pleasanter and less dangerous than in the last century, while many of the most hazardous of occupations have entirely disappeared. Higher incomes are thus more easily earned, which would seem to most of us to make us 'better off'.

Economists and economic historians have recently attempted to cope with such criticisms of their traditional tools. To some, the advantages which stem from the use of standardised methods of measurement and from the link which they have with measures of money incomes have stifled doubts; they are essentially content to define welfare within the confines of national income analysis. Others, however, have made attempts to adjust conventional measures to make them more representative of lay ideas of welfare. Using a method proposed by Usher (1980), Williamson (1984) has attempted to adjust indices of real income to take account of gains in life expectancy, concluding as a result that 'conventional indices of real income growth may understate true living standard growth by 25 per cent or more' with the greatest effects being seen in the second half of the nineteenth century and the first third of the twentieth. Thus British growth is seen, on these grounds, to have accelerated much more sharply since the middle of the eighteenth century than is suggested by more conventional measures. Williamson (1984) has also attempted to estimate the cost of 'urban disamenities', though here concluding that the cost was small, a conclusion that is hotly debated (Pollard 1981).

Despite their impact on conventional measures, it is likely that such adjustments do not go far enough. Williamson (1984) begins his discussion with the words: 'Like all concepts of economic value, the value of longevity gains has two multiplicative parts: price and quantity.' He and Usher concentrate, therefore, on measuring quantity, in the form of numbers of people living extra years, and price, in the form of an assessment of the price those people are prepared to pay for an improvement in their chances of survival. These computations, however, ignore the fact that typically individuals do not enjoy perfect health from the moment they are born until the moment that they drop down dead. As Oddy (1982: 121) has pointed out, we know very little about the health of people in the past, as opposed to knowing a great deal about why they died; common sense and contemporary observation both suggest, however, that societies, and subgroups within societies, with higher levels of life expectation also have less ill-health than do societies with lower levels of life expectation. In other words, not only have people in Europe come to live longer, but they are also probably healthier *at each age* until their death than they were two hundred years ago.[3] This is a notable addition to welfare (and probably also a notable addition to the productive capacity of the economy) but one that has been almost entirely ignored.

It is very easy to suggest ways in which measured trends in national income should be adjusted for improvements in welfare and to demonstrate that such adjustments would be substantial. There are, however, formidable obstacles in making the adjustments. There are two principal difficulties. First, it is important to consider how far the improvements are truly exogenous to increases in real income as it is conventionally measured. Second, there may be a substantial problem of double counting; how can we separate, for example, the effects of increased life expectancy from the effects of improved health?

Usher and Williamson differ substantially when discussing whether improvements in life expectancy are truly exogenous. This point is extremely important; if all the improvements in health and life expectation were 'bought' by people devoting part of their current consumption expenditure specifically to 'buy' improved health and longer life, then there would be no reason to adjust measured national income for improvements in health and mortality. As Williamson rightly argues, Usher assumes 'that all mortality changes ... are exogenous to the household, totally independent of household investments in health via the mix in and the level of C (current consumption) itself' (1984: 160). Usher justifies this assumption on the basis that:

I feel that the environmental component of observed mortality rates is a large enough portion of the total that the bias in treating mortality rates as though they were largely environmental need not have a significant impact on our results.

(1980: 251)

Williamson argues, by contrast, that Usher does not take sufficient account of 'endogenous household response to changes in health technology, like lower fuel prices offering better food preparation or warmer residences', or of 'endogenous changes in mortality attributable to workers' investment in health, made possible by increases in income' (1984: 162). For this reason, Williamson does not consider that the whole of the increase in life expectancy should be used in adjusting national income, although he believes that over time an increasing proportion has been exogenously determined.

---

[3] For a contrary view, however, see Riley and Alter (1986).

Similar objections can be raised to all the other adjustments which have been proposed. To the extent that increased leisure has been bought by investment in capital equipment, that improvement is already subsumed within increasing income. Similarly, as Williamson suggests, current consumption of fuel may warm houses and thus improve health. The relative degree of endogeneity and exogeneity in such improvements is very subjective; while Williamson quotes McKeown and Record to the effect that:

change in the character of these infectious diseases, essentially independent of human intervention, may have been responsible for not less than one-fifth and – as a very rough estimate – for not more than one-third of the nineteenth century mortality decline

it seems wrong to regard such estimates as having any degree of precision (1984: 164, quoting 1962: 119).

A second cause of difficulty lies in the extent of double counting that may be involved when imputations are made for more than one improvement to welfare. More leisure and less hard work may lead, for example, to better health and a longer life; imputing separately for leisure, health and mortality changes will, therefore, considerably overstate the size of the improvement in welfare. It is not unreasonable to conclude, in fact, that imputations to national income may be more trouble than they are worth. They complicate measures which, for all their faults and difficulties, have the advantages of familiarity and, more important, of easy translation, as Usher put it, into goals which people might want the economy to achieve.

It is important to recognise that very similar criticisms can be levelled against other ways of measuring changes in living standards. Each – mortality, morbidity, diet or housing conditions – presents only a partial view of reality, while attempts at combining them give rise to the problems of double counting. It would be as problematical to adjust mortality statistics for changes in income as to do the reverse. It only requires the reading of Mayhew, Booth or Rowntree, or any one of a host of nineteenth-century novelists, to see that the position of the working class was so poor in so many ways that no single method of description is likely to do it justice.

The measurement of nutritional status through anthropometric investigation has two definite advantages over the more traditional measures. First, it is a net measure, summing up various different influences, both positive and negative, on the human body. Second, it is a measure of output rather than, like income or diet, a measure of inputs into health or welfare. In neither respect is nutritional status unique. Mortality is pre-eminently an output measure. Income is, to some extent and over normal ranges, a net measure, for people partly adjust their consumption and their activity to actual as well as potential earnings.

Of course, an individual has very little or no control over his or her height, in contrast to some control, perhaps, over his or her death or income. In other words, height, and the nutritional status in childhood and adolescence which it measures, are exogenous to individuals, though not entirely so to families.

In three other respects, height would be an inferior measure to real income or real wages, assuming that they could be correctly and convincingly measured. First, unlike income or wages, height reflects welfare only over the period of physical growth, although that welfare can affect the rest of life.

Second, simply because height is a net measure, reflecting the interaction of so many influences on the growing body, it is often very difficult to discover which of those influences is paramount at a given time, or to discover whether changes in height should be attributed to changes in one influence or another. There is no equivalent in the study of height to the partitioning of changes in real wages into those caused by movements in prices and those caused by movements in wages.

Third, the functional relationship between nutritional status and welfare is much less clearly determined than is the relationship between income and welfare. Although there is much room for dispute about the exact relationship, within normal ranges of income it makes some sense to assert that doubling one's income will double one's welfare or utility. We cannot, at the moment at least, make a statement of this kind about nutritional status and welfare, although further study of the relationship under many different sets of circumstances may lead us to be able to do so in the future.

The measurement of nutritional status by height is not, therefore, a panacea or instant solution to the standard of living debate. On the other hand, it is both a valid measure and one which has an important contribution to make. Let us now see what it tells us.

7.2 NUTRITIONAL STATUS, HEALTH AND INCOME, 1750–1850

7.2.1 Nutritional status, real income and real wages

The new evidence which studies of height bring to the standard of living debate is set out again in figure 7.1, which incorporates for the classical period of the Industrial Revolution the evidence of military recruits from the working class and from Marine Society boys from the London slums.

Our evidence of nutritional status is contrasted, in figure 7.2, with three recent calculations of changes in real wages for blue-collar workers. The first series is that calculated by Lindert and Williamson (1983b: 13) for 'all blue-collar' workers. The second is the result of our calculation for the same group of a 'new' series for real wages during the Industrial Revolution from Lindert and Williamson (1983b, 1985), incorporating corrections to the series which underlies their calculation of 'trends in real adult-male full-time earnings' (1985: 151, table 3, col. 2). The third series is drawn from a study by L. D. Schwarz (1985) of wages and the cost of living in London, which makes use of another Lindert and Williamson series for living costs in southern England.

It is convenient to examine these series in two parts, with a break in the 1820s. The moving average of heights of male adults shows a gradual rise between the 1740s and the 1820s, although this cuts through points substantially above the average in the 1760s and 1770s, somewhat below the average in the late 1780s and 1790s and considerably above the average again up to the 1820s. The Marine Society series also shows an overall increase over the period, composed of a stable or slightly falling series to the 1790s and a sharp rise thereafter. There are some signs of a similar increase in the heights of boys at Sandhurst.

All three real wage series diverge from an earlier tradition that real wages rose during the second half of the eighteenth century (Hunt and Botham 1987: 380–1). The series derived from the recent work of Lindert and Williamson shows an increase of 37.8 per cent between 1781 and 1827 (from a value of 53.7 to 74.0), while the original Lindert and Williamson series for blue-collar workers shows an increase of 22.6 per cent between 1751 and 1827 or of 37.9 per cent between 1781 and 1827. In both cases, however, the greater part of the increase is thought to have occurred after 1810; before that date there are only minor fluctuations around a constant level. By contrast, the Schwarz series falls steeply from about 1755 to about 1800 before rising equally steeply thereafter until the end of the series in the 1850s. Schwarz argues (1985: 31) that the finding of falling real wages can be generalised to 'many parts of England' but this finding – and that of Lindert and Williamson – has been disputed by Hunt and Botham, who find substantially rising wages in north Staffordshire (1987). They calculate real wage increases of 10.2 per cent between 1751 and 1792 for general labourers, of 8.9 per cent between 1750 and 1792 for

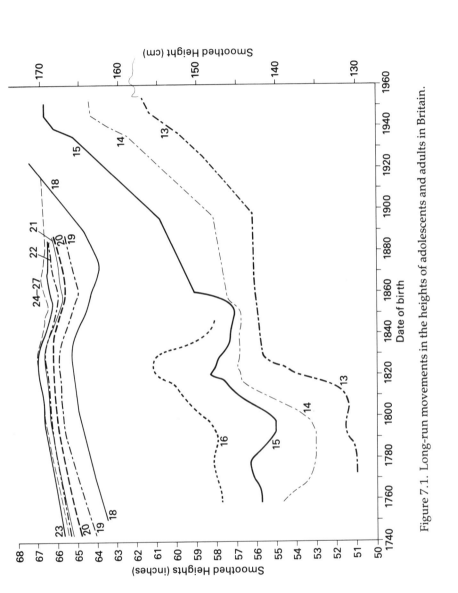

Figure 7.1. Long-run movements in the heights of adolescents and adults in Britain.

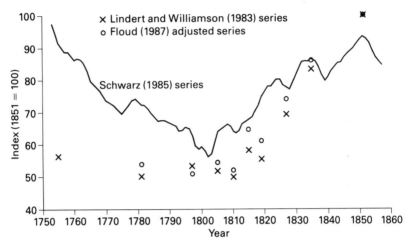

Figure 7.2. Real wages, 1750–1860. Notes: (1) Lindert and Williamson 1983 series for all blue-collar workers. (2) Floud 1987 adjusted version of series 2. (3) Schwarz 1985 series for bricklayers' wages in London, adjusted by the Phelps Brown and Hopkins price series, 10 year average.

craftsmen and of 36.5 per cent between 1750 and 1794 for skilled potters (1987: 390–3).

It needs emphasis that, as has often been stated, most of the 'bounce' in all the real wage series comes from movements in prices rather than in wages; this puts great pressure on the accuracy of compilation of price series and on the weights used in their aggregation. In particular, the national Lindert and Williamson series, which are also used by Schwarz, are substantially affected by the inclusion of rents, based on 'a few dozen cottages in Trentham, Staffordshire' (1983b: 9), which show somewhat different movements from the rent series for other houses in north Staffordshire collected by Hunt and Botham (1987: 388). The fragility of generalisations from that area to the whole of England and Wales is clear from the contrast between the findings of Hunt and Botham and those of Schwarz. None of the series refer to Scotland or to Ireland.

It is difficult, on this basis, to summarise evidence on real wage movements in order to compare them with the height series. The Schwarz series for London should bear some relationship to the Marine Society series – although one is for adult bricklayers and the other for unskilled teenagers – and, indeed, the rapid rise during and after the Napoleonic Wars appears in both series, although the fall before that is much more marked in the Schwarz series. As for the adults, the supposed national series and that for north Staffordshire, as well as the consensus of prior interpretations, concur in showing modest overall increases between 1750 and 1820, which they share with the height series, although it is important to repeat that most of the real wage movement occurs after 1800. The correspondence is, therefore, reasonably good, although the importance of differences in regional trends is clear.

After the 1820s, however, the series diverge markedly. Heights then began to fall while the Lindert and Williamson series shows an increase of 1.51 per cent per annum between 1819 and 1851; even Crafts' series for personal consumption rises by 1.24 per cent per annum from 1820 to 1850 (1985: 143), whilst their combination (Lindert and Williamson 1985: 151) rises by 0.9 per cent per annum between 1819 and 1851. Schwarz's London series also shows a marked rise.

It was such estimates that led Williamson, for example, to state that (1985: 18):

Unless new errors are discovered, the debate over real wages is over: the *average* worker was much better off in any decade from the 1830s on than in any decade before 1820. The same is true of *any class* of worker in [his] table 2.8 (Farm laborers, middle group, artisans, white-collar).

while, he feels, neither unemployment, pauperism, urbanisation nor longevity levels or trends seriously detract from this conclusion (1985: 19–28). Yet the evidence of heights certainly does so.

7.2.2 Mortality

What light can other evidence throw on these patterns and on the conflict between them? Figure 7.3 reproduces Wrigley and Schofield's (1981) calculations of changes in expectation of life at birth in England and Wales. In this summary form, these figures do not tell us directly about changes in the age-pattern of deaths, but they are a much better general indicator than crude death rates. As figure 7.3 shows, life expectancy reached its second lowest point between 1541 and 1901 in the quinquennium centred on 1731, at 27.9 years. There was then a sharp improvement in the middle and later parts of the eighteenth century, although only to the levels that had been reached in the first part of that century, and a further improvement in the first quarter of the nineteenth century. Wrigley and Schofield write of their index that (1981: 236):

After 1731 there was recovery and fairly steady improvement, though the early 1740s, the 1760s and the early 1780s were all periods of relapse from

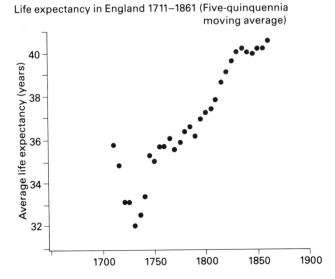

Figure 7.3. Life expectancy in England, 1711–1861 (five-quinquennia moving average). Source: Wrigley and Schofield 1981, p. 230.

the rising trend in expectation of life. Thereafter there was a decline in the scale of fluctuations in the quinquennial estimates of e° [expectation of life at birth], and between 1781 and 1826 expectation of life at birth improved from about 35 years to 40 years, though after this there was no significant change for a further half-century.

Thereafter, as Wrigley and Schofield point out, 'e° was only about two years higher than in the reigns of Elizabeth and James I' (1981: 236). Reconstitution studies also suggest a substantial improvement in e° and in infant mortality in the last fifty years of the eighteenth century, but much less change after that (Wrigley and Schofield 1981: 249–53). These changes occurred despite marked rises in fertility.

The Scottish picture is more complex. Flinn sees the period from 1760 to 1781 as showing 'a fairly benign picture of mortality' (1977: 229) except in the far north and the Highlands and Hebrides, but comments of the succeeding period to 1800 that 'There is no period for which the evidence of mortality is more difficult to evaluate than this' (1977: 237). There seems, however, to have been a rise in mortality in many areas. For the country as a whole, life expectancy at birth in the 1790s was probably somewhat higher than in England and Wales; the Scottish figure was 39.4 years, with only the Western Lowlands substantially lower, while the figures in England and Wales were 37.3 for the quinquennium centred on 1791, and 36.8 for that centred on 1796 (Flinn 1977: 270; Wrigley and Schofield 1981: 230). The evidence of heights is unequivocal in seeing a Scottish advantage during this period, although one that is substantially eroded thereafter.

In the nineteenth century, Scottish mortality levels seem to have shown little change, despite some short-term crises, during the first 30 years. Thereafter, 'the period from 1832 to 1855 was to be one of the worst in modern Scottish history, with frequent, severe crises rising to a peak in 1847, and only falling away in the late 1850s' (Flinn 1977: 371). It was at this period that Scottish height advantages seem to have been significantly reduced. There is thus a remarkable concordance between Flinn's accounts and the testimony of the recruitment data as they pertain to Scotland.

Irish population history, and with it the history of mortality, is made very difficult by lack of records. There is some evidence of declining mortality in the late eighteenth and early nineteenth centuries, although on a limited scale. By the census of 1841, just before the devastating famine, Irish mortality levels were 'slightly higher than Great Britain' (Mokyr and O'Grada 1984: 483). Infant mortality rates, however, are thought to have been higher than those in other European countries, although they were probably declining.

Our knowledge of the age-pattern of deaths in all parts of Britain and Ireland is much less certain, until the advent of civil registration in England and Wales in 1837 and in Scotland in 1855. In 1839 in England and Wales there were 151 deaths of infants under one year per thousand live births and the infant death rate stayed at around this level, fluctuating between 164 and 135 per thousand, for the remainder of the nineteenth century, showing a sustained fall only after 1900. The Scottish rate, at around 120 significantly lower than the English in the 1850s, also stayed very stable until the early years of the present century, falling somewhat later than the English. In both countries, the infant death rate, and to a lesser extent the death rate for older people, fell significantly later and less rapidly than the death rate for the age-group 2–45; deaths in this latter group began to decline in the 1870s.

For earlier periods, since Wrigley and Schofield's methods of estimation do not make it possible to estimate the age-structure of deaths, it is necessary to rely on the relatively fragmentary evidence of reconstitution studies. These seem to show that the infant mortality rate in England and Wales may have declined from quite high levels in the first half of the eighteenth century to about 135 per thousand for males and 122 per thousand for females. These levels were significantly below those that were to be experienced for several decades after 1838 (Wrigley and Schofield 1981: 249). There are, therefore, good grounds for thinking either that infant mortality rates did not share in the general improvement around the time of the Napoleonic Wars or that they rose more rapidly than adult rates in the second quarter of the century. The Scottish evidence suggests that the latter is more likely; mortality in Glasgow rose substantially in the second quarter of the nineteenth century, and Flinn dates the turning-point for the younger age-groups to the cholera epidemic of 1832; even after the epidemic mortality subsided in the 1850s, mortality in the under-five group 'remained appreciably higher than it had been in 1821 and 1831' (Flinn 1977: 377).

The Scottish experience points to one of the most striking features of mortality in the eighteenth and nineteenth centuries, the impact of urbanisation. Flinn ascribes the poor mortality of Scotland in the second and third quarter of the nineteenth century largely to this factor.

> The principal explanation must lie in the pace of urbanisation. In the cities of the first half of the nineteenth century there was virtually no effective sanitation, little or no street cleaning, and a totally inadequate supply of pure drinking water. In the absence of water closets for all but the wealthiest, sewage disposal was by cesspits or removal in carts. House-building could not keep pace with demand, and overcrowding reached terrifying levels. It was a system ideally designed for the maximum spread of killing infections.
>
> (Flinn 1977: 19)

In addition, as Flinn points out, disease spread to the countryside as infections caught in the towns were brought back to the villages and farms.

The situation in England and Wales was little different, as observers such as the Rev Thomas Malthus soon realised.[4] Although, in a recent study of mortality patterns, Woods is right to emphasise the immense regional diversity, it remains true that the large towns showed enormous excess mortality at all ages above that of the countryside. In 1861, for example, male expectation of life at birth in

---

[4] In the fourth edition of the *Essay on Population* Malthus commented of mortality that:

> The causes of most of our diseases appear to be so mysterious and probably are really so various, that it would be rashness to lay too much stress on any single one; but it will not perhaps be too much to say, that *among* these causes we ought certainly to rank crowded houses, and insufficient wholesome food, which are the natural consequences of an increase of population faster than the accommodation of a country with respect to habitations and food will allow.
>
> (1807: 565, quoted in Wrigley 1986: 8).

Bristol, Birmingham, Leicester, Derby, Manchester, Sheffield, Hull, Newcastle and Liverpool and in many parts of inner London was less than 35 years, while 'several rural districts in the south, the West Midlands and the south west had male life expectancies at birth of over 50 years' (Woods 1984: 43). Factor analysis suggests a more complex pattern, emphasising infant mortality, which underlay these figures:

in urban-industrial south Lancashire and west Yorkshire male infant and child mortality, and female mortality in late adulthood, are relatively more important elements in the structure of age-specific mortality than is the mortality of other age groups.

In London, by contrast, mortality was dominated by high male infant mortality and by the high mortality of adult males (Woods 1984: 62). In Ireland, too, urban infant mortality was 'far in excess' of that in rural areas (Mokyr and O'Grada 1984: 484). We have seen in chapter 6 that environmental conditions in infancy and early childhood are particularly influential in determining nutritional status and height.

7.2.3 The disease environment

We have looked at three ways of describing the mortality experience of eighteenth- and nineteenth-century Britain, in terms of the time-specific, age-specific and region-specific incidence of death. But people die of specific causes – even if they are often difficult to determine – and we must therefore examine the pattern of cause-specific death rates.

It should be said that there is very little evidence about cause-specific death rates before the 1840s. In Scotland, as in England and Wales, the main source is the bills of mortality of various cities, which only cover relatively small parts of the population and in which diagnosis is, to say the least, inexact. Such evidence does not show any noticeable decline in death rates from infectious diseases, with the exception of smallpox:[5]

First, throughout the first half of the nineteenth century, the common infectious diseases regularly accounted for over 60 per cent of all deaths. Second,

---

[5] There is considerable controversy over the impact of inoculation on the decline of smallpox and of that decline on the course of mortality as a whole (Razzell 1977). An intriguing but unsubstantiated link between that controversy and the evidence of heights is provided by the work of Landauer and his collaborators, who argue that the stress induced by inoculation and vaccination can itself produce growth in height (1964, 1973).

tuberculosis, under-registered as it almost certainly was in these sources, was overwhelmingly the largest single killing disease. Third, the lethal impact of smallpox and, to a lesser extent, of measles, declined significantly during this period. Fourth, fever and whooping cough, important killers at all times in the nineteenth century, did not noticeably diminish during this period.

(Flinn 1977: 389)

Moreover, tuberculosis continued as a major cause of death in Scotland well into the twentieth century, although it was overtaken in the 1870s by the bronchitis and pneumonia complex and other infectious diseases, notably influenza, began later to rival it in importance. Ireland differed from this overall pattern only in that smallpox declined more slowly there than elsewhere; in 1841, for example, 'smallpox accounted for 13.3 per cent of all deaths under five in Connacht and 8.4 per cent in Leinster' although on the more developed eastern seaboard the rates were much lower (Mokyr and O'Grada 1984: 485).

Evidence for England and Wales is extremely sparse before the coming of civil registration, but McKeown argues that infective diseases were even more virulent in earlier periods and that, important though they were, their impact may indeed have been declining at the time of the beginning of civil registration:

Although information about individual diseases is lacking, there is little doubt that mortality from at least two major airborne infections – tuberculosis and smallpox – had fallen before 1838. There is reason to believe that there was also a significant decrease of deaths from water- and food-borne diseases ... Of the vector-borne diseases, plague had virtually disappeared before the beginning of the eighteenth century, and it is unlikely that malaria was ever an important cause of death in the British Isles; however, the decline of typhus undoubtedly contributed to the reduction of mortality in the pre-registration period.

(McKeown 1976: 72)

The mortality history of England and Wales, Scotland and Ireland thus suggests that the early and middle decades of the nineteenth century were marked by very high levels of death from infectious diseases and, in particular, from the diarrhoeal diseases, from tuberculosis and from bronchitis and pneumonia, all of which are closely associated with malnutrition in the less-developed countries of today. The impact of the Irish famine of the late 1840s is a graphic illustration. What is unclear, unfortunately, is the extent to which, except in such a case as Ireland in the famine, this mortality pattern reflects the pattern of morbidity. Our height measures, after all, obviously reflect the nutritional experience of those who did not die in infancy or childhood; what grounds are there for thinking that mortality levels or causes have any relevance to their physical growth?

7.2.4 *Morbidity*

In discussing the health of the people in the nineteenth century, Derek Oddy argues that:

The nature of the available evidence is such that positive data on health and normal physical development are scarce, while evidence of mortality and morbidity can be found in abundance from a variety of sources. Studies of health tend to rationalise the use of whatever evidence is available: ill-health becomes the reciprocal of health, with the result that the emphasis is over-whelmingly on bodily disorders. Such studies become works of historical epidemiology rather than of human health and physical development. What is missing is a description of healthy late Victorian *Homo sapiens*.

(Oddy 1982: 121)

Oddy therefore seeks evidence of the health of the people in studies of nutrition and physical development, including those of height. Unfortunately the physical development which is being measured is itself greatly but not by any means entirely affected by the disease environment. In other words, one cannot escape from the need to delineate ill-health, either in describing the health of the people or in explaining the pattern of physical growth.

Oddy is, however, optimistic in his view that there is an abundance of evidence on morbidity patterns, or at least that the evidence is easily usable. The major problem is that we know a lot about death, but very much less about the impact of disease on those who survived; even case–fatality rates, the number of those who died as a proportion of those with the disease, were rarely recorded or discussed. In *The People's Health, 1830–1910*, for example, F. B. Smith presents a very full discussion of diseases, based on extensive research, but is forced to concentrate almost entirely on death rates as evidence. Part of the problem, of course, is that case–fatality rates varied enormously. In discussing scarlet fever, for example, he comments that:

Throughout the period case mortality was highest among infants under twelve months old, approaching 50 per cent, falling to about 27 per cent among two- to four-year olds. But the incidence of the disease appears to have been highest among children aged four to eight.

(Smith 1979: 136)

but in 1894 the medical officer of health for Brighton calculated that the overall case–fatality rate in Brighton was 1:62, as against 1:19 in London (Smith 1979: 140). Where diseases were not notifiable, even less is known and the pattern is bewildering. In discussing diarrhoea in infancy Smith comments that:

Attacks in infants were always acute with a *probable* high case fatality rate. The illness lasted about a week in a strong child and death was often preceded by distressing convulsions, while young babies and weaklings could be carried off in less than 48 hours. Other members of the family, especially the children, were generally also affected, indicating, amongst other causes, poor food handling and much personal dirtiness.

(Smith 1979: 85)

Yet the evidence from less-developed countries is of diarrhoea as an endemic disease, with relatively low case–fatality rates beyond infancy compared to other infections.

Our knowledge of childhood morbidity is thus patchy and unsatisfactory, although it all seems to point to increased morbidity, as well as mortality, among the poor of the urban areas. It was not until 1907, however, that Mrs Barbara Drake demonstrated by a study of cases in Westminster that there was:

a close link between low income, poor housing and high morbidity and mortality among both infants and mothers. In general, twice as many infants in low-income families in poor housing were sickly or dead.

(Smith 1979: 124)

In summarising the evidence of mortality and morbidity, it seems likely that there was some deterioration both in the late eighteenth century and, particularly, in the second quarter of the nineteenth century. The combination of poverty and urbanisation appears to have been lethal for many members of the working class and for their children and, we must presume, damaging for many more. The experience of rural Ireland is instructive; as Mokyr and O'Grada put it (1984: 486): 'While the Irish were widely thought to be wretchedly poor and backward, the numerous comments on their health and good looks are indicative of the quality of the potato diet', an impression confirmed by our evidence of their height. Potatoes and milk, and perhaps also the oatmeal of the Scots, seem to have provided a healthy and balanced diet for those who did not have to fight off urban disease.

7.2.5 Urbanisation and housing conditions

Like much else in eighteenth- and nineteenth-century Britain, urban living conditions were essentially a problem of poverty, as Rowntree's title *Poverty: A Study of Town Life*, makes clear. While the state of working-class housing varied enormously from one part of the country to another, from the cellar dwellings of Liverpool to the relative affluence of Sheffield's houses, housing was throughout the country not only an essential charge on family income but the 'largest single fixed charge' in working-class budgets, consuming anywhere between 9 and 15 per cent of incomes at the end of the nineteenth century and probably much the same throughout our period (Burnett 1986: 147).

During the first part of the nineteenth century, however, the most striking fact about working-class housing was the speed of increase in numbers of houses and other dwellings, as urban areas expanded at an extraordinary rate. As Burnett (1986: 57) shows, the overall growth in the population of urban areas was over 25 per cent per decade between 1801 and 1851, much faster than the underlying increase in the whole population, while some towns grew much faster. The increase in the physical area of towns was much less and, in addition, the advent of the railway meant that in cities such as London large areas of working-class housing were demolished to make way for lines and stations while demolition also took place to create wider streets and to remove slums. While sometimes undertaken for laudable motives, the result of such action was almost always to worsen the pressure on the housing that remained. Workers, unable to live at more than walking distance from their place of work, were forced to cram into the housing in city centres, where the houses of the rich of previous eras were turned into the slums of the present. Only much later in the century, with the coming of cheap trains, was this pressure alleviated at all.

As Burnett and others (George 1925; Chapman 1971; Daunton 1983) have shown, the result of the pressure of demand on a limited geographical area was to produce a housing stock and housing conditions of bewildering complexity and variety. While the solution to the 'housing question' eluded Victorian reformers, their efforts and those of the myriads of small builders intertwined with custom and fashion and with changing real incomes to create an hierarchy of housing provision – cellars, tenements, lodging houses, back-to-backs, terraces, workshops and tied houses, philanthropic dwellings – through which working-class families moved as their incomes waxed and waned over the life-cycle. Census and other studies show a degree of mobility which was very large by modern standards, as families sought to adjust their housing to their income and to the number to be sheltered.

For those in primary or secondary poverty, this balance resulted in housing of indescribable horror. Contemporary accounts are legion, emphasising the cold, the damp, the intolerable smell of the eighteenth- and nineteenth-century city dwellings, from which middle-class visitors, themselves no strangers to bad drains and inadequate heating, recoiled in disgust. As Edwin Chadwick found in his two great enquiries, into the 'Health of Towns' and the 'Sanitary Condition of the Working Class', these conditions bred disease and death. For those already malnourished by poverty in the sense that they could only afford a meagre diet, the additional claims on their bodies stemming from the need to combat cold, polluted water, foetid air and lack of living space must have often been intolerable; their nutritional status, as the heights of the children of the Marine Society from the slums and rookeries of London so eloquently show, was appalling. Rickets was only the most visible of the deficiency diseases from which they suffered (Loomis 1970).

Compelling evidence of the effect of urbanisation comes from the trends in differentials in heights which were described in chapter 5. As the discussion there showed, both Scots and English urban areas showed declining trends in height differentials, bringing them closer over time to the heights of Londoners. These latter were consistently lower in the eighteenth and nineteenth centuries than the heights of other groups which we can measure, testifying to the effect of living conditions in what was and remained by far the largest urban area. Yet, as the factory and other enquiries showed, the children of other areas soon matched the deprivation shown by the Marine Society.

Differentials between heights in the urbanising English counties and those in the rural English counties were also reduced and then reversed, while the heights of men from the Scots rural counties and from Ireland remained greater. It seems likely that this narrowing of differentials between urban and rural areas in England derived from one, or both, of two factors; first, it may be that the worsening disease environment in the towns spread outwards into the countryside around them, particularly as transport improved during the course of the period. Second, it is well known that demands for labour from the towns, particularly in the North and Midlands, exerted upward pressure on wage levels in the countryside and reduced the differentials between urban and rural wages in those areas. Both factors would reduce these geographic differentials, but it is difficult to discriminate between them, particularly as the experience of the southern rural counties of England was rather different, at least so far as wage levels were concerned; there, the corn-growing regions were notorious for their low wage levels and for the unavailing efforts of the local upper classes to promote emigration and to reduce the burden of poor relief. It would be necessary to draw larger samples and to discriminate more clearly between different part of rural England to settle these issues.

7.2.6 *Diet and consumption*

In the light of the evidence on mortality, morbidity and urbanisation, it is perhaps not surprising that few historians have found evidence of substantial improvements in the diet of the working-class population. Burnett (1979) surveys trends in the consumption of imported foodstuffs, where import duties provide reasonably accurate estimates; alterations in duties and in prices are complicating features, but Burnett found a substantial reduction in sugar consumption per capita between 1801 and 1821, followed by gradually falling consumption until 1840, when consumption per head was at only half the level of 1801; there was then a gradual increase to 1845 and a sharp increase thereafter. As for tea, consumption fell slightly in the 1820s and 1830s but rose in the 1840s (1979: 26). The evidence of malt charged for duty also indicates a fall in beer consumption 'from the beginning of the century down to 1851'. All this leads Burnett to the view that (1979: 29):

> Our conclusion must be that there does not seem to be any evidence of a general rise in consumption trends over the period 1815–50. The trend in sugar and beer was downwards until 1845, tea was practically stationary throughout the same period, while bread consumption probably rose only after 1847. Sugar and beer are perhaps the best indicators of working class standards (tea was already a near necessity, and its consumption highly inelastic), and on their evidence those standards were tending to fall rather than rise.

Burnett also constantly emphasises the extent of adulteration of foodstuffs which took place in the eighteenth and nineteenth centuries. In another survey, Brinley Thomas (1985) also finds little increase in consumption of basic foodstuffs and, emphasising the importance of imports from Ireland, Scotland and Wales, throws doubt on some of the more 'optimistic' interpretations of the success of English agriculture in feeding a growing population.

Such 'pessimistic' conclusions remain deeply controversial, however, and arguments over consumption have been at the heart of the standard of living debate. Crafts (1985b: 98), for example, emphasises that in the measurement of overall consumption growth it is 'liable to be misleading' to discuss food consumption alone. Agricultural goods became relatively expensive between 1760 and 1820, 'whilst items like cotton clothing became much cheaper and at no time did workers spend all their budgets on food'. Thus Crafts accepts that current estimates of food consumption support a picture of deterioration; other consumption was growing even if it is impossible to tell exactly who was buying the goods.

As Crafts implies, it is the distribution of consumption, both by geography and by income, which is crucial but unknown. As an example, Thomas (1985: 148–9) cites the 'plight of the agricultural population of southern England, where the vast majority depended on wheat' but were forced to switch consumption to potatoes, allowing them to 'survive on the lowest possible wage'. Hunt (1986) has also emphasised the diversity of regional wage trends between 1760 and 1850, which tend to complicate any generalisation about the working class as a whole.

In addition, there remained substantial differences in the diet of different peoples within Britain and Ireland. Cullen, for example, emphasises the complexity of the Irish diet in the eighteenth and nineteenth centuries; far from the population being solely dependent on potatoes, the Irish population continued to consume substantial quantities of meat and dairy products while potatoes served as a substitute for breadgrains. They were also important as feed for pigs, and pork and bacon production rose markedly from the middle of the eighteenth century. But within Ireland there were several distinct regions, concentrating for example on cereal – pulse production or on dairying, where the pattern of seasonal production and consumption was entirely different (Cullen 1981: 104–8). Similar regional differentiation was marked within England, Wales and Scotland.

These differences in diet, partly but not wholly linked to the income levels of the different regions, make generalisation difficult and undermine attempts to derive the nutritional characteristics of British and Irish diet as a whole. Were it not for the evidence of heights, it would not be easy to conclude that there had been improvement in the diet of any large section of the working class during the period of the Industrial Revolution.

7.2.7 Income distribution

There is no doubt that, in addition to changing regional patterns, there were substantial changes in the relative incomes of different social and occupational groups within the working class, as well as distributional changes affecting all classes. These are apparent in the height differentials which were estimated and discussed in chapter 5. As was emphasised there, the height data demonstrate declining differentials within the working class, particularly before 1820; by that point, the differentials between the different occupational groups had been considerably reduced while, after the 1820s, the differentials remained relatively stable and small.

This pattern conflicts very seriously with that described by Williamson (1985). His discussion of inequality trends emphasises contrasting trends before and after 1820 but in a very different manner. He believes that (1985: 72–3):

there was a rise in inequality across the century following 1760. The inequality drift was universal, since the income shares at the top rose, the shares at the bottom fell, the relative pay of the unskilled deteriorated, and the earnings distribution widened . . .

The pay ratio and earnings distribution data clearly document an egalitarian leveling across the Napoleonic period, perhaps starting as early as the 1780s. These trends are reversed following the wars, with a surge in wage inequality from the 1820s to mid-century . . . The post-Waterloo period was one of consistent inequality movements.

There is simply no sign of such trends in the height data, which suggest that the early part of the Industrial Revolution was marked by a lessening of differentials between the nutritional status of different groups within the working class, with very little trend in differentials during the half century after 1820. It is of particular interest, therefore, that a recent critique of Williamson by C. H. Feinstein (1988), based on a detailed examination of many of the data sources, has similarly concluded that there was little trend in inequality during the nineteenth century and that the Kuznets curve which Williamson discerned did not in fact exist.

7.2.8 Productivity change

Even though the improvements in nutritional status up to the birth cohorts of the 1830s are impressive, it is not certain that these improvements increased the strength and endurance of those who laboured by hand sufficiently to affect overall labour productivity. After all, even with the improvements, the levels of heights remained very low by modern standards. Comparisons with workers in the third world today are dubious, considering the different genetic and epidemiological contexts, but it is of relevance to remember that many individuals today who are of comparable height to the British of the early 1800s are capable only of bursts of activity rather than sustained heavy work. The British working class appears to have lived near enough to the margin for it to be conceivable that the falls in nutritional status for those reaching adulthood around the 1850s which are suggested by the height series may have been accompanied by drops in physical labour productivity and that the large later increases in height may have helped a recovery of productivity levels.

It is also possible that improvements in childhood nutritional status, if they helped to produce the substantial increase in life expectations which occurred before the 1820s, could have contributed to increased productivity through extending the working life. Unlike today, where retirement from work is a reality for most of the population and increased life expectancy therefore has little effect on the numbers of producers in the economy, a decline in deaths before 1850 had substantial effects on the number of workers and thus on the output of the economy. The link with nutritional status is, however, too tenuous at the moment for this to be more than a matter of speculation.

7.2.9 A Synthesis, 1750–1850

How are we to put together all this evidence on living standards before 1850? For the greater part of the period, the height data indicate substantial though gradual improvement which would be hard to discern on the evidence of mortality, morbidity, diet or housing alone. For the very end of the period, for those born after 1830, the height evidence is consistent with those types of evidence, which concur in finding at best little improvement in living conditions and at worst deterioration. For this crucial later period, the exceptional evidence is that provided by estimates of real wages and real income, which seem to indicate impressive increases at the time when heights decline.

One way to reconcile these conflicts is simple; it is to disbelieve one or other source. Indeed, while Feinstein's major criticisms of Williamson's work are directed at his calculations of earnings inequality, many of the same criticisms apply to Williamson's calculations of real wages, particularly those of the white collar groups. Yet there are sufficient alternative computations of real wage gains, some by different methods, which concur in seeing improvements from the 1820s onwards, that simply to reject the real wage evidence out of hand would be foolish.

The evidence about nutritional status provided by measurements of height is, as has been argued above, of a different kind from the evidence of other indicators. Like mortality, it is a net measure of output but, unlike mortality, it sums up in a net measure a number of environmental conditions which are not extreme enough to result in death. Despite the many caveats which must be attached to its use, a measure of nutritional status does comprehend the joint effects of income, of the disease environment, of living conditions and of work effort. As such, the measure suggests that, even if there were substantial gains in real incomes or in real wages for the working class in the second quarter of the nineteenth century, these were more than outweighed by other features of the environment – urbanisation, disease, diet and possibly work intensity. If our focus is on those Victorians who reached adulthood at mid century, then the decline in mean heights of those born between the 1820s and the 1850s is a strong argument indeed for the pessimistic interpretation of the impact of industrialisation on the British working class. It should also shift the attention of historians away from the time of the Napoleonic Wars towards the second quarter of the nineteenth century.

If one takes a longer view, however, this conclusion is reversed, since the evidence of heights suggests that there was significant improvement in nutritional status over the whole of the century between 1750 and 1850. If that is taken as the period of industrialisation, then gains in nutritional status – not necessarily to be attributed to industrialisation, since so many occurred at the time of the Napoleonic War, before the 1820s – were somewhat greater than the checks to improvement in physical growth that were imposed thereafter. It also seems that significant inequalities within the working class, as shown by height differentials, narrowed during the late eighteenth and early nineteenth century and then remained roughly constant.

The contribution of the evidence of heights is, therefore, twofold. First, it reinforces the view that the early period of the Industrial Revolution saw significant gains for the working class as a whole and for some of the most deprived groups within it; this is shown not only by the narrowing of differentials but also by the experience of the children of the Marine Society. Second, it demonstrates forcibly that, if there were significant gains in real incomes for the working class between the 1820s and the 1850s, they were bought at a very high price.

It is interesting, last, to speculate about the long-term effects of the dramatic changes in mean height which occurred in the second quarter of the nineteenth century. As chapter 6 suggests, deprivation and disease in early childhood have particularly severe consequences upon nutritional status and physical growth; it is not surprising that the 'Hungry Forties' and perhaps even hungrier thirties should have produced the effects which we see in our figures. But chapter 6 also suggests that such effects can be felt in the very long-term, affecting the life and death chances of the children of the 1830s and 1840s as they grew into adulthood and old age. In other words, we should expect to see the echoes of the experience of the early part of the nineteenth century as we examine the later part; it is to that task that we now turn.

7.3 NUTRITIONAL STATUS, HEALTH AND INCOME, 1850–1914

7.3.1 Nutritional status

As figure 7.1 shows, the decline in heights of the second quarter of the century persisted into the cohorts born in the 1850s and 1860s. Thereafter, there was a rise which gradually reversed the decline of the previous period, so that by the time of the cohort born just before the First World War it is likely that mean heights had recovered and perhaps slightly surpassed the levels reached in the birth cohorts of the 1820s.

This would have been a surprising conclusion to those commentators, such as Major-General Sir Frederick Maurice, who read the evidence of recruiting statistics at the end of the nineteenth century to imply the decline of the health and fitness of the British race. It would also have surprised the military authorities who examined recruits during the First World War. Maurice calculated in 1902 that 'out of every five men who are willing to enlist only two are fit to become effective soldiers' ('Miles' 1902: 79) and saw in this evidence of the physical state of the nation 'a far more deadly peril than any that was presented by the most anxious period of the South African War' (1902: 86).

What particularly alarmed Maurice and a number of his contemporaries was that it seemed that there had been and was continuing physical deterioration among the working class, with the effect that 'the great body of the nation itself is decaying in health and physical vigour' ('Miles' 1902: 82) and would, moreover, as it bred, reproduce itself in ever more stunted and unhealthy a form. Maurice, like others such as Shee and like earlier writers such as Cantlie and Freeman-Williams, was convinced that progressive physical deterioration had set in and that only a massive programme of education of the lower classes in better parenthood might stand a chance of averting catastrophe (Maurice 1903: 52; Shee 1903; Cantlie 1885; Freeman-Williams 1890). Unless something were done, the nation would be unable to defend itself, a fear that was reinforced by the statement of the Inspector-General of Army Recruiting that (PP 1903 xi: para. 150):

The one subject which causes anxiety in the future as regards recruiting is the gradual deterioration of the physique of the working classes from whom the bulk of the recruits must always be drawn.

It was concern such as this which led to the setting-up by the Government of the Inter-Departmental Committee on Physical Deterioration, partly in order to examine the recruiting statistics on which Maurice had relied. The Committee (PP 1904 xxxii) refused to believe the evidence of the statistics and, on the basis of numerous expert medical witnesses, argued that health had been improving during the last decades of the nineteenth century, while accepting that the nutrition and health of the working class were certainly not at acceptable levels.

In one sense, both Maurice and the Committee were wrong; the raw recruiting statistics did suggest a deterioration but our statistical corrections for the effects of truncation and the changing height standard convert that deterioration into a gradual improvement (Floud, Gregory and Wachter 1985). What is not at issue is that working-class health was still deplorable.

It would be tedious and unnecessary to examine the later part of the nineteenth century as closely as we have the earlier part. As we have argued above, the evidence of Rowntree and his contemporaries, early in the twentieth century, demonstrates forcibly the levels of absolute poverty which still obtained at that time among the working class. What we have to explore, therefore, is the transition from the appalling conditions which the height and other data suggest were experienced by the working class in mid century to the slightly improved conditions of the Edwardian era.

7.3.2 *Real income and real wages*

Until very recently, there has been little controversy about the course of real incomes or real wages in the period between 1850 and 1914, certainly none that rivals the standard of living debate that was described above. It was accepted, first, that there were gradual improvements during the 1850s and 1860s, the period of the so-called 'Great Victorian Boom', although most increases were concentrated at the end of the period. Second, it was accepted that the period of the so-called 'Great Depression' between 1873 and 1896 saw substantial improvements in real wages for those in employment, primarily as a result of falls in the prices of foodstuffs and other imported goods. Last, it was believed that there was a check to and even reversal of real wage growth after 1896 and particularly in the early years of the twentieth century; much of the substantial labour unrest of

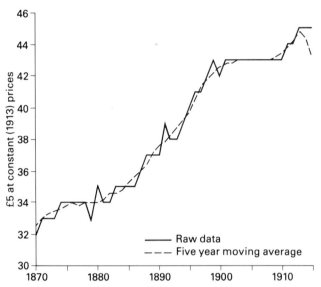

Figure 7.4. Consumers' expenditure per capita at constant (1913) prices, 1870–
1915. Source: Feinstein 1972, table 17.

that period of the 'Strange Death of Liberal England' was attributed
to that cause. Figure 7.4 shows, for example, the course of real incomes
calculated by Feinstein (1972).

This picture presented by the older work on real wages conflicts
in detail, though not perhaps too seriously, with the picture drawn
by using height as an index of nutritional status. Both see some improvement for the working classes towards the end of the century.
The improvements indicated by the height data are rather minimal
and relatively later than those shown by the older series of wages,
which might cause some surprise.

Recently, however, considerable doubt has been thrown on this
accepted pattern of change in real incomes and real wages and new
work accords rather better with the evidence of heights. This new
work has been based on two detailed re-examinations of the wage
and price series collected initially by Bowley and Wood and on a
supplementation of their series by others. Although much of this re-
working is still in progress at the time of writing, initial indications
are that the traditional picture is defective in two respects; first, the
improvement in real wages between the 1870s and the 1890s has been
overstated and, second, the check or decline in real wages in the
first decade of the twentieth century has similarly been overestimated.

In other words, the improvement to real wages is now thought to have been more smoothly distributed over the whole period from the 1860s to 1914 and the overall improvement is less than had previously been thought.

Substantially more research needs to be devoted to the course of real wages and real income in this period and to seeking a reconciliation between the different estimates. It is clear, however, that this research is likely to conclude that there were marked real wage gains during the half century before 1914. During this period, therefore, by contrast with the situation in the previous period, the evidence of heights coincides with the evidence of real wage gains in suggesting a considerable improvement in the welfare of the British working class. It is uncertain whether the new results on real wages will prove more durable than the old ones. But if they do, they raise an interesting question. Why should real wages and nutritional status have improved together in the late nineteenth century after their marked divergence in the early nineteenth century? To address this question we need to explore other aspects of welfare.

7.3.3 Mortality and morbidity

With the advent of civil registration of deaths in England and Wales in 1837 and in Scotland in 1855, it is possible to write with much greater certainty about mortality in the later than in the earlier part of the nineteenth century, although changes in the classification of disease and the cause of death still cause many problems.

The overall course of mortality is clear: as Winter puts it, there has been 'an astonishing change' in life expectation at birth (1982: 100):

which in England and Wales in 1861 stood at 40.5 years for men and 43.0 years for women. Sixty years later, after the First World War, the 50 year mark was passed for women but not yet for men. Ten more years were added to life expectation at birth for both sexes by 1951. It was only in the 1960s that infants born in England and Wales were likely to survive to the Biblical lifespan of threescore years and ten.

A similar improvement occurred in Scotland. There the rising death rates continued into the mid 1870s, but 'By 1881 mortality was in retreat in all parts' and there was a fall of 32 per cent in death rates between 1871 and 1911, a trend which continued in the twentieth century (Flinn 1977: 384). However, the small advantage of Scottish rates over those of England and Wales disappeared around 1900 and since then Scottish mortality has been consistently higher than that of England and Wales.

Within the context of this general improvement, considerable significance for our purposes lies in its age-structure. Mitchison (1977: 39–40), following Greenwood, puts it in this way:

> for children under 15 mortality had begun to fall in the first half of the 1870s; of the 15–24s, females benefited at the same time and males in the next quinquennium. For those of middling age the benefit began in the 1880s for women and in the 1890s for men. For the elderly, i.e. over 45, improvement of any significant kind for both sexes was delayed until early this century ... For neither sex did infant mortality fall significantly until the twentieth century.

This pattern of improvement appears to have been common to all types of areas of the country, so that there was no significant lessening of the gap between urban and rural death rates until the time of the First World War; urban rates were consistently much higher than those of the rural areas.

The causation of these deaths has been explored in great detail by Thomas McKeown and his collaborators (1976). One of McKeown's many contributions to historical epidemiology has been to develop a fourfold taxonomy of mortality in terms of the methods by which the diseases are transmitted: air-borne micro-organisms, water- and food-borne micro-organisms, other micro-organisms, and other conditions. Table 7.1, adapted from *The Modern Rise of Population*, shows how McKeown divides causes of mortality into these four groups and gives the death rates per million from each during the period immediately after 1848, when civil registration and recording of the causes of mortality began. The main conclusions bear repetition:

> Of the fall in mortality which occurred between 1848–54 and 1971, three quarters were associated with conditions attributable to micro-organisms and one quarter with non-infective conditions. Forty per cent of the reduction was due to airborne diseases, 21 per cent to water- and food-borne diseases and 13 per cent to other infections ... The proportion of the decline between 1848–54 and 1971 which occurred by the turn of the century ... was 30 per cent for all diseases, 37 per cent for the infections and 10 per cent for conditions not attributable to micro-organisms.
>
> (1976: 56)

For that period of the second half of the nineteenth century, as Woods and Woodward (1984: 30) succinctly put it:

> Most of the decline in the last half of the nineteenth century is attributable to the reduction in three particular sets of diseases. They are: tuberculosis; cholera, typhus, typhoid; scarlet fever. To account for changes in these

Table 7.1. *McKeown's classification of the causes of mortality, 1848–1854.*

	Death rate per million	
I Conditions attributable to micro-organisms	12 965	
[1] Air-borne diseases	7259	
Tuberculosis (respiratory)		2901
Bronchitis, pneumonia, influenza		2239
Whooping cough		423
Measles		342
Scarlet fever and diphtheria		1016
Smallpox		263
Infections of ear, pharnyx, larynx		75
[2] Water- and food-borne diseases	3562	
Cholera, diarrhoea, dysentery		1819
Tuberculosis (non-respiratory)		753
Typhoid, typhus		990
[3] Other conditions	2144	
Convulsions, teething		1322
Syphilis		50
Appendicitis, peritonitis		75
Puerperal fever		62
Other infections		635
II Conditions not attributable to micro-organisms	8891	
Congenital defects		28
Prematurity, immaturity, other diseases of infancy		1221
Cerebrovascular disease		890
Rheumatic heart disease		64
Other cardiovascular disease		634
Cancer		307
Other diseases of digestive system		706
Other diseases of nervous system		316
Nephritis		615
Other diseases of urinary system		107
Pregnancy and childbirth (excluding sepsis)		130
Violence		761
Old age		1447
Other		1665
All diseases	21 856	

Source: McKeown 1976: 54–62.

particular diseases would be to explain up to 75 per cent of the reasons for the general fall in mortality.

and McKeown himself sees the main explanation for their decline to be environmental and to be, in particular, the result of nutritional improvements.

McKeown's findings, and particularly his suggestion that the mortality decline was largely attributable to improvements in nutrition, have not gone unchallenged. His argument that mortality changes were more significant than fertility changes in causing the modern rise of population (McKeown 1976: 38–40) was clearly flawed and Wrigley and Schofield reached the opposite conclusion, while Winter and others have argued that McKeown was too ready to dismiss the significance of medical intervention in the mortality improvement (Wrigley and Schofield 1981: 244; Winter 1982: 111). More recently, Szreter has suggested that McKeown's case rests too much on the history of a single cause of mortality, respiratory tuberculosis, and that in general McKeown has severely underestimated the role of preventive public health measures (Szreter 1986b).

Despite these criticisms of his interpretation, McKeown's classification of the causes of death is useful and points to the major significance of diseases caused by the spread of micro-organisms, in particular the air- and water-borne diseases, in the mortality experience of the middle of the nineteenth century, particularly when compared to their significance in Britain today. In view of the age-structure of the decline in mortality, it is particularly significant that tuberculosis was a major cause of death in young adults, the group in which the mortality decline began. Between 1851 and 1910, nearly four million people died in England and Wales from tuberculosis and more than one-third of those deaths occurred in the 15–34 age-group; over 40 per cent of deaths in that age-group were attributed to tuberculosis (Cronje 1984: 83).

This raises the question of whether resistance to some types of disease is more affected by undernutrition than others. As we saw in chapter 6, viral and intra-cellular bacterial diseases are most affected by undernutrition, but in practice third-world studies do not usually differentiate between these and other types of infection. One reason for this is theoretical: the effects of undernutrition on the immune system are so complex that the severity of all infections is exacerbated to a greater or lesser extent by undernutrition. The second reason is practical: it is not feasible to attempt to identify the causal agents for all common childhood complaints which, as we have seen, are the main cause of high rates of morbidity and mortality in the third world.

For reasons which were explained above, we still know far too little about morbidity and the disease environment in the nineteenth century, including the period after 1850. Progress in the recording of the incidence and cause of death was not accompanied by systematic recording of morbidity or even of case–fatality rates. Only in exceptional cases, such as the tuberculin test which reveals whether an individual has ever suffered from tuberculosis, is it possible to measure exposure to infection. In that case, Cronje reports that in London in 1930–31, the test showed that (1984: 81–2):

58.3 per cent of the children in the sample aged between 10 and 15 reacted positively to the test, while among the 14- and 15-year-olds the proportion was as high as 82.2 per cent. Other surveys indicated almost universal exposure in European cities where, on average, 20 per cent of children had been infected by the time they were two; 50 per cent by the time they were five; 90 per cent of children under 15; while 97 per cent of adults reacted positively to a tuberculin test.

While it is possible that exposure was slightly lower in rural communities, these figures are certainly indicative of the extent of risk which was run by all sections of the community in the nineteenth century. What is particularly interesting is that the British figures for exposure relate to a period long after the nineteenth-century decline in tuberculosis mortality. It seems likely that the rates of exposure in nineteenth-century British towns were very much higher, comparable to those in European cities, since otherwise the case–fatality rates would have been impossibly high. What has to be explained, therefore, as McKeown and others have realised, is the decline in mortality from a disease to which most of the population continued to be exposed.

McKeown's explanation was that the change was the result of improved nutrition, but he had no direct evidence for this suggestion; nutrition plays the part, in his elegant argument, of the residual explanation. He eliminates all the other possibilities such as improvements in medical care and a change in the virulence of the disease; that which is left is nutritional improvement. His difficulty was that he had no direct means of measuring nutritional change.

It is in this context that the evidence of nutritional status as measured by height is so intriguing. It will be remembered that the increase in heights, after the severe decline of the middle of the century, began with the cohorts born in the 1860s and that there was a gradual but consistent increase thereafter. If this improvement reflects an improvement in nutritional status, then one would expect to see the benefits of this improvement in the shape of declining morbidity and mortality as these cohorts aged; in addition, if conditions continued to improve, their improved nutritional status in childhood would be reinforced by better nutritional status in adolescence and adulthood.

The cohort born in 1860 reached the ages of 15–24 between 1875 and

1884; its members experienced middle age, as defined at that time to include the ages 25–44, between 1880 and 1904, and old age – from the age of 45 onwards – from 1905 onwards. Now recall Greenwood's characterisation of the age-specific fall in death rates: for children under 15, mortality began to fall between 1870 and 1875; for males aged 15–24, between 1875 and 1880; for males of middling age, the 1890s; for the elderly over 45, early this century. The match is amazingly close. In other words, the fall in mortality in late nineteenth century England and Wales follows almost exactly the pattern that we would expect from the evidence of nutritional status. The height data make the link between nutrition (although in a wider sense) and mortality which McKeown could only infer. The data also provide concrete support for the assertions made by Kermack, McKendrick and McKinlay (1934) that the pattern of the decline of mortality – in which each successive cohort exhibited relatively lower mortality throughout life – could best be explained by improvements in the health of children.

Despite this striking result, some puzzles remain. The most obvious is that of infant mortality, which did not decline significantly until the twentieth century. Why did not infant mortality respond to improved nutritional status in ways similar to those affecting mortality at later ages?

One answer is that, even if improvements in nutritional status enabled children and adults increasingly to fight off the major air-borne diseases, there still remained many diseases capable of killing infants. The problem is complicated by the fact that our statistics do not distinguish clearly between deaths immediately following birth, in the neo-natal period, and deaths later in the first year of life. Many deaths immediately following birth may be attributed to birth defects, to the practices of doctors and midwives or to the cross-infections common in lying-in hospitals, together with the general state of public health.

Some results from the Narangwal study, discussed in chapter 6, emphasise the importance of distinguishing between different age-groups when assessing the relative effects of improved nutrition and health care on mortality rates. It was found that infant mortality was reduced much more in villages where children received only health care than in those in which they and their mothers received only nutrition care – the figures were 45 and 24 per cent respectively, with an infant mortality rate in control villages of 128 per thousand. Health care was still more important if infants under 1 month old were excluded – the corresponding figures were then 50 and 7 per cent, with a mortality rate of 53. By contrast, health and nutrition care were of equal importance in reducing mortality rates in the first month of life (excluding stillbirths), and also in children aged between 1 and 3 years – the corresponding figures were about 40 per cent in all cases, with mortality rates of 79 and 19 (although the differences for the older children were not significant).

The greater importance of improved nutrition for children between 1 and 3 years than for infants over a month old (which, as we saw in chapter 6, was reflected in height growth) is also indicated by the dramatic reduction in mortality rates which had already occurred as a result of the agricultural 'green revolution' in Punjab in the 1960s. If the figures for the Narangwal control villages in the early 1970s are compared with figures for a neighbouring area in the late 1950s, the reduction in mortality was 60 per cent for children aged 1–3 years, and 36 per cent for infants over 1 month old (mortality rates in the late 1950s were 48 and 83 respectively).

Kielmann and colleagues (1983: 193–211) suggest several possible factors which might explain these differences – in particular, improved pre-natal nutrition for mothers was probably important in reducing neo-natal death rates; infants, however, were unlikely to benefit from nutrition supplements until breast-feeding became inadequate in the second half of infancy; health care is particularly important in preventing infant deaths because conditions which result in death at this age often require fast curative interventions. The last two factors, at least, are relevant to nineteenth-century Britain, even though conditions in Punjab are otherwise not directly comparable. This suggests that it may be important to distinguish the response of infant mortality from that of mortality at later ages to improvements in nutrition on the one hand, and sanitation and health care on the other, in nineteenth- and early twentieth-century Britain.

Nevertheless, and despite the protection afforded by breast-feeding, many infants died from the complex of diarrhoeal and respiratory diseases which are so common a cause of death in the third world today. The evidence of the prevalence of endemic and epidemic disease in British cities even in the late nineteenth century is also overwhelming and, to modern eyes, horrifying. In London between 1861 and 1870, for example, no East End district had a combined death rate from typhus and typhoid of less than 110 per 100 000 population; Luckin suggests that case–fatality rates were as high as 20–45 per cent for typhus and 15–20 per cent for typhoid, indicating morbidity of at least 400 per 100 000 in those poor areas, while the whole of the London area experienced rates probably over 200 per 100 000 (Luckin 1984: 104–10). There was, however, a substantial decline in mortality and presumably in morbidity between 1870 and 1900; Luckin suggests that case–fatality rates, at least from typhus, remained stable over the period (1984: 115).

But less dramatic diseases remained endemic; many mid-nine-teenth-century reformers saw high levels of infant mortality as a sure sign of insanitary conditions of public and private life and as a spur to public health measures, in particular improvements in water supply and sewage disposal. But these improvements were often slow to come, partly because the connection was sometimes disputed by those who sought to blame the morals and behaviour of the working class or other undoubted evils such as adulterated food (Thompson 1984: 128–9). And despite the improvements which did slowly come in a town such as Bradford, it is difficult to discern any immediate impact on infant mortality; Thompson calculates that between 1876 and 1899 the death rate from gastro-intestinal infections (diarrhoea, atrophy and debility, convulsions) rose from 72.2 per 1000 to 75.6 per 1000, representing 44 per cent of all infant deaths at each date. Mortality from respiratory infections (bronchitis, pneumonia and pleurisy) de-clined only slightly from 30.1 per 1000 to 28.6 per 1000 and represented 18 per cent of infant deaths in 1876–80 and 17 per cent 20 years later (1984: 138–9). She attributes these death rates to 'glaring inadequacies in domestic sanitary provision, to the general disregard of hygiene ... and to the practice of feeding infants artificially'. Much the same can be said of infant mortality in all the other major British cities and in many smaller communities, such as the colliery communities studied by Buchanan where the diarrhoeal diseases were endemic and, as he points out (1985: 149): 'The fact that contemporaries, especially medical officers, did not make constant reference to stomach complaints is probably due to their acceptance as inevitable events.'

Thompson and others have emphasised the pervasive association between infant mortality and poverty. Whatever the complexity of the causal relationships, it is a fact that the shockingly high death rates of infants did not decline until the period when gradual improve-ments in real incomes and real wages in the latter part of the century were trickling through to the whole of the working class and were supplemented by better public sanitary provision (Szreter 1986b). At the same time, those children who survived into childhood did benefit from improvements in nutritional status and were increasingly able to fight off the diseases which would, in previous generations, have killed them. In terms of what we know about the interactions between infection and nutritional status, this suggests that children were able to catch up in growth after the infections which they were almost bound to have caught in infancy and childhood and that the gaps between those infections grew longer, allowing both for catch-up and for survival since their resistance and strength could be restored.

This discussion of mortality and morbidity describes, but does not in many ways explain, the improvements which occurred in the late nineteenth century and which were probably related to improved nutritional status. In attempting to do this, we need to examine other components of working-class living standards.

7.3.4 Diet and housing

There seems little doubt that there was a gradual improvement in working-class diet during the latter part of the nineteenth century, although the accounts of Booth (1902) and Rowntree (1901) caution against any assumption that malnutrition had disappeared. Burnett (unpublished) emphasises rising consumption of a number of imported foodstuffs, in particular sugar, and the general fall that is known to have occurred in the prices of imported foods; this fall plays a major role in the measurement of real wages and is therefore subsumed within the discussion above. The rise in real wages, modified by the recent work of Gazeley and Feinstein (unpublished), thus shows the maximum effect which such dietary improvements had.

In addition, some writers doubt whether the improvements were as substantial as Burnett implies. Oddy has calculated the nutritional content of a number of working-class dietary and budget studies conducted between 1887 and 1901. These show a mean daily intake per capita for the working class of 2100 kilocalories, but the intake of the lower income groups was much less than this average; the intake for Rowntree's class A, those living in primary poverty, was as low as 1578 kilocalories, a level insufficient to sustain hard physical activity or growth. Only those in Rowntree's class D, the artisan group, showed a level of consumption significantly higher than the average, in terms both of energy and of protein content. For most of the working class, bread and potatoes continued to be the staple element of the diet and, as Oddy puts it (1970: 322):

Nor was there much opportunity for improvement in families which, on average, already spent 58 per cent of their income on food. Money spent on foods such as bread, flour and potatoes produced energy cheaply, but resulted in a stodgy diet, and in these families over 61 per cent of calories were obtained from such carbohydrate sources.

This led to expenditure on what seemed to some middle-class consumers to be frills, in order to make the food palatable, and therefore to expenditure with little direct food value. It is partly this, Oddy suggests, that leads to:

the apparent paradox between the rise in real wages and the low standards of nutrition and health which observers noted at the end of the nineteenth century. It may suggest that we should be less certain that the rise in real wages or the fall in food prices led to increased food consumption, an argument which ignores environmental, physiological, and psychological factors in working class life.

It is likely, however, that there were improvements in the quality of food, which would not be revealed by nutritional analyses. Burnett argues that, from mid-century, there was increased awareness of and public pressure to reduce the extent of adulteration of food (1979: 240–67). This led to ineffective legislation in 1860 and to more effective laws in 1872 and 1875, but Burnett also suggests that a noticeable improvement in food quality took place irrespective of legal enforcement. Since adulteration, though by no means confined to working-class foods, was particularly a problem with foods sold in small quantities, it seems likely that these improvements contributed to better nutritional status. A further source of improvement sprang from the increased use of gas for cooking, which gave access to cooking methods which helped to conserve the energy value of food.

Food and housing, as Rowntree and others found, continued to take up almost all the income of the working class, although tobacco, alcohol and other forms of leisure consumption were growing in importance. Those two main items were together responsible for between 60 and 75 per cent of working-class expenditure, with expenditure on fuel and light adding a further 5–10 per cent (Gazeley 1987). As with diet, it seems likely that the quality of housing was improving in late nineteenth-century Britain, although many black spots remained in the dense urban areas. The worst overcrowding of the first part of the century was, however, alleviated by improved transport which allowed workers to live further from their jobs and by the slightly more spacious housing which was built as a result in the suburbs. This combined with urban sanitary improvements to diminish the inequalities in health which had been so marked a feature of Chadwick's findings in the 1840s, although many remained to be re-emphasised by Titmuss one hundred years later and by the Black Report in the 1970s (Chadwick 1844; Titmuss 1943; Black 1980).

But, as Burnett emphasises (1986: 166) for 'a substantial section of the working class' though not, certainly, for those whose hovels in York were described by Rowntree, higher real incomes and a lessening of crowding brought major changes to the pattern of home and family life. Some credit must also be given to the great Victorian reformers and to the society which gave them support enough to carry moral outrage into practical change. For most of history, the kinds of conditions which are reflected in the short heights of the British working class had been regarded as the inevitable lot of the great majority of human beings. Such attitudes altered in this period and this alteration certainly helped to bring about the improvement in nutritional status which we have described.

7.3.5 A synthesis, 1850–1914

There is little doubt that the second half of the nineteenth century, or more precisely the fifty-five years from 1860 to the outbreak of the First World War, saw significant improvements in the nutritional status of the British people and that these improvements were reflected in reductions in mortality and morbidity levels. The evidence of mean heights correlates so well with that of mortality that this inference is fully justified.

Nevertheless, it would be inappropriate to overemphasise the scale of the change. Average male heights recovered from the very low levels which they had reached in the middle of the nineteenth century, but the recovery brought them by the time of the First World War only to the levels which they had achieved nearly a century earlier. This pattern, together with the different strands which go to make up nutritional status, suggests that it was only by the end of the nineteenth century that improvements in real wages, and in public health and other sanitary measures, compensated the British working class for the horrors of urban and industrial life which they had borne in the second quarter of the century.

It only requires reading of Rowntree's study, however, to be aware of how miserable the nutritional status and standard of living of the working class continued to be at the beginning of this century. In addition, although we have little direct evidence of the nutritional status of the upper classes of Edwardian society, there is no reason to believe that the extent of inequality and consequent difference in nutritional status between the upper, middle and working classes had significantly diminished. At that time, Army recruits had mean heights at approximately the same level as the 3rd centile of the modern distribution, similar to the levels of the children of town artisans revealed in the British Association publications of the early 1880s; the boys of Christ's Hospital were slightly taller, at around the 10th centile of the modern distribution both in the 1870s and in the early years of the twentieth century, but both were much shorter than the children of the professional classes reported by the British Association, who were consistently shown to be at about the 25th centile of the modern distribution. In other words, class distinction remained acute.

7.4 NUTRITIONAL STATUS, HEALTH AND INCOME, 1914–1980

In one sense, there is little mystery about the relationship between nutritional status, health and income in the period since 1914; they all improved. In another way, however, the relationships between nutritional status and outcomes such as health and mortality in adult life are almost as mysterious in the twentieth century as in the nineteenth. This is particularly so because we know too little about the exact course of adolescent or adult heights between the cohorts represented in our military samples, born at the end of the nineteenth century, and the cohorts represented in the 1980 survey of adult heights and weights taken by the Office of Population Censuses and Surveys. As chapter 4 showed, for the intervening period we must rely on a small number of surveys of relatively specialised groups within the population. Even for children's heights, which were supposedly monitored throughout the period by the school medical service, the failure to expand those measurements into a national anthropometric survey means that we must rely on the work of Boyne, Aitken and Leitch (1957) in collecting such measurements, on the work of Harris (1988) in collecting published series from school medical officers' reports and on the work of Cameron (1979) in collating and analysing the records of London children.

In general, these estimates suggest that there was a sustained but slow increase in heights between the World Wars, followed by a more rapid increase after the Second World War which may have come to an end in the 1960s, although there is some evidence for its continuance into the 1970s. These changes in nutritional status can be compared with measures of real incomes such as Feinstein's index of real per capita consumers' expenditure which is shown in figure 7.5. The comparison shows a close correspondence between changes in height and in per capita national income or variants of it, which has also been found in other studies of the modern developed world (Floud 1983, 1984; Steckel 1983; Brinkman, Drukker and Slot 1985). Steckel also found that the level of income inequality had a significant effect, in addition to the effect of national income per capita; it is thought that income inequality has diminished in Britain for much

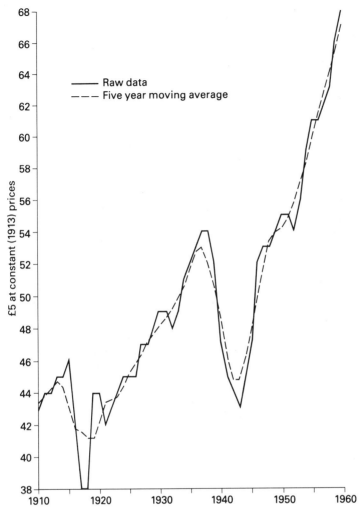

Figure 7.5. Consumers' expenditure per capita at constant (1913) prices, 1910–1960. Source: Feinstein 1972, table 17.

of the twentieth century and particularly since 1945, although the trend has been reversed in the 1980s.

In addition, the overall level of infant mortality has fallen markedly since the beginning of the century, just as the overall level of life expectation has risen. Whatever the balance between improved nutritional status and medical care in reducing the incidence and the effects of disease, the major diseases which killed the young in the nineteenth century have largely been controlled, while the diseases of the old have a different relationship to nutritional status. This is not to argue that there is not a link between childhood nutritional status and subsequent life chances; the work of Marmot and Waaler described in the last chapter clearly shows that there is. But the quantitative impact of that link is much weaker than was the link between nutritional status and child morbidity and mortality in the age of high infant mortality.

What still requires much more investigation, however, are the reasons for the continued differences in nutritional status between different regional and socio-occupational groups which are shown by anthropometric surveys to have been a feature of the inter-war period and to persist today. The evidence of the heights of the upper classes in nineteenth-century England, such as the records of Sandhurst, presents what Fogel (1987) has called 'the Peerage Paradox'. That is, it appears paradoxical that the children of the aristocracy, who were possessed of immense wealth and therefore the ability to purchase all that they wished to consume, were not taller in the nineteenth century, as tall as the children of the upper classes today. They were, as the Sandhurst evidence shows, as tall as the mean of the British male population today, but that is still shorter than the height of the upper classes. In addition, it is paradoxical that, as Hollingsworth (1977) discovered, death rates among the aristocracy were slow to fall to modern levels.

This 'peerage paradox' can be resolved for the nineteenth century by remembering, as we were continually forced to do when examining the evidence of real wages and incomes, that income or wealth are not the sole influences on nutritional status. It is true that we do not know enough about the food of upper-class children in the last century and it is possible that the 'nursery food' to which generations of upper- and middle-class children became addicted was less than adequate nutritionally. But it is clear that the children of the aristocracy could not, in any case, be isolated totally from the overall disease environment; in an age in which Prince Albert could die of typhoid fever, how could children escape from water- and air-borne diseases which could seriously affect their nutritional status and physical growth?

As the recent work of Rosenbaum shows, it is likely that the paradox as far as heights were concerned disappeared by the end of the nineteenth century; the boys of Eton and other public schools were as tall then as they are now. But, although the heights of members of the working class have increased substantially, marked class differences still remain. Hence the modern version of the peerage paradox: instead of needing to explain the low heights of the rich within a poverty-stricken society, we now need to explain the low heights of the poor within an affluent society.

This paradox, if there is one, is common to almost all developed countries; only Sweden seems to be an exception in showing no relationship of mean height to class or social status, though even in Sweden there are associations between geographical region and height. In all these countries, extreme poverty has long been avoided by income support schemes, infant mortality and morbidity has been enormously reduced and the general income level of the population is both far higher and more equally distributed than in less-developed countries. It thus seems clear that, although the overall trends in height over time may indeed reflect the elimination of much poverty and disease in the developed world, both the current variation in height and nutritional status within that world – both within and between the countries which make it up – and to some extent the trends in the most recent past, cannot owe much to the traditional causes of such variation. These countries, Britain among them, are today so rich, and have been so rich for so long, that malnutrition and epidemic or endemic disease seem unlikely determinants of height variation.

There is, nevertheless, strong evidence for the continued effect of socio-economic status on physical growth in the twentieth century. In the inter-war period, for example, the work of Bernard Harris has demonstrated links between the mean height of children and the level of unemployment in the communities in which they grew up (1988). In the modern world, Rona, Swan and Attman (1978) have demonstrated an association between height and parental social class, sibship size and the unemployment of parents while Smith, Chinn and Rona (1980) show that such associations and the resulting differentials are established before children enter school at the age of 5. By contrast, Lindgren reported that in Sweden in 1976: 'No significant differences between socio-economic strata defined by father's occupation and family income were found either for height or weight for ages at PHV, PWV and menarche' (1976: 501).

It is possible, of course, that income differences are not responsible for such class differences in height. It is certainly conceivable that psychological and emotional support of infants and children differs between social groups. Other possibilities might be differences in the amount of work effort or other physical activity required in different classes, or even inherited characteristics. But, of these, only the last could conceivably affect children as young as the age of 2, when class differences can be found, and it seems most unlikely that genetic inheritance could explain marked class differences in countries such as Britain which have high levels of social and geographical mobility. The evidence of Sweden, where income differences have been much reduced but where behavioural differences between white-collar and manual workers are still evident also suggests the primacy of income as a determinant. But exactly how income exerts its influence – whether through the quality or quantity of the diet, through warmth, housing density or other mechanism – still remains undetermined.

Late twentieth-century Britain remains, therefore, a country in which rich and poor, north and south, are distinguished by height as well as by other features of class and status. Those distinctions of nutritional status may be less obvious than they were one or two hundred years ago, but they still mark for life those who are poor, ill or deprived.

8

Conclusions

The last chapter ended on a sombre note and, indeed, the history of nutritional status in Britain is one of unfulfilled potential. Over the last two hundred years, Britain's economy and society has not enabled all its citizens to grow to their full stature, to enjoy good health or to contribute fully to the productive capacity of the nation. All too often, there have been gross inequalities; the accidents of birth have been reflected in such contrasting lives as those led by the stunted boys of the Marine Society in the slums of London or by the children of the aristocracy in the Royal Military Academy. Yet, over that last two hundred years, there has also been improvement, a reduction in the worst inequalities and an increase in the number of those whose nutritional status enables them to walk tall.

The main conclusions of this book can be simply stated. They are, first, that it is possible to write an anthropometric history of Britain and Ireland since 1750. Although many imperfections remain and although there is still much scope for argument about the detail of statistical procedures, the evidence from the records of military recruits can be used to make reasonable inferences about the height and nutritional status of the bulk of the population, the working class. More study is required, on the basis of larger samples than it has been possible to draw, of specific occupational and geographical groups, but the broad outline is clear.

Second, that broad outline shows that average nutritional status has markedly increased in Britain since 1750, but the increase has not been smooth nor uninterrupted. The concept of a secular trend in height must be discarded. Height grew in the period of the Industrial Revolution, fell back in the middle of the nineteenth century, gradually climbed back to its previous peak by the time of the First World War, grew slowly between the World Wars and then accelerated after World War Two.

Third, the overall growth in height was accompanied both by a reduction in inequalities between social and geographical groups in

325

the population and by a reordering of those inequalities. The unskilled working class appear to have benefited from the early period of the Industrial Revolution and height differentials never again reached the dramatic levels shown by the evidence from the Marine Society and Sandhurst. Yet substantial social inequality remains. Geographical inequality too remains, but in a very different form to that which it had in the eighteenth century. Scotland has lost its advantage, but even more dramatic has been the improvement in average nutritional status in urban areas and particularly in London. The fear of national degeneration from the effects of urbanisation, so prevalent in the late nineteenth century on the basis of observation of the bodies of city-dwellers, has been removed.

Fourth, it is suggested that the effects of urbanisation and in particular of the disease environment which came with it, provide the main explanation for the irregular pattern of growth in height during the eighteenth and nineteenth centuries. It seems likely that the early part of the Industrial Revolution led to an absolute as well as relative increase in the welfare and nutritional status of the working class, but that the impact of urban growth eroded this increase and even led to decreases in average height as larger proportions of the working-class community were subjected to town life. This erosion and decrease took place despite well-attested rises in real wages for the bulk of town dwellers. This finding is the main contribution of this book to the lengthy debate about the standard of living of the British working class.

Fifth, it is apparent that during the latter part of the nineteenth century nutritional status in Britain benefited from the combined impact of rising real wages and the gradual improvement of public health. Increases in the quantity and quality of diet acted in a synergistic relationship with other factors influencing nutritional status to enable human bodies in Britain increasingly to combat the respiratory and water-borne diseases which were the scourge of periods earlier than the latter years of the nineteenth century. It is in this respect that this book contributes to another debate, that about the causes of the decline in mortality at the end of the nineteenth century. While the evidence does not point clearly to the simple relationship of improved nutrition with declining mortality which was posited by McKeown, both the existence and the timing of growth in height after the 1870s strongly suggest that improved nutritional status was soon reflected, except for infants, in declining mortality.

It has not been possible to measure directly the impact of nutritional status on labour productivity in Britain, but the evidence presented here strongly suggests, sixth, that the improved health, strength and longevity which stem from improved nutritional status deserves to be taken much more seriously as a cause of increased productivity than it has been normal for economists and historians to do. When the results from this book are combined both with knowledge derived from modern studies in the developing world that nutritional status is particularly vulnerable to trauma and insult in early life, and with evidence that such insults are reflected in morbidity throughout life and ultimately in length of life itself, they show that economists must take a much longer view of the causation of changes in labour productivity.

This book is thus both a contribution to the dismal science of economics and to the more hopeful sciences of history and human biology. It demonstrates that economic growth can have great costs, seen in the bodies of the men, women and children of eighteenth- and nineteenth-century Britain, but that such economic growth can also in the long run promote growth in nutritional status and its proxy, growth in height. There is still far to go before the world achieves the current goal of the World Health Organisation, 'health for all by the year 2000', but the record of history, as of the under-developed world today, suggests that such a goal of adequate nutritional status for the peoples of the world is within our grasp. The anthropometric history of Britain has been neither a short nor a tall story; it has been a sombre tale but one which yet gives some hope.

Bibliography

Acheson, K. J., Campbell, I. T., Edholm, O. G., Miller, D. S. and Stock, M. J. 1980, 'The measurement of food and energy intake in man – an evaluation of some techniques', *American Journal of Clinical Nutrition* **35**: 1147–54

Adrianzen, B., Baertl, J. M. and Graham, G. G. 1973, 'Growth of children from extremely poor families', *American Journal of Clinical Nutrition* **26**: 926–30

Anderson, M. 1987, *The 1851 Census Enumerators Returns* (Cambridge: Chadwyck-Healy)

Armstrong, W. A. 1972, 'The use of information about occupation', *in* Wrigley, E. A. (ed.), 1972

Aron, J-P., Dumont, P. and LeRoy Ladurie, E. 1972, *Anthropologie du conscrit français d' après les comptes numériques et sommaires du recrutement de l' armée (1819–1826)* (Paris – La Haye: Mouton)

Aubenque, M. 1957, 'Note documentaire sur la statistique des tailles des étudiants au cours de ces dernières années', *Biotypologie* **18**: 202–14

Aubenque, M. 1963, 'Note sur l'évolution de la taille des étudiants', *Biotypologie* **24**: 124

Aykroyd, W. R. 1971, 'Nutrition and mortality in infancy and early childhood: past and present relationships', *American Journal of Clinical Nutrition* **24**: 480–7

Bailey, N. T. J. 1951, 'A statistical analysis of Cambridge University Health Service Records, 1948–50' *Journal of Hygiene (Cambridge)* **49**: 81–91

Bakwin, H. 1964, 'The secular change in growth and development', *Acta Paediatrica* **53**: 79–89

Bakwin, H. and McLaughlin, S. 1964, 'Secular increase in height: is the end in sight?' *The Lancet*, 5 Dec. 1964: 1195

Barker, D. J. P. and Osmond, C. 1986a, 'Infant mortality, childhood nutrition, and ischaemic heart disease in England and Wales', *The Lancet*, 10 May 1986: 1077–81

Barker, D. J. P. and Osmond, C. 1986b, 'Childhood respiratory infection and adult chronic bronchitis in England and Wales', *British Medical Journal*, 15 Nov. 1986: 1271–5

Barker, T. and Drake, M. (eds.) 1982, *Population and Society in Britain, 1850–1980* (London: Batsford Academic and Educational)

Barnicot, N. A., Bennett, F. J., Woodburn, J. C., Pilkington, T. R. E. and Antonis, A. 1972, 'Blood pressure and serum cholesterol in the Hadza of Tanzania', *Human Biology* **44**: 87–116

Baumgartner, R. N. and Mueller, W. H. 1984, 'Multivariate analyses of illness data for use in studies on the relationship of physical growth and morbidity', *Human Biology* **56**: 111–28

Baxter, R. D. 1868, *National Income* (London)

Beaton, G. H. and Ghassemi, H. 1982, 'Supplementary feeding programs for young children in developing countries', *American Journal of Clinical Nutrition* **35**: 864–916

Beddoe, J. 1870, 'On the stature and bulk of man in the British Isles', *Memoirs of the Anthropological Society of London* **3**: 384–573

Belavady, B. 1966, 'Nutrition and efficiency in agricultural labourers', *Indian Journal of Medical Research* **54**: 971–6

Bengoa, J. M. 1974, 'The problem of malnutrition', *World Health Organisation* **28**: 3–7

Billy, G. 1980, 'Microevolution and exogamy', *in* Schwidetzky, I., Chiarelli, B. and Necrasov, O. (eds) 1980 *Physical Anthropology of European Populations* (The Hague: Mouton)

Biswas, M. and Pinstrup-Anderson, P. 1985, *Nutrition and Development* (Oxford: Oxford University Press)

Black, Sir D. 1980, *Report of the Working Group on Inequalities in Health*, republished in Townsend *et al.* 1988

Blaxter, K. and Waterlow, J. C. 1985 *Nutritional Adaptation in Man* (London: John Libbey)

Bliss, C. and Stern, N. 1978, 'Productivity, wages and nutrition', parts 1 and 2, *Journal of Development Economies*, 5 Dec. 1978: 331–62 and 363–98

Bodmer, W. and Cavalli-Sforza, L. 1971, *The Genetics of Human Populations* (San Francisco: W. H. Freeman)

Bolsakova, M. D. 1958, 'Observations on changes in the physical development of children in the USSR', *Abstracts of World Medicine* **23**: 465

Booth, C. 1902, *Life and Labour of the People of London* (London)

Bowley, A. L. 1900, *Wages in the United Kingdom in the Nineteenth Century* (Cambridge: Cambridge University Press)

Bowley, A. L. and Burnett-Hurst, A. R. 1915, *Livelihood and Poverty* (London: Ratan Tata Foundation)

Boyne, A. W. and Leitch, I. 1954, 'Secular change in the height of British adults', *Nutrition Abstracts and Reviews* **24**: 255–69

Boyne, A. W., Aitken, F. C. and Leitch, I. 1957, 'Secular changes in height and weight of British children, including an analysis of measurements of English children in primary schools, 1911–1953', *Nutrition Abstracts and Reviews* **27**: 1–18

Bridges, J. H. and Holmes, T. 1873, *Report to the Local Government Board on Proposed Changes in Hours and Ages of Employment in Textile Factories*, PP 1873 lv

Brinkman, H. J., Drukker, J. W. and Slot, B. 1985, 'Height and income: a new method for the estimation of historical national income series', mimeo, University of Groningen

British Association for the Advancement of Science 1883, *Final Report of the Anthropometric Committee* (London: British Association). Page references are to the report as published in C. Roberts 1878 *A Manual of Anthropometry* (London: Churchill)

Buchanan, I. 1985, 'Infant feeding, sanitation and diarrhoea in colliery communities, 1880–1911', *in* Oddy, D. and Miller, D. 1985

Bulwer, W. 1836, *Monarchy of the Middle Classes* (London: Richard Bentley)

Burnett, J. 1979, *Plenty and Want* (London: Scolar Press)

Burnett, J. 1986, *A Social History of Housing, 1815–1985*, (London: Methuen)

Cameron, N. 1979, 'The growth of London schoolchildren 1904–1966: An analysis of secular trend and inter-county variation', *Annals of Human Biology* 6: 505–25

Cannadine, D. 1984, 'The present and the past in the English Industrial Revolution', *Past and Present* **103**: 131–72

Cantlie, J. 1885, *Deterioration Amongst Londoners* (London: Parkes Museum of Hygetic)

Carrion, J. M. M. 1986, 'Estatura, Nutricion y Nivel de Vida en Murcia, 1860–1930', *Revista de Historia Economica* 4: 67–99

Cathcart, E. P., Hughes, D. E. R., and Chalmers, J. G. 1935, 'The physique of man in industry', *Industrial Health Research Board Report* 71, HMSO

Cecil, R. L. 1947, *A Textbook of Medicine*, 7th edn. (Philadelphia and London: W. B. Saunder)

Chadwick, E. 1844, *see* Flinn, M. W. 1965

Chambers, R., Longhurst, R. and Pacey, A. (eds.) 1981, *Seasonal Dimensions to Rural Poverty* (London: Frances Pinter)

Chamla, M.-C., 1964, 'L'Accroissement de la stature en France de 1880 à 1960; comparaison avec les pays d'Europe occidentale', *Bulletins de la Société d' Anthropologie de Paris* T6, 40th series, 1964: 210–78

Chandra, R. K. 1980, *Immunology of Nutritional Disorders* (London: Edward Arnold)

Chapman, S. D. (ed.) 1971, *The History of Working-class Housing: A Symposium* (Newton Abbot: David and Charles)

Chen, L. C. and Scrimshaw, N. S. 1983, *Diarrhoea and Malnutrition: Interactions, Mechanisms, and Interventions* (New York: Plenum)

Chinn, S. and Rona, R. J. 1984, 'The secular trend in the height of primary school children in England and Scotland from 1972–1980', *Annals of Human Biology* **11**: 1–16

Chirikos, T. N. and Nestel, G. 1985, 'Further evidence on the economic effects of poor health', *Review of Economics and Statistics* **67**: 61–9

Clements, E. M. B. 1953, 'Changes in the mean stature and weight of British children over the past 70 years', *British Medical Journal*, 24 Oct. 1953: 897–902

Clements, E. M. B. and Pickett, K. G. 1952, 'Stature of Scotsmen aged 18 to 40 years in 1941', *British Journal of Social Medicine* 6: 245–52

Clements, E. M. B. and Pickett, K. G. 1957, 'Stature and weight of men from England and Wales in 1941', *British Journal of Preventive and Social Medicine* **11**: 51–60

Cleveland, William S. 1979, 'Robust locally weighted regression and smoothing scatterplots', *Journal of the American Statistical Association* **74**: 829–36

Clode, C. M. 1869, *The Military Forces of the Crown* (London)

Cohen, A. C. 1959, 'Simplified estimators for the normal distribution when samples are singly censored or truncated', *Technometrics* **1**: 217–37

Cohen, A. C. Jr. and Woodward, J. 1953, 'Tables of Pearson–Lee–Fisher Functions of singly truncated normal distributions', *Biometrics* **9**: 489–97

Cone, T. E. 1961, 'Secular acceleration of height and biologic maturation in children during the past century', *Journal of Pediatrics* **59**: 738–40

Correa, H. 1975, 'Measured influence of nutrition on socio-economic development', *World Review of Nutrition and Dietetics* **20**: 1–48

Crafts, N. F. R. 1985a, 'English workers' real wages during the Industrial Revolution: some remaining problems', *Journal of Economic History* **45**: 139–44

Crafts, N. F. R. 1985b, *British Economic Growth during the Industrial Revolution* (Oxford: Clarendon Press)

Crafts, N. F. R. 1987, 'British economic growth, 1700–1850; some difficulties of interpretation', *Explorations in Economic History* **24**: 245–68

Cronje, G. 1984, 'Tuberculosis and mortality decline in England and Wales, 1851–1910', *in* Woods, R. and Woodward, J. 1984

Cropper, M. L. 1981, 'Measuring the benefits from reduced morbidity', *American Economic Review* **71**: 235–40

Cruickshank, R., Standard, K. L. and Russell, H. B. L. 1978, *Epidemiology and Community Health in Warm Climate Countries* (Edinburgh: Longman)

Cullen, L. M. 1981, 'Population growth and diet, 1600–1850', *in* Goldstrom, J. M. and Clarkson, L. A. 1981: 89–112

Cuthbertson, B. 1776, *Cuthbertson's System for the Complete Management and Economy of a Battalion of Infantry* (Bristol: Rouths and Nelson)

Dalrymple, C. 1761, *Military Essay* (London: D. Wilson)

Damon, A. 1965, 'Stature increase among Italian-Americans: environmental, genetic or both?' *American Journal of Physical Anthropology* **23**: 401–8

Danmarks Statistik 1963, Statistik Aarbog (Kobenhavn)

Dasgupta, P. and Ray, D. 1985, 'Inequality, malnutrition and unemployment: a critique of the competitive market mechanism', *Centre for Economic Policy Research Discussion Paper* no. 50

Daunton, M. J. 1983, *House and Home in the Victorian City* (London: Arnold)

Distad, N. M. 1972, 'Jonas Hanway and the Marine Society', *History Today* **23**: 6

Drake, M. 1908, 'A study of infant-life in Westminster', *Journal of the Royal Statistical Society* **71**: 678–86

Efron, B. 1979, 'Bootstrap methods: another look at the jacknife', *Annals of Statistics* **7**: 1–26

Efron, B. 1986, 'Comment on Wu', *Annals of Statistics* **14**: 1301–4

Efron, B. and Gong, G. 1983, 'A leisurely look at the bootstrap', *The American Statistician* **37**: 36–48

Elderton, E. M. 1914, 'Height and weight of schoolchildren in Glasgow', *Biometrika* **10**: 288–339

Engerman, S. L. and Gallman, R. E. 1986, *Long-term Factors in American Economic Growth*, Conference on Research in Income and Wealth, vol. 41 (Chicago: University of Chicago Press)

Eveleth, P. B. and Tanner, J. M. 1976, *Worldwide Variation in Human Growth* (Cambridge: Cambridge University Press)

Falkner, F. and Tanner, J. M. 1986, *Human Growth*, 3 vols, 2nd edn. (New York: Plenum)

FAO 1962, *Nutrition and Working Efficiency* (FFHC Basic Study 5)

FAO 1987, *The Fifth World Food Survey 1985* (Rome: FAO)

FAO/WHO/UNU 1985, *Energy and Protein Requirements*, Report of a Joint FAO/WHO/UNU Expert Consultation. WHO Technical Report Series 724, (Geneva: WHO)

Feigin, R. D. 1977, 'Resumé of the discussion concerning recommendations for dietary intake during infection', *American Journal of Clinical Nutrition* **30**: 1548–52

Feigin, R. D. 1981, 'Interaction of infection and nutrition', *in* Feigin, R. D. and Cherry, J. D. *Textbook of Pediatric Infectious Diseases* (Philadelphia: W. B. Saunders): 17–24

Feinstein, C. H. 1972, *National Income, Expenditure and Output of the United Kingdom, 1855–1965* (Cambridge: Cambridge University Press)

Feinstein, C. H. 1981, 'Capital accumulation and the Industrial Revolution' *in* Floud, R. C. and McCloskey, D. N. 1981, vol. 1

Feinstein, C. H. 1988, 'What really happened to real wages? Trends in money wages and the cost of living in the United Kingdom 1880–1913', *mimeo*

Feinstein, C. H. 1988, 'The rise and fall of the Williamson curve', *Journal of Economic History*, **48**: 699–729

Fergus, W. and Rodwell, G. F. 1874–5, 'On a series of measurements for statistical purposes, recently made at Marlborough College', *Journal of the Anthropological Institute* **4**: 126–30

Flinn, M. W. (ed.) 1965, *Report on the Sanitary Condition of the Labouring Population of Great Britain*, by Edwin Chadwick (Edinburgh: Edinburgh University Press)

Flinn, M. W. 1974, 'Trends in real wages, 1750–1850', *Economic History Review* **27**: 395–413

Flinn, M. W. (ed.) 1977, *Scottish Population History from the Seventeenth Century to the 1930s* (Cambridge: Cambridge University Press)

Floud, R. C. (ed.) 1974, *Essays in Quantitative Economic History* (Oxford: Clarendon Press)

Floud, R. C. 1979, *An Introduction to Quantitative Methods for Historians*, 2nd edition (London: Methuen)

Floud, R. C. 1983, 'The heights of Europeans since 1750: a new source for European economic history', *mimeo*; also published as 'Wirtschaftliche und soziale Einflusse auf die Korpergrossen von Europaern seit 1750', *Jahrbuch für Wirtschaftsgeschichte* 1985: 93

Floud, R. C. 1984, 'Measuring the transformation of the European economies: income, health and welfare', *Centre for Economic Policy Research Discussion Paper* 33

Floud, R. C. and McCloskey, D. N. (eds.) 1981, *The Economic History of Britain since 1700* (Cambridge: Cambridge University Press)

Floud, R. C., Gregory, A. and Wachter, K. W. 1985, 'The physical state of the British working class, 1870–1914: evidence from Army recruits', *National Bureau of Economic Research*, Working Paper 1661

Floud, R. C. and Wachter, K. W. 1982, 'Poverty and physical stature', *Social Science History* **6**: 422–52

Fogel, R. W. 1984, 'Nutrition and the Decline in Mortality since 1700: some preliminary findings', *NBER Working paper* 1802

Fogel, R. W. 1986a, *Long-term Changes in Nutrition and the Standard of Living*, Proceedings of Section B7, Ninth International Economic History Congress, Bern

Fogel R. W. 1986b, 'Nutrition and the decline in mortality since 1700: some preliminary findings', *in* Engerman, S. L. and Gallman, R. E. (eds.) 1986

Fogel, R. W. 1987, 'Biomedical approaches to the estimation and interpretation of secular trends in equity, morbidity, mortality and labor productivity in Europe, 1750–1980', *mimeo*, Center for Population Economics, University of Chicago

Fogel, R. W. 1989, *Without Consent and Contract: The Rise and Fall of American Slavery* (New York)

Fogel, R. W., Pope, C. L., Scrimshaw, N., Temin, P. and Wimmer, L. T. 1986, 'The aging of Union Army men: a longitudinal study', *mimeo*, Center for Population Economics, University of Chicago

Forsdahl, A. 1977, 'Are poor living conditions in childhood and adolescence an important risk factor for arteriosclerotic heart disease?' *British Journal of Preventive and Social Medicine* **31**: 91–5

Fortescue, Sir J. 1909, *The County Lieutenancies and the Army 1803–14* (London: Macmillan)

Fox, R. H. 1953, 'A study of the energy expenditure of Africans engaged in various rural activities'. Ph.D. thesis, University of London

Fraser, J. 1939, *Sixty Years in Uniform* (London: Stanley Paul)

Freedman, D. 1981, 'Bootstrapping regression', *Annals of Statistics* **9**: 1218–28

Freeman-Williams, J. P. 1890, *The Effect of Town Life on the General Health* (London)

Friend, G. E. 1935, *The Schoolboy: a Study of his Nutrition, Physical Development and Health* (Cambridge: Heffer)

Frisancho, A. R. and Baker, P. T. 1970, 'Altitude and growth', *American Journal of Physical Anthropology* **32**: 279–92

Galton, F. 1874, 'Notes on the Marlborough School statistics', *Journal of the Anthropological Institute* **4**: 130–5

Galton, F. 1875–6, 'On the height and weight of boys aged 14, in town and country public schools', *Journal of the Anthropological Institute* **5**: 174–81

Gandevia, B. 1976, 'Some physical characteristics, including pock marks, tattoos and disabilities, of convict boys transported to Australia from Britain c. 1840', *Australian Paediatric Journal* **12**: 6–13

Gandevia, B. 1977, 'A comparison of the heights of boys transported to Australia from England, Scotland and Ireland, c. 1840, with later British and Australian developments', *Australian Paediatric Journal* **13**: 91–7

Gandevia, B. and Gandevia, S. 1975, 'Childhood mortality and its social background in the first settlement at Sydney Cove, 1788–1792', *Australian Paediatric Journal* **11**: 9–19

Gazeley, I. 1987, 'The cost of living and real wages for urban workers in late Victorian and Edwardian Britain', *mimeo*

George, M. D. 1925, *London Life in the Eighteenth Century* (London: Routledge and Kegan Paul)

Gilbert, A. N. 1976, 'An analysis of some eighteenth century Army recruiting records', *Journal of the Society for Army Historical Research* **54**: 38–47

Gilbert, J. T. (ed.) 1893, *Documents Relating to Ireland, 1795–1804* (Dublin: Joseph Dollard)

Gilboy, E. W. 1936, 'The cost of living and real wages in eighteenth century England', *Review of Economic Statistics* **18**: 134–43

Golden, M. 1985, 'The consequences of protein deficiency in man and its relationship to the features of kwashiorkor', *in* Blaxter, K. and Waterlow, J. C. 1985: 169–85

Goldstrom J. M. and Clarkson, L. A. 1981, *Irish Population, Economy and Society: Essays in Honour of the Late K. H. Connell* (Oxford: Clarendon Press)

Greene, L. S. and Johnston, F. E. 1980, *Social and Biological Predictors of Nutritional Status, Physical Growth and Neurological Development* (New York: Academic Press)

Greenwood, A. 1913, *The Health and Physique of School Children* (London: King)

Greenwood, M. 1936, 'English death rates, past, present and future', *Journal of the Royal Statistical Society* **99**: 674–707

Greulich, W. W. 1957, 'A comparison of the physical growth and development of American born and native Japanese children', *American Journal of Physical Anthropology* **15**: 489–515

Greulich, W. W. 1976, 'Some secular changes in the growth of American-born and native Japanese children', *American Journal of Physical Anthropology* **45**: 553–68

Gurney, J. M. 1979, 'The young child: protein–energy malnutrition', *in* Jelliffe, D. B. and Jelliffe, E. F. P. 1979: 185–216

Hanway, J. 1757, *Letter from a Member of the Marine Society* (London)

Harris, B. 1989, 'Medical inspection and the nutrition of school-children in Britain, 1900–1950', unpublished Ph.D. thesis, London University

Harriss, B. 1984, *Exchange Relations and Poverty in Dryland Agriculture: Studies of South India* (New Delhi: Concept Publishing Co.)

Heald, F. P. 1979, 'The adolescent', *in* Jelliffe, D. B. and Jelliffe, E. F. P. 1979: 239–52

Hennock, E. P. 1987, 'The measurement of urban poverty: from the metropolis to the nation, 1880–1920', *Economic History Review* **40**: 208–27

Hewett Joiner, G. (n.d.), 'The business of charity: the management of the London Marine Society, 1756–1786', *mimeo*

Hewett Joiner, G. (n.d.), 'The pea-jacket of charity: John Fielding, the London police and the origins of the British Marine Society', *mimeo*

Hewett Joiner, G. 'In the interest of poor boys: the evolution of the British Marine Society, 1756–1814', unpublished paper

Hiernaux, J. 1965, 'Heredité, milieu et morphologie', *Biotypologie* **26**: 1–36

Hiernaux, J. 1982, *Man in the Heat: High Altitude and Society* (Springfield, Illinois: Thomas)

Historical Statistics of Italy 1861–1965, 1978 (Rome)

Hollingsworth, T. H. 1977, 'Mortality in the British peerage families since 1600', *Population* **32**: sp. 323–52

Horner, L. 1837, 'Practical application of physiological facts', *Penny Magazine* **6**: 270–2

Hunt, E. H. 1973, *Regional Wage Variations in Britain 1850–1914*, (Oxford: Clarendon Press)

Hunt, E. H. 1986, 'Industrialization and regional inequality: wages in Britain, 1760–1914', *Journal of Economic History* **46**: 935–66

Hunt, E. H. and Botham, F. W. 1987, 'Wages in Britain during the Industrial Revolution', *Economic History Review* **40**: 380–99

Hutchins, J. H. 1940, *Jonas Hanway, 1712–1786* (London: S.P.C.K.)

Illsley, R. 1955, 'Social class selection and class differences in relation to still births and infant deaths', *British Medical Journal* **2**: 1520

Jackson, A. A. 1985, 'Nutritional adaptation in disease and recovery', *in* Blaxter, K. and Waterlow, J. C. 1985: 111–25

Jayne, R. E. 1929, *Jonas Hanway: Philanthropist, Politician and Author, 1712–1786* (London: Epworth)

Jelliffe, D. B. and Jelliffe, E. F. P. 1979, *Human Nutrition: A Comprehensive Treatise* Vol. 2: *Nutrition and Growth*. (New York: Plenum Press)

Jelliffe, E. F. P. 1975, *Protein–calorie Malnutrition of Early Childhood: Two Decades of Malnutrition: A Bibliography*. Introduction (Slough: Commonwealth Agricultural Bureaux)

Johnston, B. F. 1977, 'Food, Health, and Population in Development' *Journal of Economic Literature* **15**: 897–907

Jones, W. O. 1972, *Marketing Staple Food Crops in Tropical Africa* (London: Cornell University Press)

Keddie, J. A. G. 1956, 'Heights and weights of Scottish schoolchildren' *British Journal of Preventive and Social Medicine* **10**: 1

Kemsley, W. F. F. 1950, 'Weight and height of a population in 1943', *Annals of Eugenics* **15**: 161–83

Kermack, W. O., McKendrick, A. G. and McKinlay, P. L. 1934, 'Death-rates in Great Britain and Sweden: some general regularities and their significance', *The Lancet*, 31 Mar. 1934: 698–703

Kielmann, A. A., Ajello, C. A. and Kielmann, N. S. 1982, 'Nutrition intervention: an evaluation of six studies', *Studies in Family Planning* **13**: 247–57

Kielmann, A. A., Taylor, C. E. and De Sweemer, C. 1983, *Child and Maternal Health Services in Rural India: The Narangwal Experiment*. Vol. 1: *Integrated Nutrition and Health Care*, (Baltimore: Johns Hopkins University Press)

Kielmann, A. A., Uberoi, I. S., Chandra, R. K. and Mehra, V. L. 1976, 'The effect of nutritional status on immune capacity and immune responses in preschool children in a rural community in India', *WHO Bulletin* **54**: 477–83

Kiil, V. 1939, *Stature and Growth of Norwegian Men During the Past 200 Years* (Oslo: Komosjpm hos Jacob Dybwad)

Knight, I. and Eldridge, J. (for the Office of Population Censuses and Surveys and the Department of Health and Social Security) 1984, *The Heights and Weights of Adults in Great Britain*, (London: HMSO)

Komlos, J. 1985, 'Stature and nutrition in the Habsburg monarchy: the standard of living and economic development in the eighteenth century', *American Historical Review* **90**: 1149–61

Komlos, J. 1986, 'Patterns of children's growth in east-central Europe in the eighteenth century', *Annals of Human Biology* **13**: 33–48

Kunitz, S. J. 1987, 'Making a long story short: a note on men's height and mortality in England from the first through the nineteenth centuries', *Medical History* **31**: 269–80

Kuznets, S. 1955, 'Economic growth and income inequality', *American Economic Review* **45**: 1–28

Lampl, M., Johnston, F. E. and Malcolm, L. A. 1978, 'The effects of protein supplementation on the growth and skeletal maturation of New Guinean schoolchildren', *Annals of Human Biology* **5**: 219–27

Landauer, T. K. 1973, 'Infantile vaccination and the secular trend in stature', *Ethos* **1**: 499–503

Landauer, T. K. and Whiting, J. W. M. 1964, 'Infantile stimulation and adult stature of human males', *American Anthropologist* **66**: 1007–28

Leighton, G. and Clark, M. L. 1929, 'Milk consumption and the growth of schoolchildren', *Lancet* **1**: 40–3

Leitch, I, and Boyne, A. W. 'Recent change in the height and weight of adolescents', *Nutrition Abstracts and Reviews* **30**: 1173–86

LeRoy Ladurie, E. 1973, 'Anthropologie de la jeunesse masculine en France au niveau d'une cartographie cantonale (1819–30)', *Le Territoire de l'Historien* (Paris: Gallimard)

Lewis, M. 1960, *A Social History of the Navy, 1793–1815* (London: George Allen and Unwin)

Lindert, P. H. 1980, 'English occupations, 1670–1811', *Journal of Economic History* **40**, 4: 685–712

Lindert, P. H. and Williamson, J. G. 1982, 'Revising England's social tables, 1688–1867', *Explorations in Economic History* **19**: 385–408

Lindert, P. H. and Williamson, J. G. 1983a, 'Reinterpreting Britain's social tables, 1688–1913', *Explorations in Economic History* **20**: 94–109

Lindert, P. H. and Williamson, J. G. 1983b, 'English workers' living standards during the Industrial Revolution: a new look', *Economic History Review* **36**: 1–25

Lindert, P. L. and Williamson, J. G. 1985, 'English workers' real wages: a reply to Crafts', *Journal of Economic History* **45**: 145–53

Lindgren, G. 1976, 'Height, weight and menarche in Swedish urban school children in relation to socio-economic and regional factors', *Annals of Human Biology* **3**: 501–28

Ljung, B.-O., Bergsten-Brucefors, A. and Lindgren, G. 1974, 'The secular trend in physical growth in Sweden', *Annals of Human Biology* **1**: 245–66

Loomis, W. F. 1970, 'Rickets', *Scientific American* **223**: 6, 77–91

Luckin, B. 1984, 'Evaluating the sanitary revolution: typhus and typhoid in London, 1851–1900', *in* Woods, R. and Woodward, J. 1984

Luft, H. S. 1975, 'The impact of poor health on earnings', *Review of Economics and Statistics* **57**: 43–57

MacMullen, J. 1846, *Camp and Barrack Room: or, the British Army as it is* (London: Edward Chapman)

Malcolm, L. A. 1970, *Growth and Development in New Guinea – A Study of the Bundi People of the Madang District*, Institute of Human Biology Papua-New Guinea Monograph series 1

Malcolm, L. 1978, 'Protein–energy malnutrition and growth', *in* Falkner, F. and Tanner, J. M. 1978: 361–8

Mann, G. V. , Roels, O. A., Price, D. L. and Merril, J. M. 1962, 'Cardiovascular disease in African pygmies', *Journal of Chronic Diseases* **15**: 341–71

Marine Society 1792, *Regulations for Admission to the Society* (London)

Marine Society 1758 onwards, *Minutes of the Marine Society*, now deposited in the National Maritime Museum, Greenwich

Marine Society 1965, *Short History of the Marine Society*, (London)

Marmot, M. G., Shipley, M. J. and Rose, G. 1984, 'Inequalities in death – specific explanations of a general pattern?' *Lancet* **8384**: 1003–6

Marshall, H. 1828, *Hints to Young Medical Officers of the Army on the Examination* of Recruits, and respecting the Feigned Disabilities of Soldiers; with Official Documents and the Regulations for the Inspection of Conscripts in the French and Russian Armies (London)

Marshall, H. 1846, *Military Miscellany* (London)

Martin, W. J. 1949, 'The physique of young adult males', *Medical Research Council Memorandum* 20

Martorell, R. 1980, 'Inter-relationships between diet, infectious disease and nutritional status', *in* Greene, L. S. and Johnston, F. E. 1980: 81–106

Martorell, R. and Habicht, J.-P., 1986, 'Growth in early childhood in developing countries', *in* Falkner, F. and Tanner, J. M. 1986, Vol. 3: 241–59

Marx, K. 1867 (repr. 1961), *Capital*, trans. S. Moore and E. Aveling (Moscow: Foreign Languages Publishing)

Mata, L. J. 1978, *The Children of Santa María Cauqué: A Prospective Field Study of Health and Growth* (Cambridge, Mass.: MIT Press)

Mata, L. J., Urrutia, J. J., Albertazzi, C., Pellecer, O. and Arellano, E. 1972, 'Influence of recurrent infections on nutrition and growth of children in Guatemala', *American Journal of Clinical Nutrition* 25: 1267–75

Maurice, Sir Frederick 1903, 'National health: a soldier's study', *Contemporary Review* 83

McGuffie, T. 1964, *Rank and File: The Common Soldier in Peace and War, 1642–1914* (London)

McKeown, T. 1976, *The Modern Rise of Population* (London: Edward Arnold)

McKeown, T. and Record, R. G. 1962, 'Reasons for the decline of mortality in England and Wales during the nineteenth century', *Population Studies* 16: 94–122

Meade, J. E. and Parkes, A. S. 1965, *Biological Aspects of Social Problems* (London: Oliver and Boyd)

Meredith, H. V. 1976, 'Findings from Asia, Australia, Europe and North America on secular change in mean height of children, youths and young adults', *American Journal of Physical Anthropology* 44: 315–26

Miall, W. E., Ashcroft, M. T., Lovell, H. G. and Moore, F. 1967, 'A longitudinal study of the decline of adult height with age in two Welsh communities', *Human Biology* 39: 445–54

Micozzi, M. S. 1985, 'Nutrition, body size and breast cancer', *Yearbook of Physical Anthropology* 28: 175–208

'Miles' (pseudonym of Major-General Sir Frederick Maurice) 1902, 'Where to get men', *Contemporary Review* 81

Mitchell, B. R. 1962, *Abstract of British Historical Statistics* (Cambridge: Cambridge University Press)

Mitchison, R. 1977, *British Population Change since 1860* (London: MacMillan)

Mokyr, J. (ed.) 1985a, *The Economics of the Industrial Revolution* (London: Allen and Unwin)

Mokyr, J. 1985b, *Why Ireland Starved: A Quantitative and Analytical History of the Irish Economy, 1800–1850* (London: Allen and Unwin)

Mokyr, J. 1987, 'Has the Industrial Revolution been Crowded Out? Some Reflections on Crafts and Williamson', *Explorations in Economic History* 24: 293–319

Mokyr, J. and O'Grada, C. 1984, 'New developments in Irish population history, 1700–1850', *Economic History Review* 37: 473–88

Mokyr, J. and O'Grada, C. 1986, 'Living standards in Ireland and Britain, 1800–1850: The East India Company Army data', *mimeo*

Morant, G. M. 1950, 'Secular changes in the height of British people', *Proceedings of the Royal Society, series B* **137**: 443–52

Morley, D. 1976, 'Measles and whooping cough', *in* Cruickshank, R., Standard, K. L. and Russell, H.B.L. 1976: 63–76

Morrison, J. F. and Blake, G. T. W. 1974, 'Physiological observations on cane cutters', *European Journal of Applied Physiology* **33**: 247–54

Mumford, A. A. 1912, 'The physique of the modern boy', *Transactions of the Manchester Statistical Society* **8**: 127–68

Nelson, W. 1954, *Textbook of Pediatrics*, 6th edn. (Philadelphia: Saunders)

Neuburg, V. E. 1983, 'The British Army in the eighteenth century', *Journal of the Society for Army Historical Research* **61**: 39–47

Nicholas, S. and Shergold, P. R. 1982, 'The heights of British male convict children transported to Australia, 1825–40', *Australian Paediatric Journal* **18**: 76–83

Nicholas, S. and Shergold, P. R. 1988, *Convict Workers: Australia, Britain and Ireland* (Cambridge: Cambridge University Press)

O'Brien, P. K. and Engerman, S. L. 1981, 'Changes in income and its distribution during the industrial revolution', *in* Floud, R. C. and McCloskey, D. N. 1981

Oddy, D. J. 1970, 'Working-class diets in late nineteenth century Britain', *Economic History Review* **23**: 314–23

Oddy, D. J. 1982, 'The health of the people', *in* Barker, T. C. and Drake, M. (eds.) 1982

Oddy, D. J. and Miller, D. S. 1985, *Diet and Health in Modern Britain* (London: Croom Helm)

Olivier, G. 1970, 'Anthropologie de la France', *Bulletins et Memoires de la Societé d'Anthropologie de Paris*, 12th series, **6**: 109–87

Olivier, G., Chamla, M. C., Devigne, G., Jacquard, A. and Iagolnitzer, E. R. 1977, 'L'accroissement de la stature en France: 1 – L'accélération du phénomène, 2. Les causes du phénomène: Analyse univariée', *Bulletins et Mémoires de la Societé d'Anthropologie de Paris*, 8th series **4**: 197–214

Orr, J. B. 1928, 'Milk consumption and the growth of schoolchildren', *Lancet* **1**: 202–3

Pacey, A. and Payne, P. (eds.) 1985, *Agricultural Development and Nutrition* (London: Hutchinson, by arrangement with FAO and UNICEF)

Passmore, R., Nicol, B. M., Rao, M. N., Beaton, G. H. and Demayer, E. M. 1974, *Handbook of Human Nutritional Requirements*, WHO Monograph no. 61 (Geneva)

Payne, P. 1987, 'Undernutrition: measurement and implications', unpublished *mimeo*

Pollard, S. 1981, 'Sheffield and Sweet Auburn: amenities and living standards in the British Industrial Revolution', *Journal of Economic History* **41**: 902–4

Pottier, J. 1985, 'Introduction', *Food Systems in Central and Southern Africa* ed. J. Pottier, pp. 1–60 (London: School of Oriental and African Studies)

Power, C., Fogelman, K. and Fox, A. J. 1986, 'Health and social mobility during the early years of life', *Quarterly Journal of Social Affairs* **2**: 397–414

PP 1806–7 iv, 167, *Papers presented to the House of Commons by Mr Secretary at War relating to the Recruiting Service*

PP 1807 iv, 319, *Account of Rates of Bounty paid to recruits for the Regular Army*

PP 1808 vii, 205, *Account of the Sum fixed in each County or Riding in England, as the Average Bounty for Substitutes in the Militia, On the late Ballot, As far as the same can be ascertained from the Returns received at this Office*

PP 1816 xii, *Return of the Expenses and Numerical Amount of the Military Establishment of Great Britain*

PP 1833 xx, 1, *First Report from Commissioners appointed to collect information in the Manufacturing Districts, relative to the employment of children in Factories*

PP 1833 xxi, 1, *Second Report of the Royal Commission on the Employment of Children in Factories*

PP 1840 xxiii, *Commission on Handloom Weavers*

PP 1860 xlii, *A Tabular statement of the Number of Seamen (including Officers), Boys, and Marines, Voted for Naval Service, and actually Borne, from the year 1756 to the present time (1859) inclusive; and of the Amount of Money Voted in each Year for the Service, specifying the different periods of War or Peace*

PP 1861 xv, 1, *Report of the Commissioners Appointed to Inquire into the Present System of Recruiting in the Army*

PP 1862 xxxiii, 1, *Annual Report of the Army Medical Department for the year 1861*

PP 1867 xv, 1, *Report of the Commissioners appointed to inquire into the Recruiting for the Army*

PP 1868–9 xxxvii, 1, *Report on the Army Medical Department for the year 1867*

PP 1873 xv, 803, *Report to the Local Government Board on Proposed Changes in Hours and Ages of Employment in Textile Factories*

PP 1890 xix, 145, *Report of the Committee appointed to inquire into certain Questions that have arisen with respect to the Militia; with minutes of evidence and appendices*

PP 1903 xi, 1, *Annual Report of the Inspector-General of Recruiting for the Year 1902*

PP 1904 xxxii, 1, *Report of the Inter-departmental Committee on Physical Deterioration*

PP 1908 lxiv, 601, *Report of the Army Medical Department for the year 1907*

PP 1911 xlvii, 27, *Report of the Health of the Army for the year 1909*

PP 1919 xxvi, 307, *Report upon the Physical Examination of Men of Military Age by National Service Medical Boards between November 1st 1917 and October 1st 1918*

Public Record Office 1981, *Royal Marines Records in the Public Record Office*, Leaflet 28 (London)

Public Record Office 1988, *Records of the War Office* (London: HMSO)

Razzell, P. 1977, *The Conquest of Smallpox* (Firle, Sussex: Caliban)

Rea, J. N. 1971, 'Social and economic influences on the growth of pre-school children in Lagos', *Human Biology* 43: 46–63

Reves, R. 1985, 'Declining fertility in England and Wales as a major cause of the twentieth century decline in mortality: the role of changing family size and age structure in inflating disease mortality in infancy', *American Journal of Epidemiology* 122: 112–26

Riley, J. and Alter, G. 1986, 'Mortality and morbidity: measuring ill-health across time', *in* Fogel, R. W. (ed.) 1986a

Rimoin, D. L., Merimee, T. J., Rabinowitz, D., McKusick, V. A. and Cavalli-Sforza, L. L. 1967, 'Growth hormone in African Pygmies', *Lancet* 2: 523–6

Roberts, C. 1874–78, 'The physical development and the proportions of the human body', *St George's Hospital Medical School Reports* **8**: 1–48

Roberts, C. 1878, *A Manual of Anthropometry, or a Guide to the Physical Examination and Measurement of the Human Body*, (London: Churchill)

Rodgers, G. B. 1975, 'Nutritonally based wage determination in the low-income labour market', *Oxford Economic Papers* **27**: 61–81

Rodriguez, M. G. (no date), *La Estadistica de Reemplazo y Reclutamiento de los Ejercitos* (Madrid)

Rona, R. J. and Florey, C. du V. 1980, 'National study of health and growth: respiratory symptoms and height in primary schoolchildren', *International Journal of Epidemiology* **9**: 35–43

Rona, R. J., Swan, A. V. and Altman, D. G. 1978, 'Social factors and height of primary schoolchildren in England and Scotland', *Journal of Epidemiology and Community Health* **32**: 147–54

Rosenbaum, S. 1988, '100 years of heights and weights', *Journal of the Royal Statistical Society*

Rotberg, R. I. and Rabb, T. K. (eds.) 1983, *Hunger and History: The Impact of Changing Food Production and Consumption Patterns on Society* (Cambridge: Cambridge University Press)

Routh, G. 1965, *Occupation and Pay in Great Britain 1906–60* (Cambridge: Cambridge University Press)

Rowntree, B. Seebohm 1901, *Poverty: A Study of Town Life* (London)

Sandberg, L. and Steckel, R. 1987, 'Heights and economic history: the Swedish case', *Annals of Human Biology* **14**: 101–10

Schofield, R. S. 1972–3, 'Dimensions of illiteracy, 1750–1830', *Explorations in Economic History* **10**: 437–54

Schreider, E. 1968, 'L'influence de l'heterosis sur les variations staturales', *L'Anthropologie* (Paris), **72**: 279–96

Schwarz, L. D. 1985, 'The standard of living in the long run: London, 1700–1860', *Economic History Review* **38**: 24–41

Schwidetzky, I., Chiarelli, B. and Necrasov, O. 1980, *Physical Anthropology of European Populations* (The Hague: Mouton)

Scrimshaw, N. S. 1977, 'Effect of infection on nutritional requirements', *American Journal of Clinical Nutrition* **30**: 1536–44

Scrimshaw, N. S., Taylor, C. E. and Gordon, J. E. 1968, *Interactions of Nutrition and Infection* (Geneva: World Health Organisation)

Shee, G. F. 1903, 'The deterioration in the national physique', *Nineteenth Century* **53**: 797–805

Skelley, A. R. 1977, *The Victorian Army at Home* (London: Croom Helm)

Smith, A. M., Chinn, S. and Rona, R. J. 1980, 'Social factors and height gain of primary schoolchildren in England and Scotland', *Annals of Human Biology* **7**: 115–24

Smith, F. B. 1979, *The People's Health, 1830–1910* (London: Croom Helm)

Smyth, J. 1961, *Sandhurst. The History of the Royal Military Academy, Woolwich, the Royal Military College, Sandhurst and the Royal Military Academy, Sandhurst, 1741–1961* (London: Weidenfeld and Nicolson)

Sofola, T. O. and Lawal, S. F. 1983, 'Bacteriological analysis of water samples from mains taps and domestic water storage tanks in metropolitan Lagos', *Nigerian Medical Practitioner* **6**: 95–8

Sokoloff, K. L. 1984, 'The heights of Americans in three centuries: some economic and demographic implications', *National Bureau of Economic Research*, Working Paper 1384 (Cambridge, Mass.)

Sokoloff, K. L. and Villaflor, G. C. 1982, 'The early achievement of modern stature in America', *Social Science History* **6**: 453–81

Spiers, E. M. 1980, *The Army and Society, 1815–1914* (London: Longman)

Spurr, G. B. 1983, 'Nutritional status and physical work capacity', *Yearbook of Physical Anthropology* **26**: 1–35

Stanhope, P. H. 1888, *Notes of Conversations with the Duke of Wellington* (London: John Murray)

Statistical Yearbook of the Netherlands (annual) (The Hague)

Statistik Arbok (annual) (Oslo)

Steckel, R. H. 1983, 'Height and per capita income', *Historical Methods* **16**: 1–7

Steckel, R. H. 1987, 'Growth depression and recovery: the remarkable case of American slaves', *Annals of Human Biology* **14**: 111–32

Steegman, A. T. 1985, 'Eighteenth century British military stature: growth cessation, selective recruiting, secular trends, nutrition at birth, cold and occupations', *Human Biology* **57**: 77–95

Stein, Z., Susser, M., Saenger, G. and Marolla, F. 1975, *Famine and Human Development: The Dutch Hunger Winter of 1944–45* (Oxford: Oxford University Press)

Steven, M. 1985, *The Good Scots Diet: What Happened To It?* (Aberdeen: Aberdeen University Press)

Stevenson, R. L. 1984 (originally published 1895), *The Amateur Emigrant* (London)

Suchy, J. 1976, 'Trend of physical development of Czech youth in the twentieth century', *Review of Czechoslovak Medicine* **18**: 18–27

Supple, B. E. 1981, 'Income and demand 1860–1914', *in* Floud, R. C. and McCloskey, D. N. 1981

Sutter, J., Izac, R. and Tran, N. 1958, 'L'évolution de la taille des Polytechniciens 1801–1954', *Population* (Paris) **3**: 373–406

Szreter, S. 1986a, 'The first scientific social structure of modern Britain, 1875–1883', *in* Bordfield, L., Smith, R. M. and Wrightson, K. (eds.), *The World We Have Gained* (Blackwell)

Szreter, S. 1986b, 'The importance of social intervention in Britain's mortality decline c. 1850–1914: a re-interpretation', *Centre for Economic Policy Research*, Discussion Paper 121

Tanner, J. M. 1962, *Growth at Adolescence* 2nd edn. (Oxford: Blackwell)

Tanner, J. M. 1966, 'The secular trend towards earlier physical maturation', *Tijdschrift voor sociale Geneeskunde* **44**: 524

Tanner, J. M. 1978, *Foetus Into Man: Physical Growth from Conception to Maturity* (London: Open Books Publishing)

Tanner, J. M. 1981, *A History of the Study of Human Growth* (Cambridge: Cambridge University Press)

Tanner, J. M. 1982, 'The potential of auxological data for measuring economic and social well-being', *Social Science History* **6**: 571–81

Tanner, J. M. and Eveleth, P. B. 1976, 'Urbanisation and growth', *in* Harrison, G. A. and Gibson, J. B. (eds.) *Man in Urban Environments*, pp. 144–66 (Oxford: Oxford University Press)

Tanner, J. M., Hayashi, T., Preece, M. A. and Cameron, N. 1982, 'Increase in length of leg relative to trunk in Japanese children and adults from 1957 to 1977: comparison with British and with Japanese Americans', *Annals of Human Biology* 9: 411–23

Tanner, J. M., Whitehouse, R. H. and Takaishi, M. 1966, 'Standards from birth to maturity for height, weight, height velocity and weight velocity: British children, 1965', *Archives of Disease in Childhood* 41: 454–71 and 613–35

Taylor, A. J. (ed.) 1975, *The Standard of Living in Britain in the Industrial Revolution* (London: Meuthen)

Taylor, J. S. 1979, 'Philanthropy and empire: Jonas Hanway and the infant poor of London', *Eighteenth Century Studies* 12: 285–305

Thane, P. M. 1981, 'Social history 1860–1914', *in* Floud, R. C. and McCloskey, D. N. 1981

Thoday, J. M. 1965, 'Geneticism and environmentalism', *in* Meade, J. E. and Parkes, A. S. 1965

Thomas, B. 1985, 'Food supply in the United Kingdom during the Industrial Revolution', *in* Mokyr, J. 1985a

Thomas, H. 1961, *The Story of Sandhurst* (London: Hutchinson)

Thompson, B. 1984, 'Infant mortality in nineteenth-century Bradford', *in* Woods, R. and Woodward, J. 1984

Titmuss, R. M. 1943, *Birth, Poverty and Wealth: A Study of Infant Mortality* (London: Hamish Hamilton)

Tobias, P. V. 1962, 'On the increasing stature of the bushmen', *Anthropos* 57: 801–10

Townsend, P., Davidson, N. and Whitehead, M. 1988, *Inequalities in Health* (Harmondsworth: Penguin Books)

Treble, J. H. 1979, *Urban Poverty in Britain, 1830–1914* (London: Batsford)

Trussell, J. and Wachter, K. W. 1984, 'Estimating the covariates of historical heights', *National Bureau of Economic Research Working Paper* No. 1455

Trustram, M. 1984, *Women of the Regiment: Marriage and the Victorian Army* (Cambridge: Cambridge Unversity Press)

Tukey, J. W. 1977, *Exploratory Data Analysis* (Reading, Mass.: Addison-Wesley)

Turner, M. (ed.) 1986, *Malthus and His Time* (Basingstoke: MacMillan)

Tuxford, A. W. and Glegg, R. A. 1911, 'The average height and weight of English schoolchildren', *British Medical Journal* 1: 1423–6

Usher, D. 1980, *The Measurement of Economic Growth* (Oxford: Blackwell)

Valaoras, V. G. 1970, 'Biometric studies of army conscripts in Greece', *Human Biology* 42: 184

Van Wieringen, J. C. 1978, 'Secular growth changes', *in* Falkner, F. and Tanner, J. M., *Human Growth* (New-York: Plenum)

Verbrugge, L. M. 1984, 'Longer life but worsening health? Trends in health and mortality of middle-aged and older persons', *Millbank Memorial Fund Quarterly/Health and Society* 62: 475–519

Villerme, L. R. 1829, 'Memoire sur la taille de l'homme en France', *Annales d'hygiene publique* 1: 551–9

Vlastovsky, V. G. 1966, 'The secular trend in the growth and development of children and young persons in the Soviet Union', *Human Biology* 38: 219–30

von Tunzelmann, G. N. 1979, 'Trends in real wages, 1750–1850, revisited', *Economic History Review* 32: 33–49

Waaler, H. Th. 1984, *Height, Weight and Mortality: The Norwegian Experience* (Oslo: Gruppe for Helsetjenesteforskning)

Wachter, K. W. 1981, 'Graphical estimation of military heights', *Historical Methods* **14**: 31–42

Wachter, K. W. and Trussell, J. 1982, 'Estimating historical heights', *Journal of the American Statistical Association* **77**: 279–303

Ward, W. P. 1988, 'Weight at birth in Vienna, Austria, 1865–1930', *Annals of Human Biology*

Wark, M. L. and Malcolm, L. A. 1969, 'Growth and development of the Lumi child of the Sepik district of New Guinea', *Medical Journal of Australia* **2**: 129–36

Waterlow, J. C. and Payne, P. R. 1975, 'The protein gap', *Nature* **258**: 113–17

de Watteville, H. 1954, *The British Soldier* (London)

Werdelin, L. 1985, 'The stature of some medieval Swedish populations', *Fornvannen* **80**: 133–40

Wernham, R. B. 1984, *After the Armada: Elizabethan England and the Struggle for Western Europe* (Oxford: Clarendon Press)

Whitehead, R. G. 1977, 'Protein and energy requirements of young children living in the developing countries to allow for catch-up growth after infections', *American Journal of Clinical Nutrition* **30**: 1545–7

Williams, B. A. and Walsh, A. H. 1968, *Urban Government for Metropolitan Lagos* (New York: Praeger)

Williamson, J. G. 1982, 'Was the Industrial Revolution worth it? Disamenities and death in nineteenth century British towns', *Explorations in Economic History* **19**: 221–45

Williamson, J. G. 1984, 'British mortality and the value of life, 1781–1831', *Population Studies* **38**: 157–72

Williamson, J. G. 1985, *Did British Capitalism Breed Inequality?* (London: Allen and Unwin)

Williamson, J. G. 1987, 'Debating the British Industrial Revolution', *Explorations in Economic History* **24**: 269–92

Winick, M. (ed.) 1979, *Hunger Disease: Studies by the Jewish Physicians in the Warsaw Ghetto*, trans. M. Osnos (New York: John Wiley)

Winter, J. M. 1980, 'Military fitness and civilian health in Britain during the First World War', *Journal of Contemporary History* **15**: 211–44

Winter, J. M. 1982, 'The decline of mortality in Britain 1870–1950', in Barker, T. C. and Drake, M. 1982

Wolanski, N. 1978, 'Secular trend in man: evidence and factors', *Colloquia in Anthropology* **2**: 69–86

Wolanski, N. 1980, 'Heterosis and homosis in man', in Schwidetzky *et al.* 1980

Wolanski, N., Jarosz, E. and Pyzuk, M. 1968, 'Heterosis effect as a causative factor in the secular trend of some continuous traits in man', *Anthropologie* **6**: 15–17

Woods, R. I. 1984, 'Mortality patterns in the nineteenth century', in Woods, R. I. and Woodward, J. 1984

Woods, R. I. and Woodward, J. H. (eds.) 1984, *Urban Disease and Mortality in Nineteenth Century England* (London: Batsford)

World Health Organisation 1974, *Handbook of Human Nutritional Requirements 1974*, WHO Monograph No. 61 (Geneva: World Health Organisation)

Wrigley, E. A. (ed.) 1972, *Nineteenth Century Society: Essays in the Use of Quantitative Methods for the Study of Social Data* (Cambridge: Cambridge University Press)

Wrigley, E. A. 1986, 'Malthus's model of a pre-industrial economy', *in* Turner, M. (ed.) 1986

Wrigley, E. A. and Schofield, R. S. 1981, *The Population History of England, 1541–1871* (Cambridge, Mass.: Harvard University Press)

Wu, C. F. J. 1986, 'Jacknife, bootstrap and other resampling methods in regression analysis', *Annals of Statistics* **14**: 1261–1300

Wyndham, C. H. 1970, 'Man's adaptation to the physical environment in South Africa', *Materialy i Prace Antropologiczne* **78**; 49–79

Index